ORIGAMI BUGS

MARC KIRSCHENBAUM

Fit to Print Publishing, Inc.
New York, New York

The diagrams in this book were produced with Macromedia's Freehand, and image processing was done with Adobe Photoshop. The Backtalk family of typefaces was used for the body text. and Trebuchet was used for the cover. Ellen Cohen assisted with the cover design and provided valuable artistic assistance. Jan Polish provided editing assistance; any remaining errors are the fault of the author.

Contents

Introduction

One of the most appealing aspects of origami is in its ability to transform a piece of paper into the unexpected. Perhaps the most impressive subject paperfolding artists have tackled is insects. Since the starting point of a square only contains four obvious appendage sources (the corners), some observers of origami pieces are surprised at how folding alone can coax a square into wings, antennae, and six legs (let alone stripes and spots). Fortunately for the origami designers out there, getting all of those extra appendages is not always so complicated. Sometime back in the 1960's, a few people independently discovered how folding the four corners of the square to the center would yield a new (smaller) square, with extra flaps that could be utilized for additional appendages. This so called "blintz" technique is still used today, and in fact, some of the models in this book make use of it. This book also explores other approaches at forming large numbers of points, so from a folding perspective you should find interesting and fun sequences to try out. From an artistic standpoint, I lean towards an abstraction of the subject at hand, but feel free to embellish on these pieces as you feel appropriate. There is also a section in this book on materials and methods, which might provide you with the creative juice to take your works to a higher level. It is my wish this book will provide many hours of enjoyment to even the most jaded origami aficionado.

Symbols and Terminology

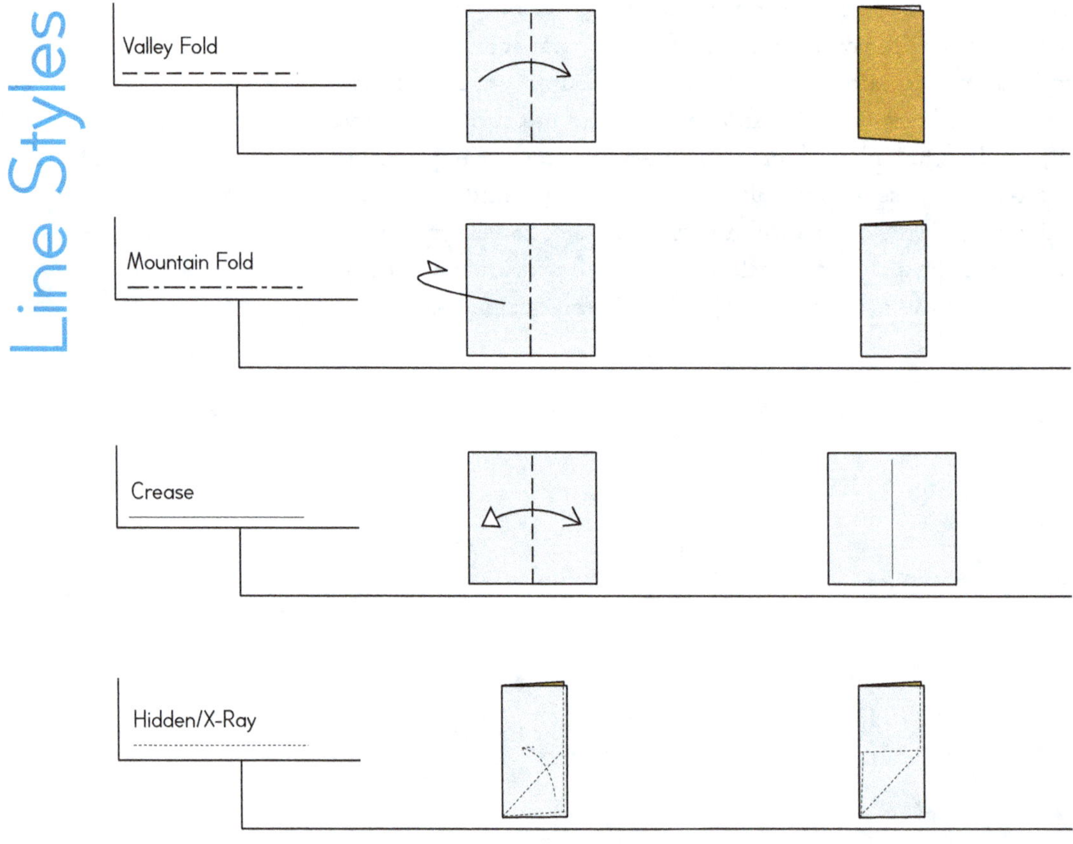

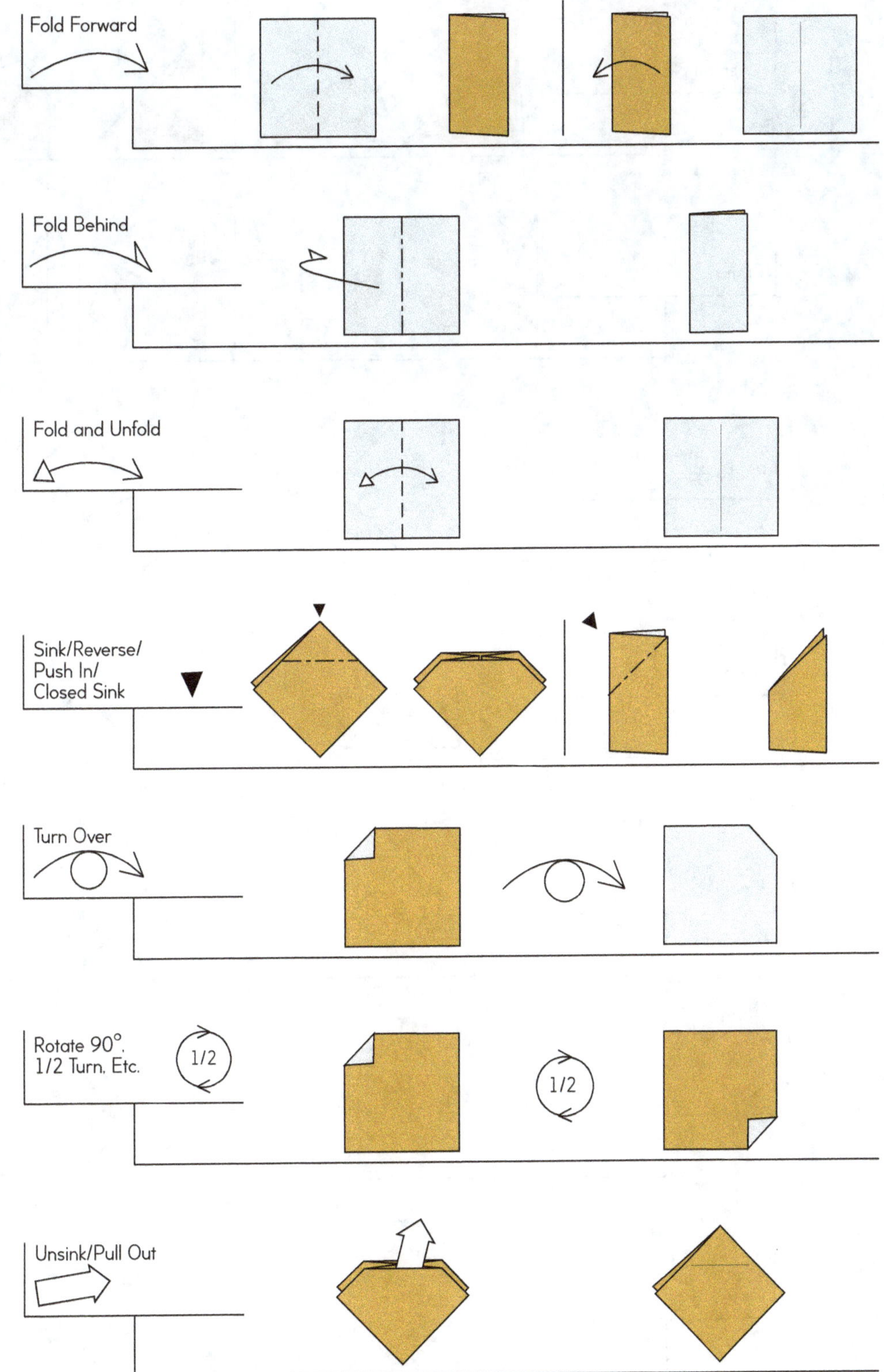
Fold Forward
Fold Behind
Fold and Unfold
Sink/Reverse/
Push In/
Closed Sink
Turn Over
Rotate 90°.
1/2 Turn. Etc.
1/2
1/2
Unsink/Pull Out

Reverse Fold

Crimp

Rabbit Ear

Squash

Petal Fold

Sink

Closed Sink

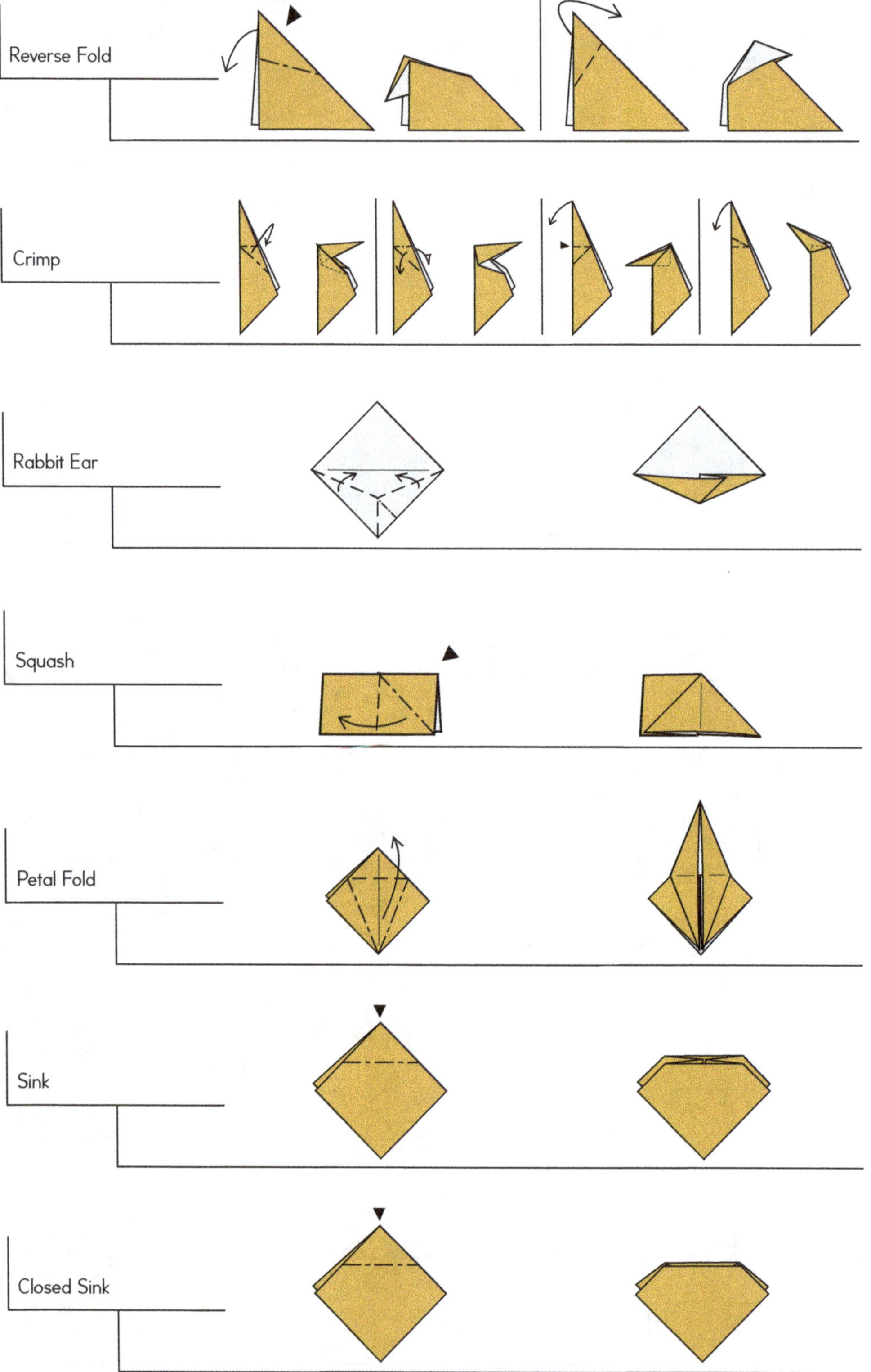

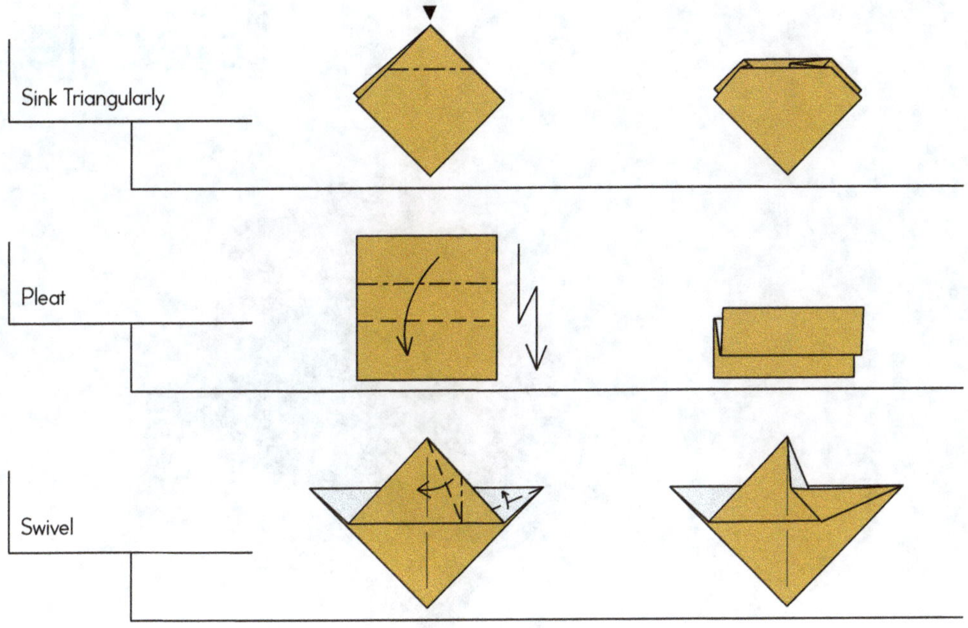

Sink Triangularly

Pleat

Swivel

Beetle

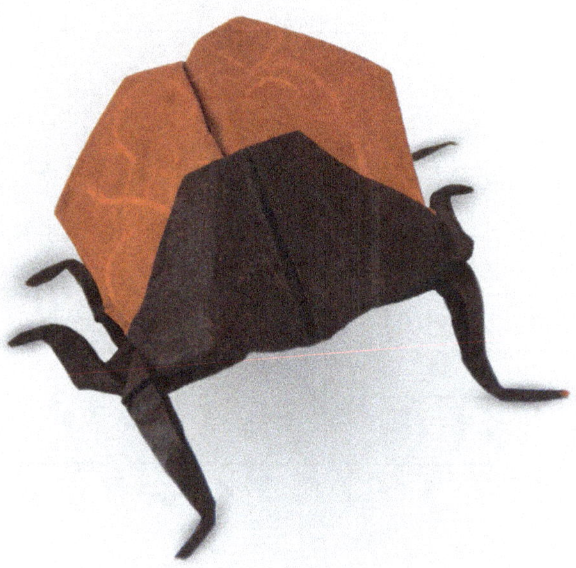

This piece makes use of the blintz technique mentioned in the introduction. The corners are folded to the center (step two), and are then partially pulled out (step six). The interesting aspect of the model is how the wings are color changed. Since those appendages come from the middle portion of the model, turning them inside out would not work. Instead, the model is predominantly white (the wing color) for most of the sequence, and then all of the other appendages are color changed. This is doable because the remainder of the points come from the edge of the square. As this is one of my easier insect designs, I have used it for a number of different teaching demonstrations. The most bizarre of these classes involved working with twelve-foot squares of paper for the students. Most of the people in the class were new to origami and had certainly not dealt with such a cumbersome size of material. The completed bugs looked great after they were hand painted to look like ladybugs. Feel free to start with a smaller square for your first attempt.

Many of the flaps in this model look alike, so it is possible to get lost. While it is nice to follow the instructions as presented, substituting a mountain-fold for a valley-fold on the legs is not going to make a noticeable difference in the finished piece.

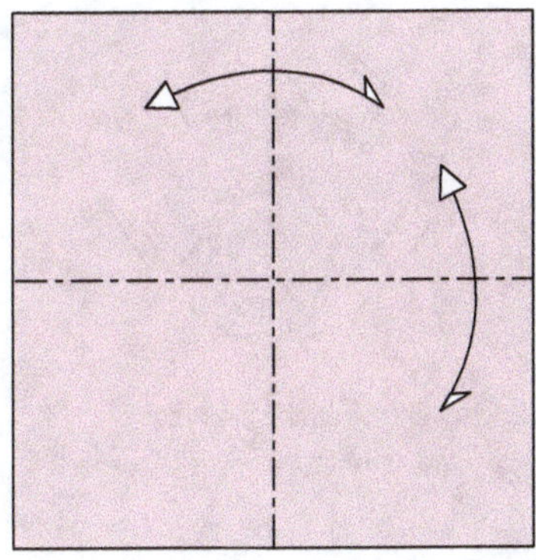

1. Precrease in half with mountain folds.

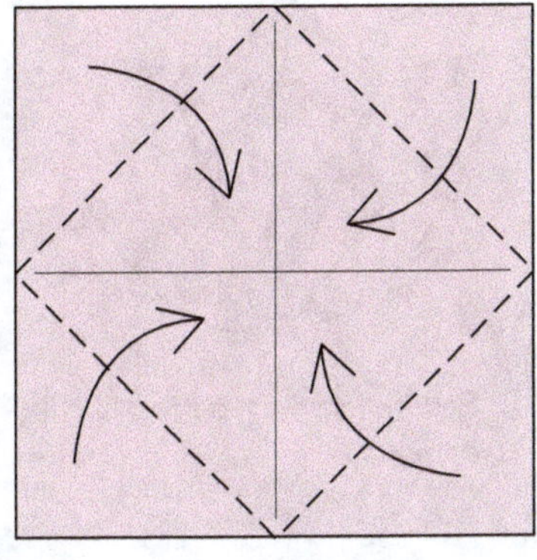

2. Valley fold the corners to the center.

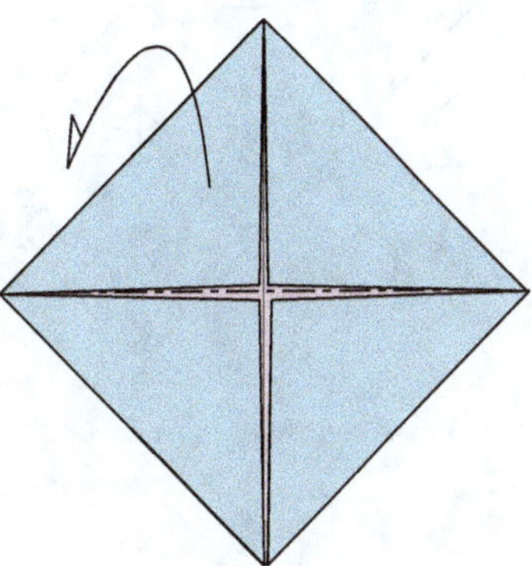

3. Mountain fold in half.

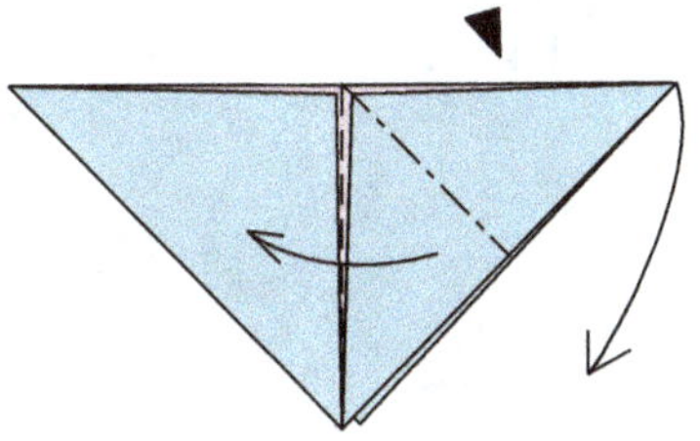

4. Squash fold.

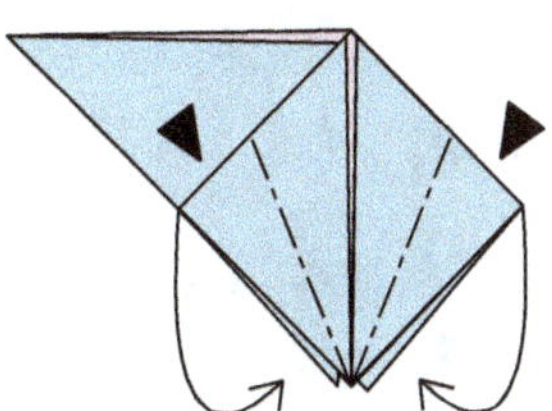

5. Reverse fold the sides.

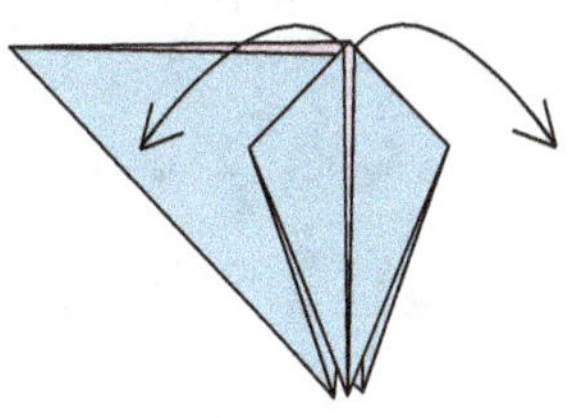

6. Unwrap the trapped corners.

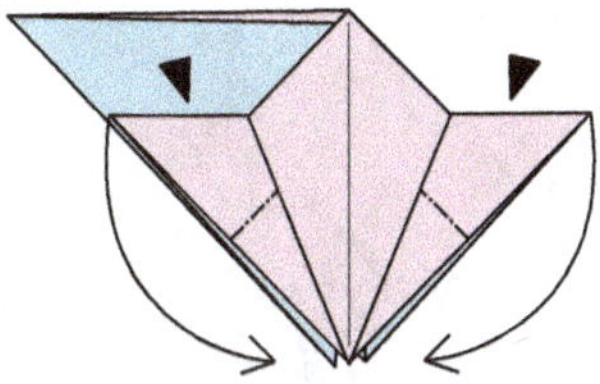

7. Reverse fold the sides.

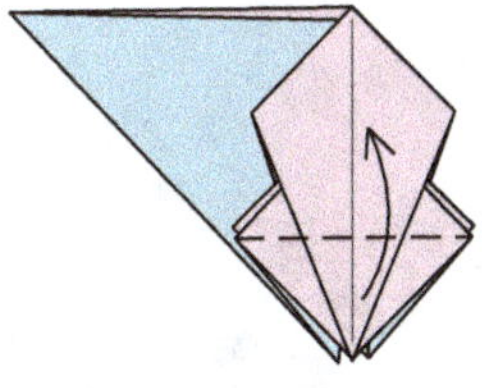

8. Valley fold the top flap up.

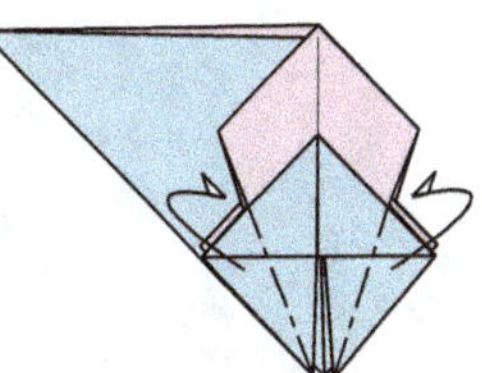

9. Mountain fold the sides, tucking the flaps into their respective pockets.

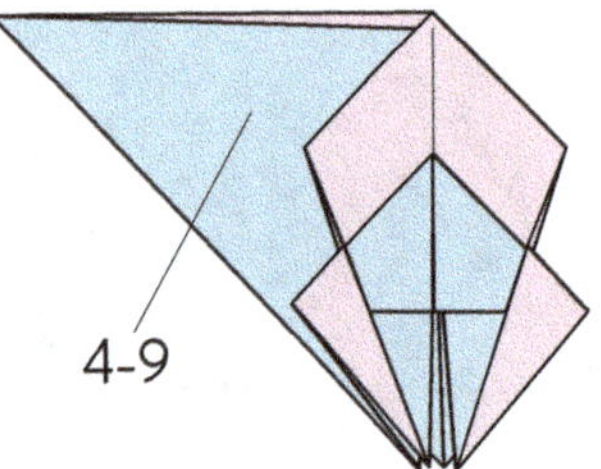

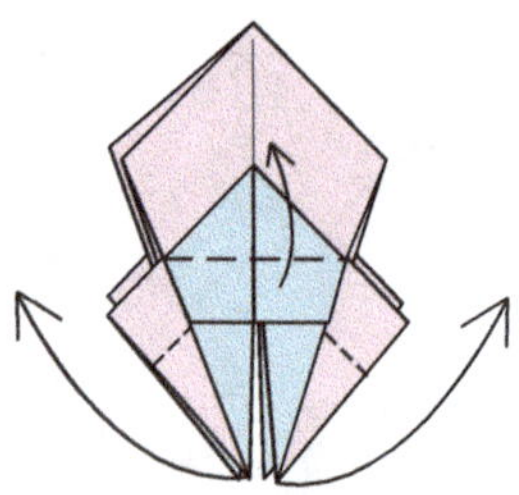

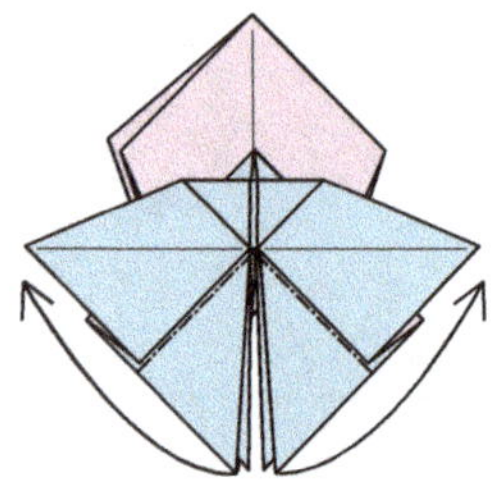

10. Repeat steps 4-9 behind.

11. Squash fold the top flaps outwards.

12. Reverse fold the next set of flaps outwards.

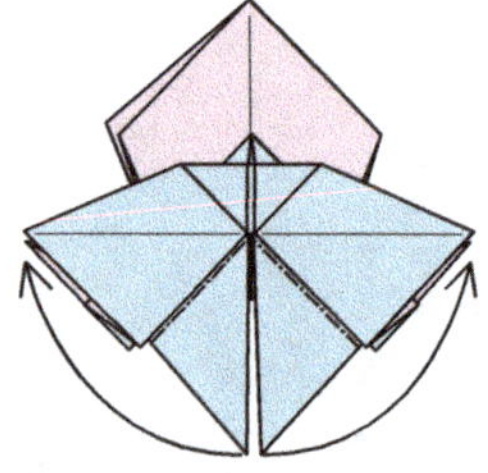

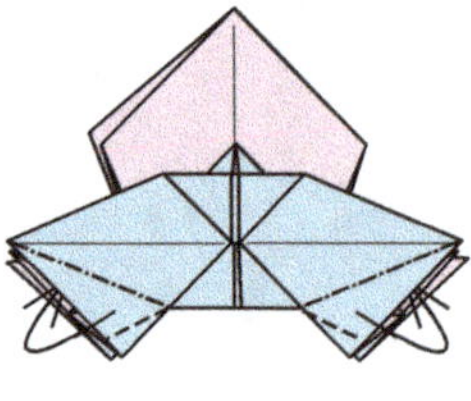

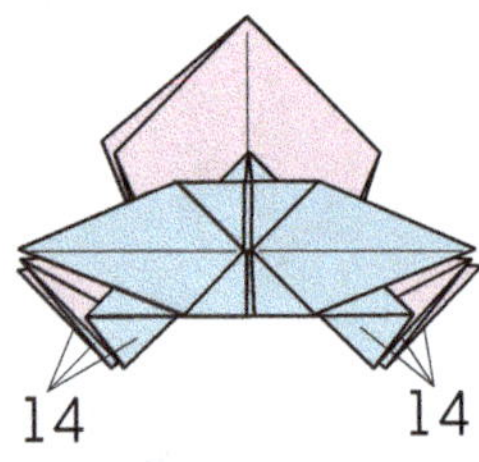

13. Reverse fold the last set of flaps.

14. Reverse fold the bottom edges.

15. Repeat step 14 on the remaining three sets of flaps.

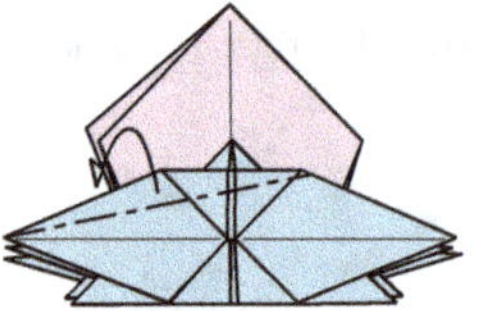

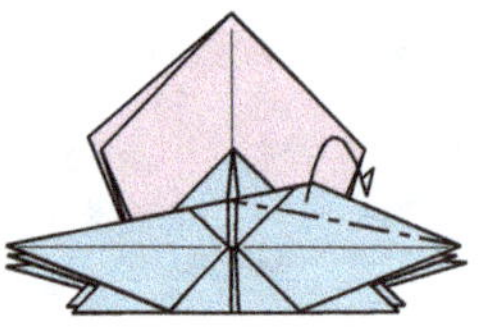

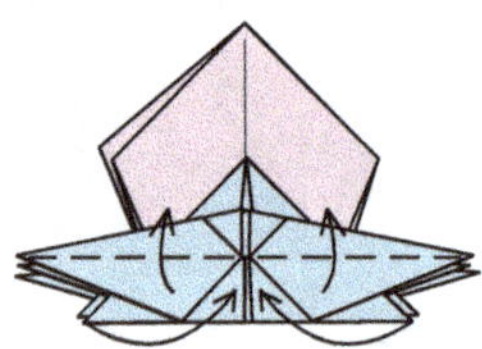

16. Mountain fold along the angle bisector.

17. Mountain fold the other side.

18. Swing the top set of flaps up, allowing the bottom corners to swing inwards and flatten.

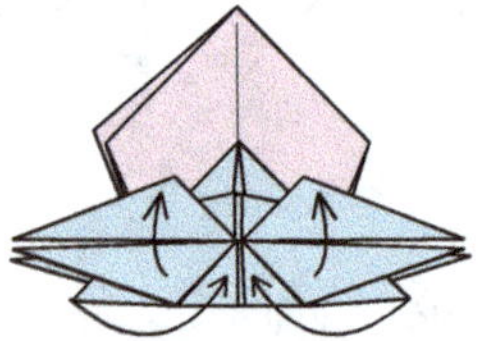

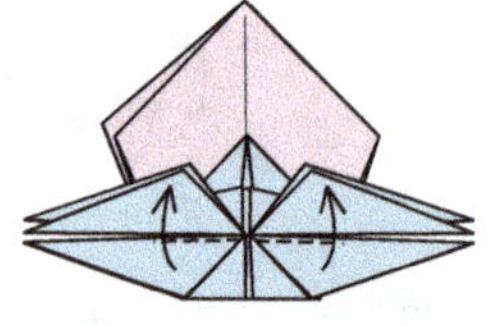

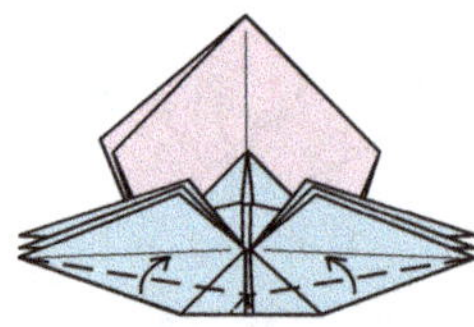

19. Swing the next set of flaps up.

20. Swing the last set of flaps up.

21. Rabbit ear the bottom edge.

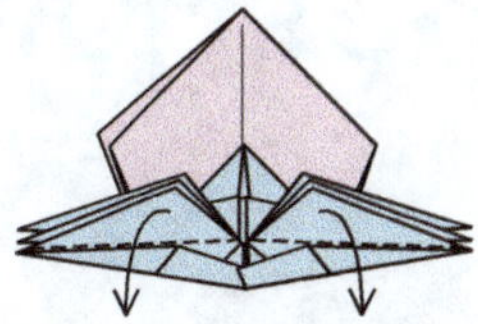

22. Swing down the top set of flaps.

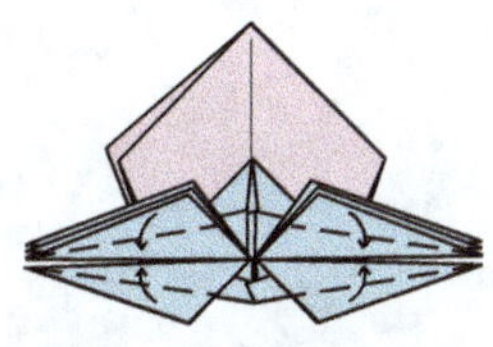

23. Valley fold the sides inward.

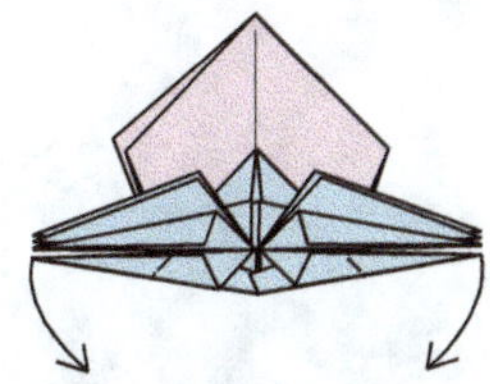

24. Reverse fold the flaps down.

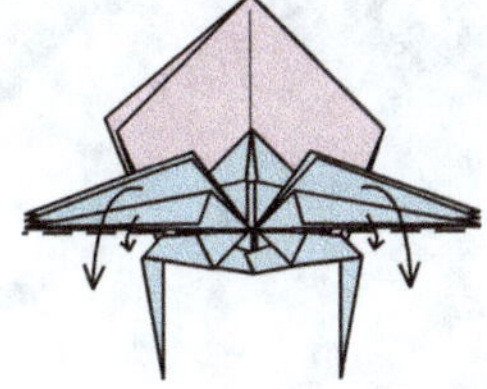

25. Swing down two sets of flaps.

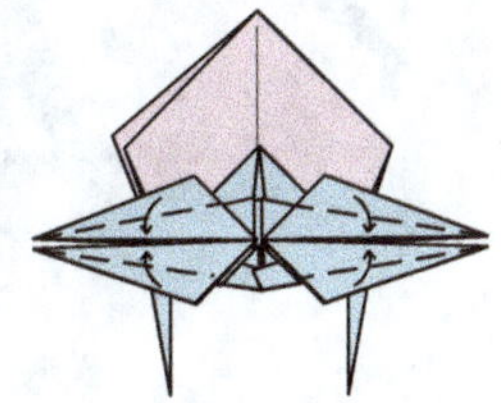

26. Valley fold the sides inward.

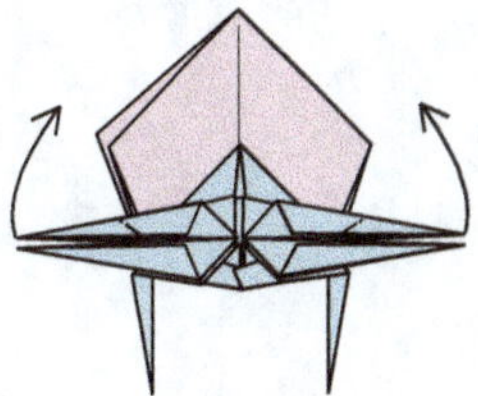

27. Reverse fold the flaps up.

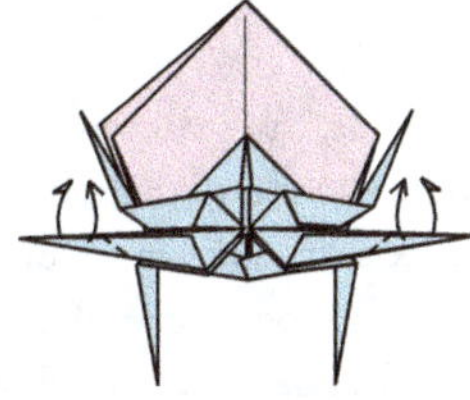

28. Outside reverse fold the flaps up.

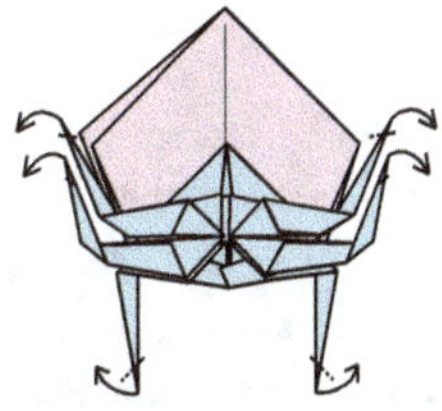

29. Reverse fold the tips of the flaps outwards.

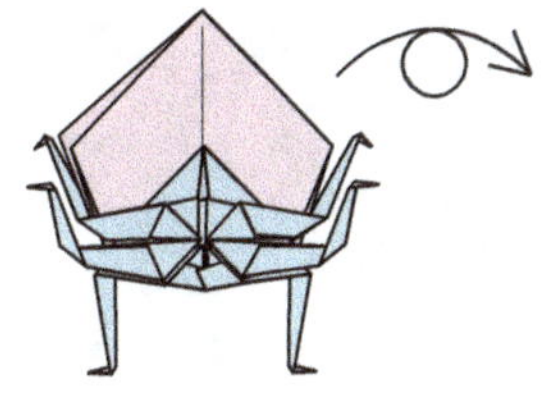

30. Turn over.

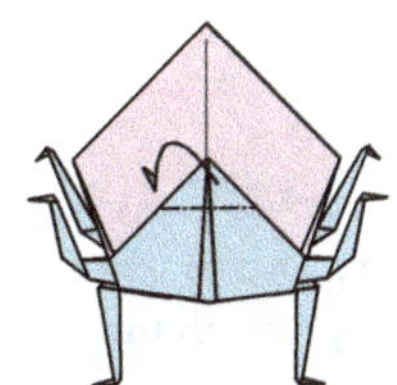

31. Mountain fold the tip of the flap.

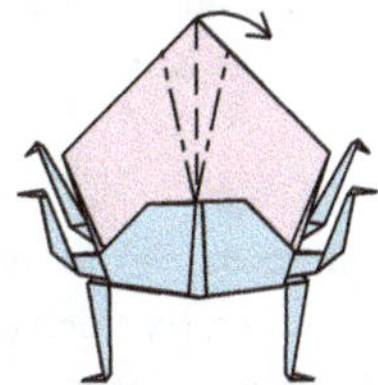

32. Reverse fold along the center, allowing the model to become convex.

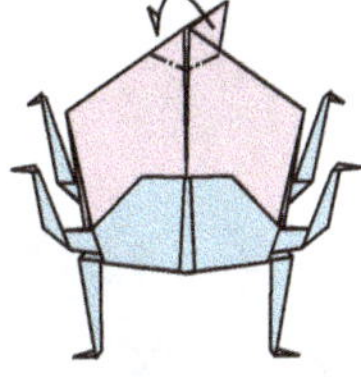

33. Mountain fold the tip, tucking it into the model.

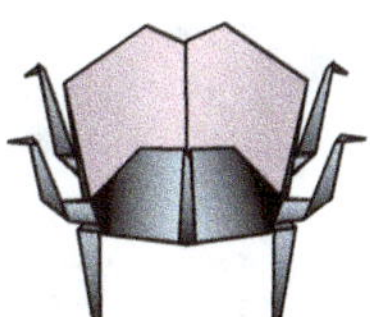

34. Completed *Beetle*.

Mosquito

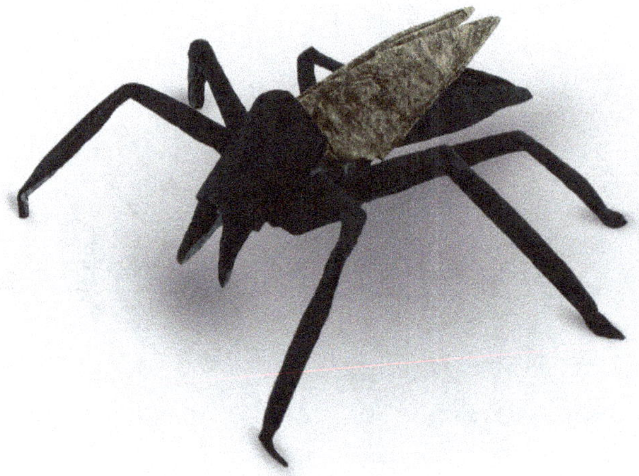

As can be seen from this model's first few steps, the structural heritage is the same as the *Beetle's*. Still, both works manage to look very different; in the *Mosquito*, the body and legs are made narrower through sinking. In essence the legs for both models are about the same length, but the ones for the *Mosquito* appear to be much longer, as the body section is made to be relatively smaller. I did have a blast folding it from tissue paper; it is kind if neat to see how thin the legs can get while working with that medium. The mosquito model Alice Gray (origami pioneer and former Entomologist) made for the American Museum of Natural History inspired this piece.

The biggest trick to make this model look right is to use thin paper, but you can try thicker material for practice. As with the *Beetle*, many of the folds for the thinning of the legs are not too critical.

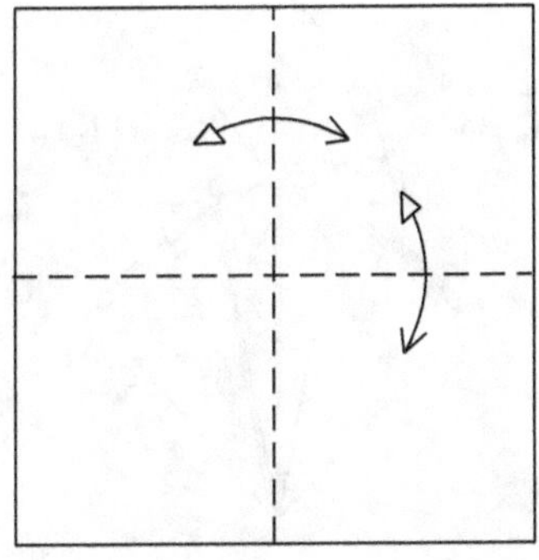

1. Precrease in half both horizontally and vertically.

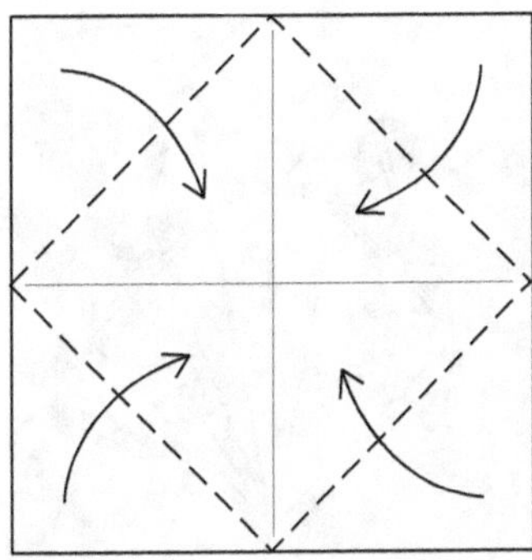

2. Valley fold the corners to the center.

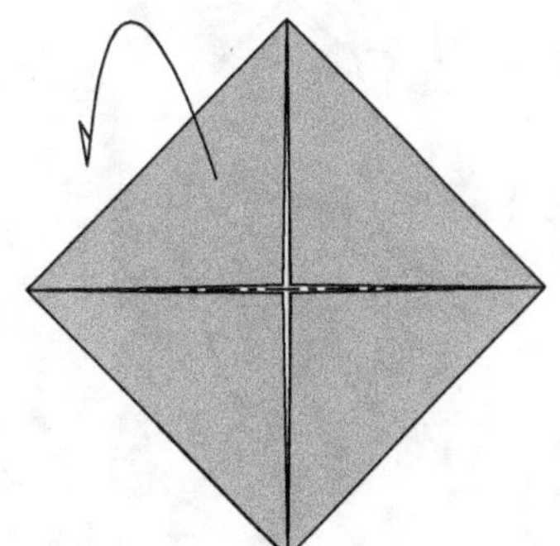

3. Mountain fold in half.

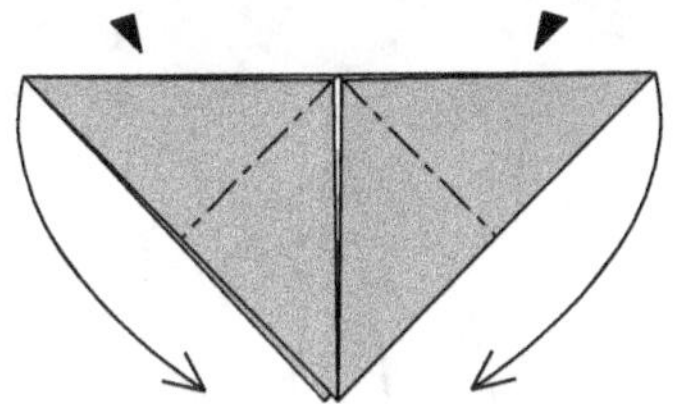

4. Reverse fold the sides.

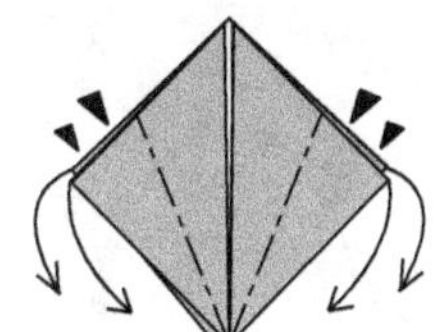

5. Reverse fold four times.

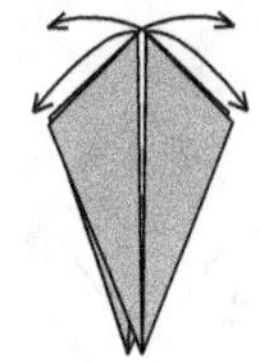

6. Unwrap the four corners.

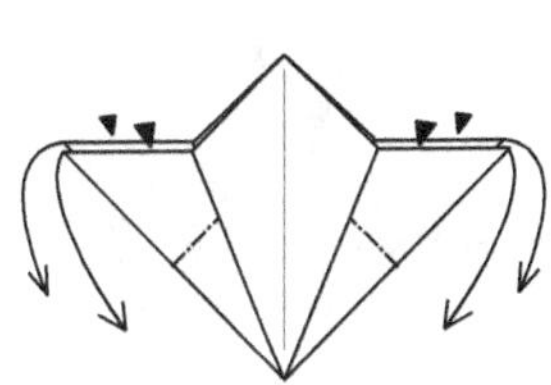

7. Reverse fold four times.

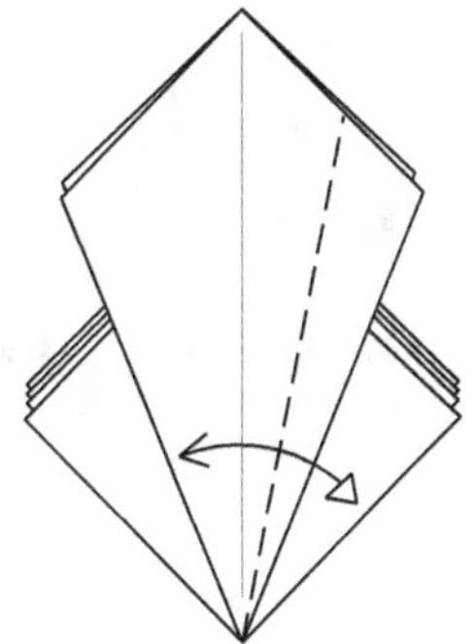

8. Precrease.

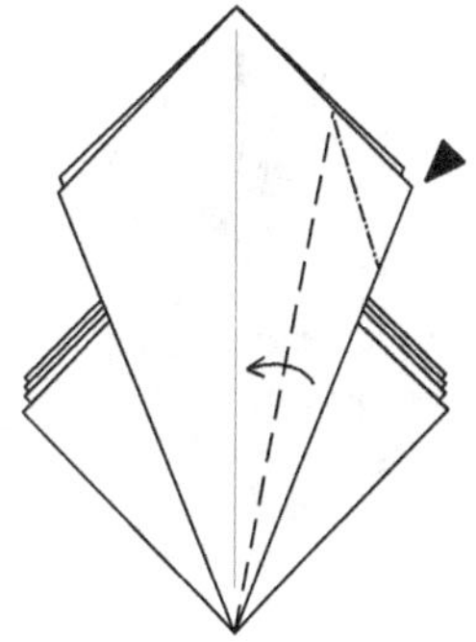

9. Valley fold while spread squashing the top.

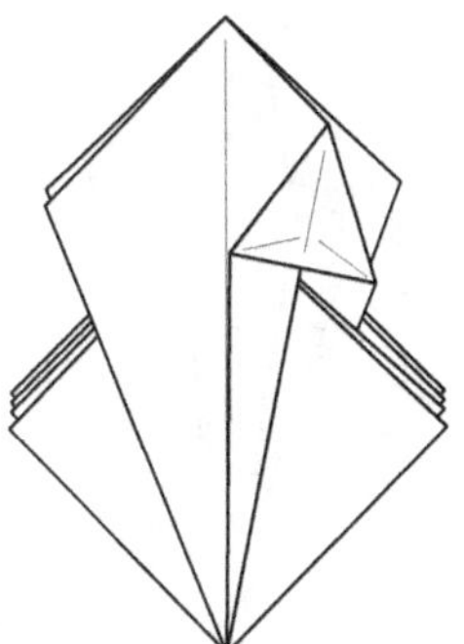

10. Repeat steps 8-9 on the other three corners.

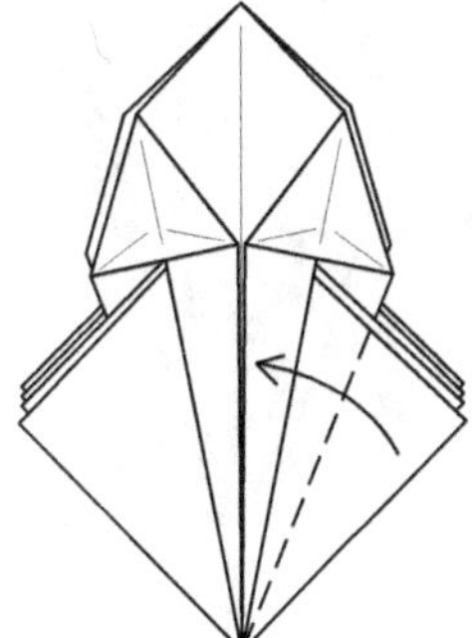

11. Valley fold to the center.

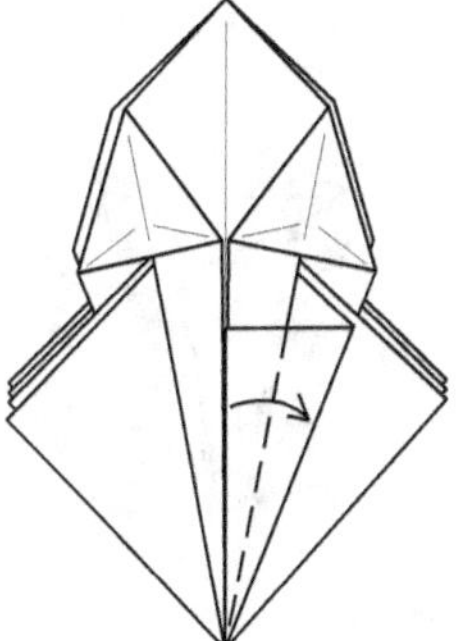

12. Valley fold along the angle bisector.

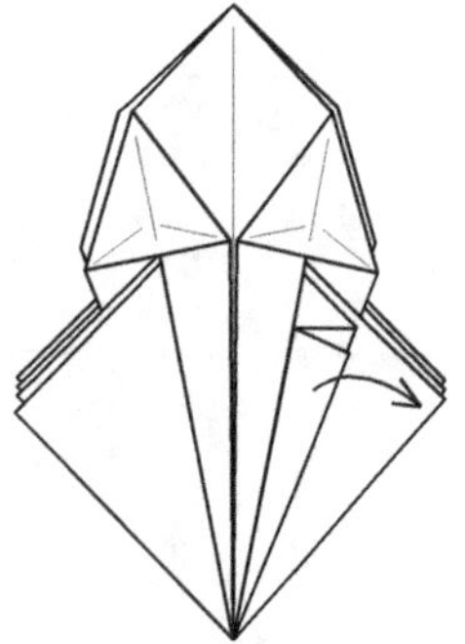

13. Unfold the pleat.

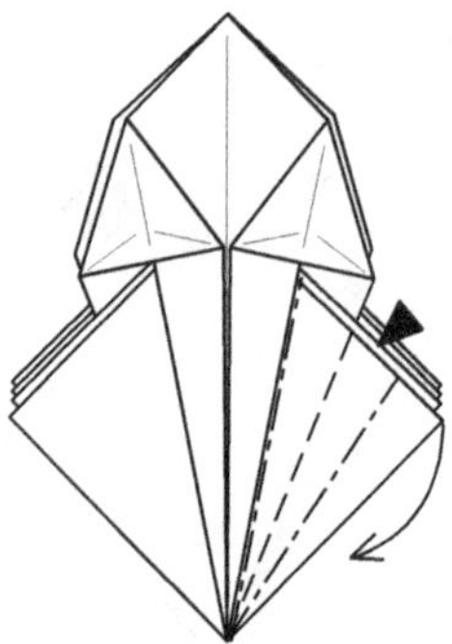

14. Reverse fold in and out along the existing creases.

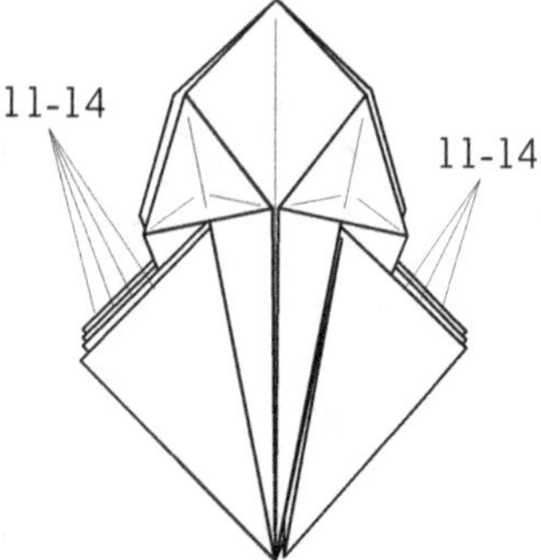

15. Repeat steps 11-14 on the remaining seven flaps.

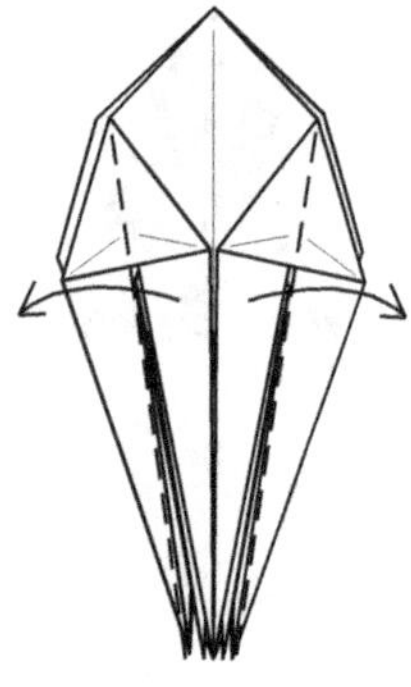

16. Valley fold the top flaps outwards.

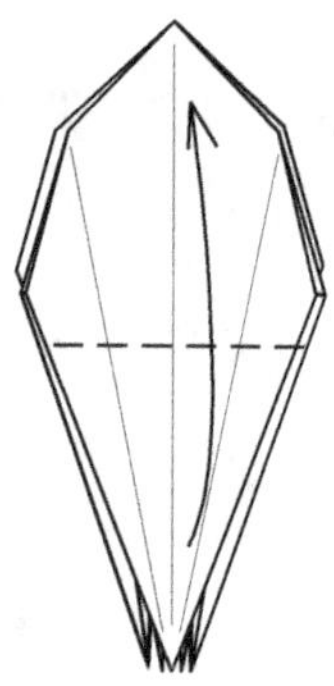

17. Valley fold up as far as possible.

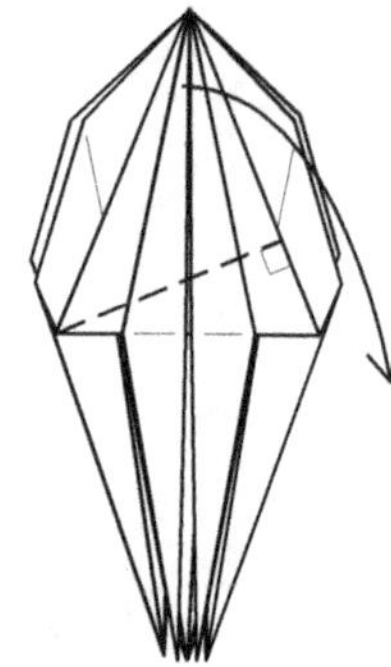

18. Valley fold over.

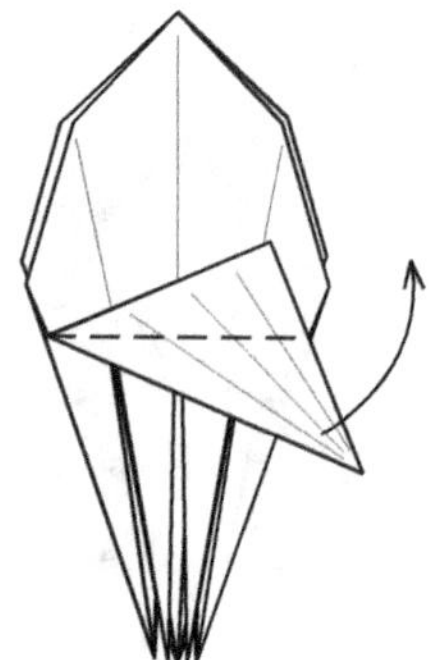

19. Valley fold up.

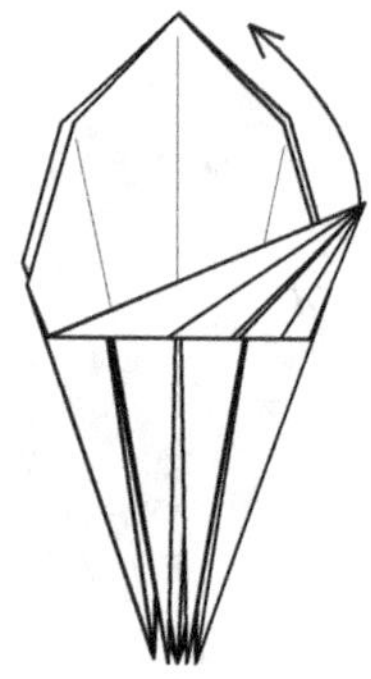

20. Unfold the pleat.

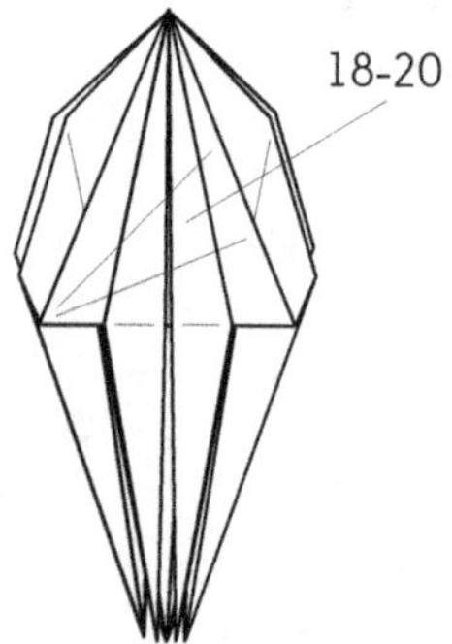

21. Repeat steps 18-20 in mirror image.

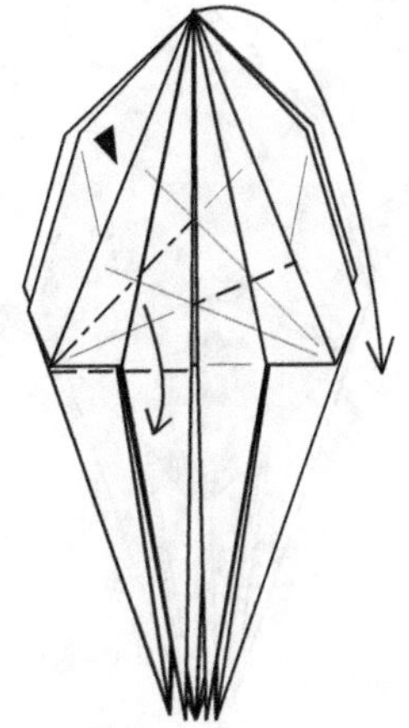

22. Squash fold.

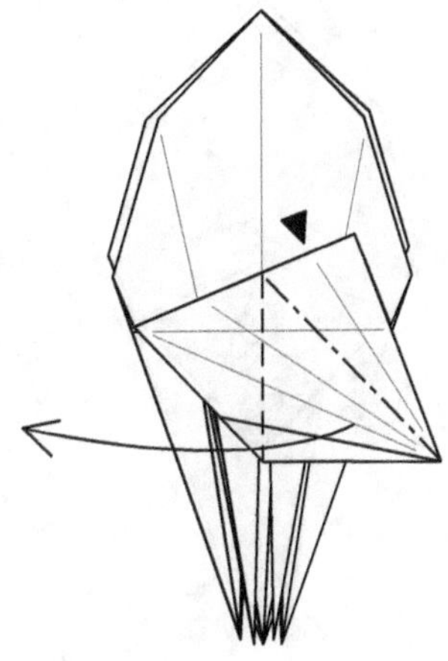

23. Squash fold.

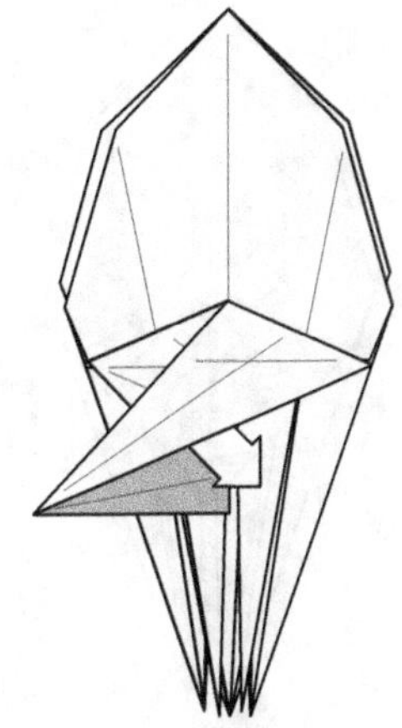

24. Pull out the inner layers.

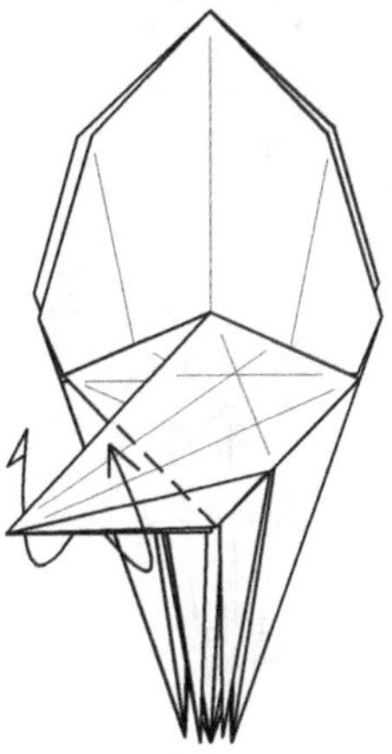

25. Outside reverse fold.

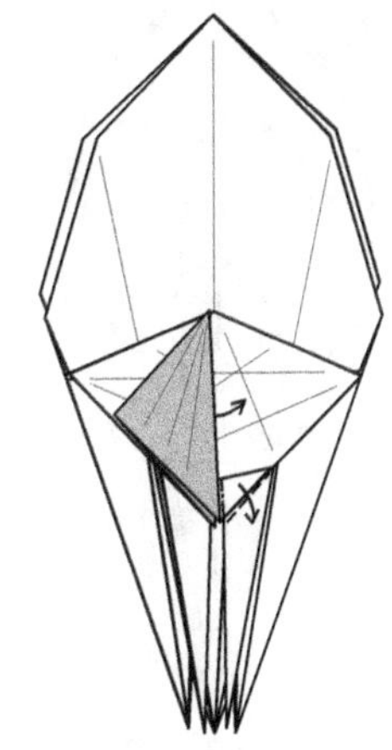

26. Pull out two layers and swivel down to flatten.

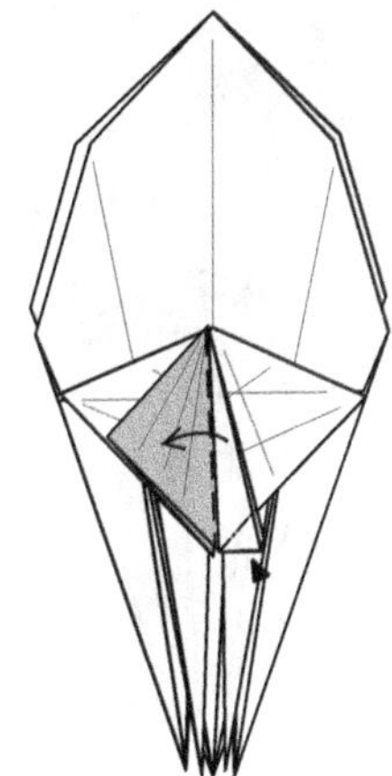

27. Squash fold.

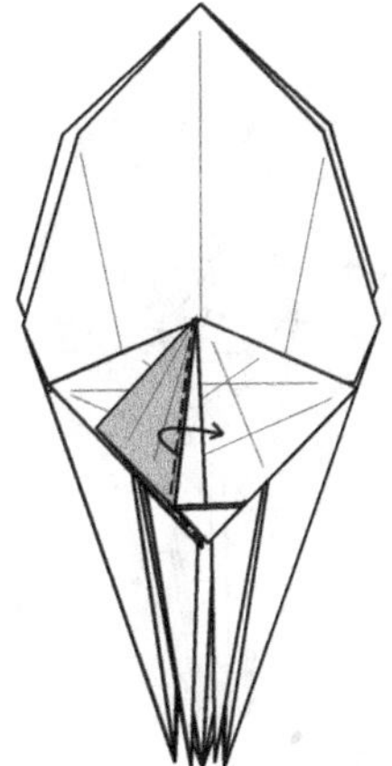

28. Wrap around two layers.

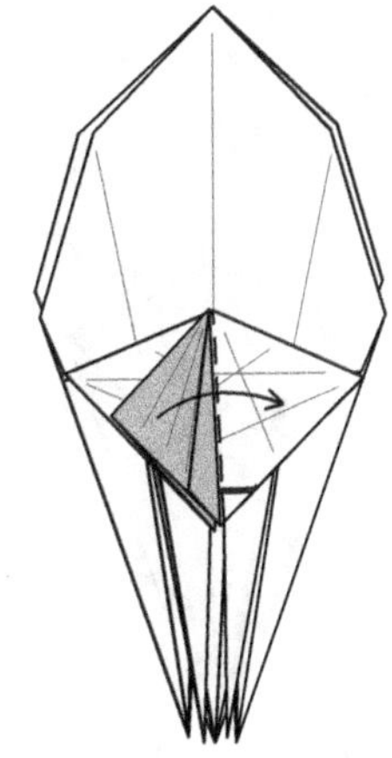

29. Swing over two flaps.

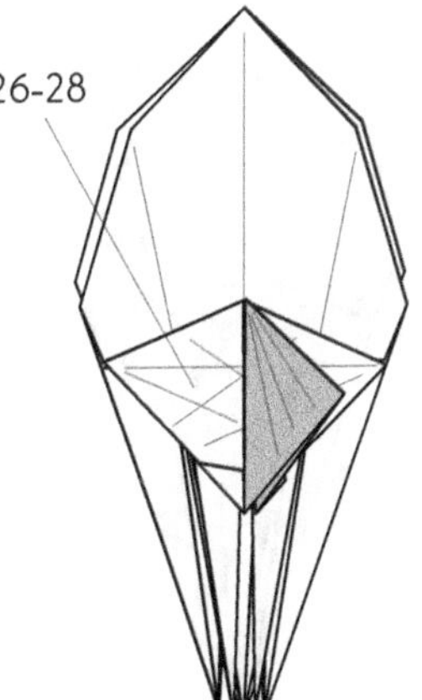

30. Repeat steps 26-28 in mirror image.

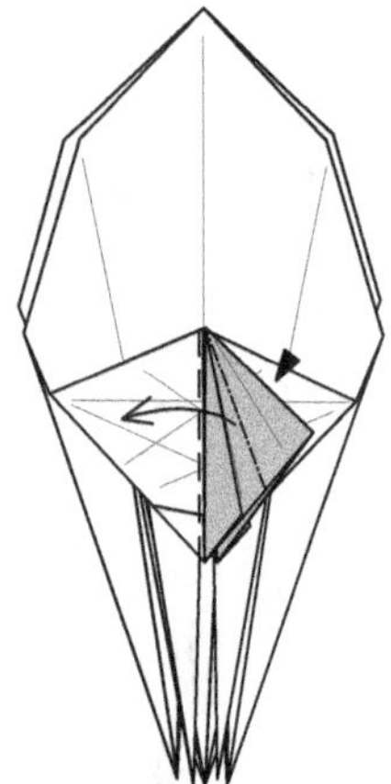

31. Squash fold.

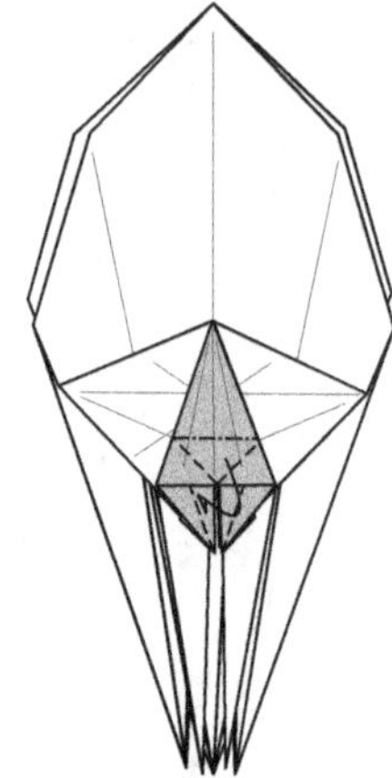

32. Petal fold under.

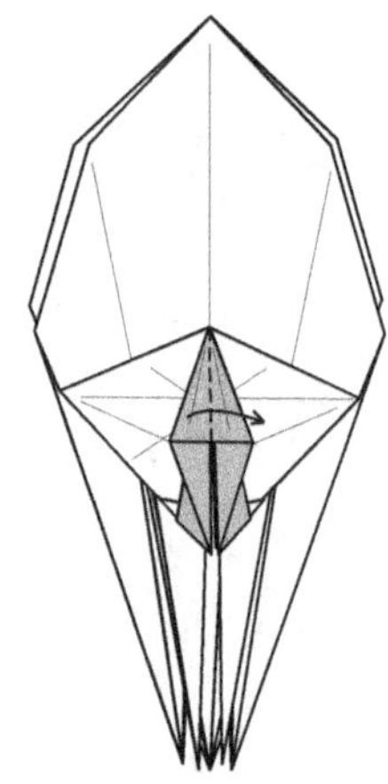

33. Swing over one flap.

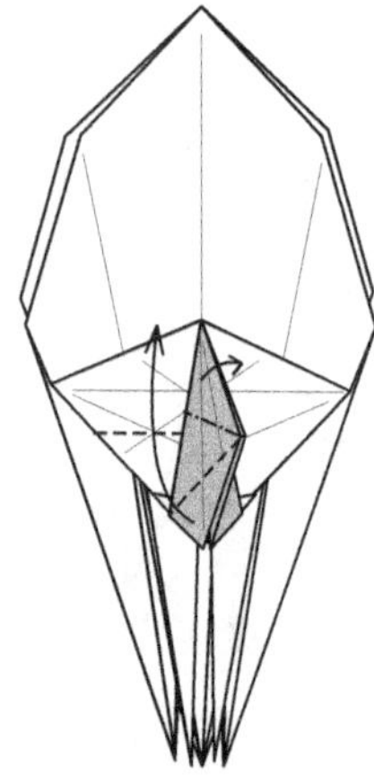

34. Valley fold up, while swiveling over the top layer.

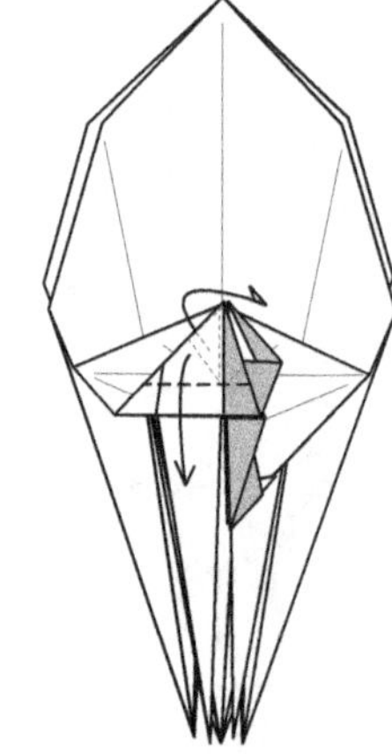

35. Valley fold down while swiveling over.

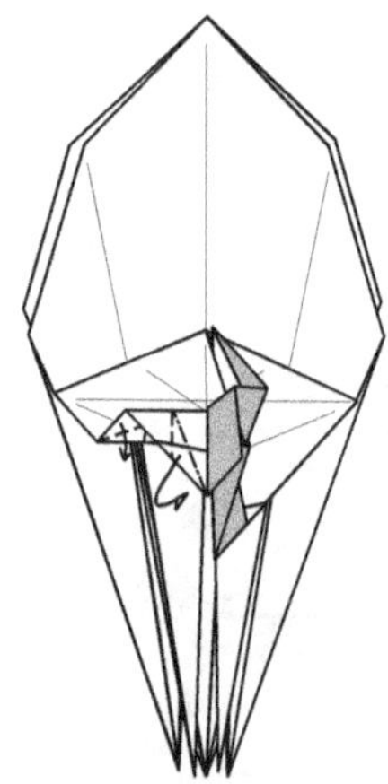

36. Swivel fold under along the angle bisector.

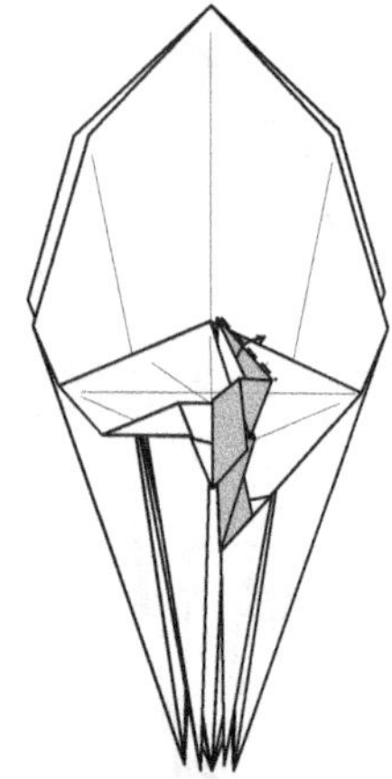

37. Valley fold the top edge up, swiveling out the trapped paper.

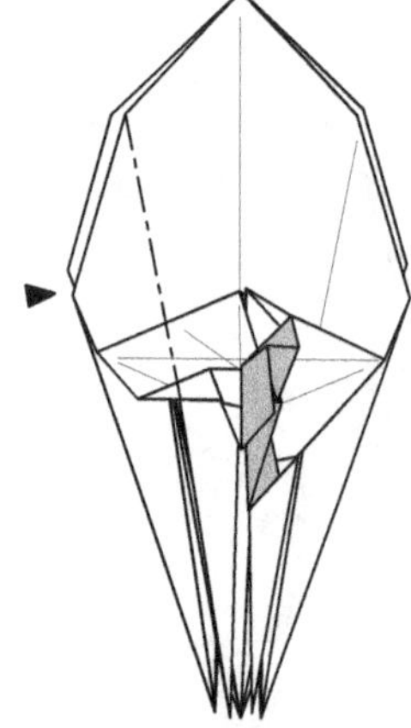

38. Closed sink along the existing crease.

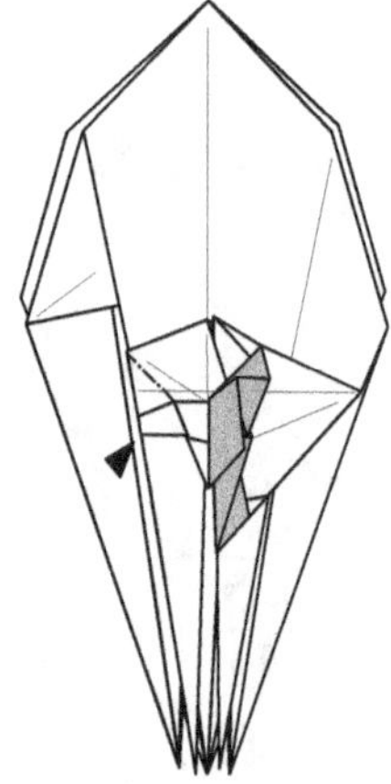

39. Reverse fold the corner.

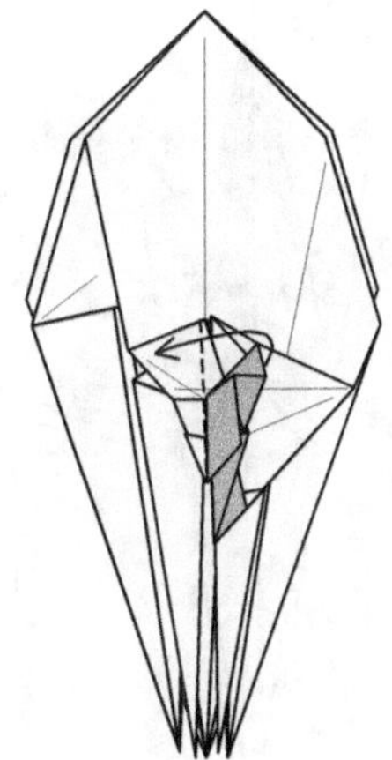

40. Valley fold over.

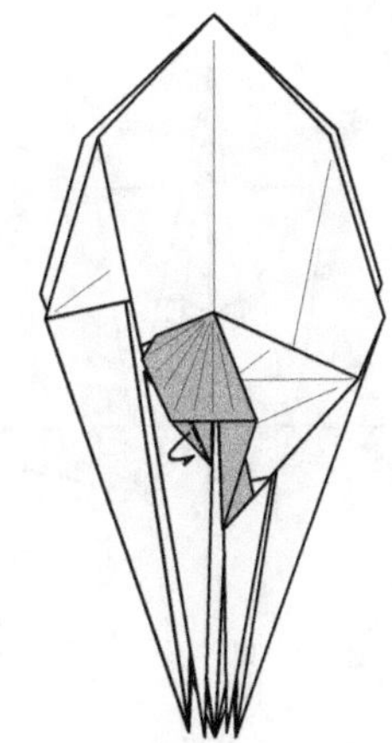

41. Mountain fold.

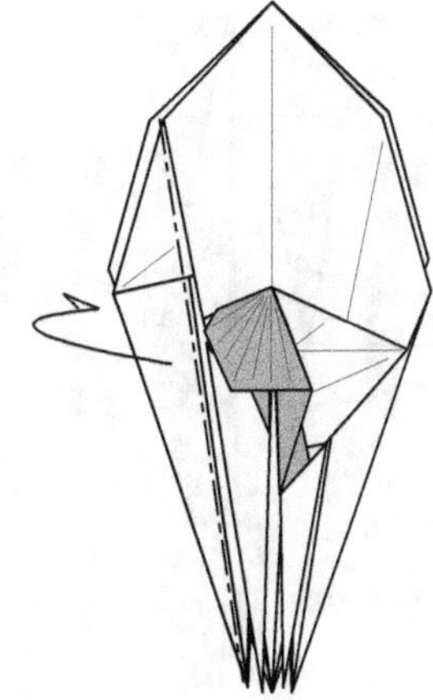

42. Mountain fold.

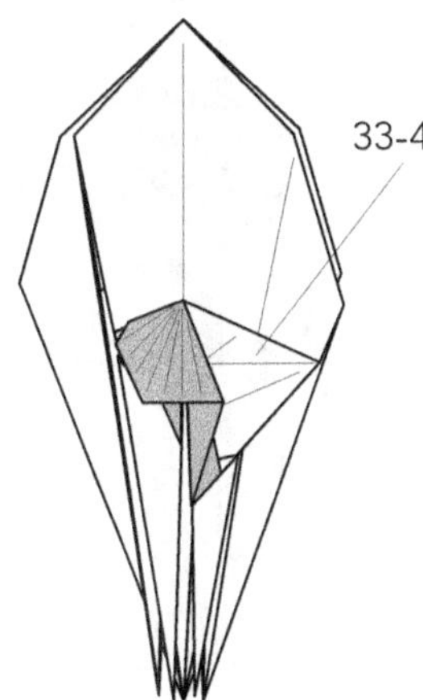

43. Repeat steps 33-42 in mirror image.

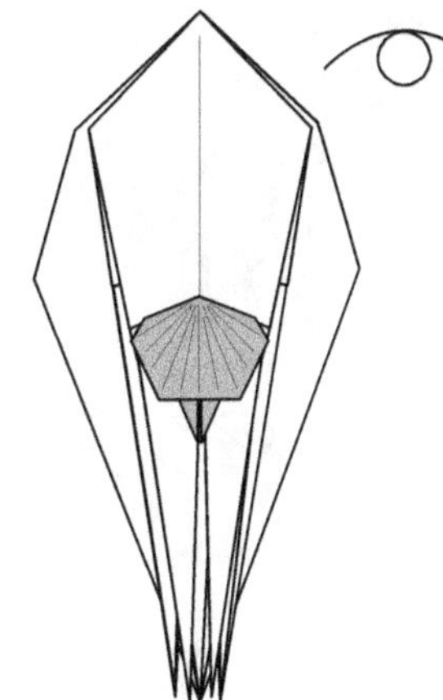

44. Turn over.

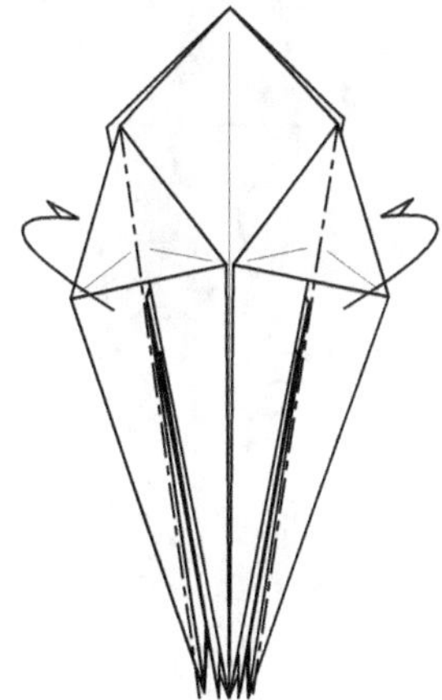

45. Mountain fold.

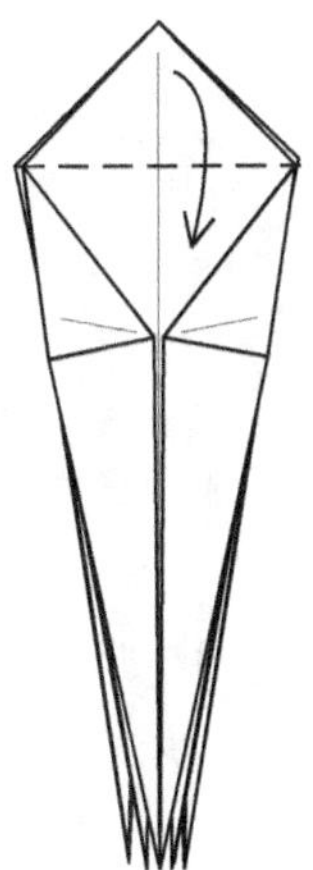

46. Valley fold.

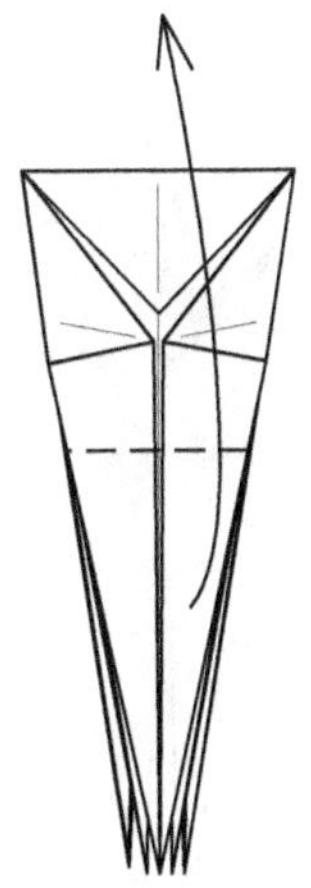

47. Valley fold up as far as possible.

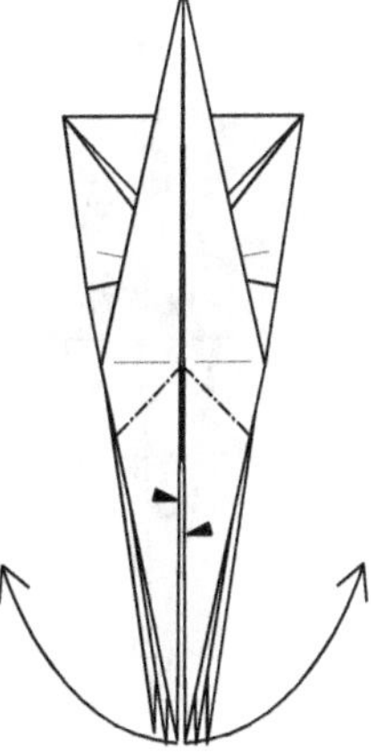

48. Reverse fold the top set of flaps, distributing the layers evenly.

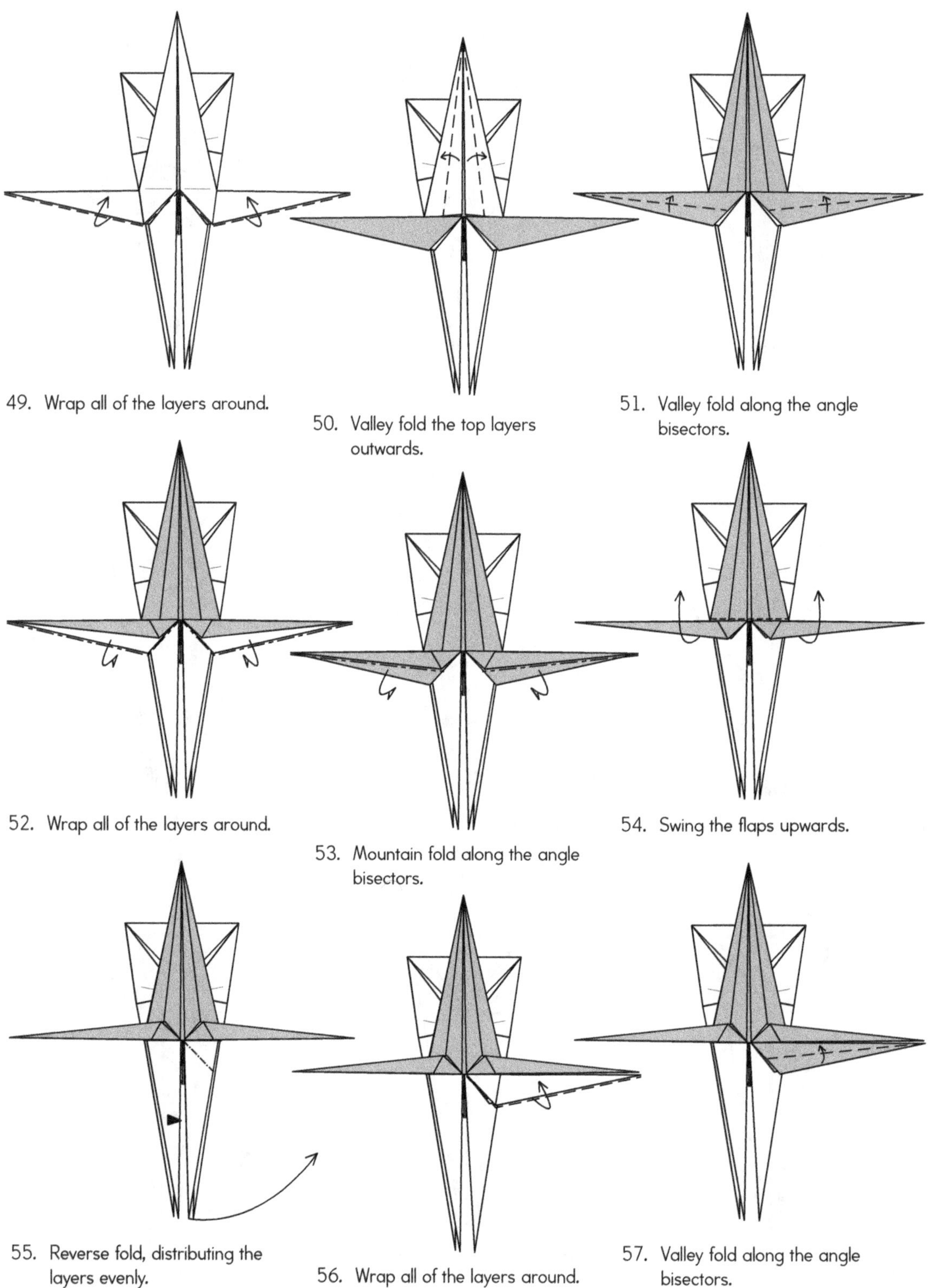

49. Wrap all of the layers around.

50. Valley fold the top layers outwards.

51. Valley fold along the angle bisectors.

52. Wrap all of the layers around.

53. Mountain fold along the angle bisectors.

54. Swing the flaps upwards.

55. Reverse fold, distributing the layers evenly.

56. Wrap all of the layers around.

57. Valley fold along the angle bisectors.

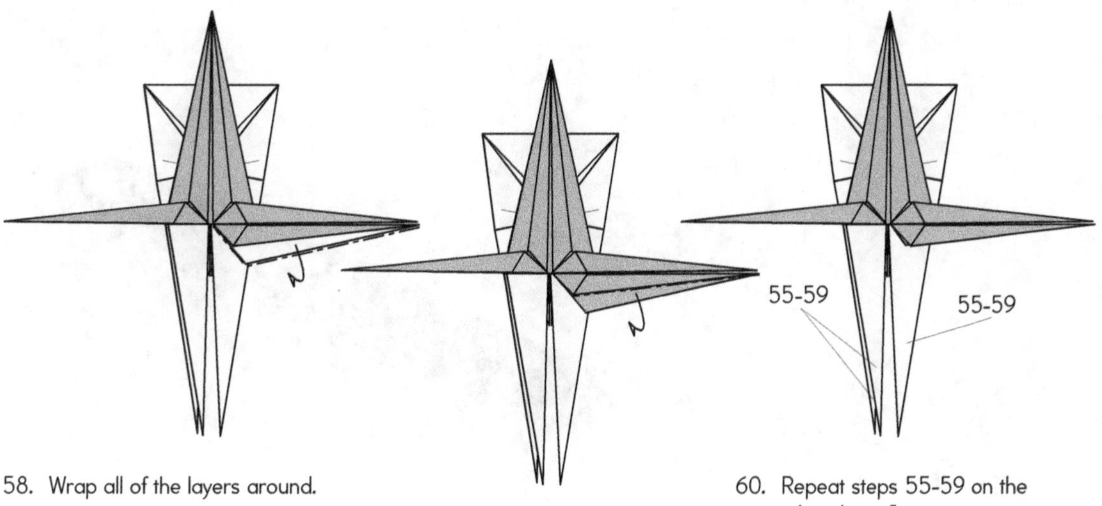

58. Wrap all of the layers around.

59. Mountain fold along the angle bisectors.

60. Repeat steps 55-59 on the other three flaps.

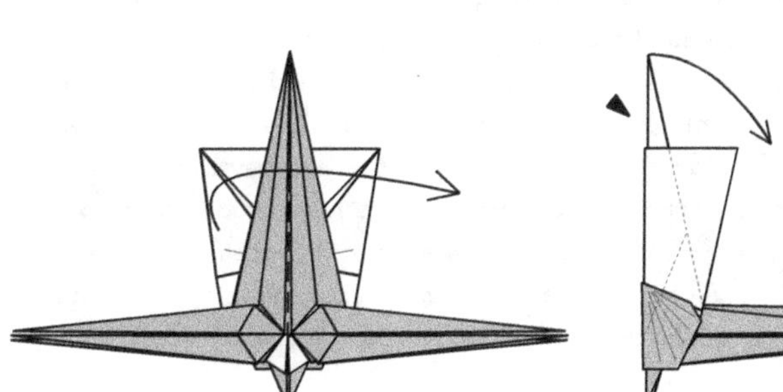

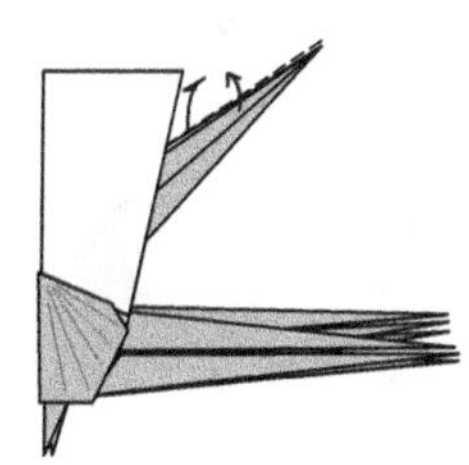

61. Valley fold the model in half.

62. Reverse fold.

63. Slide the outer layers of the abdomen up.

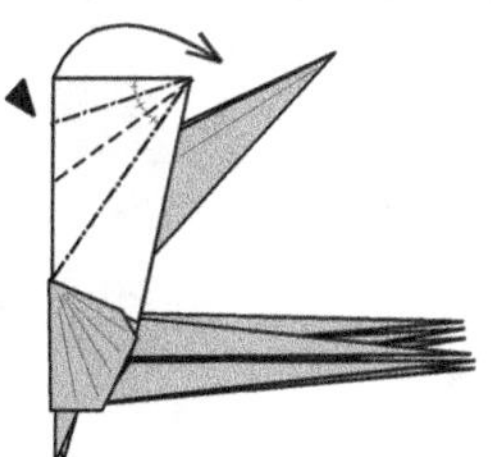

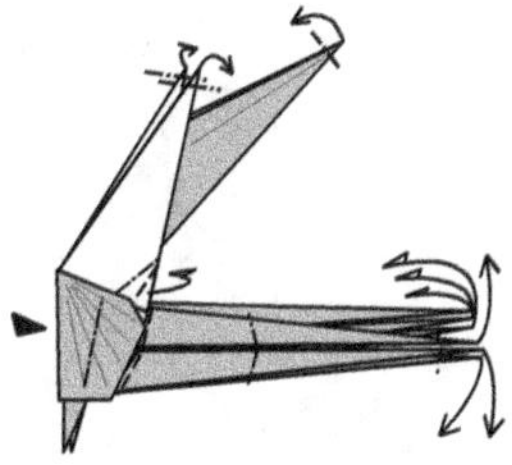

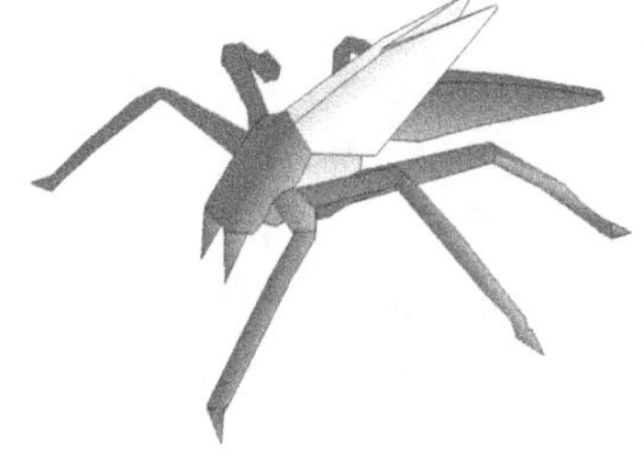

64. Reverse fold in and out, allowing the resulting pleat to fall inside the tail.

65. Reverse fold the tips of the wings and abdomen. Round out the body and wings. Position the legs to taste.

66. Completed *Mosquito*.

Cankerworm

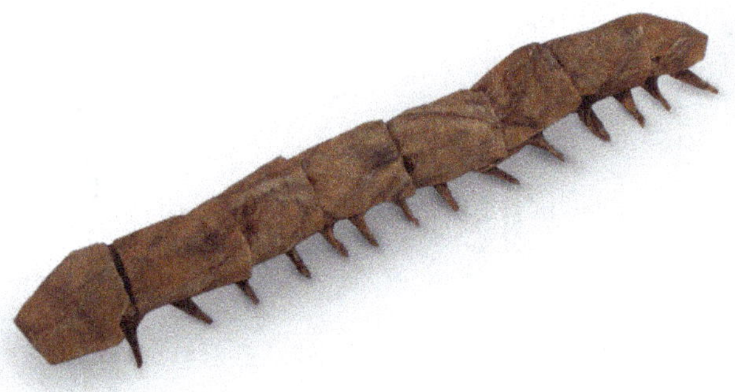

About

Although it might not be obvious, the method for coaxing this many legs is similar to the blintz technique (used in the previous two models). The idea is that all of the major appendages are derived from around the perimeter of the square. The pleating formed in step five is an exaggerated blintz, creating even more corners. The original incarnation of this model did not have the body-pleating step seventy-four depicts, but I find it allows for more dynamic posing. In case you were wondering what a cankerworm is, think of how a caterpillar metamorphoses into a butterfly; analogously, the cankerworm changes into a moth. It is distinctive from the caterpillar family as there are no serrations.

Tips

In the last few steps of the sequence, the legs seem to be pulled out from nowhere. As the legs are linked with each other, pulling on one leg might cause its neighbor to unfold. The key is to locate the tip of each leg, and pinch each one flat from its vertex. This balancing act will pay off, as the appendages will appear to be more distinct.

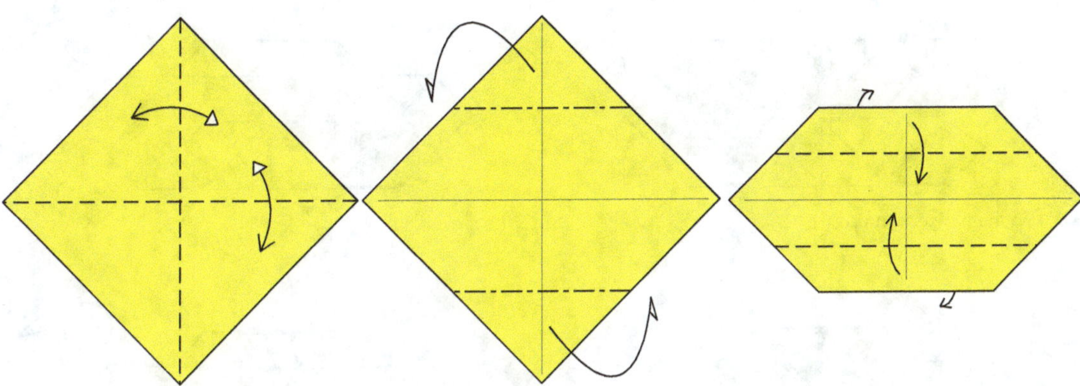

1. Precrease along the diagonals.

2. Mountain fold the corners to the center.

3. Valley fold the edges to the center, flipping the flaps from behind to the surface.

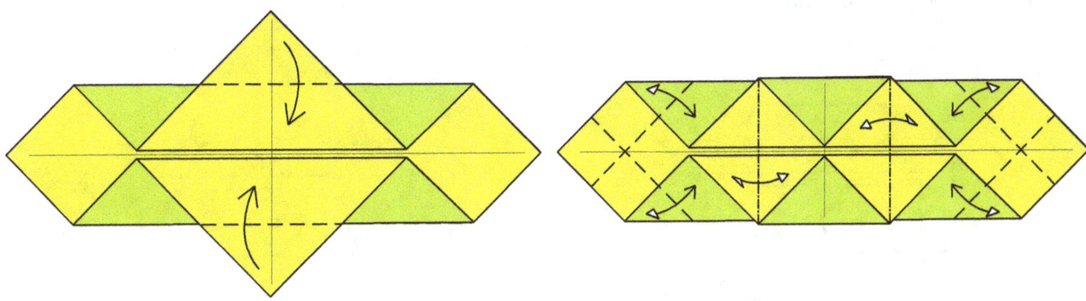

4. Valley fold the corners to the center.

5. Precrease using mountain folds and valley folds where indicated.

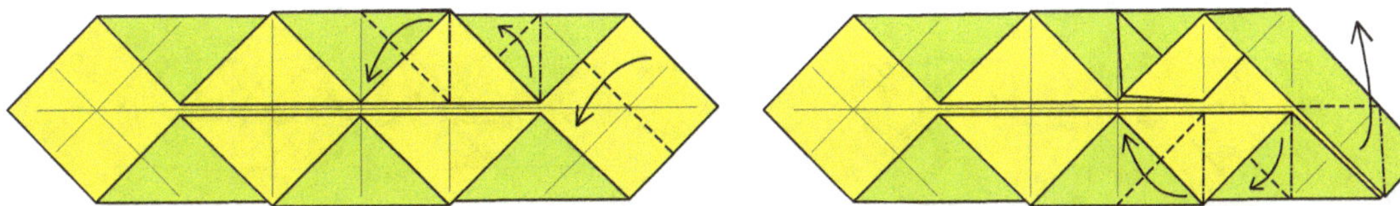

6. Form multiple swivel folds as indicated, working from the center outwards.

7. This is similar to the previous step, but this time the original corner is squashed upwards.

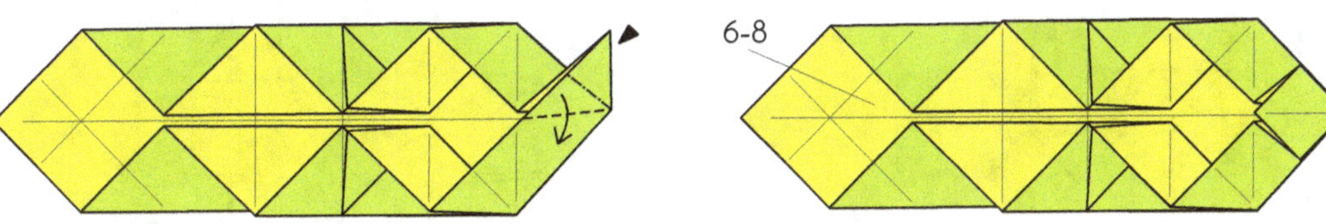

8. Squash fold.

9. Repeat steps 6-8 in mirror image.

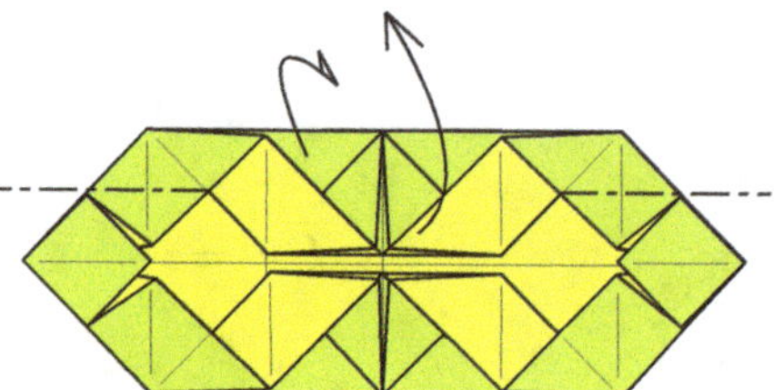

10. Flip the top section up.

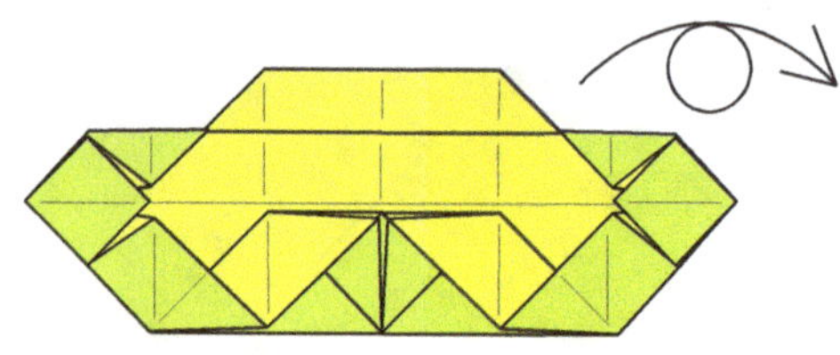

11. Turn over.

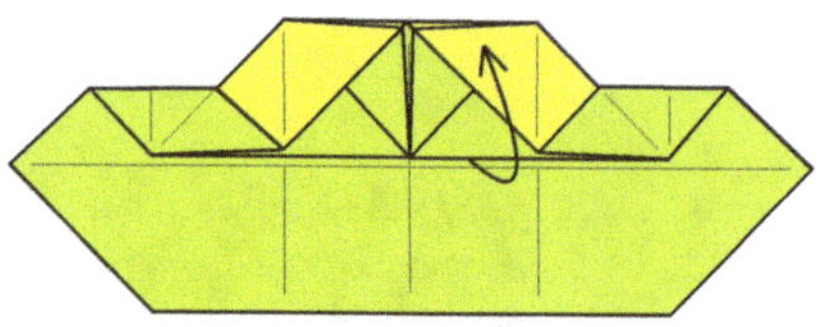

12. Bring the single layer around to the surface. This is essentially a closed sink.

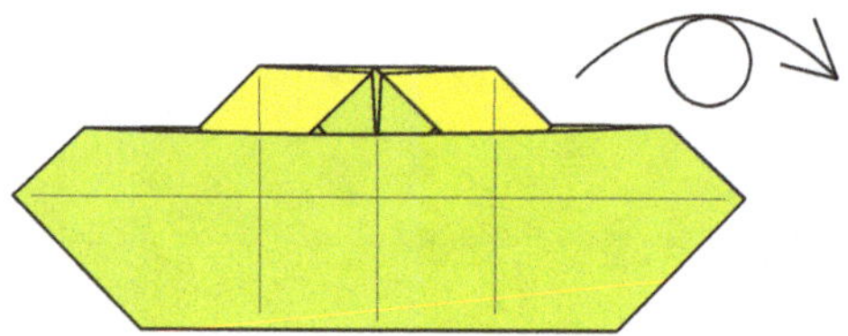

13. Turn over.

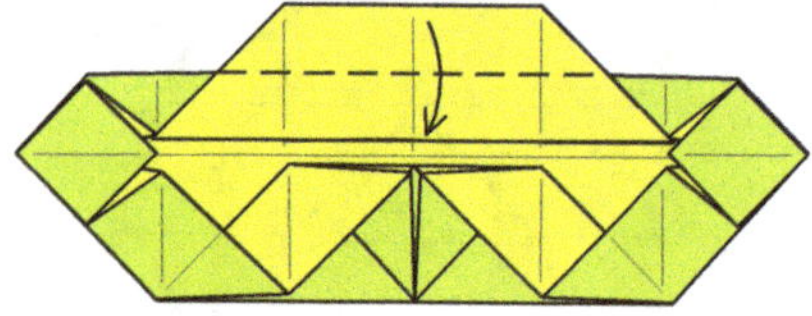

14. Valley fold to the center, flipping the triangular flap from behind to the surface.

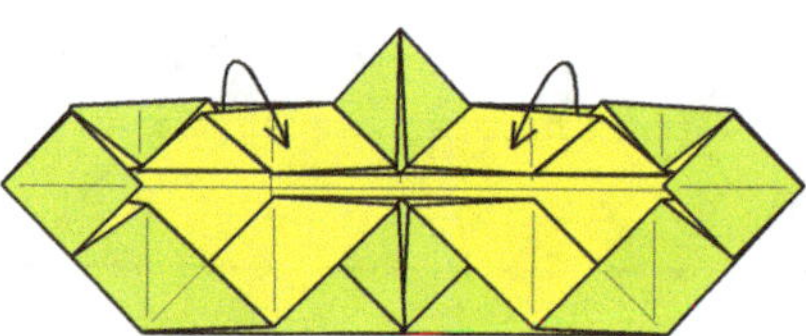

15. Wrap a single layer around at each side.

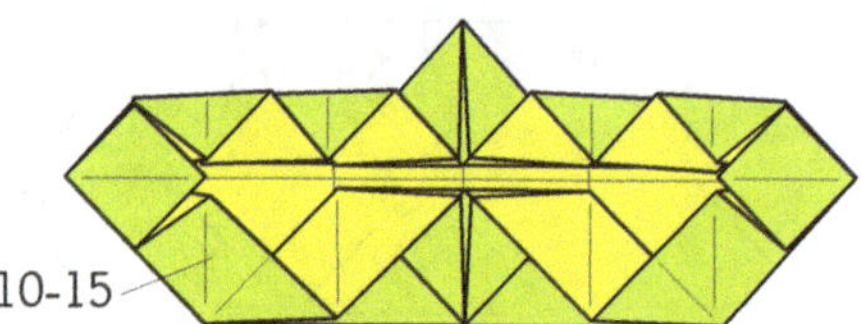

16. Repeat steps 10-15 at the bottom.

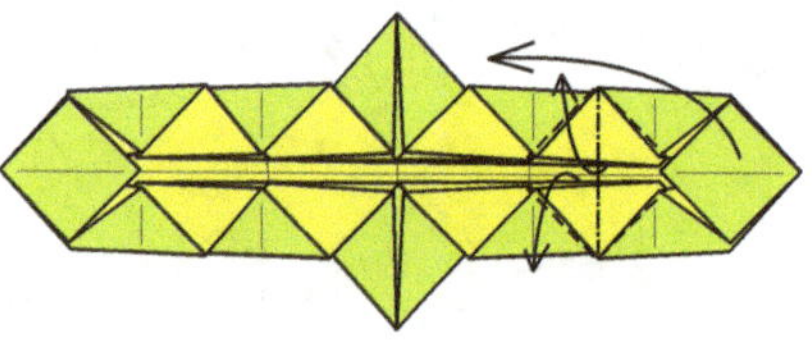

17. Fold the flap to the center, while reverse folding two layers at each side.

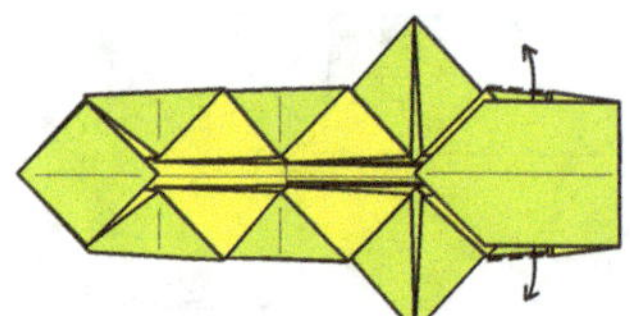

18. Pull out the trapped flap at each side.

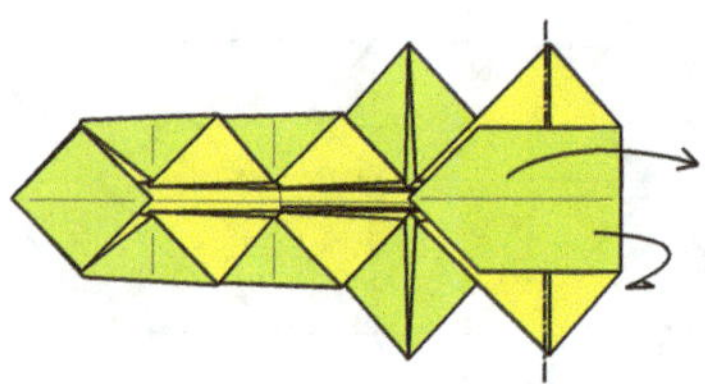

19. Flip the flap as indicated.

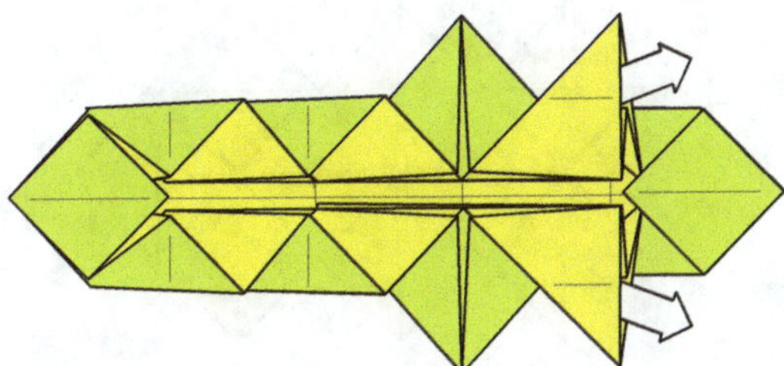

20. Unsink the indicated regions. You will have to open up the model a bit to do this.

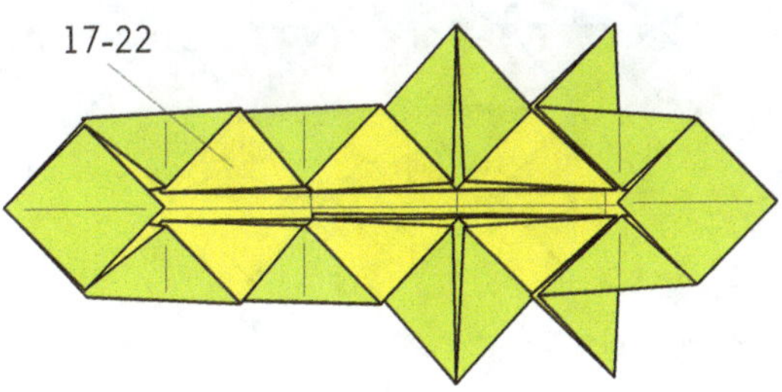

21. Valley fold the flaps over.

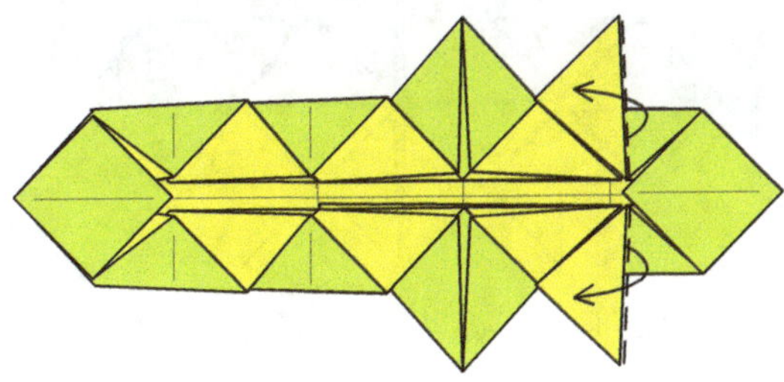

22. Wrap around a single layer where indicated.

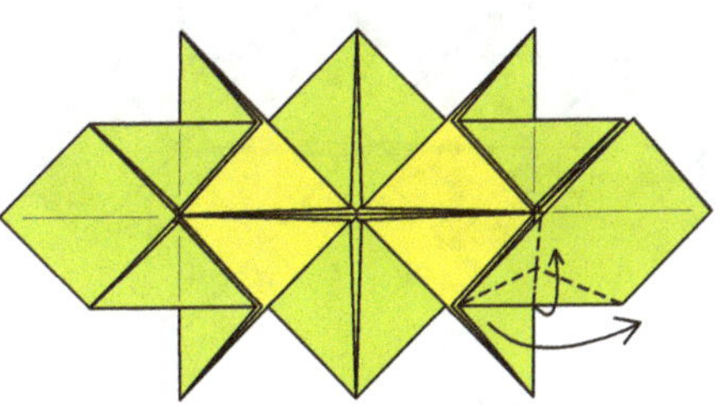

23. Repeat steps 17-22 in mirror image.

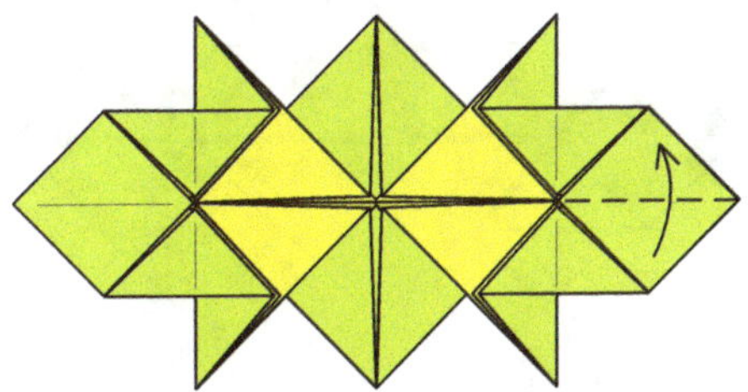

24. Valley fold one flap lightly.

25. Valley fold the flap over while incorporating a reverse fold.

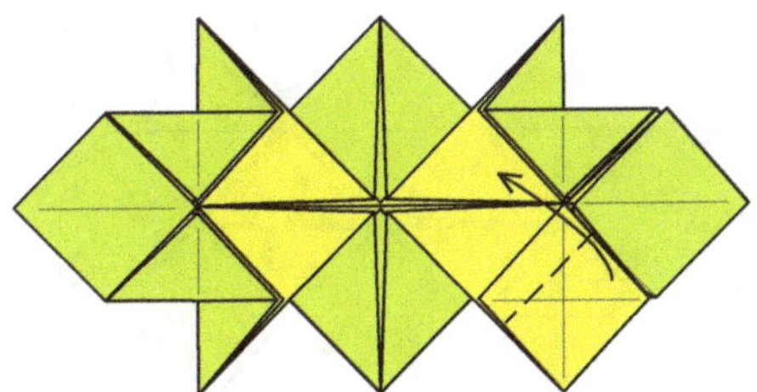

26. Lightly valley fold the flap across as far as possible.

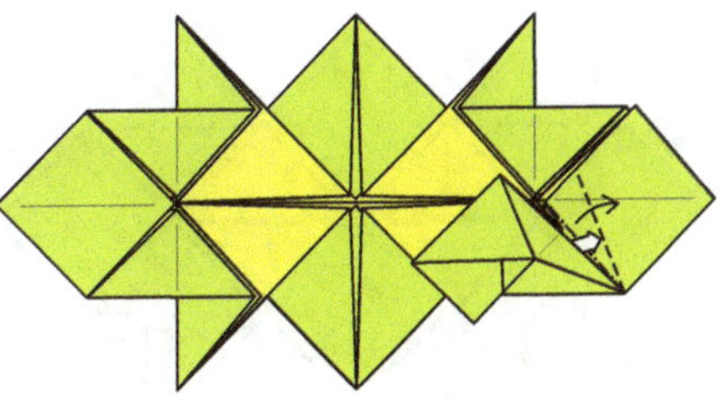

27. Lightly pleat the top layer outwards, releasing the trapped single layer.

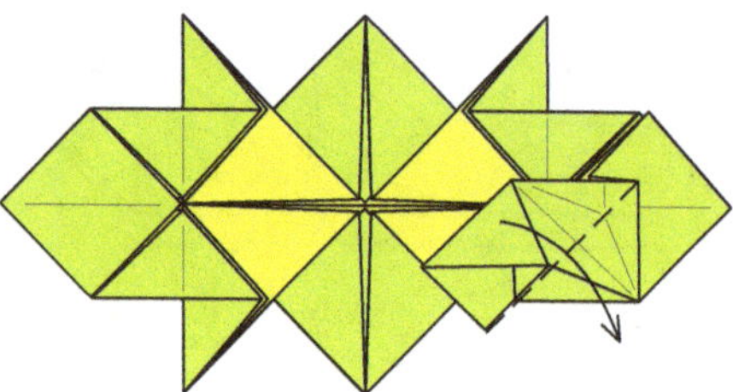

28. Valley fold the flap over.

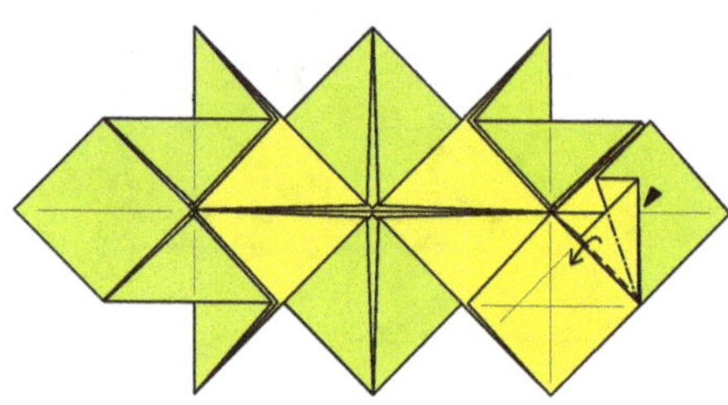

29. Squash fold.

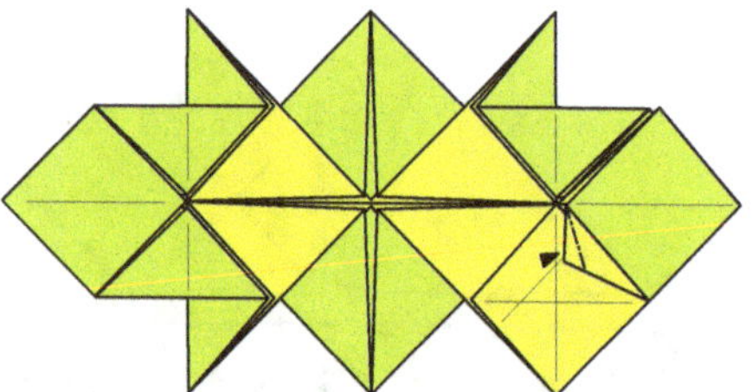

30. Reverse fold.

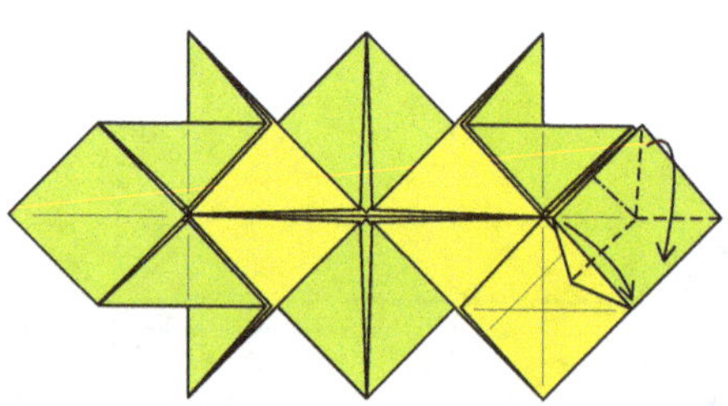

31. Valley fold the flap down while swiveling.

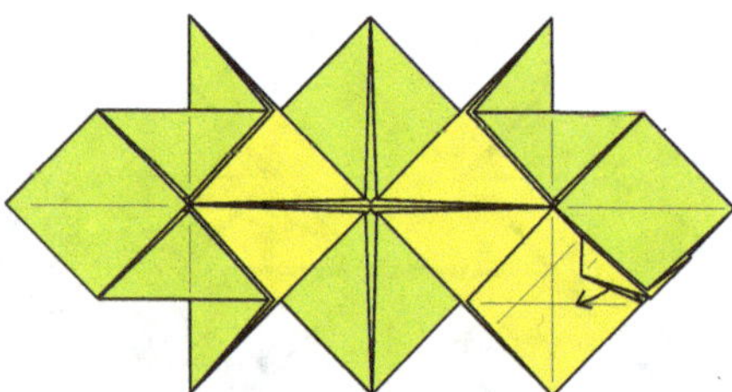

32. Pull out a single layer.

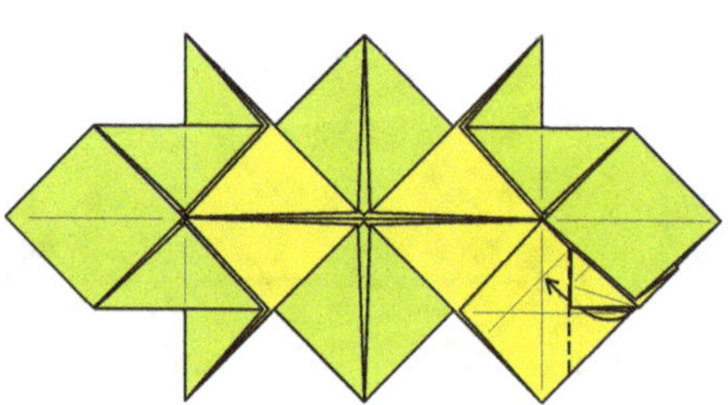

33. Pull the corner through. This is similar to a reverse fold.

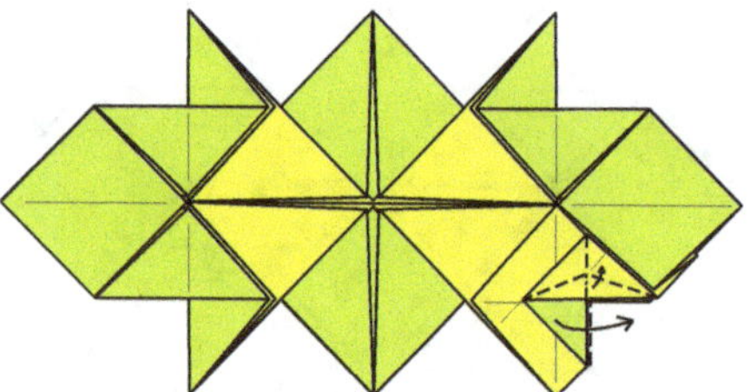

34. Valley fold over while incorporating a reverse fold.

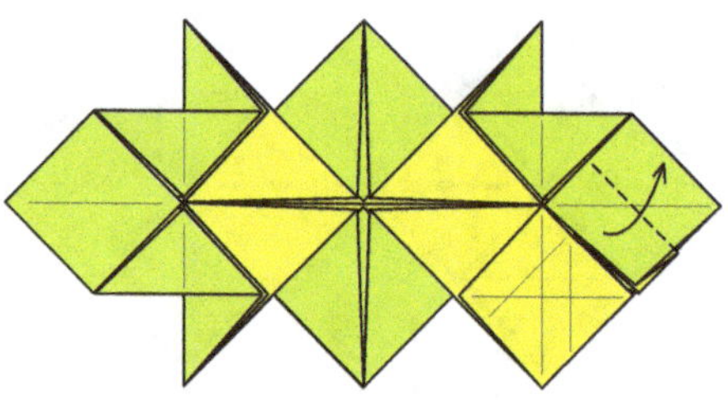

35. Lightly valley fold the top layer.

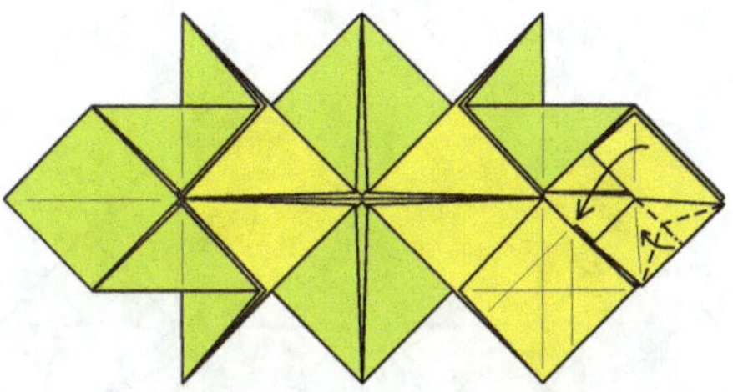

36. Swing the flap over while incorporating a reverse fold.

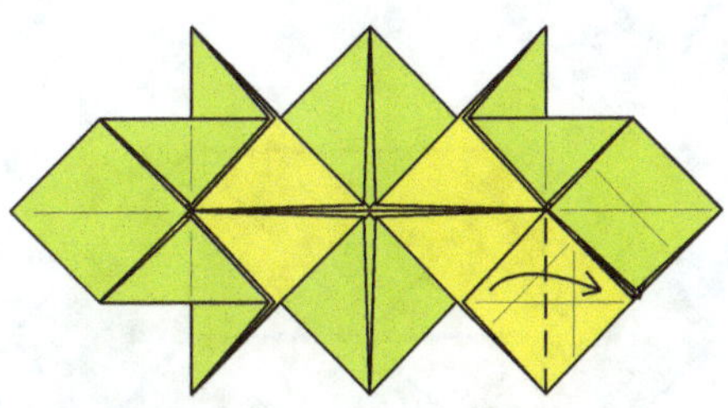

37. Swing the flap over.

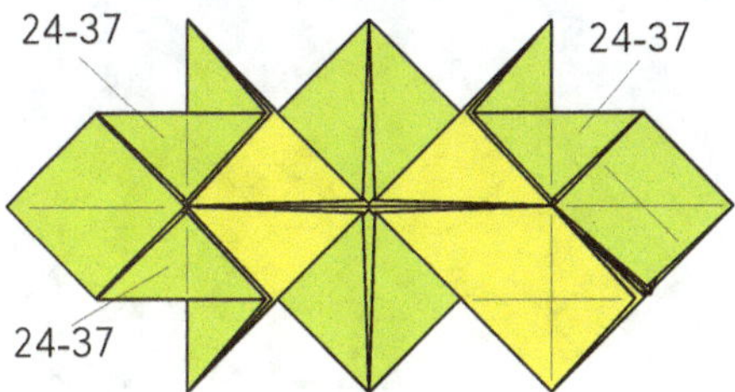

38. Repeat steps 24-37 where indicated.

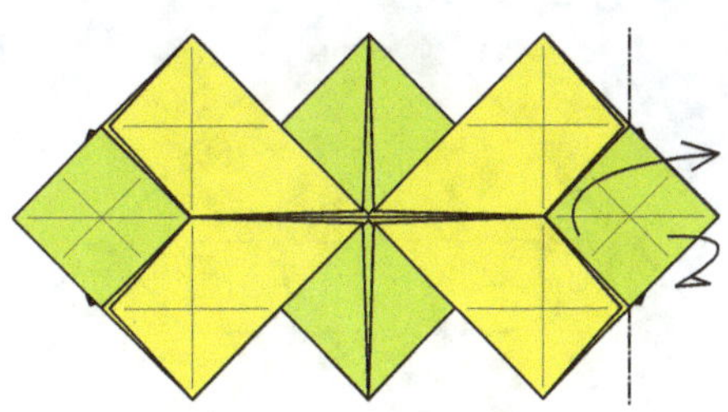

39. Flip the top flap behind.

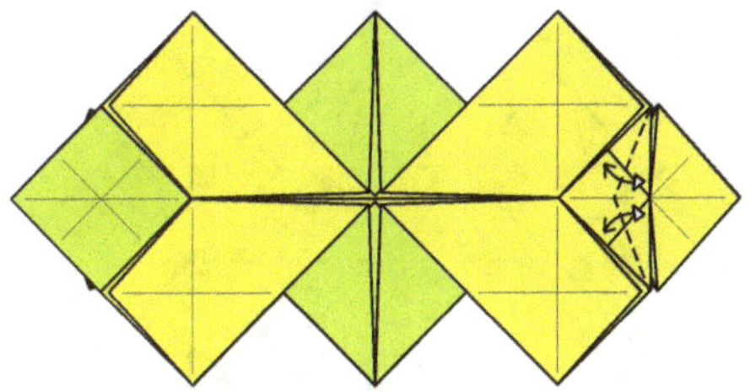

40. Precrease.

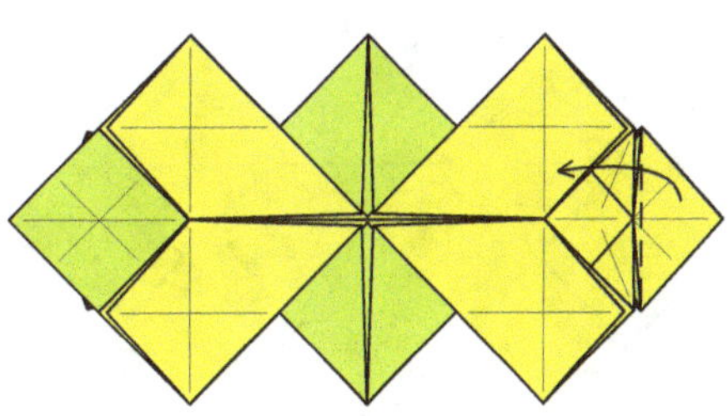

41. Flip the flap back to the surface.

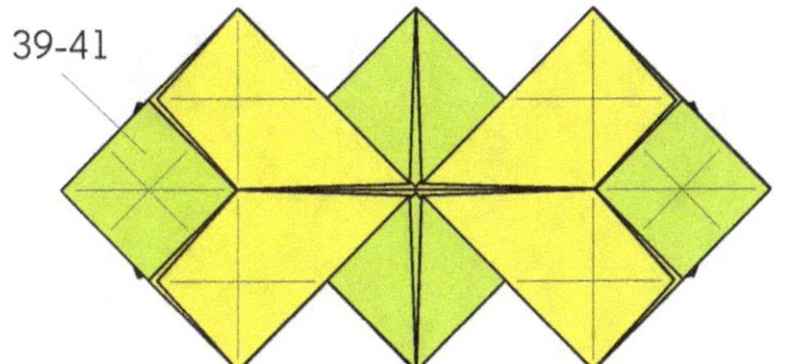

42. Repeat steps 39-41 on the other side.

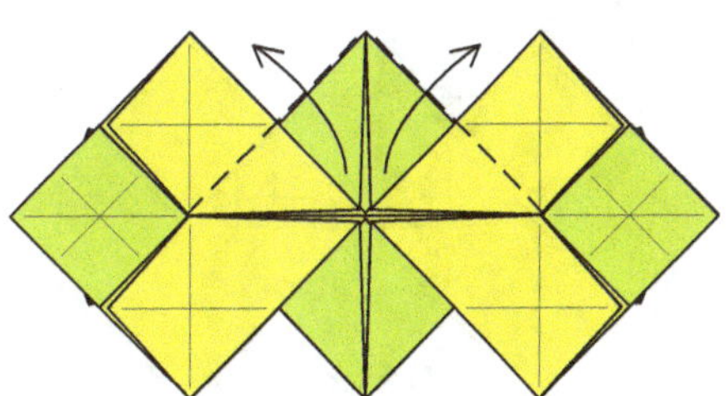

43. Valley fold the top flaps outwards.

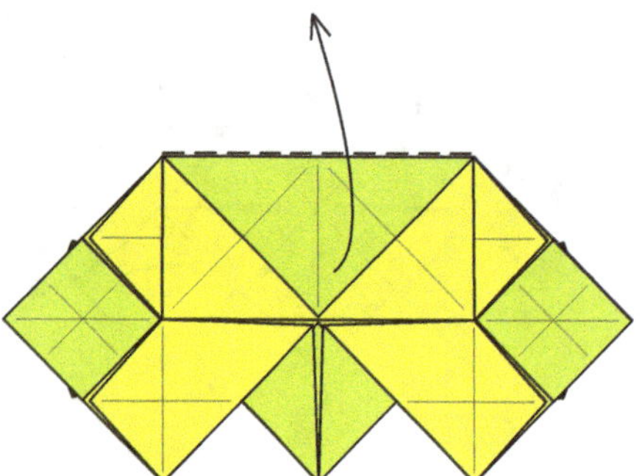

44. Swing the flap up.

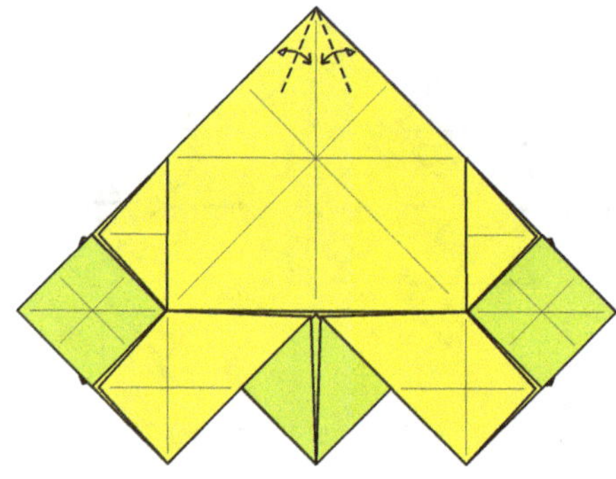

45. Precrease along the angle bisectors.

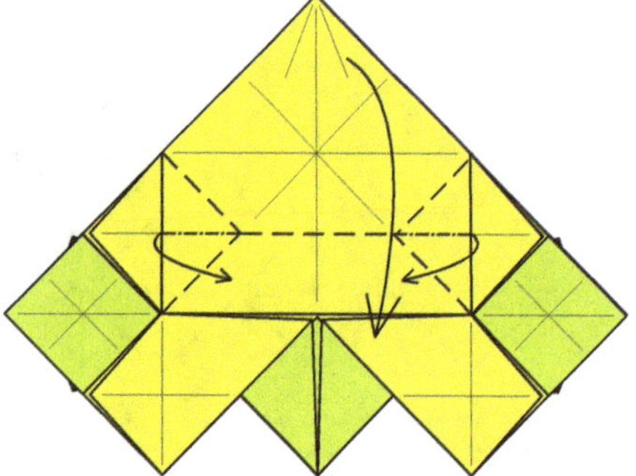

46. Valley fold the flap down while reverse folding the sides.

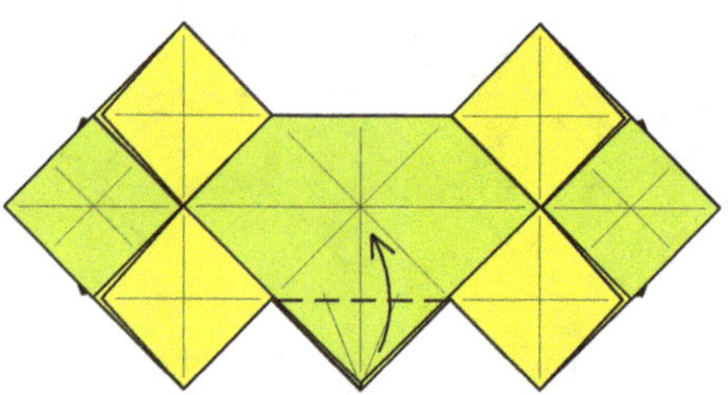

47. Valley fold the flap up.

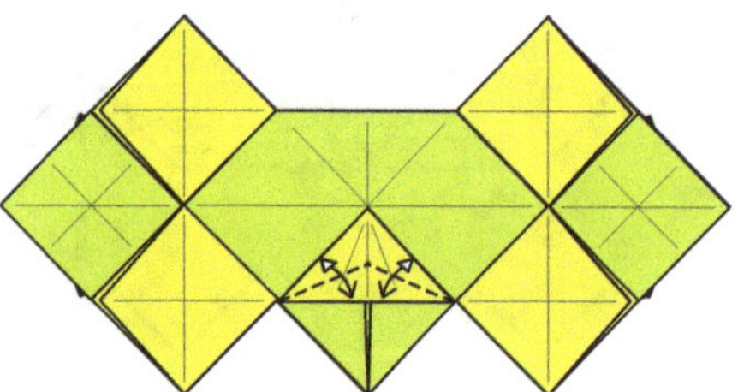

48. Precrease along the angle bisectors.

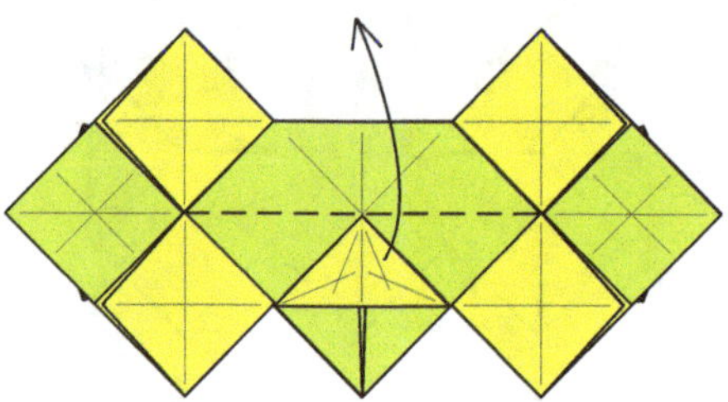

49. Valley fold the flap up, while unfolding the top section.

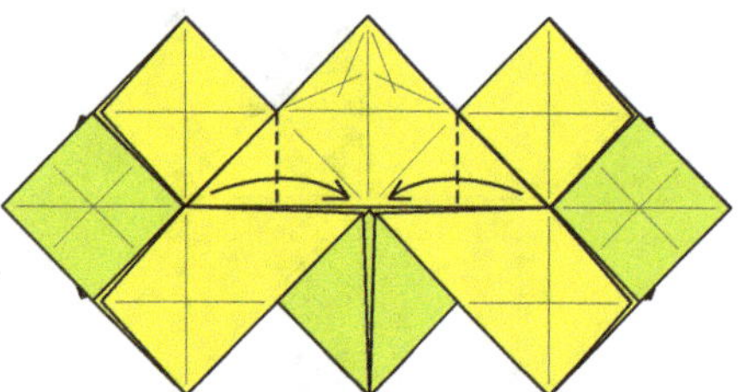

50. Valley fold the flaps to the center.

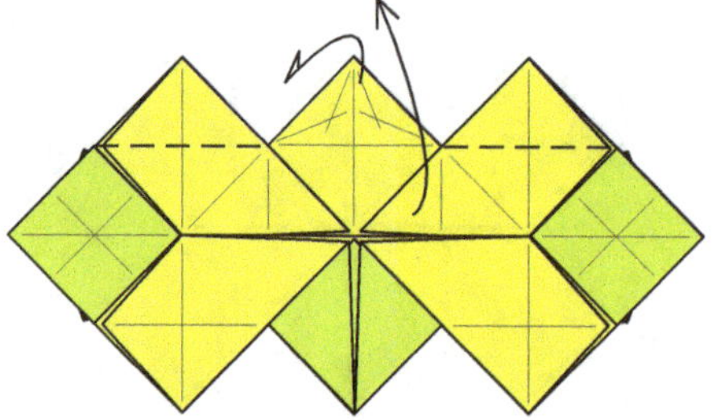

51. Valley fold the top section upwards, allowing the center flap to flip behind.

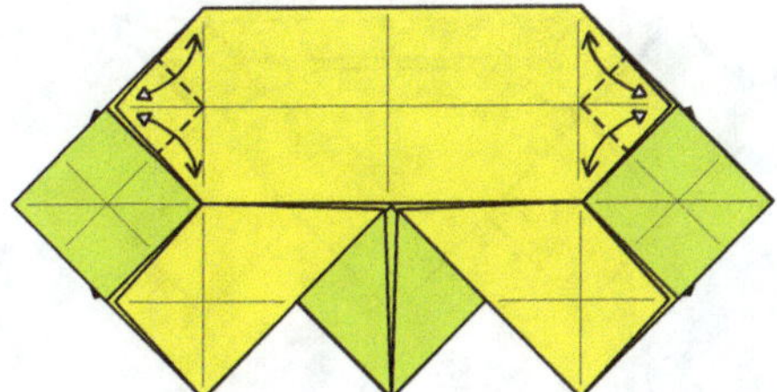

52. Precrease the top flaps.

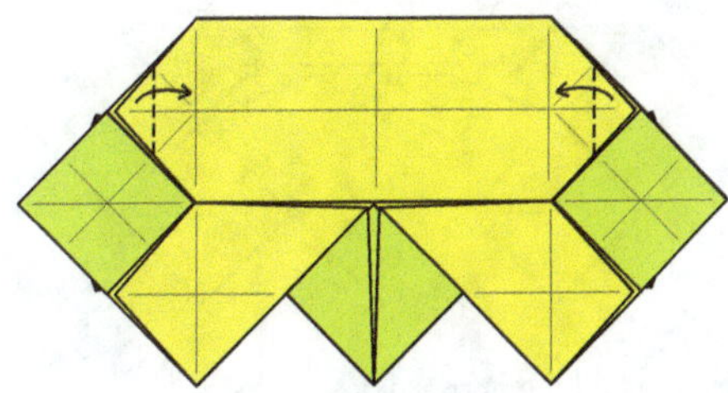

53. Valley fold the flaps inward.

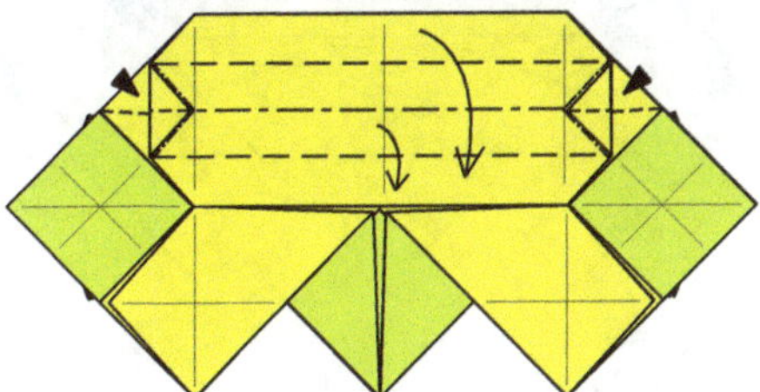

54. Push the sides in while pleating the top single layer down.

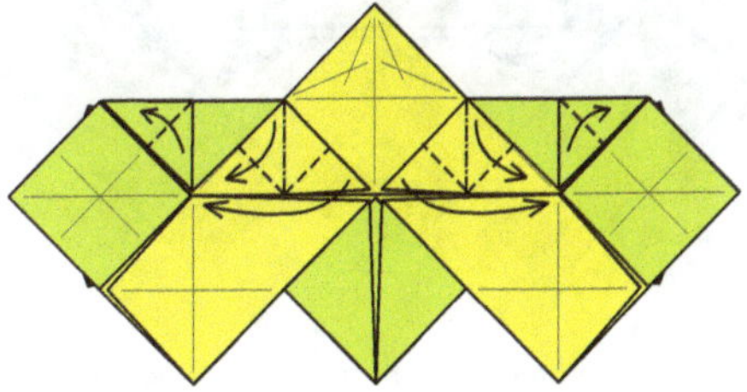

55. Form a series of multiple swivel folds.

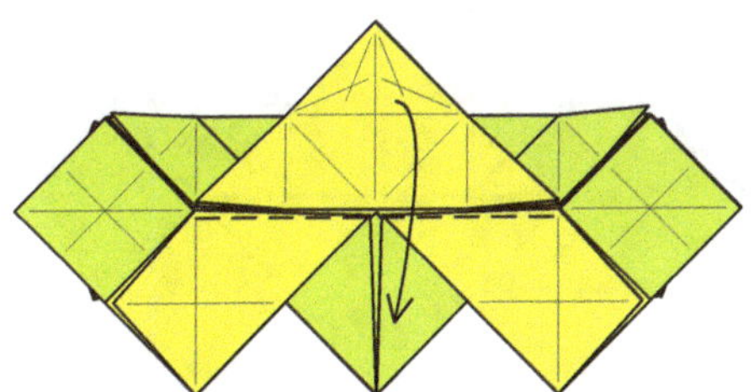

56. Swing the top flap down.

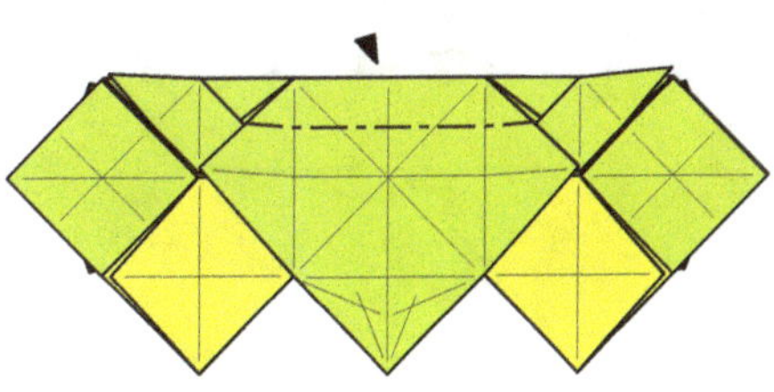

57. Sink the top flap halfway.

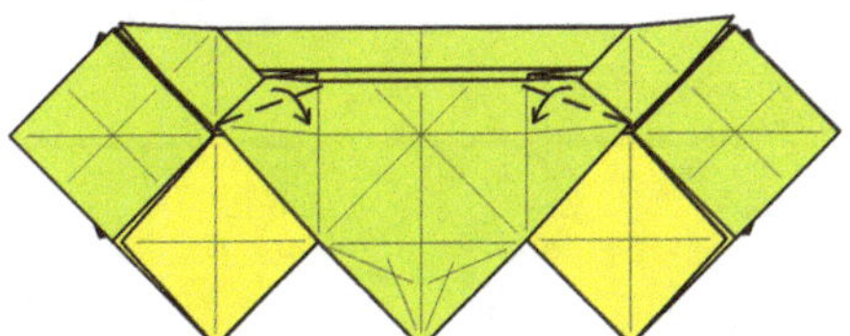

58. Valley fold the top corners along the angle bisectors. Tiny squashes will naturally form.

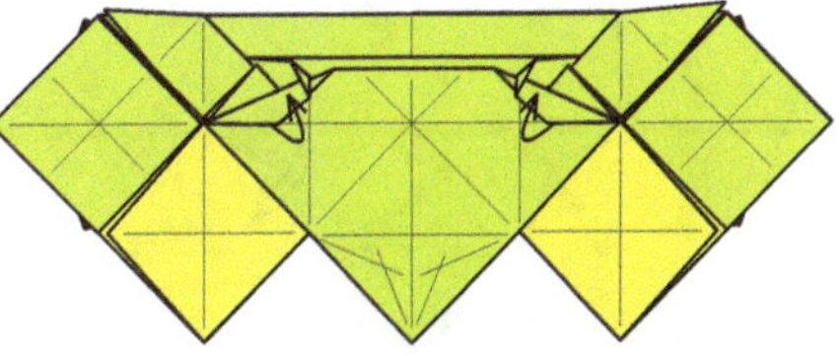

59. Wrap around a single layer to the surface. This is essentially a closed sink.

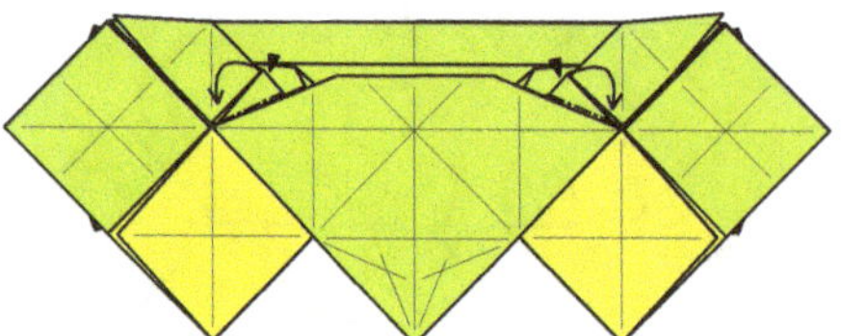

60. Reverse fold the corner flaps.

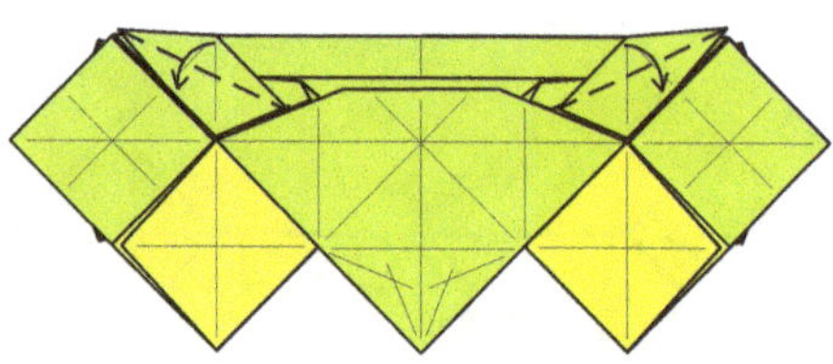

61. Valley fold down.

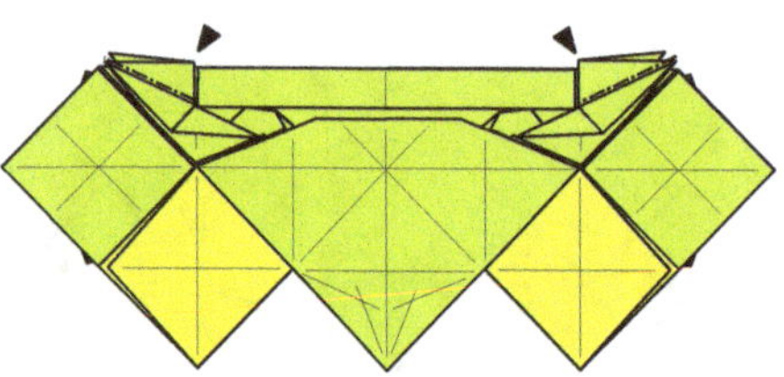

62. Sink the indicated corners (similar to reverse folding in and out).

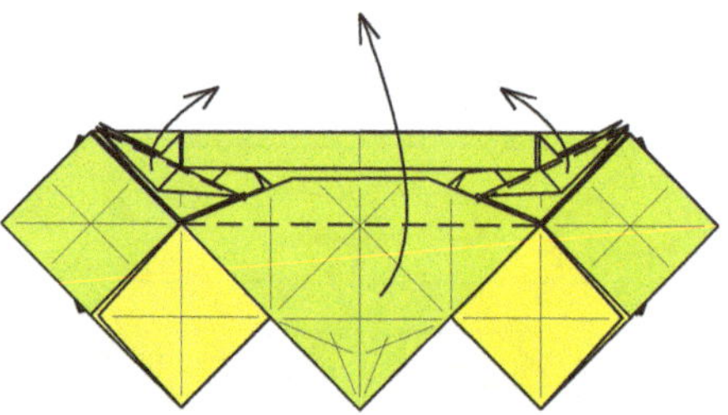

63. Valley fold the indicated flaps back up.

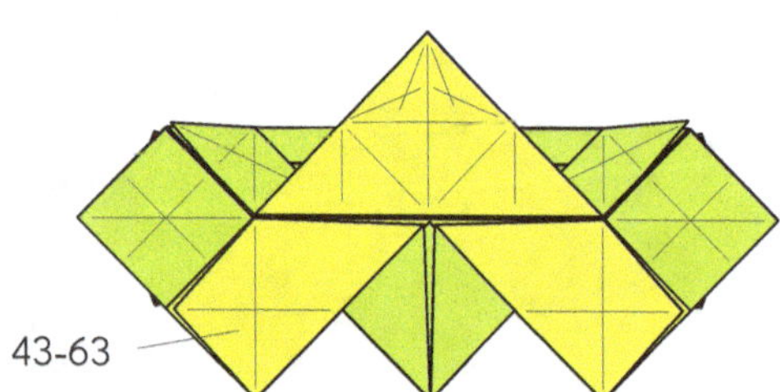

64. Repeat steps 43-63 on the bottom.

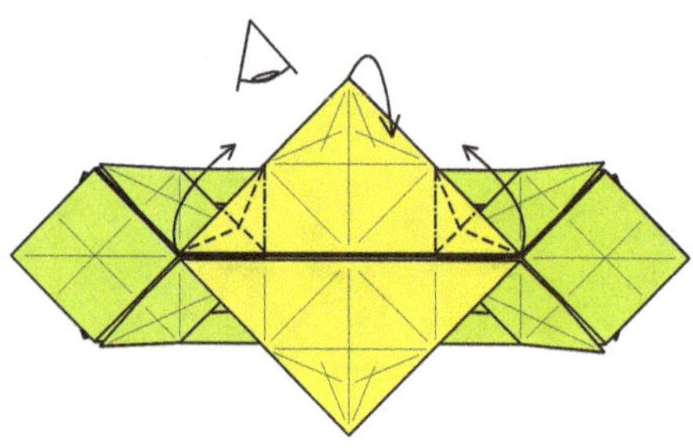

65. Lift the top flap at 90° and reverse fold the sides. The model will no longer lie flat.

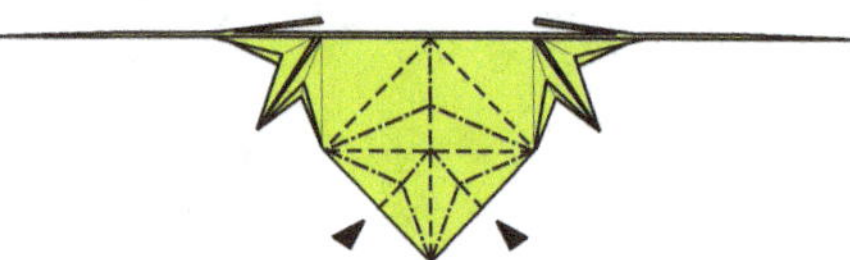

66. View from previous step. Collapse the flap using the existing creases.

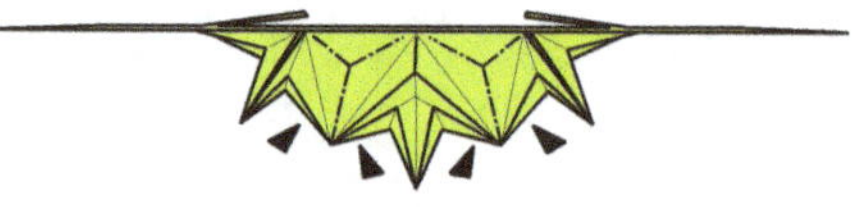

66. Pinch the indicated regions, spreading apart the five legs evenly.

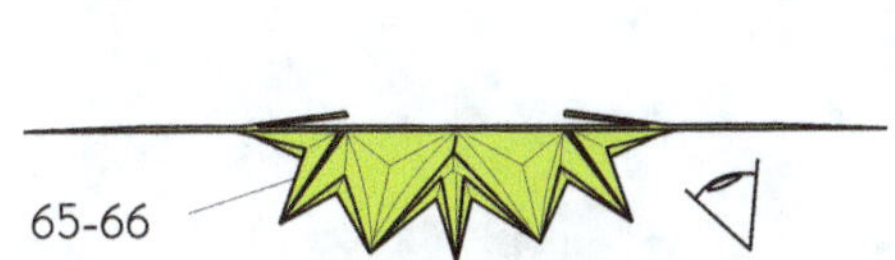

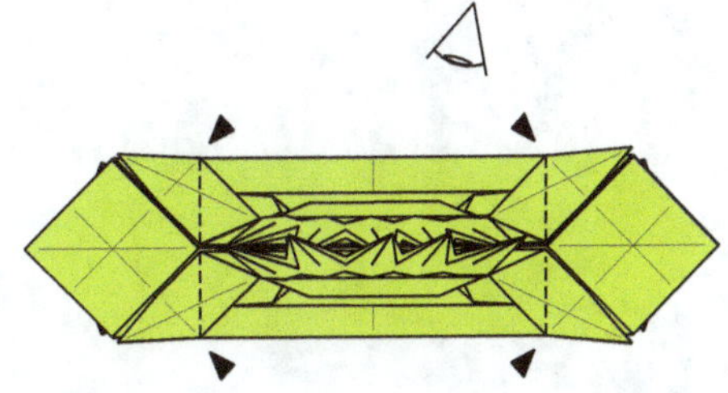

67. Repeat steps 65-66 on the other side.

68. View from previous step. Invert the four indicated corners. They will not lie flat.

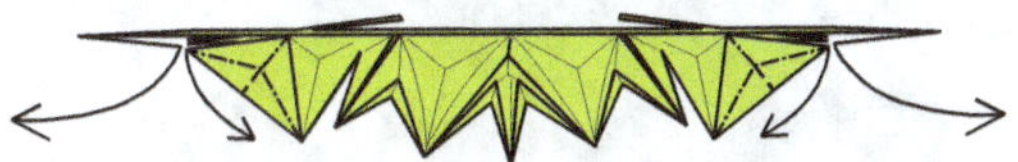

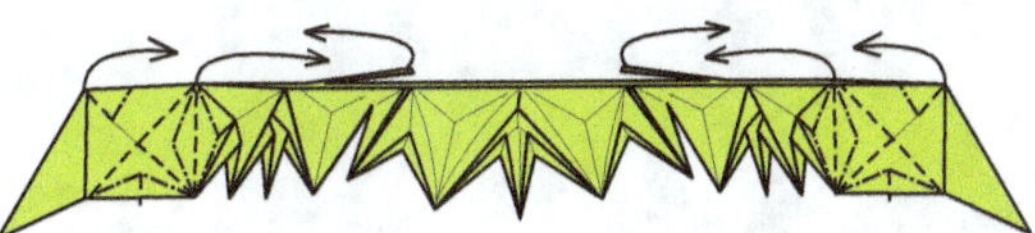

69. Reverse fold the indicated regions and repeat behind. Open out the front and back sections, pulling out the original corners.

70. Collapse the legs, forming a small crimp at each end. Swing over the top flaps in the directions indicated.

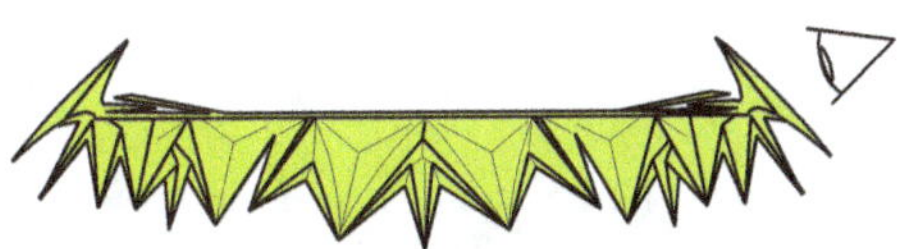

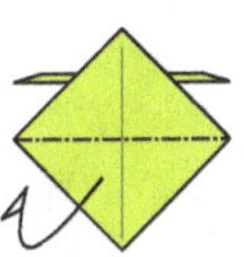

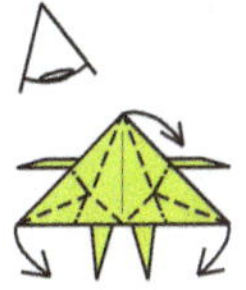

71. The legs are complete, but can be narrowed more easily when step 74 is completed.

72. View from previous step. Mountain fold.

73. Rabbit ear the side points down.

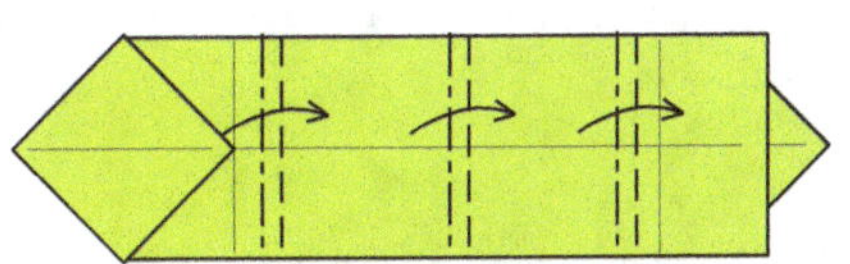

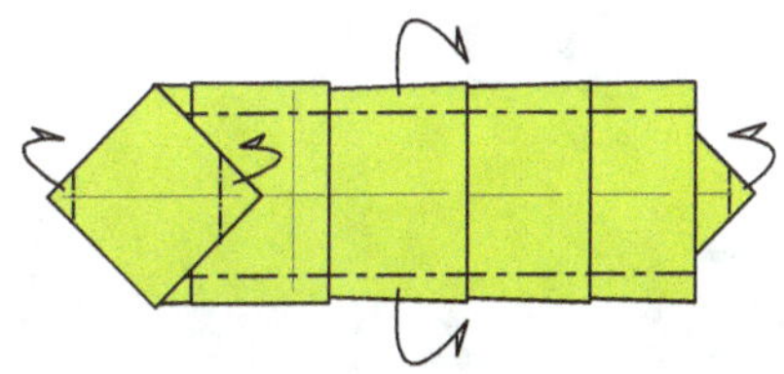

74. Pleat the body.

75. Mountain fold where indicated.

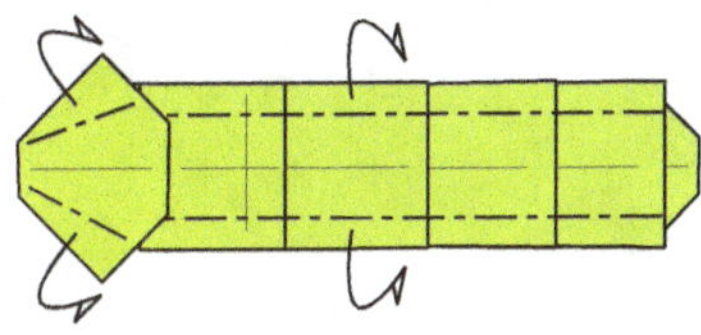

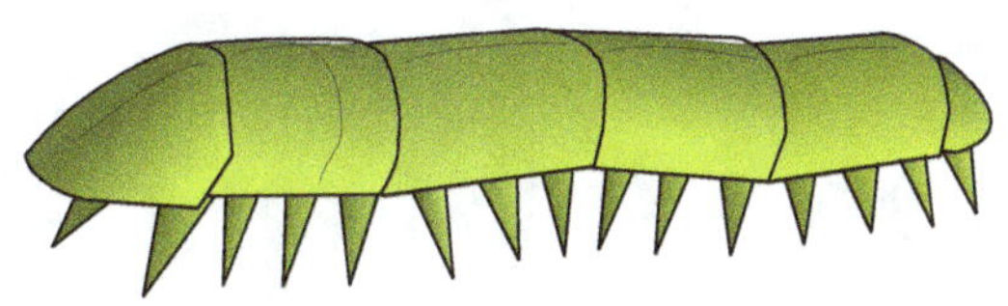

76. Round out the body and shape to taste.

77. Completed *Cankerworm*.

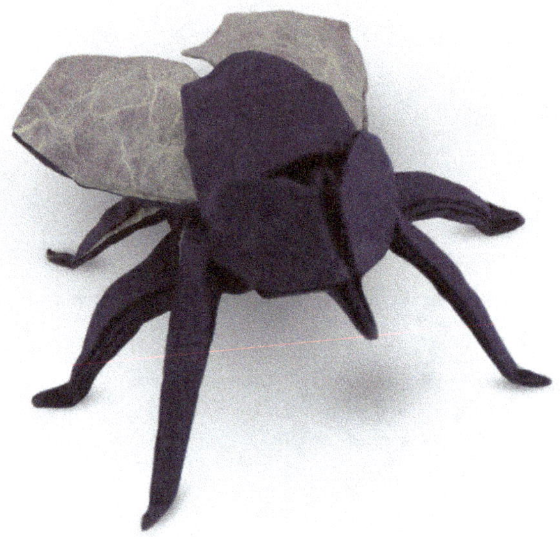

About

The design for this model is both the oldest and the newest in this book. When it was first introduced in 1986, the legs were thicker, and the folding sequence was not as straightforward. Thoughout the years minor improvements were added to make the legs thinner and the body easier to shape. This is the first piece in this book to feature legs coming from the middle portion of the square. Utilizing more of the paper for appendages tends to make for more efficient models. When folding this work, I use colors such as purple and green to accentuate the cartoonish approach.

Tips

Step eighteen might look like a lot of folds, but many of them are along existing creases. If you do one side at a time and work from the inside towards the outer edge, it is not too hard. In step sixty-three, everything needs to be done more or less simultaneously; folding the legs down will provide the slack necessary to fold the front flaps out.

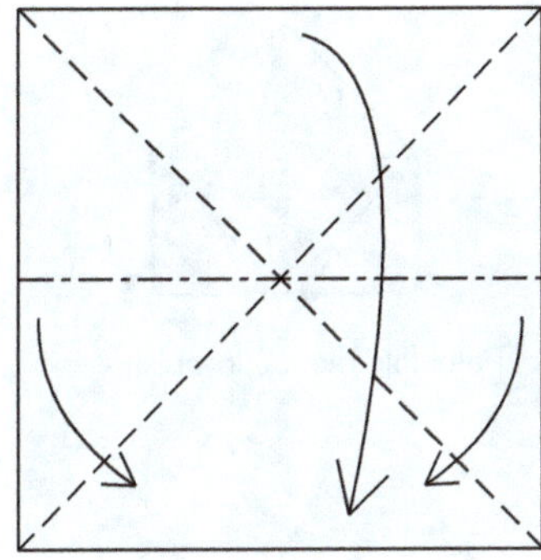

1. Collapse down (Waterbomb Base).

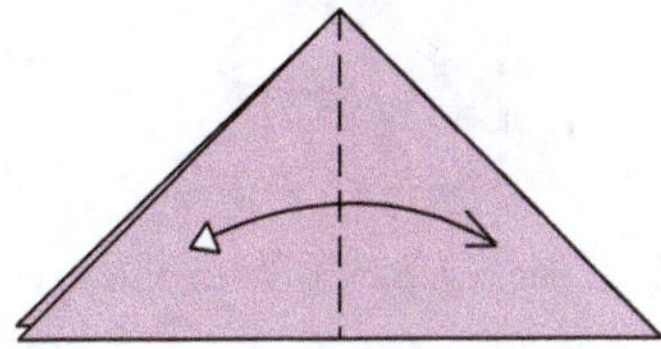

2. Precrease by swinging the flap back and forth.

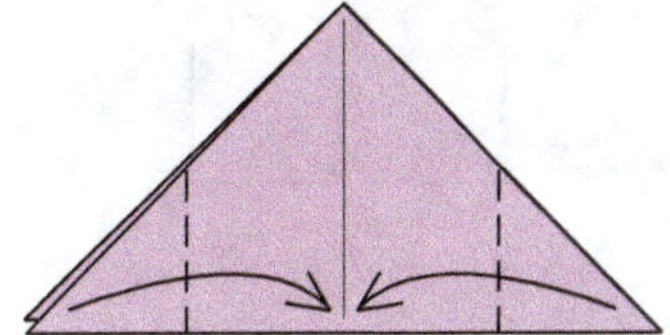

3. Valley fold the sides to the center.

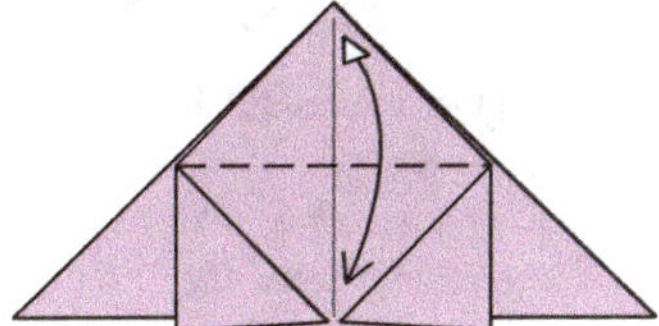

4. Precrease the flap in half.

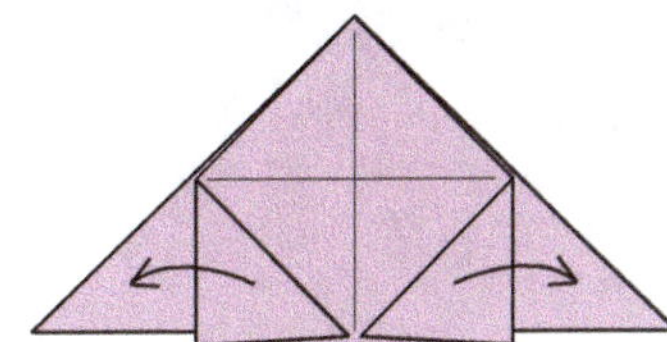

5. Open out the side flaps.

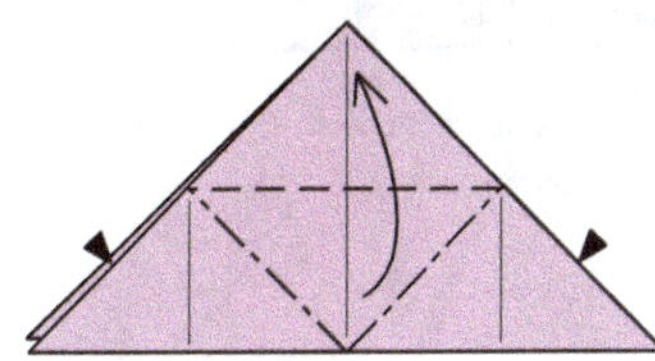

6. Petal fold upwards.

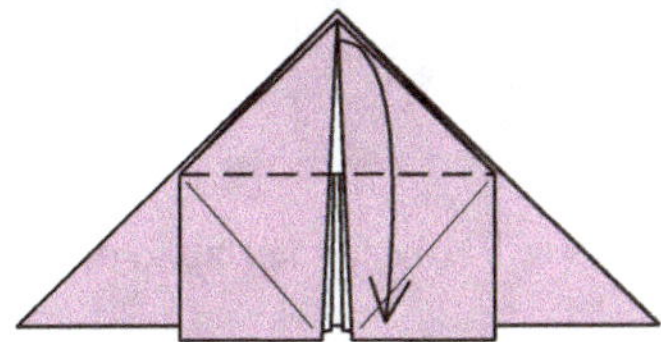

7. Valley fold the top flap down.

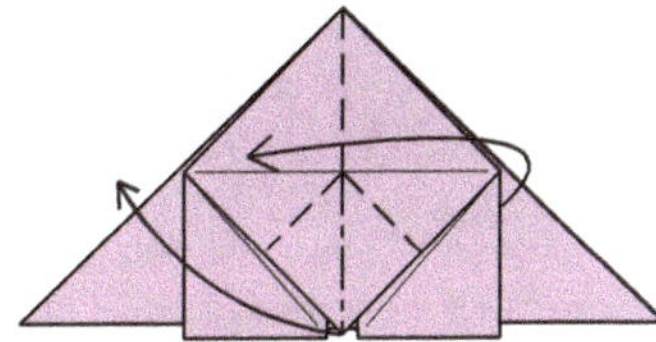

8. Swing over, while incorporating a reverse fold.

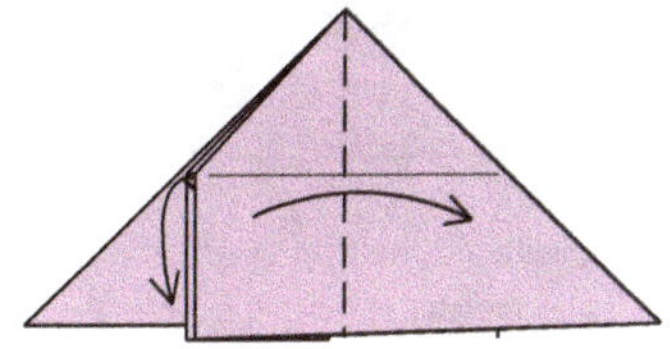

9. Swing the flap back, allowing the center flap to come undone.

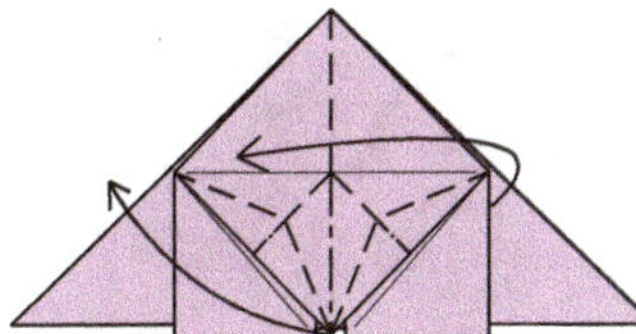

10. Swing over, while adding another set of reverse folds on the flap.

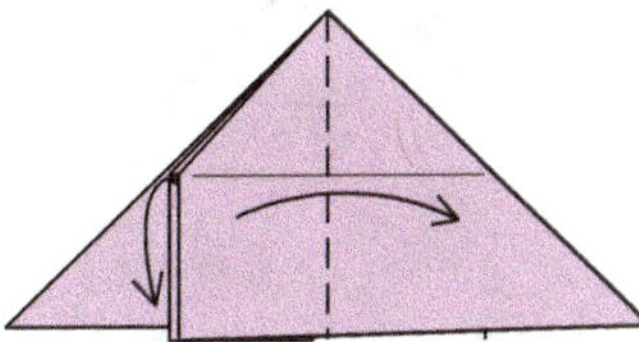

11. Swing the flap back, allowing the center flap to come undone.

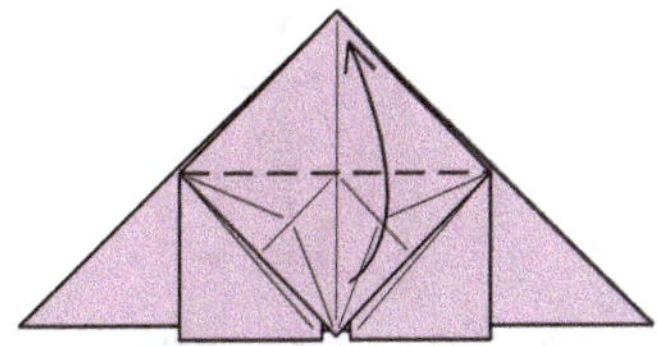

12. Swing the flap up.

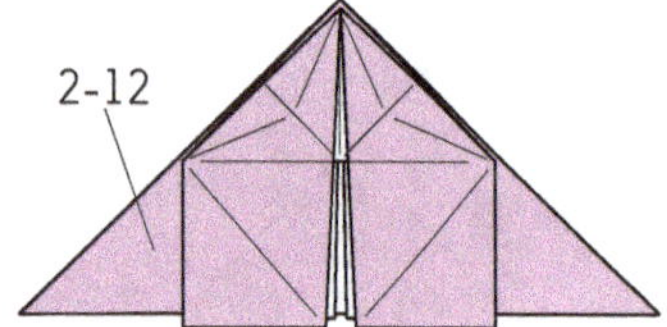

13. Repeat steps 2-12 behind.

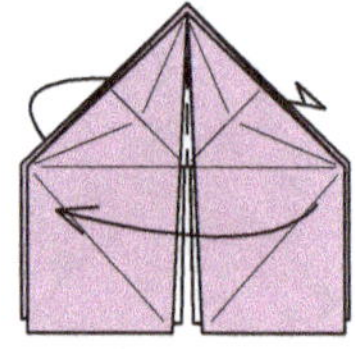

14. Swing a flap over at each side.

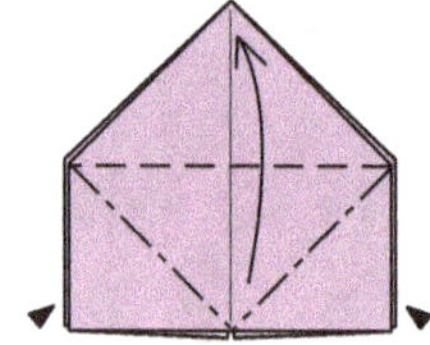

15. Petal fold the top layer up.

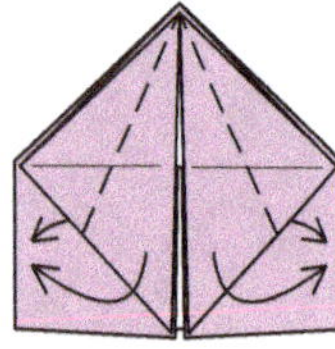

16. Outside reverse fold the top flaps.

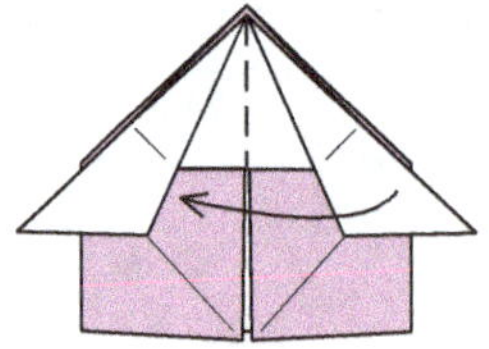

17. Swing over one flap.

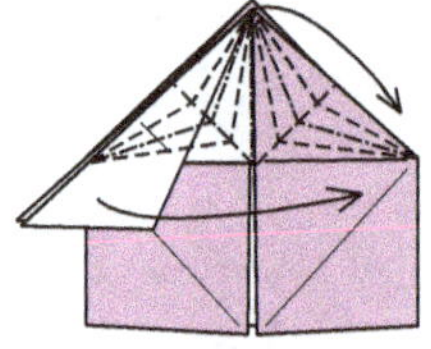

18. Swing the flap back, while inserting a series of reverse folds. The mountain folds lie along existing creases.

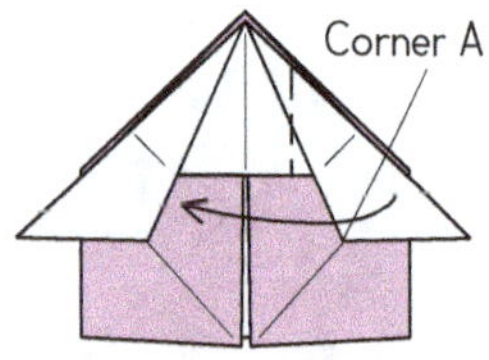

19. Valley fold the flap over as far as possible, ensuring corner A lies along the center.

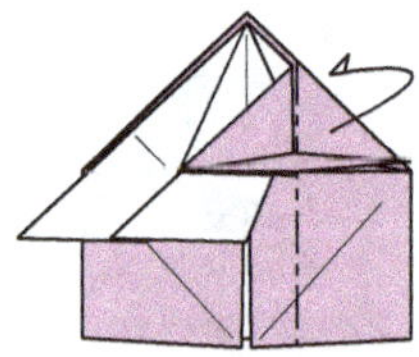

20. Mountain fold the back flap to align with the top edge.

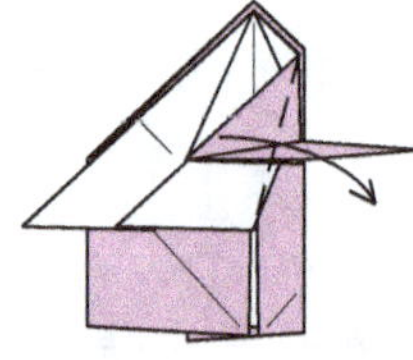

21. Valley fold the top flap outwards.

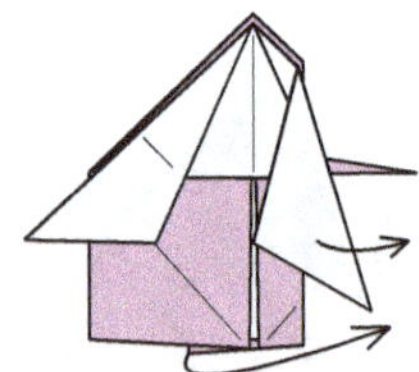

22. Unfold the top pleat and swing the back flap out.

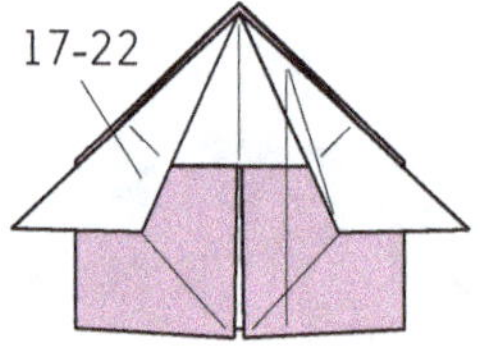

23. Repeat steps 17-22 in Mirror image.

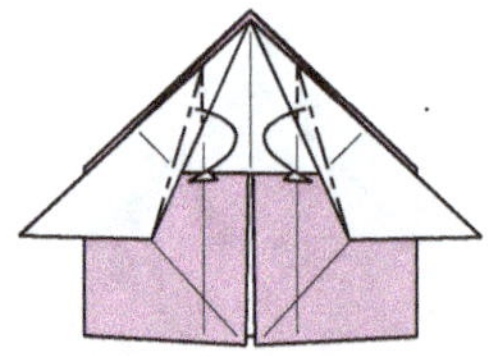

24. Swivel the top layers under along the existing creases. The top flap will curl slightly.

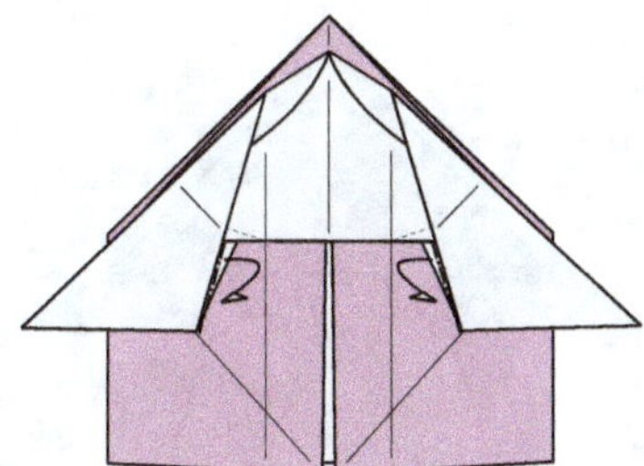

25. Swivel the protruding edges behind along the existing creases.

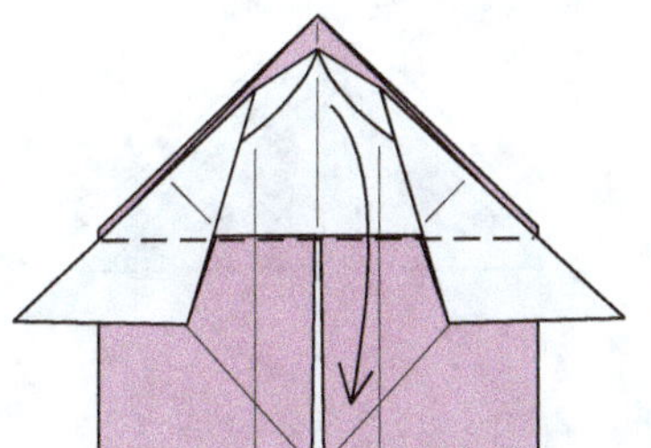

26. Valley fold the top flap down.

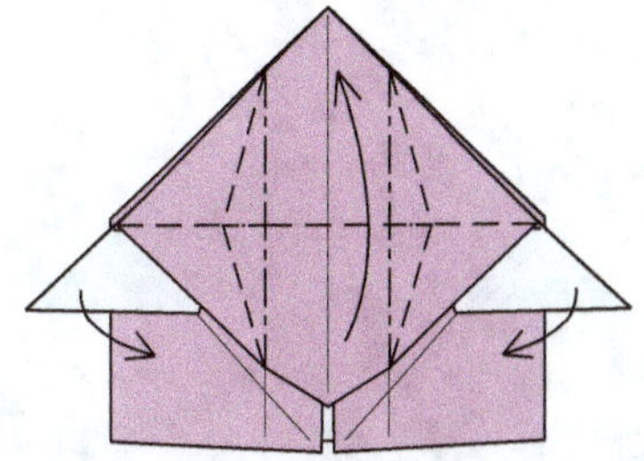

27. Valley fold the flap back up, while crimping in the sides. The model should lie flat again.

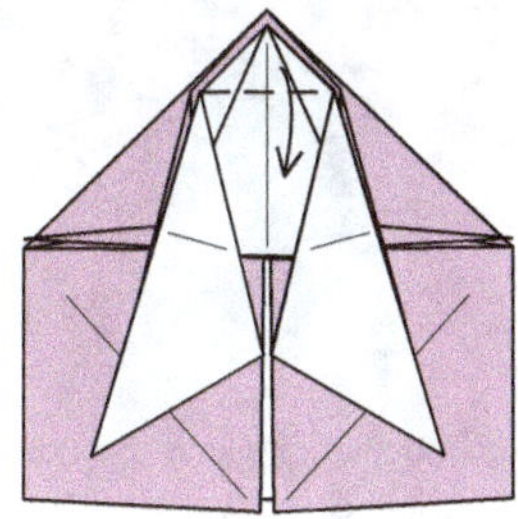

28. Valley fold the top flap down.

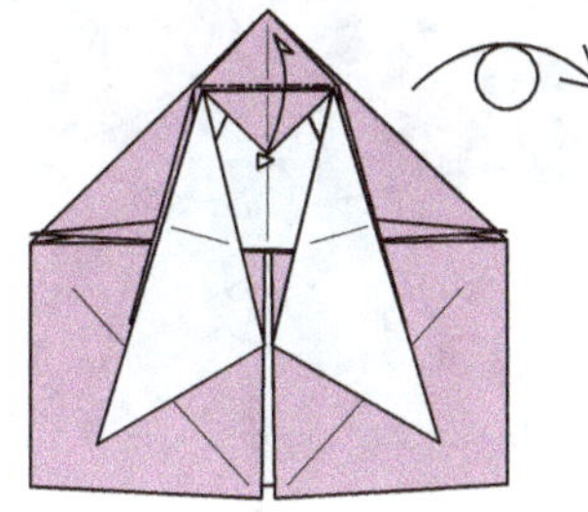

29. Precrease the top flap. Turn over.

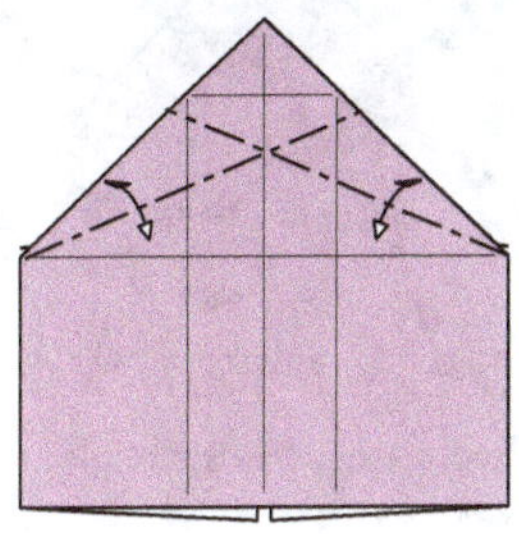

30. Precrease with mountain folds.

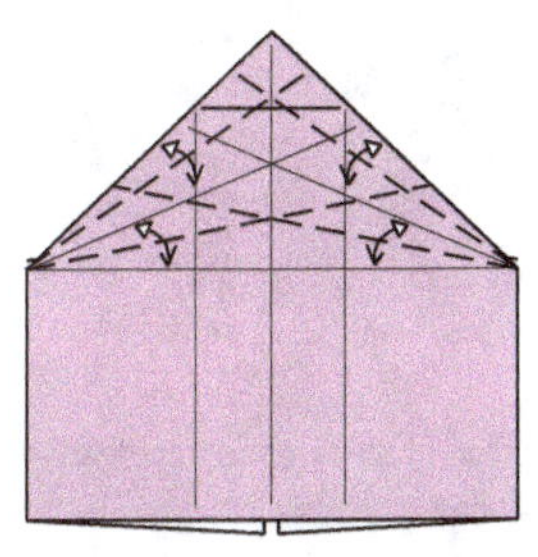

31. Add additional precreases along the angle bisectors.

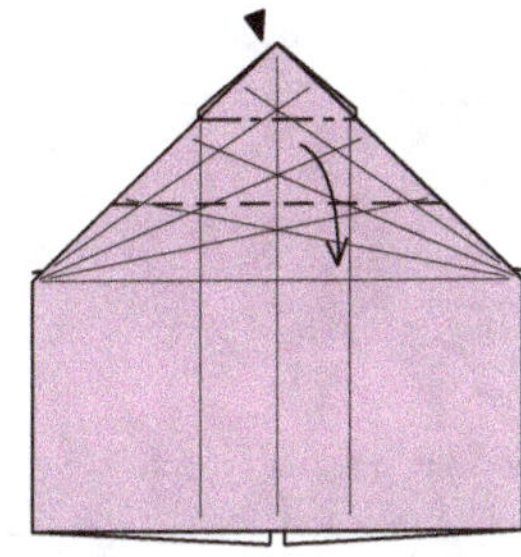

32. Spread squash down.

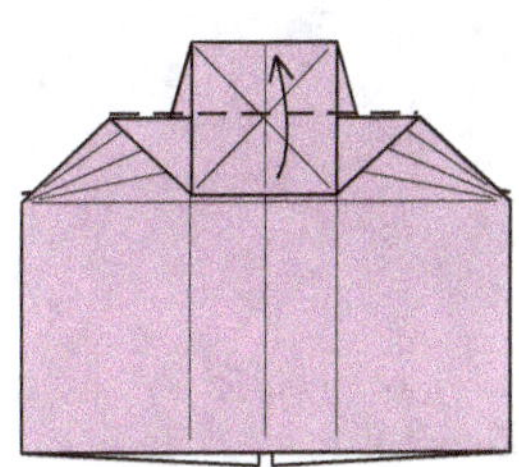

33. Valley fold up.

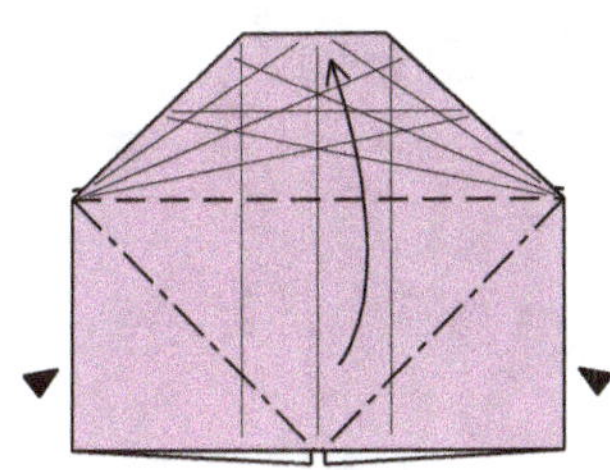

34. Petal fold up.

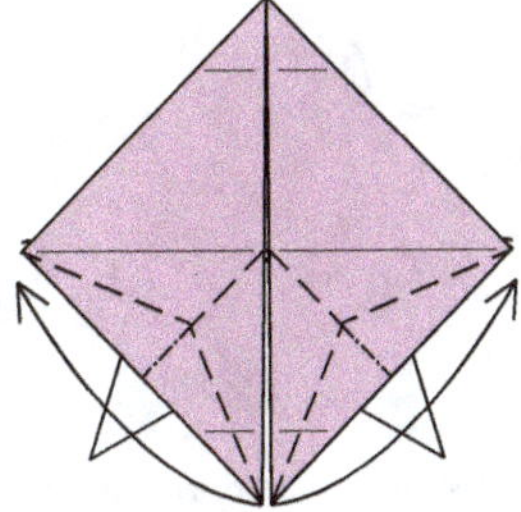

35. Rabbit ear the flaps outwards.

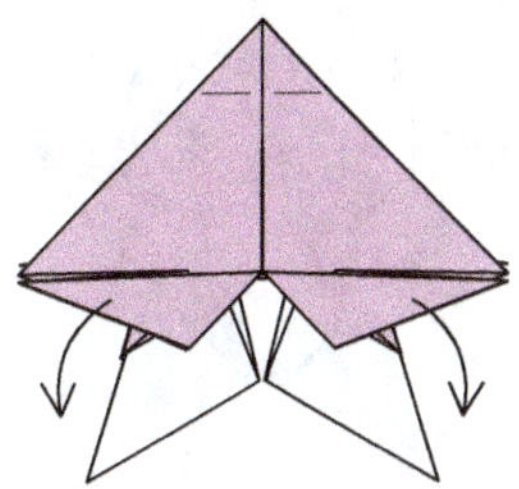

36. Unfold the rabbit-ears.

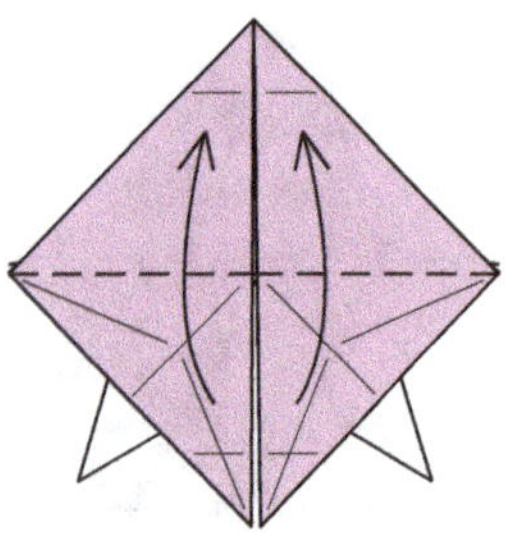

37. Valley fold the two flaps up.

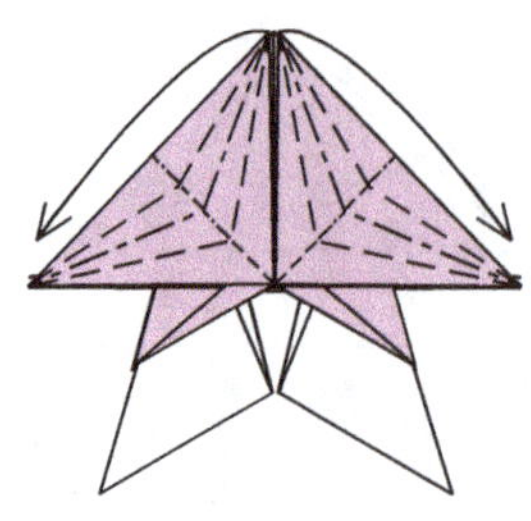

38. Form a series of reverse folds on the two flaps.

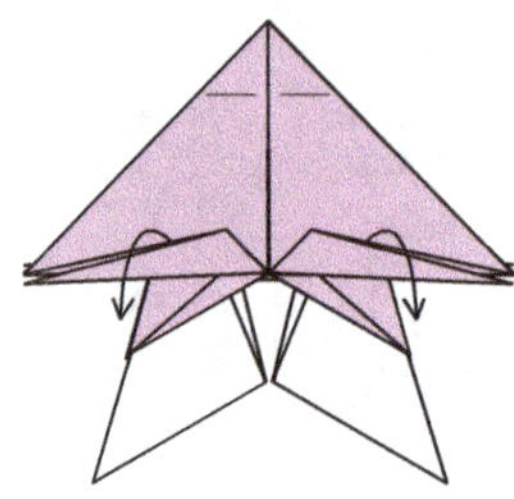

39. Swing the two thick sections down.

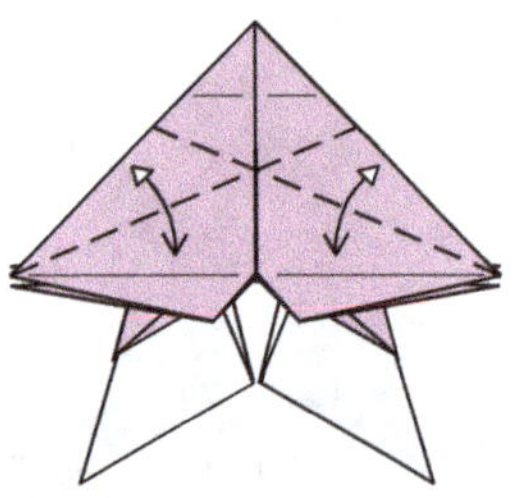

40. Precrease along the angle bisectors.

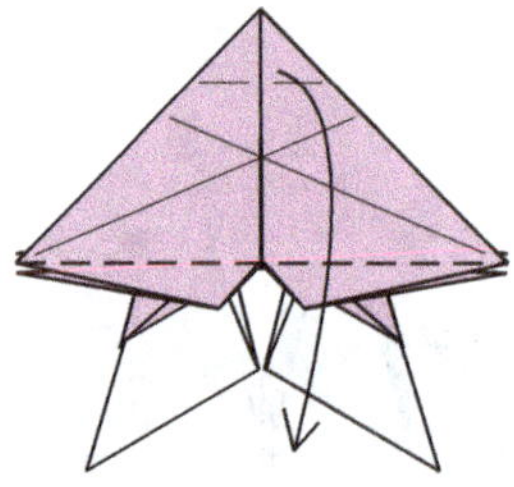

41. Swing the flap down.

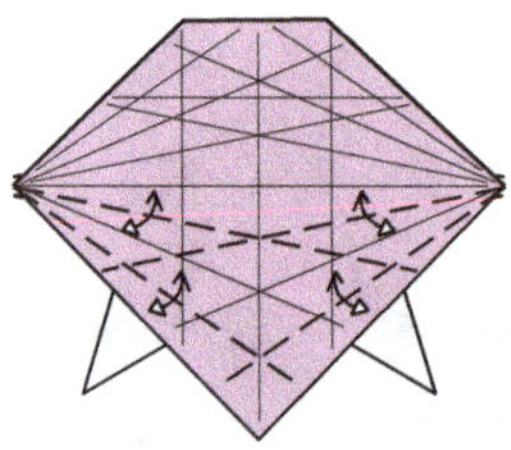

42. Add additional precreases along the angle bisectors.

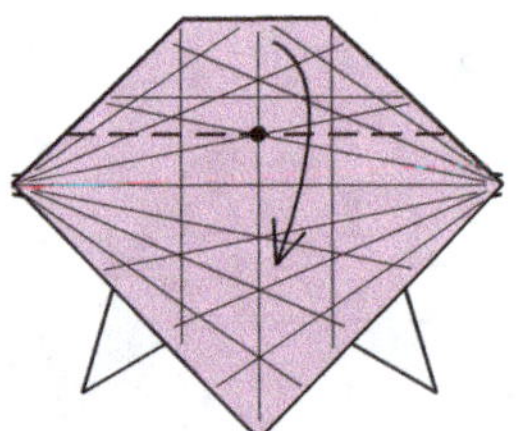

43. Valley fold the thick section down, noting the dotted reference point.

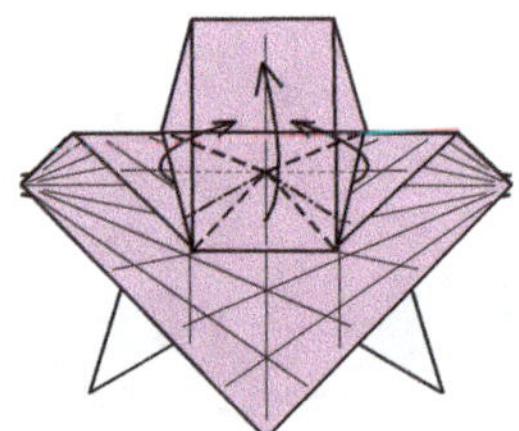

44. Bring one flap up along its pivot point, reverse folding the sides as far as possible.

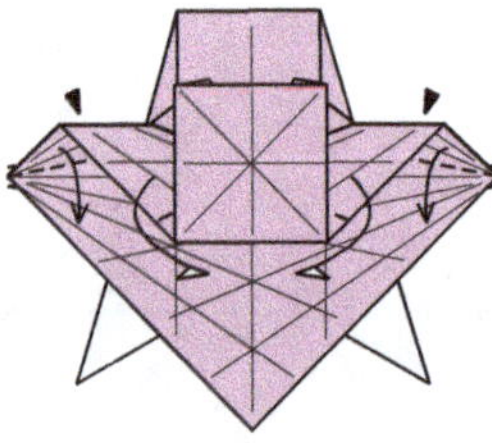

45. Swivel the sides, using the existing crease as a guide.

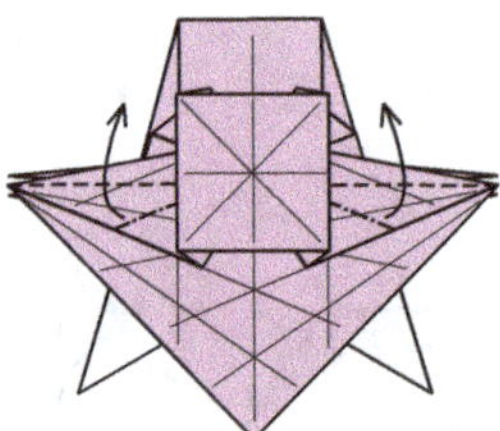

46. Swivel the sides up.

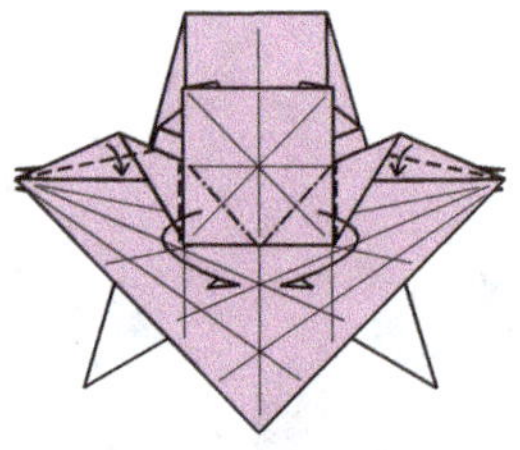

47. Swivel the sides down, allowing the center flap to come to a point.

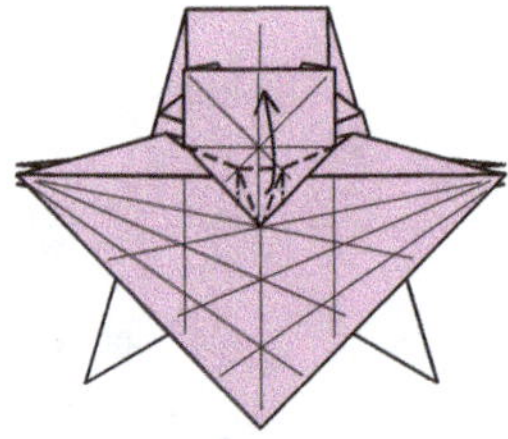

48. Collapse the thick center flap upwards.

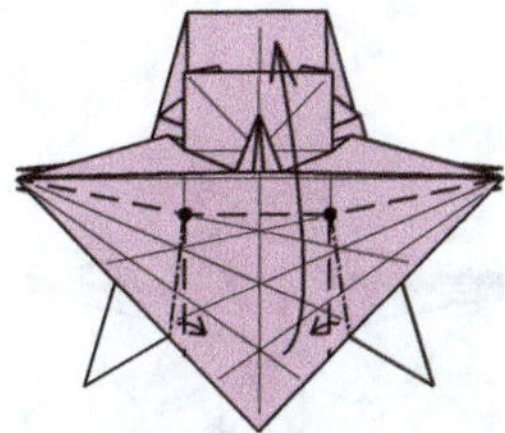

49. Valley fold the flap up, while swiveling in the sides. The valley-folds lie along existing creases.

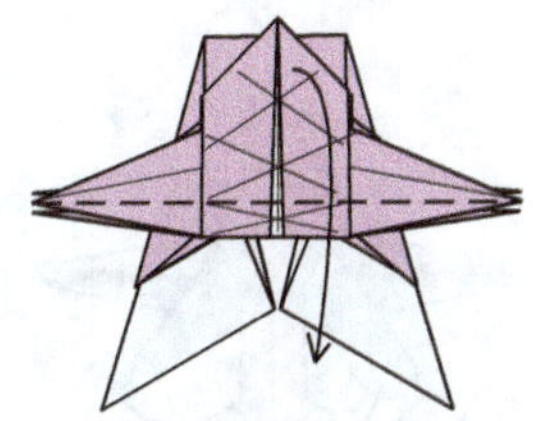

50. Valley fold the flap down.

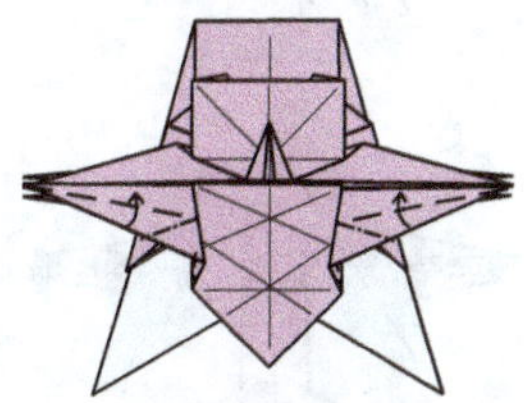

51. Valley fold the edges up, while allowing the sides to swivel outwards.

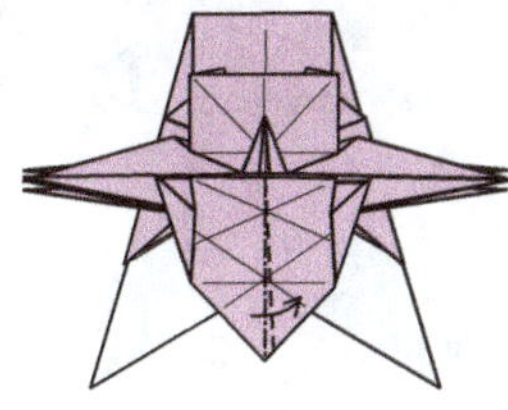

52. Form a tiny pleat. This will cause the flap to become slightly concave.

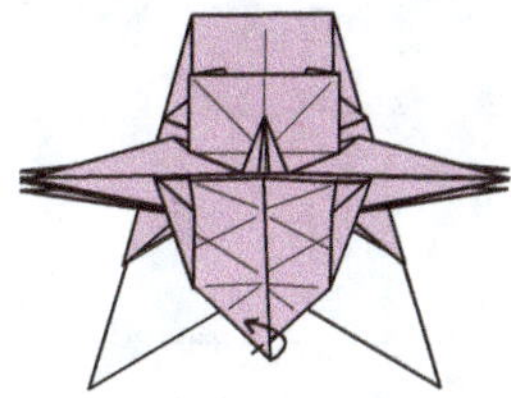

53. Valley fold the protruding corner to lock.

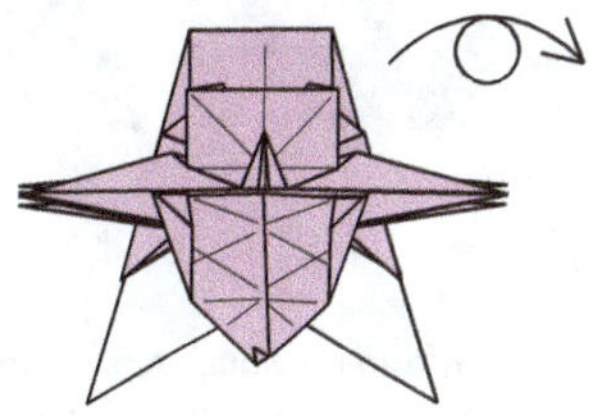

54. Turn over.

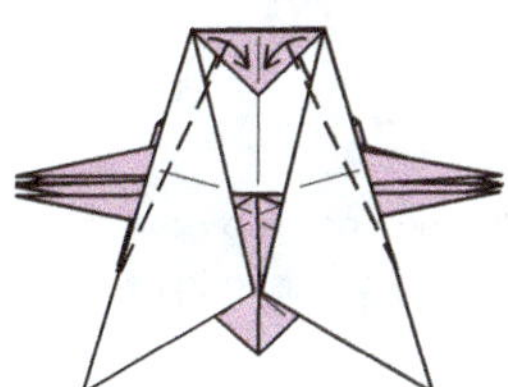

55. Valley fold the corners to the center.

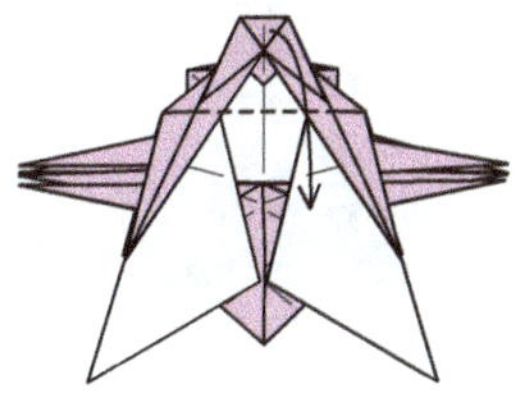

56. Valley fold the flap down, aligning it with the folded edge beneath.

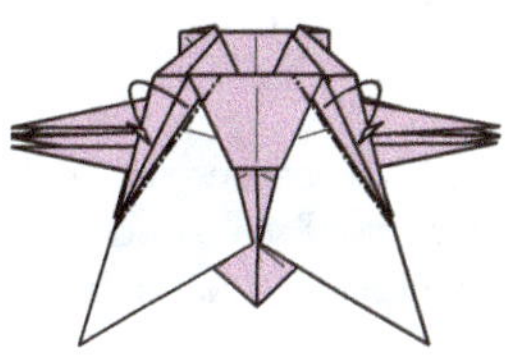

57. Mountain fold the top edges inside.

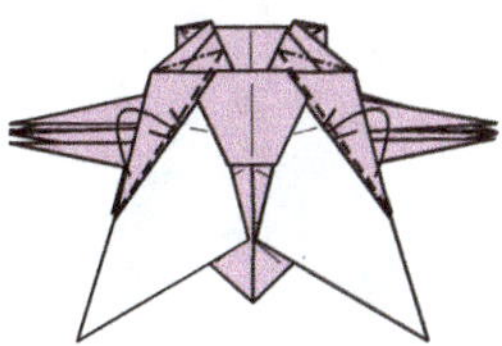

58. Valley fold the side edges inside, allowing a swivel to form at the top corners.

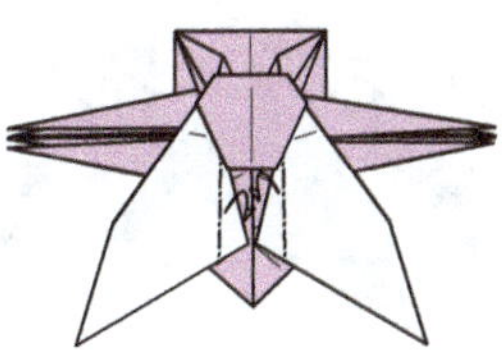

59. Mountain fold the sides of the flaps.

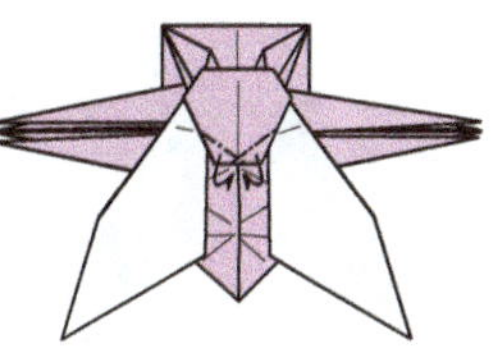

60. Shape the center flap with mountain folds.

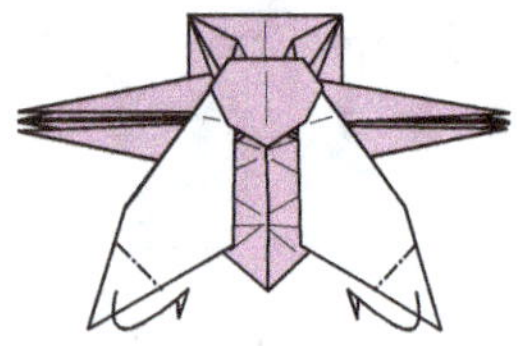

61. Mountain fold the tips of the flaps.

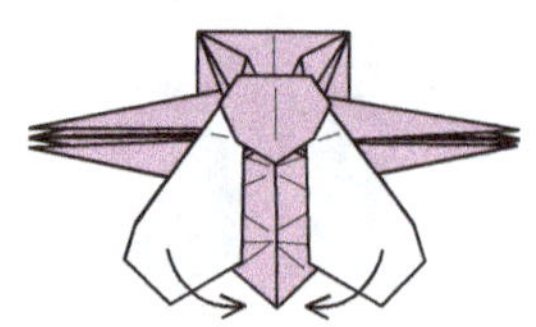

62. Pull the flaps towards the center.

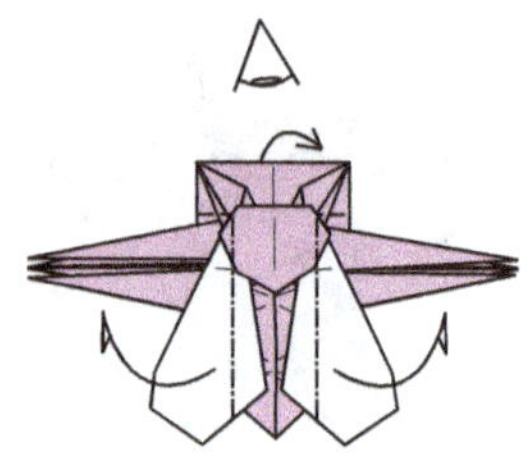

63. Round the sides downwards. Pull the front flap straight up.

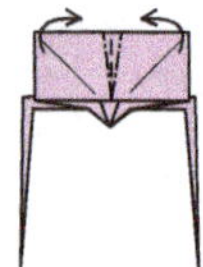

64. View from previous step. Form a tiny pleat along the center.

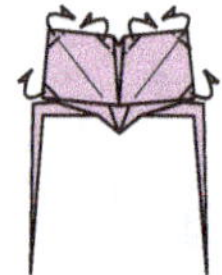

65. Round the sides with mountain folds and reverse folds.

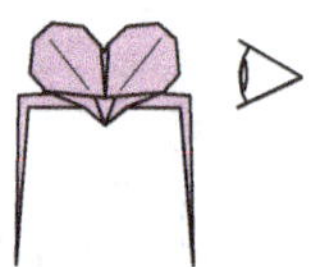

66. Complete.

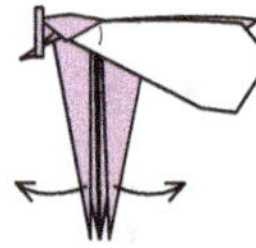

67. View from previous step. Pull the top two flaps outwards. Repeat on the other side.

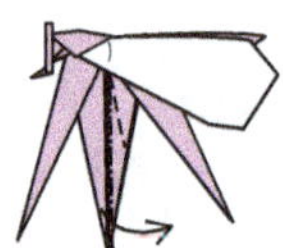

68. Pleat the center flap in half. Repeat on the other side.

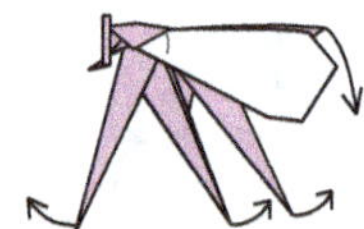

69. Pull the back flap down and shape the legs to taste.

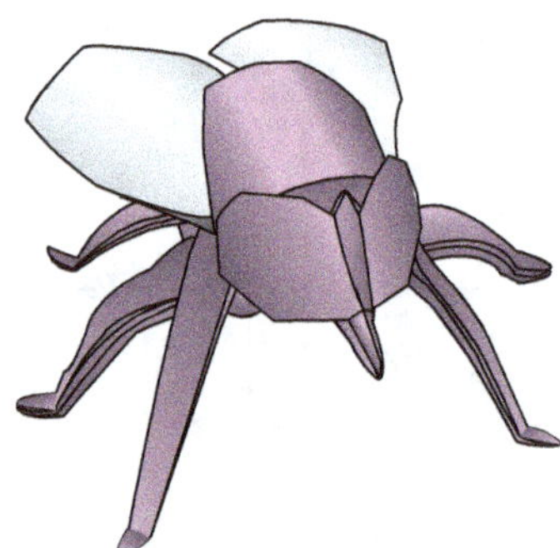

70. Completed *Fly*.

Housefly

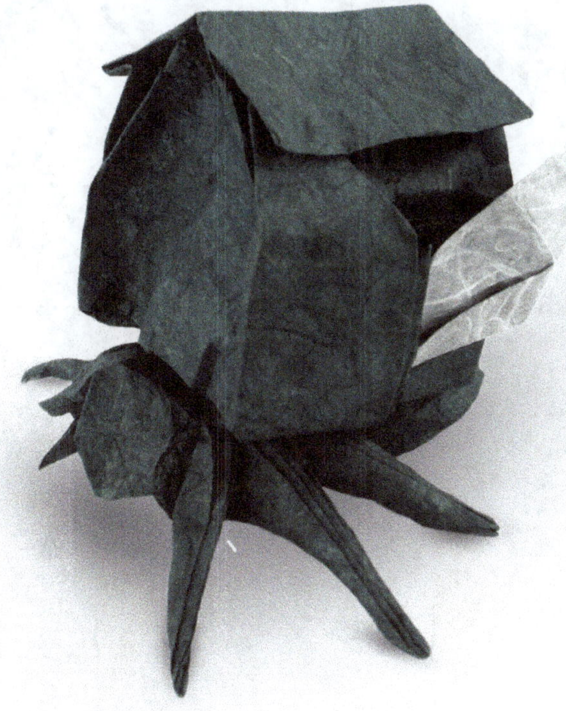

About

Continuing with the fly motif, this piece takes the word "housefly" literally, as the completed model is a house with fly-like appendages. The idea came about from some silly conversations with my friends from OrigamiUSA. As expected, I could not start with standard bug appendage layouts. The few avenues I tried out yielded similar levels of efficiency, but I like the final incarnation for its cohesiveness and somewhat simple structure. One long point opens out into the house and tail, while two center shorter flaps become wings. Another long point is made thinner and then pleated up to form the legs and head. This does result in some fairly thick legs, so larger paper is preferable. If you are going for a life-sized model, it is not clear if it should be as big as a house, or a small as a fly.

Tips

The final step is where everything comes together. To give the illusion of the abdomen being connected to the legs, you might need to adjust the valley-fold from step seventy. Also note that the pinches that form the roof (step seventy-two) will cause the front and back of the house to become slightly concave.

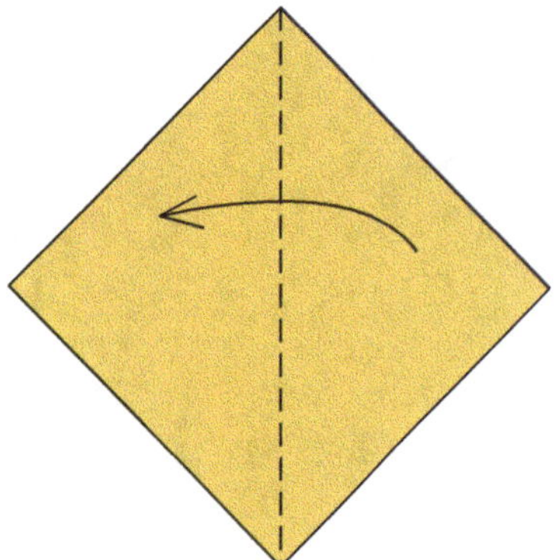

1. Valley fold in half.

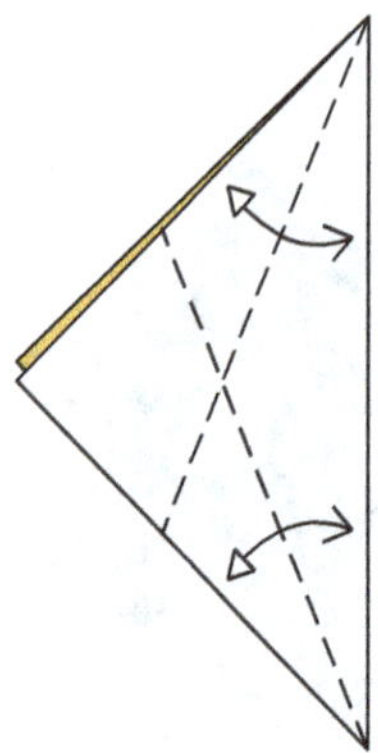

2. Precrease along the angle bisectors.

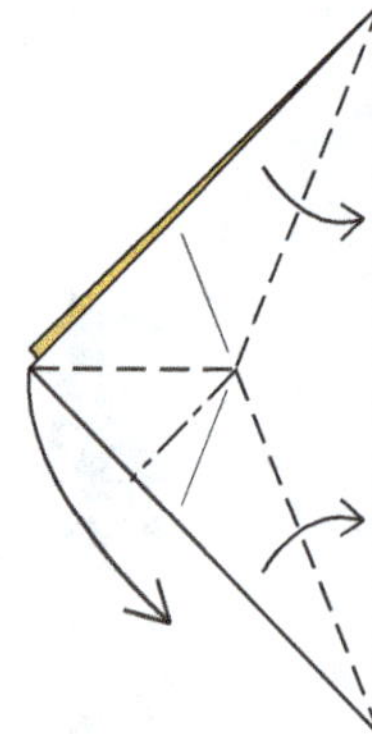

3. Rabbit ear the flap down.

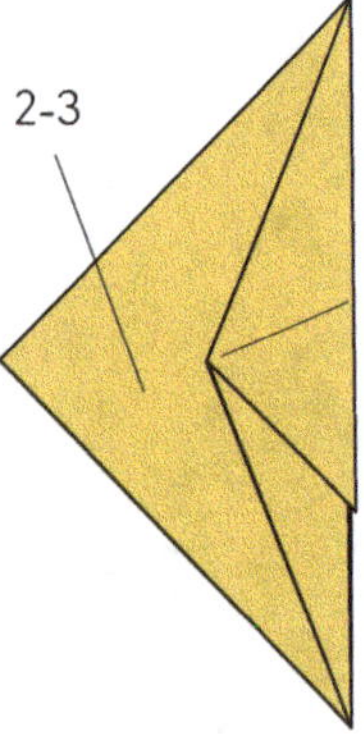

4. Repeat steps 2-3 behind.

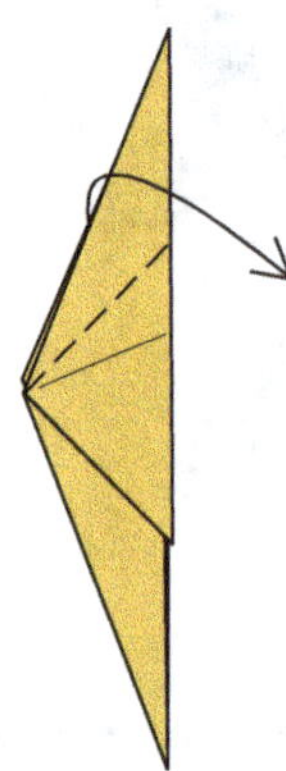

5. Valley fold the flap towards the crease.

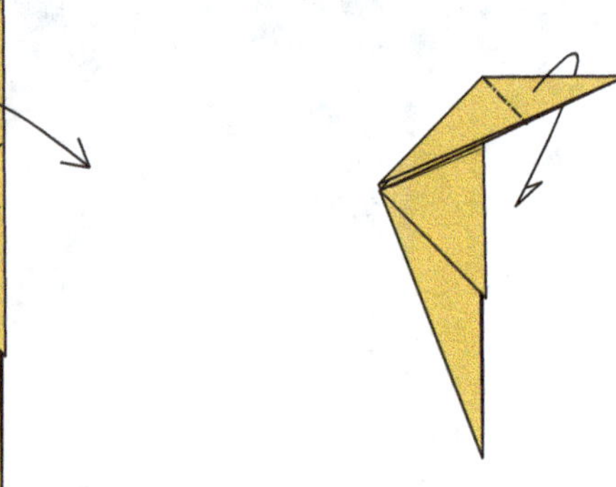

6. Mountain fold the flap to lie against the edges.

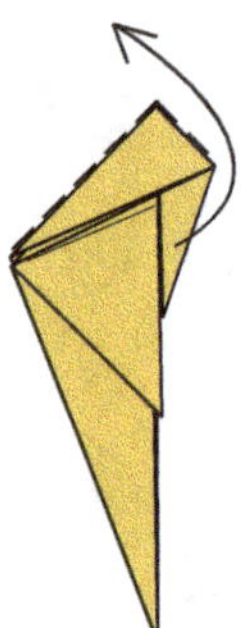

7. Unfold the flap.

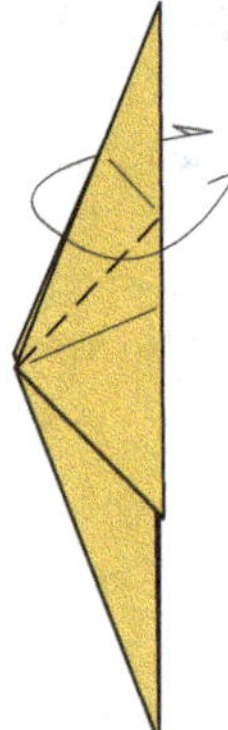

8. Outside reverse fold along the existing creases.

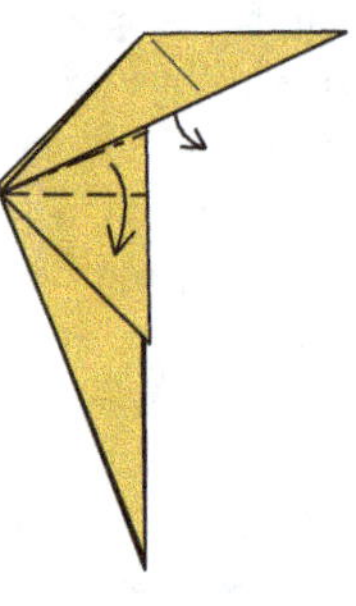

9. Pull out a single layer while pleating downward.

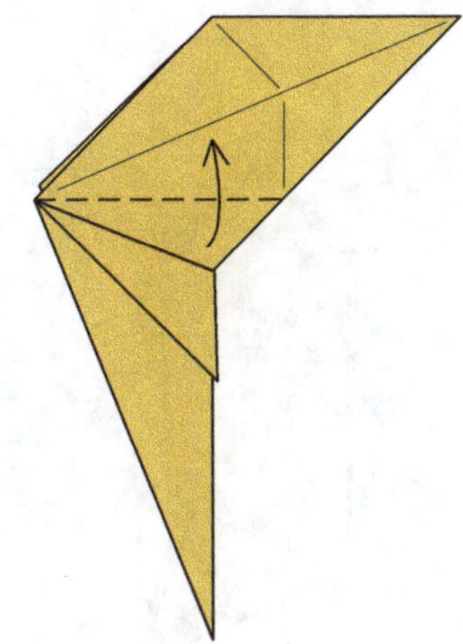

10. Valley fold up.

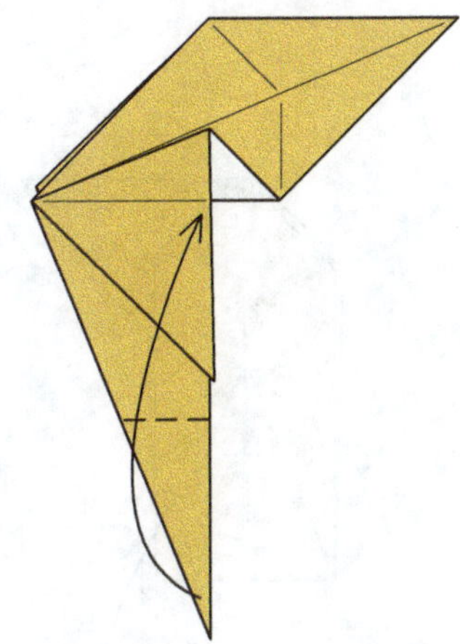

11. Valley fold up.

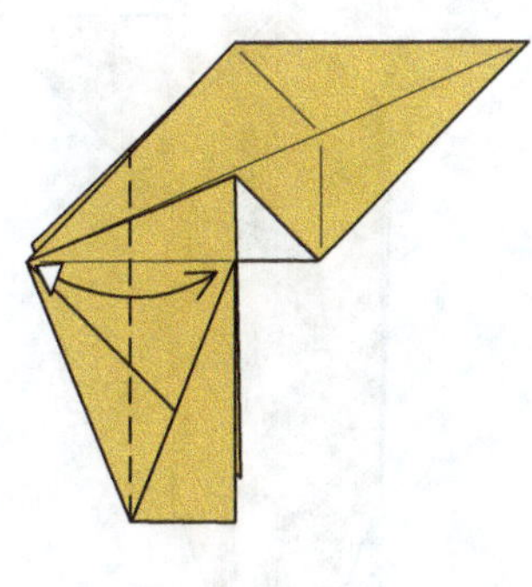

12. Precrease.

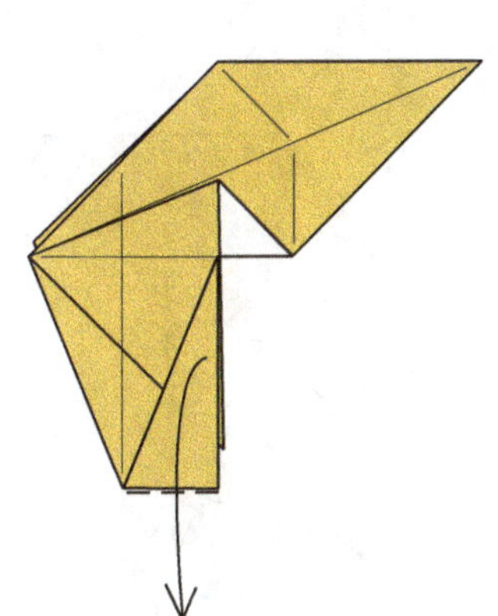

13. Swing the flap down.

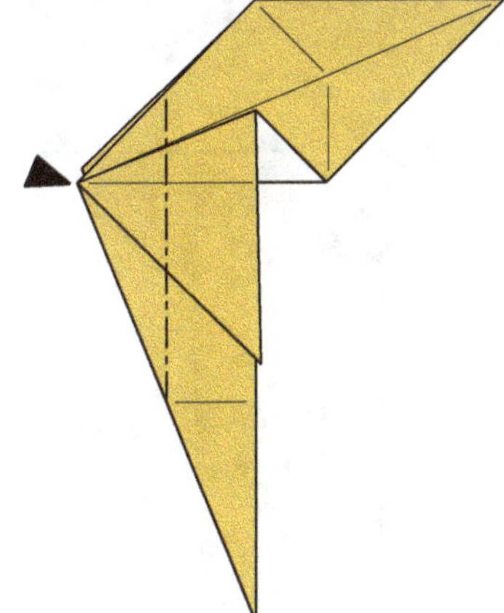

14. Sink the flap.

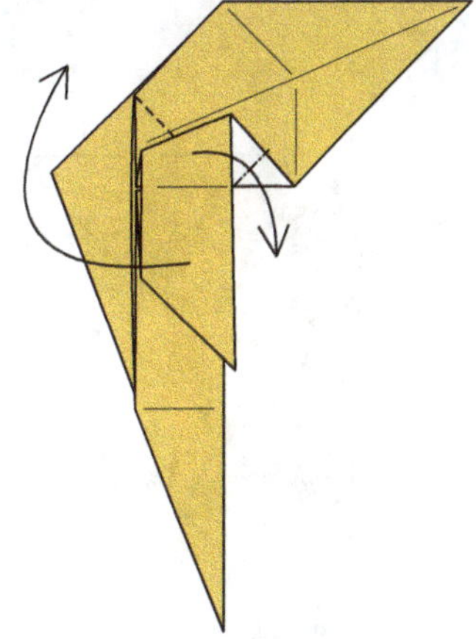

15. Twist the top flap and flatten.

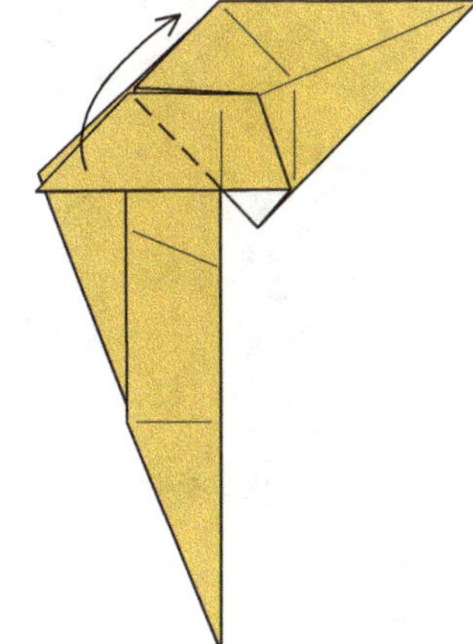

16. Valley fold up.

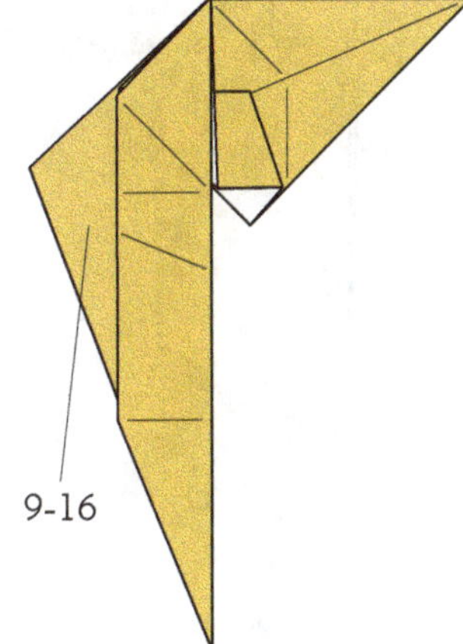

17. Repeat steps 9-16 behind.

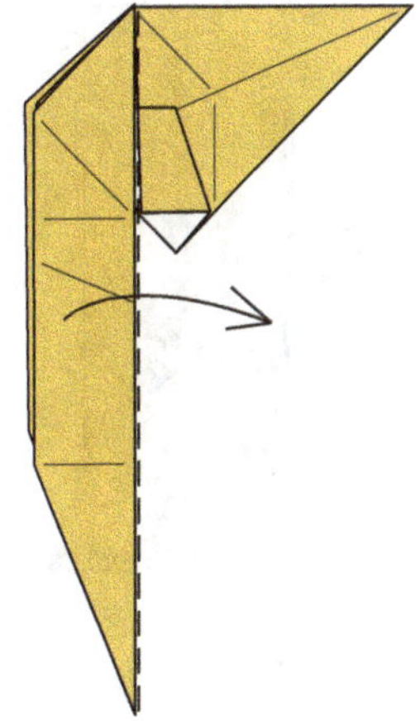

18. Open out the large flap.

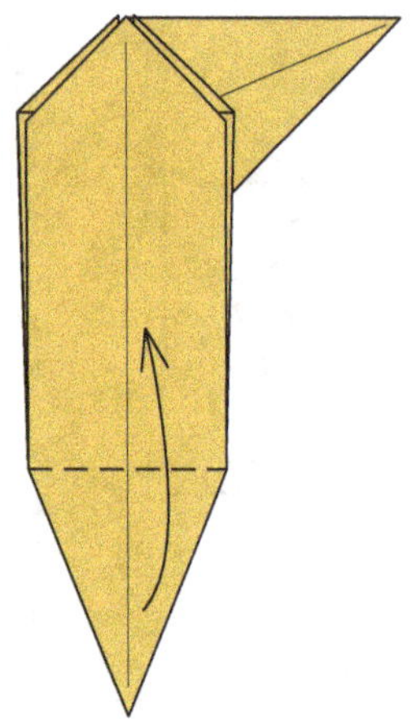

19. Valley fold up.

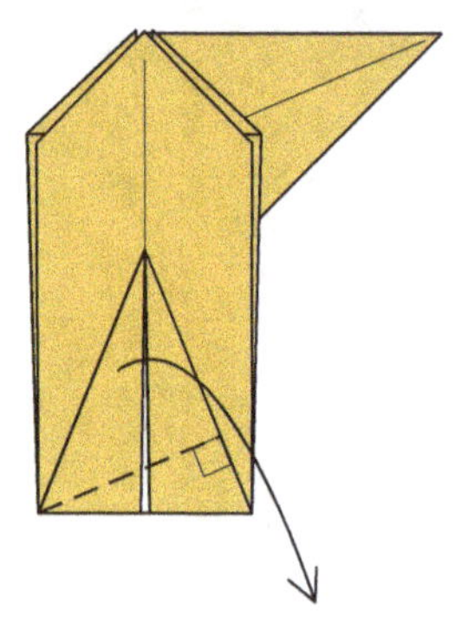

20. Valley fold down.

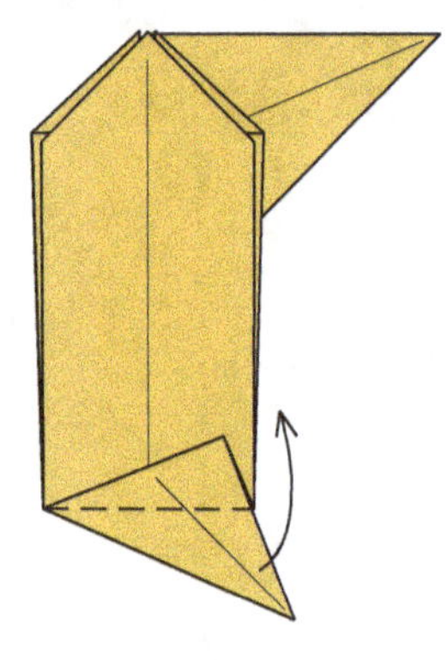

21. Valley fold up.

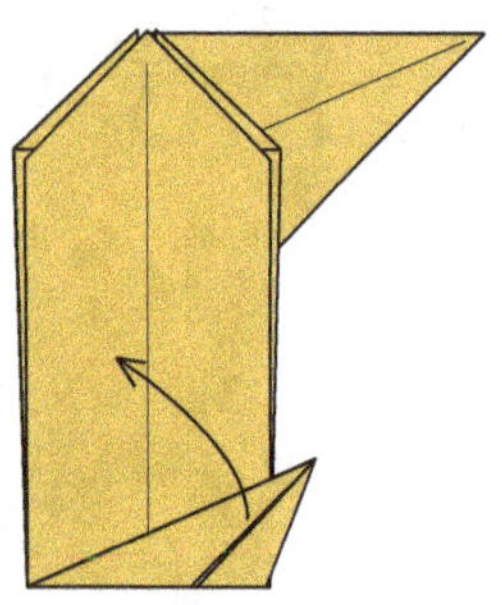
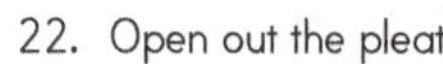

22. Open out the pleat.

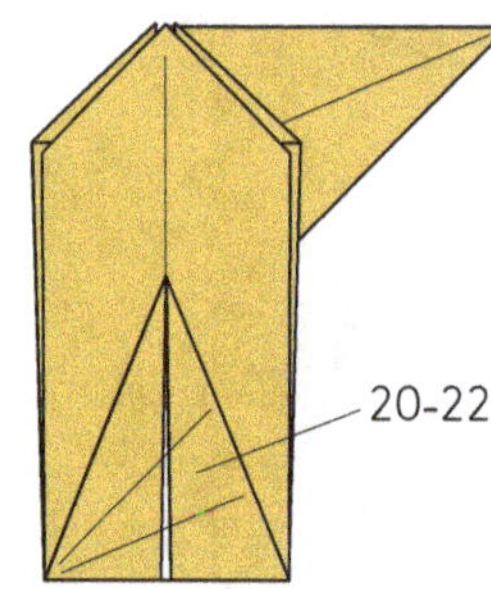

23. Repeat steps 20-22 in mirror image.

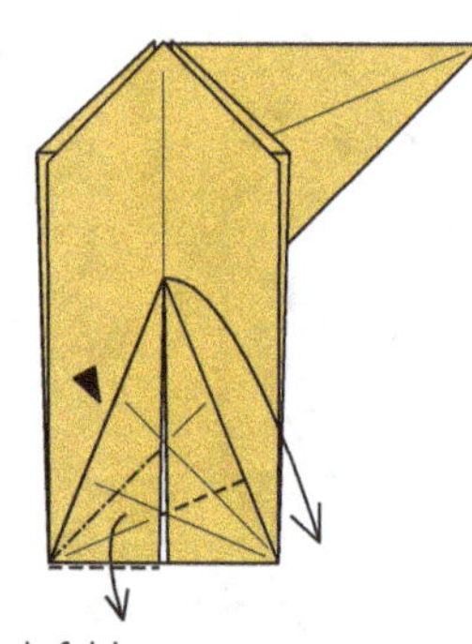

24. Squash fold.

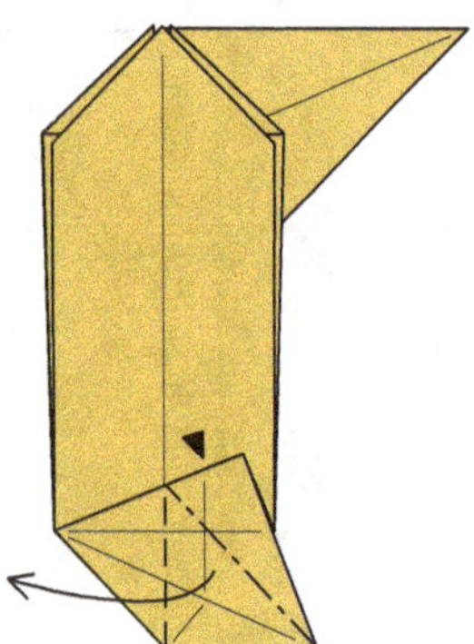

25. Squash fold.

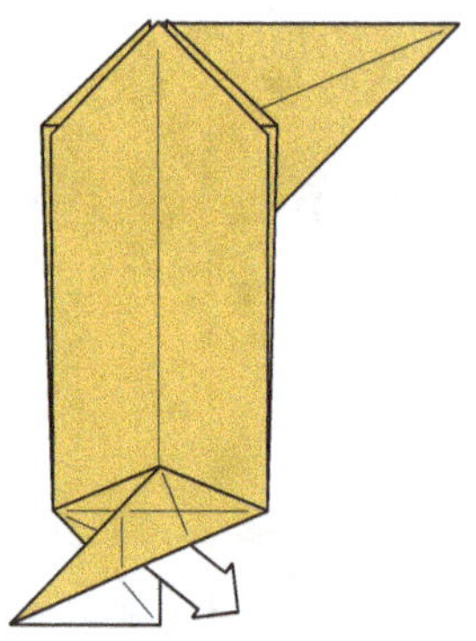

26. Pull out a single layer and flatten.

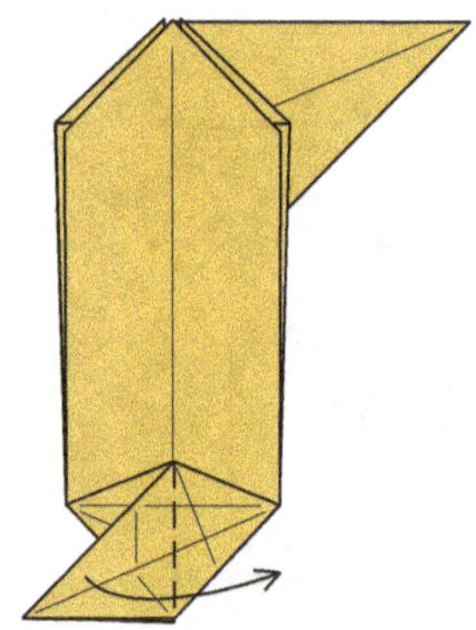

27. Swing the flap over.

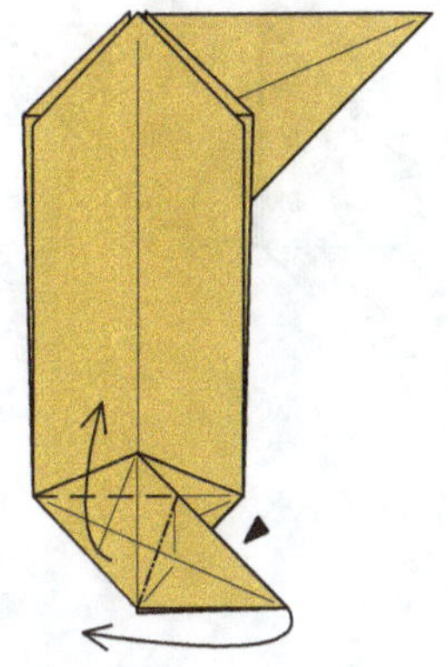

28. Squash fold.

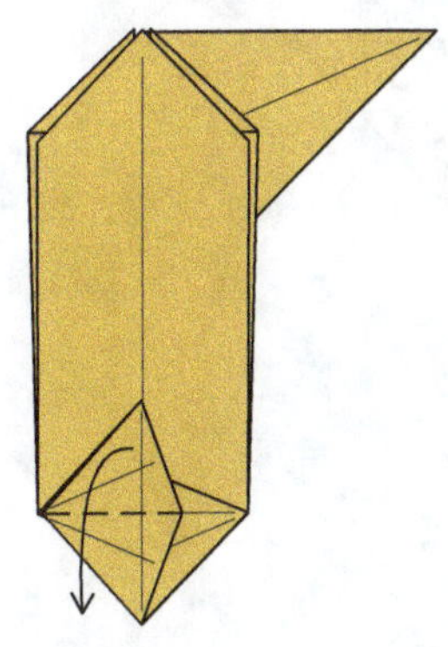

29. Valley fold down.

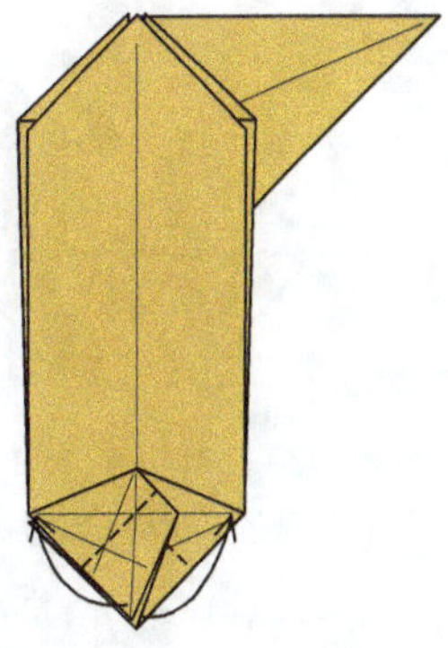

30. Valley fold the bottom flaps to the side corners, allowing the side flap to spread flat.

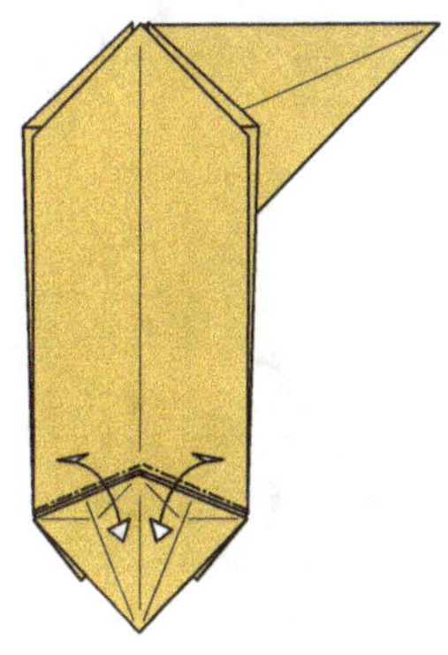

31. Precrease with mountain folds.

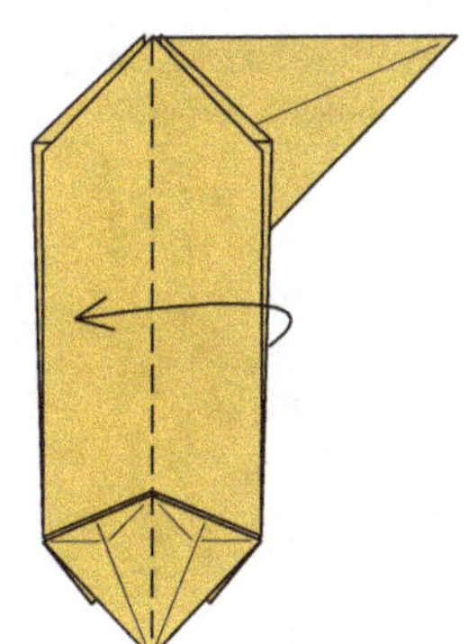

32. Valley fold the flap in half.

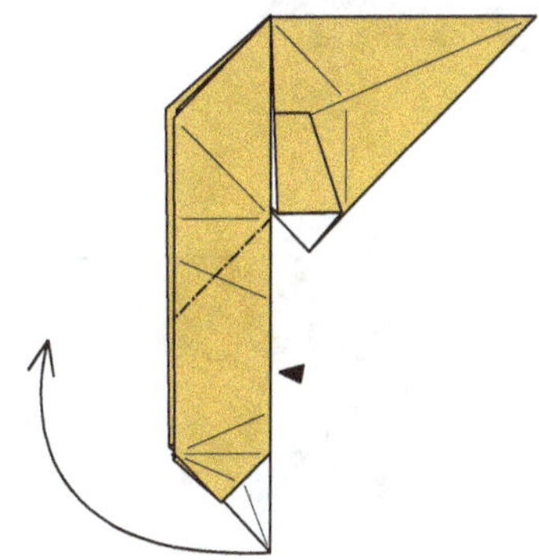

33. Reverse fold the flap.

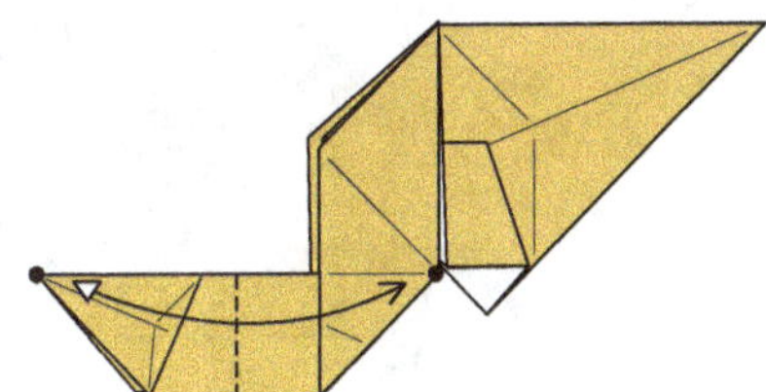

34. Precrease.

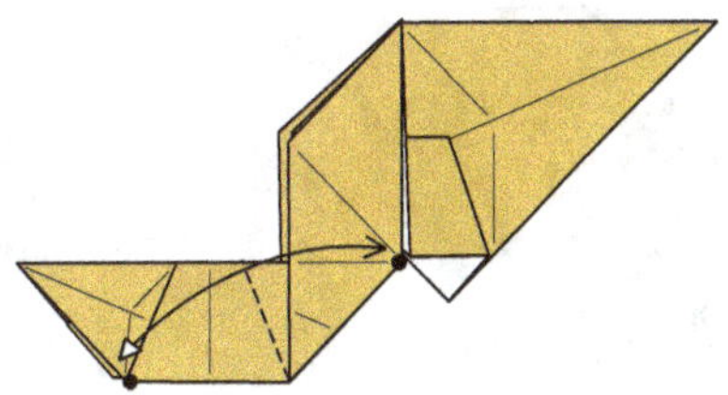

35. Precrease.

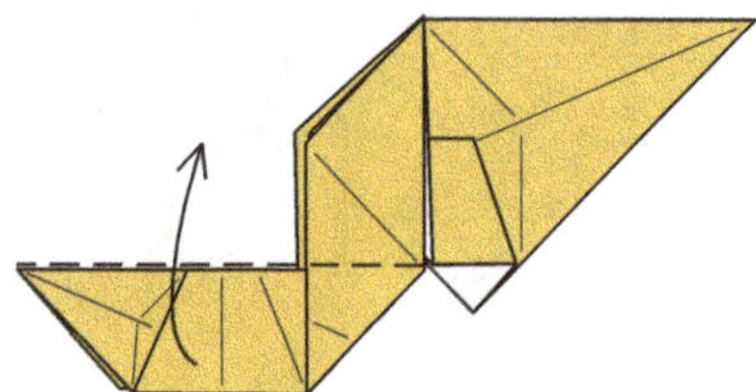

36. Open out the flap.

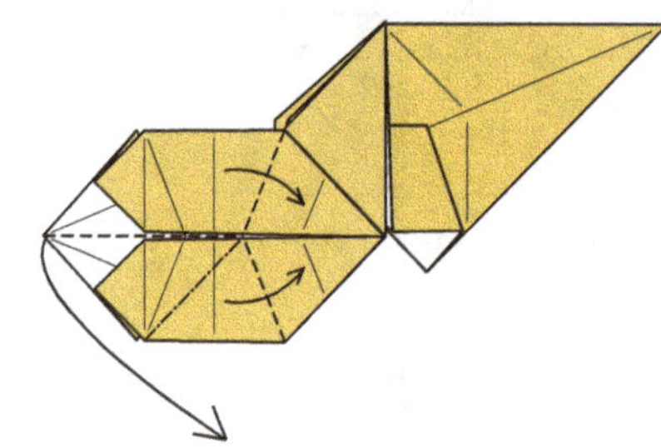

37. Rabbit ear the flap.

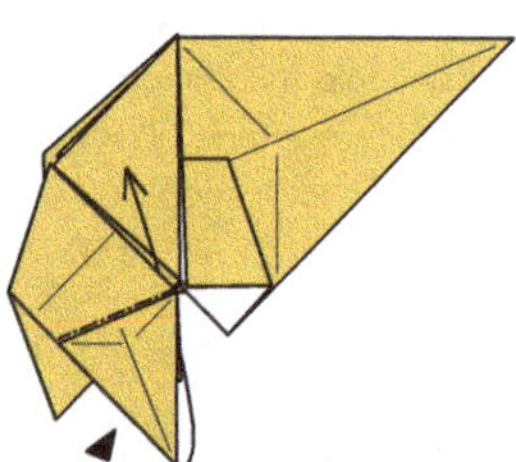

38. Reverse fold.

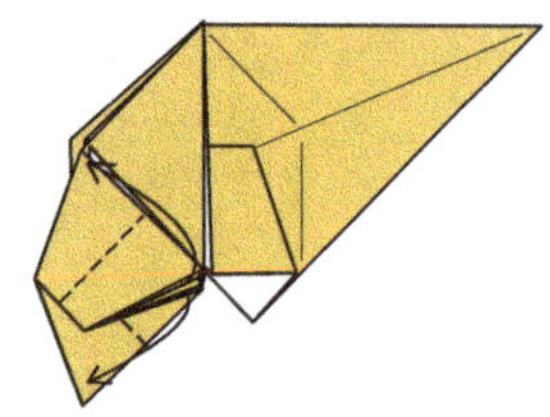

39. Valley fold the sets of flaps to the side corners.

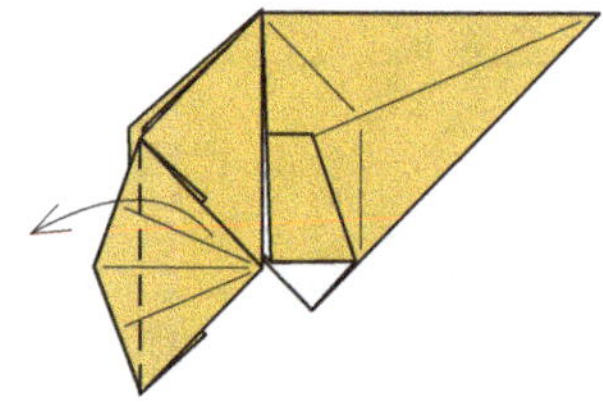

40. Valley fold the top flap.

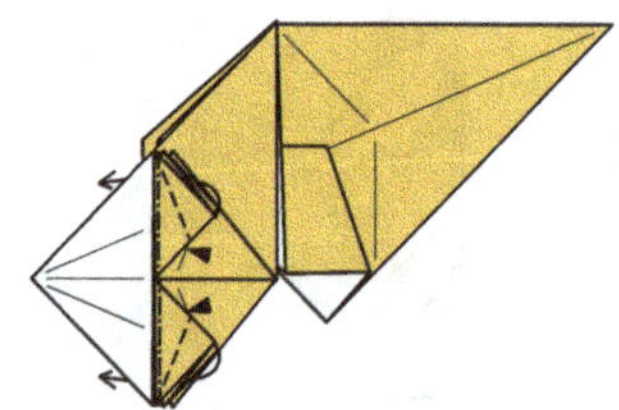

41. Reverse fold in and out.

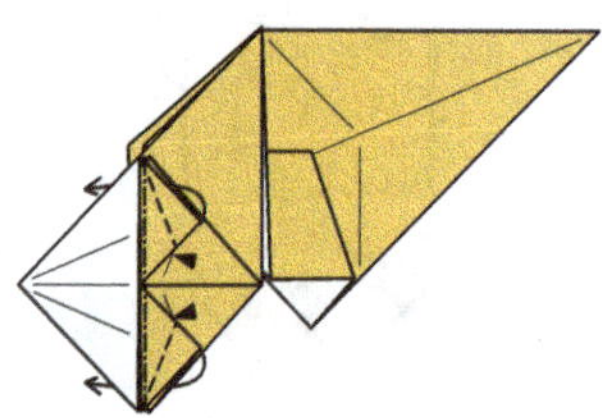

42. Reverse fold the next set of flaps in and out.

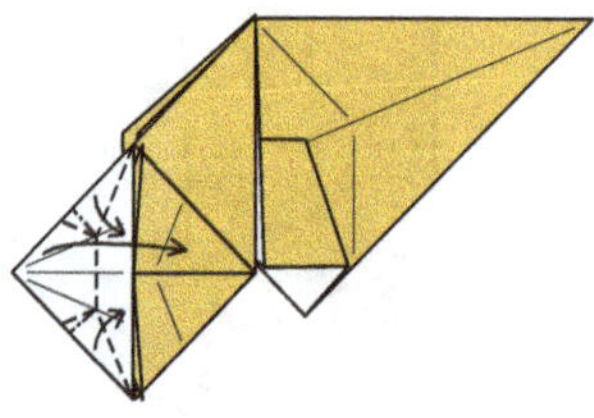

43. Valley fold along the angle bisectors while swiveling in the sides.

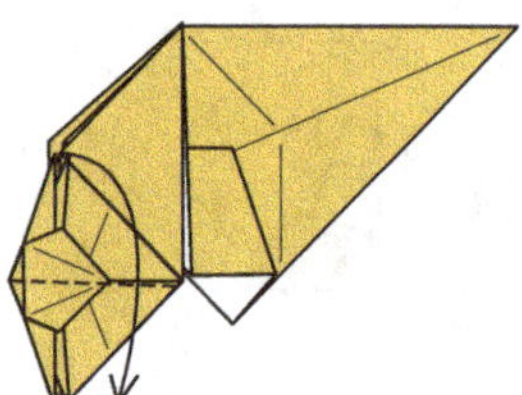

44. Valley fold down.

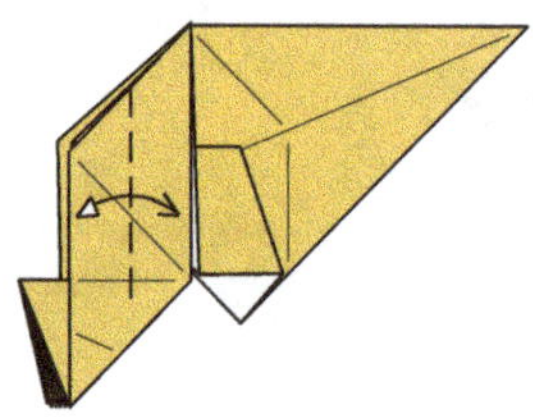

45. Precrease the top two layers in half.

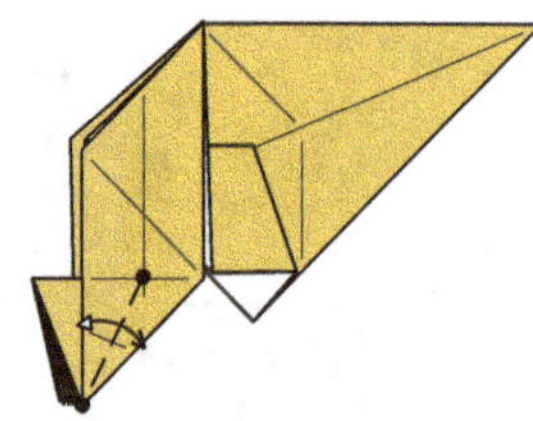

46. Precrease the top two layers, noting the indicated intersection.

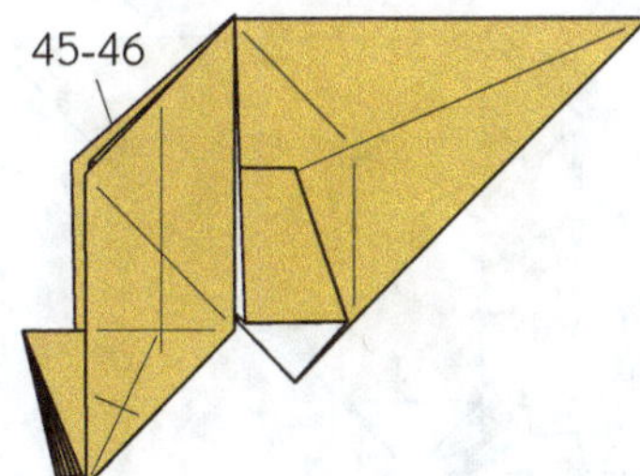

47. Repeat steps 45-46 behind.

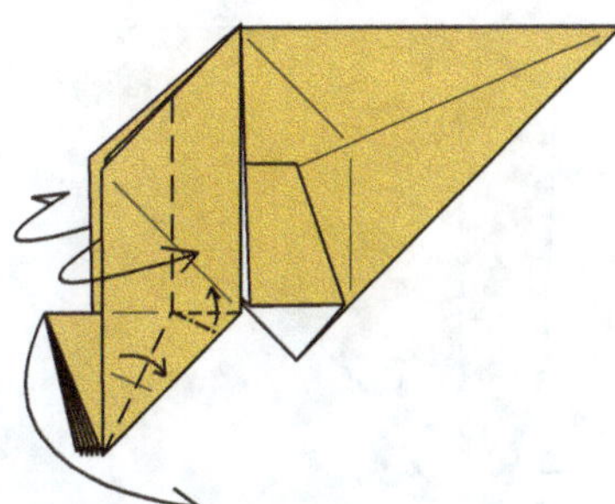

48. Valley fold the outer layers along the existing creases, allowing the bottom section to crimp downwards.

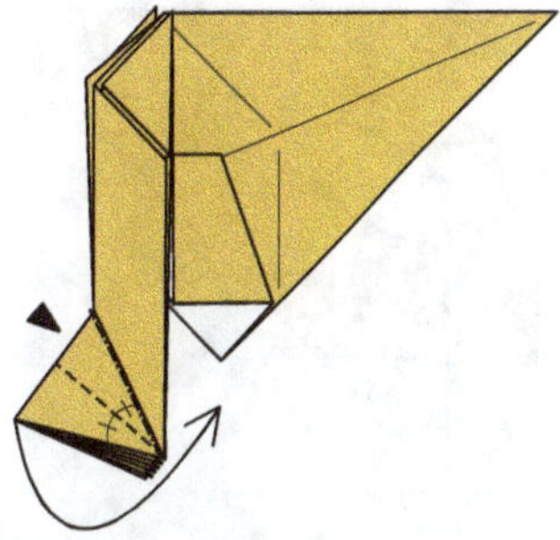

49. Reverse fold the bottom cluster of flaps in and then out along the angle bisector.

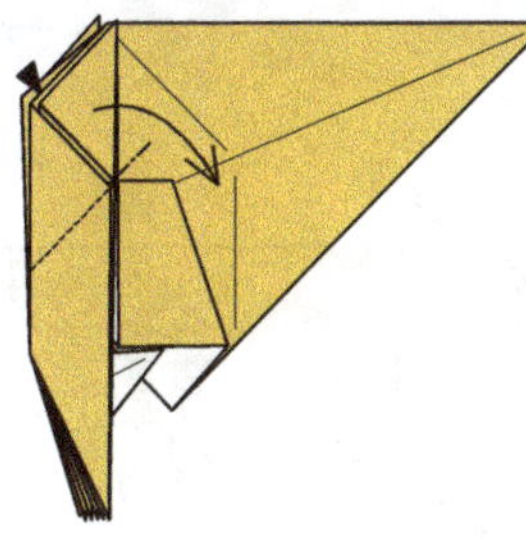

50. Reverse fold the trapped flap down.

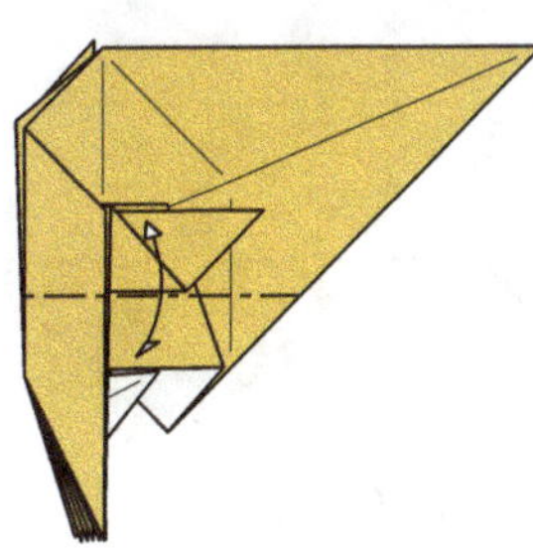

51. Precrease with a mountain fold.

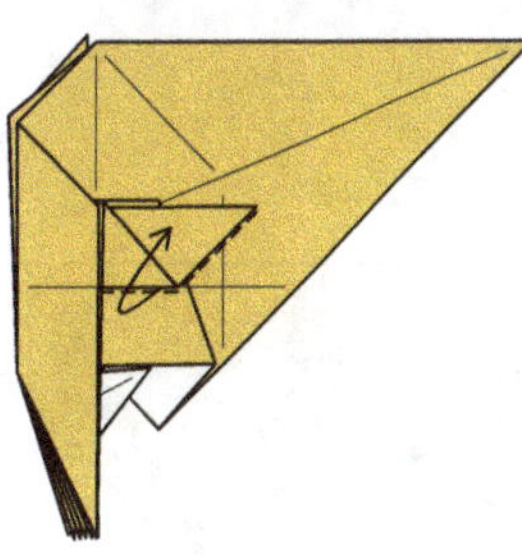

52. Wrap a single layer around from behind.

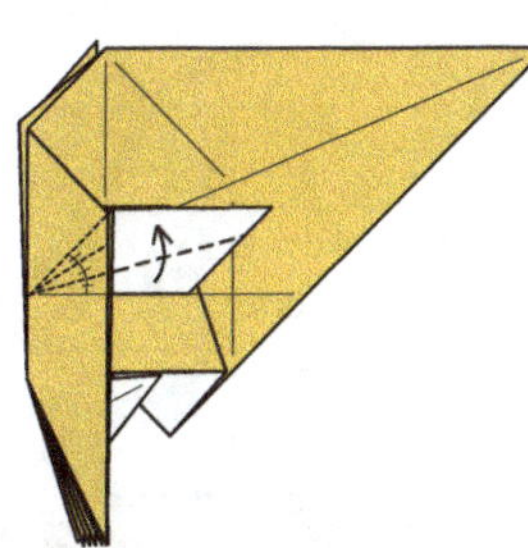

53. Valley fold along the angle trisector.

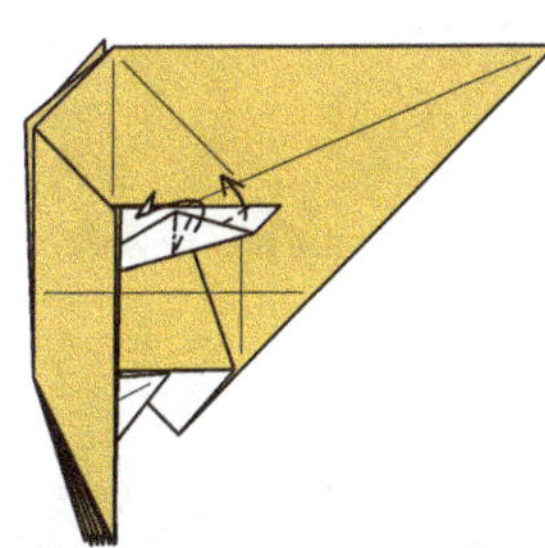

54. Valley fold up while swiveling in.

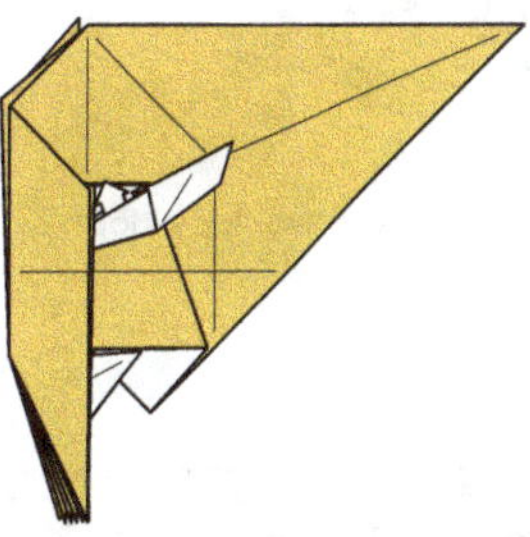

55. Unsink a single layer.

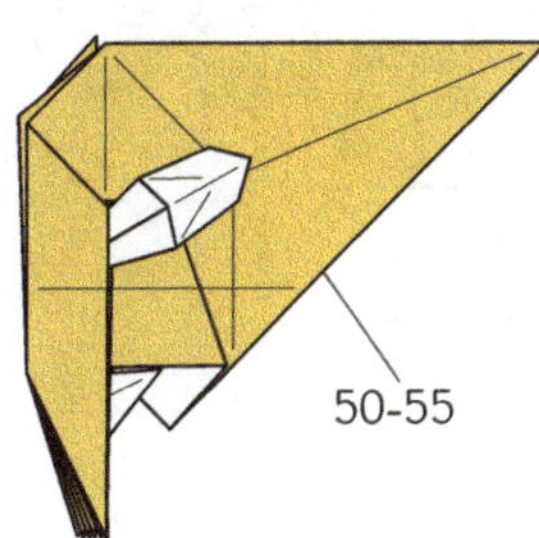

56. Repeat steps 50-55 behind.

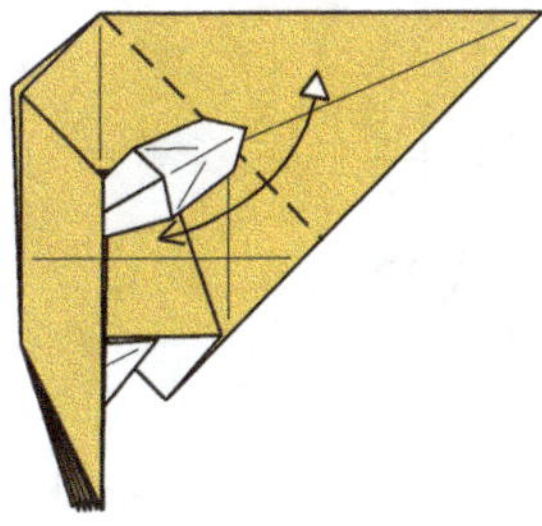

57. Precrease the large flap.

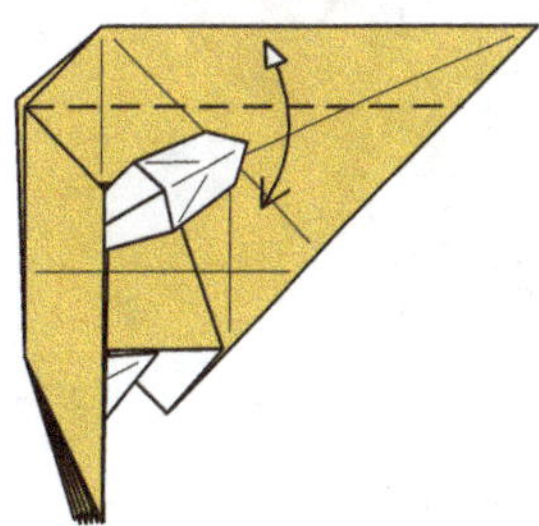

58. Precrease again.

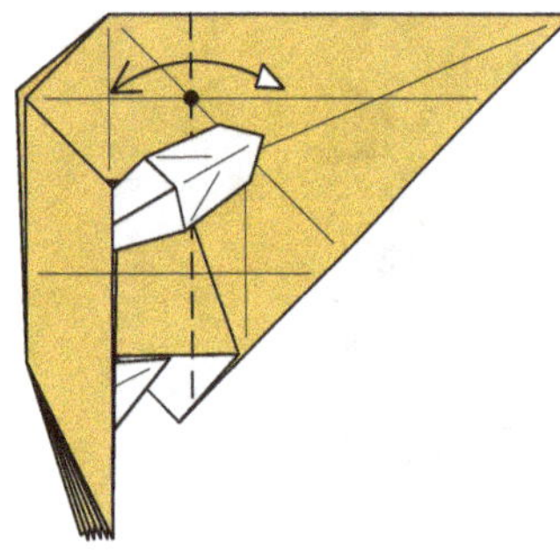 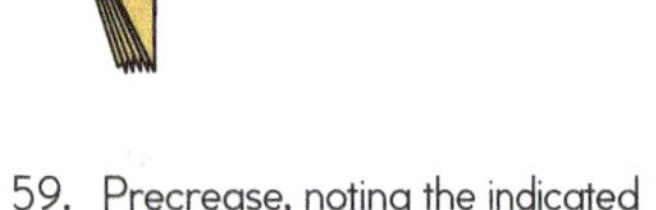

59. Precrease, noting the indicated intersection.

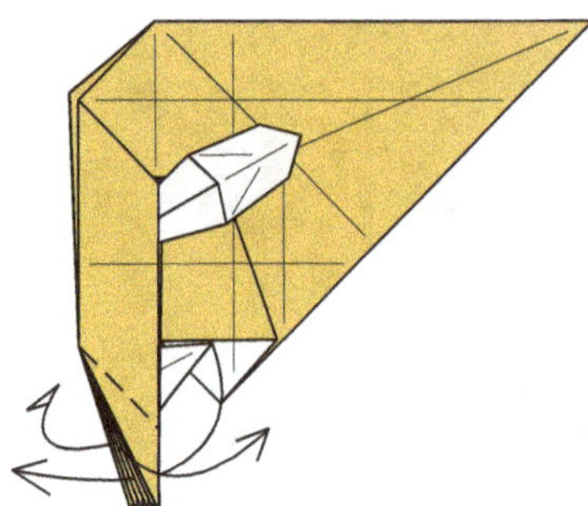

60. Valley fold three flaps over at each side, allowing the white flap to flip to the other side.

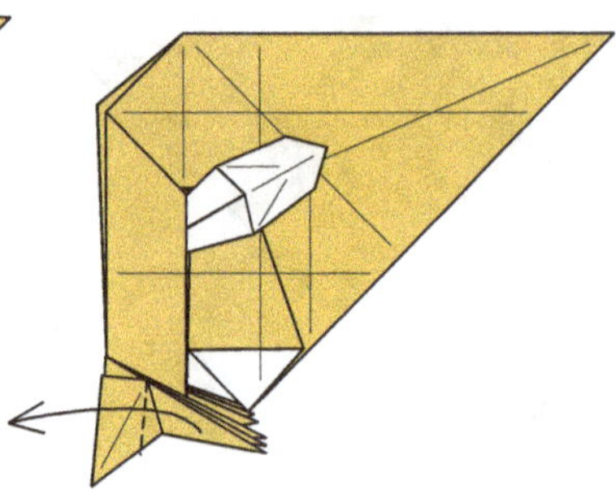

61. Valley fold one flap over.

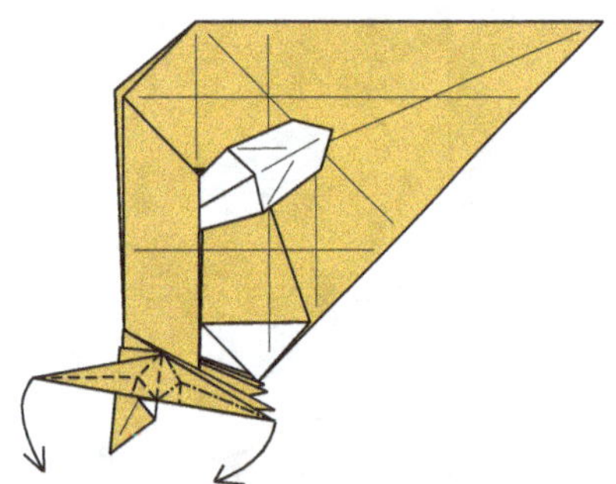

62. Rabbit ear two flaps down.

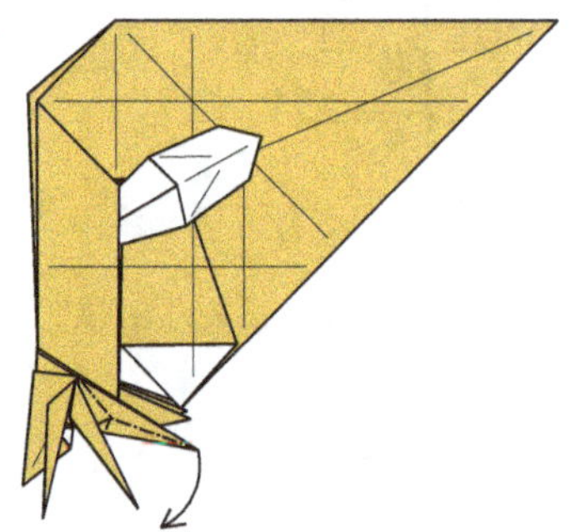

63. Rabbit ear the flap down.

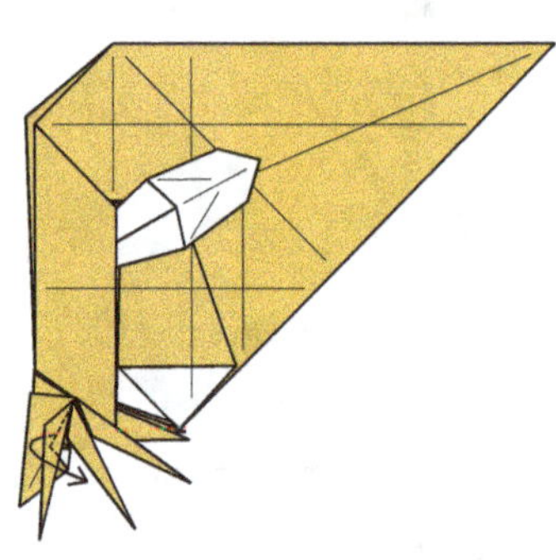

64. Pull around the trapped single layer to the surface.

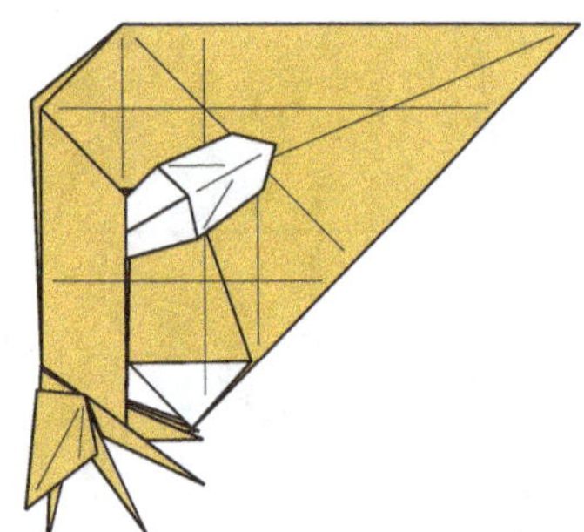

65. Repeat steps 61-64 behind.

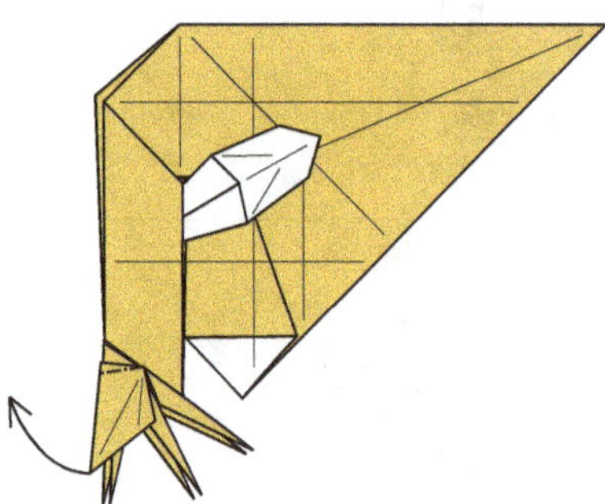

66. Slide the front flap upwards.

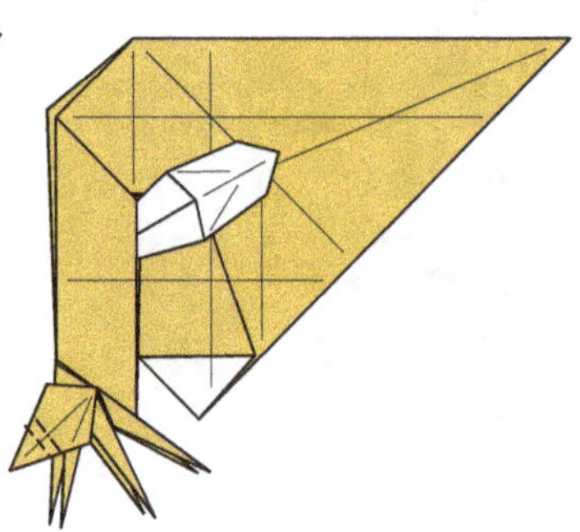

67. Crimp the tip of the flap.

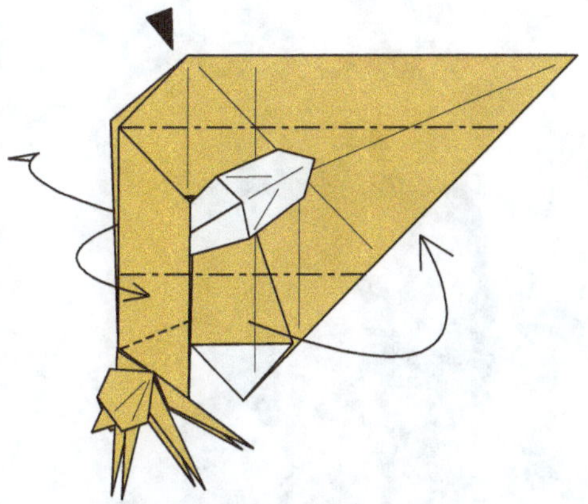

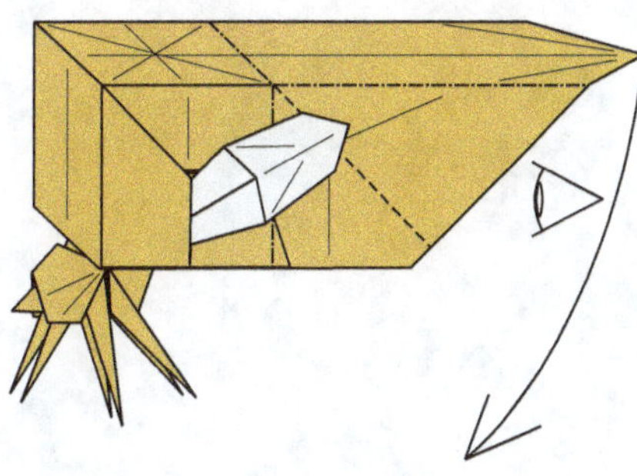

68. Spread apart the sides into a boxlike shape, pressing the bottom flaps into the sides of the structure as much as possible.

69. Fold the back section down while reverse folding in the sides (which will overlap on the inside).

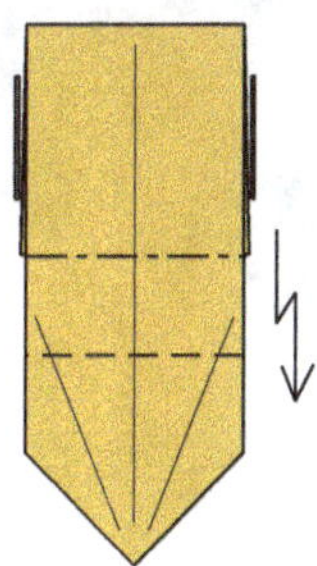

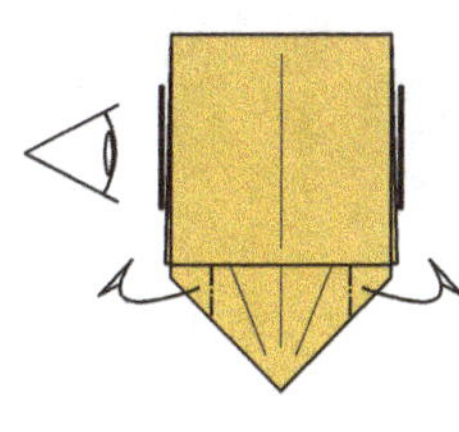

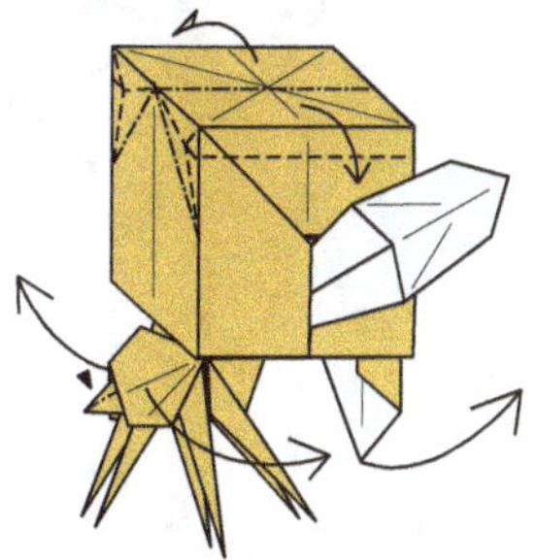

70. View from previous step. Pleat the flap up.

71. Lightly swivel the sides back at about 90°.

72. View from previous step. Pinch the sides of the roof down. Sink the tip of the nose. Raise the tail, positioning it close to the legs. Shape the model to taste.

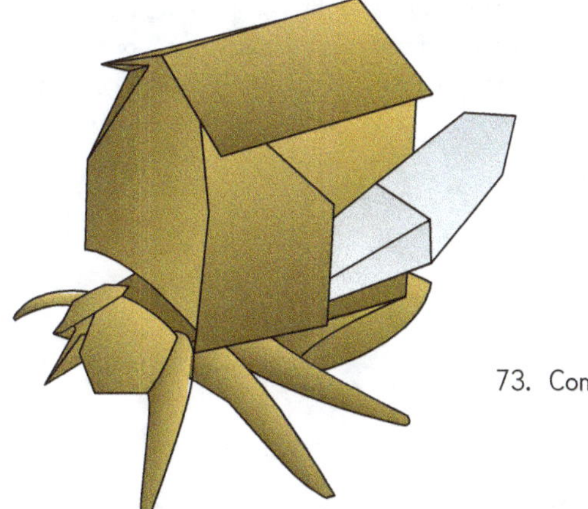

73. Completed *Housefly*.

Cockroach

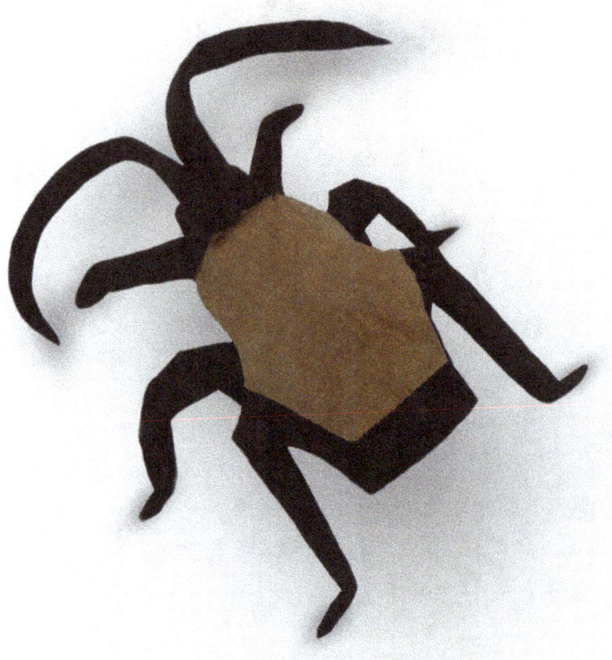

About

For this piece, I took the structure used in the *Fly* but shifted the leg portion up, allowing for extra long antennae. Neil Elias pioneered the boxy style back in the 1960's, and it works well for flaps that do not need to taper off too much. My parents like to keep one in their kitchen, lest one might not realize they are in a New York apartment.

Tips

If you are new to the box-pleating style, step fifty-one might seem strange. If you can imagine the tip of a waterbomb base (i.e., step one of the *Fly*) sunk in and out repeatedly, the results would be similar.

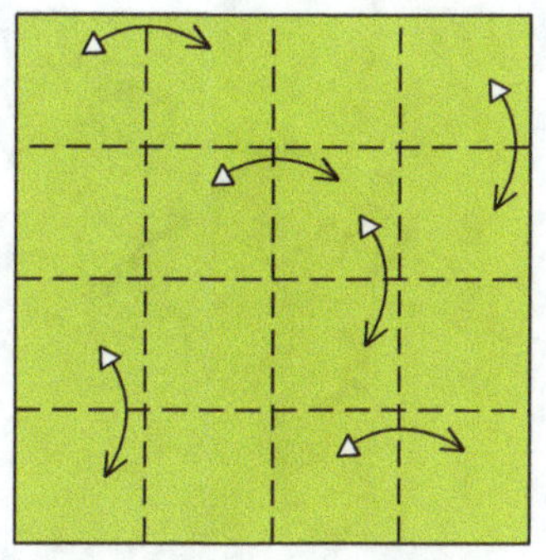

1. Precrease into fourths.

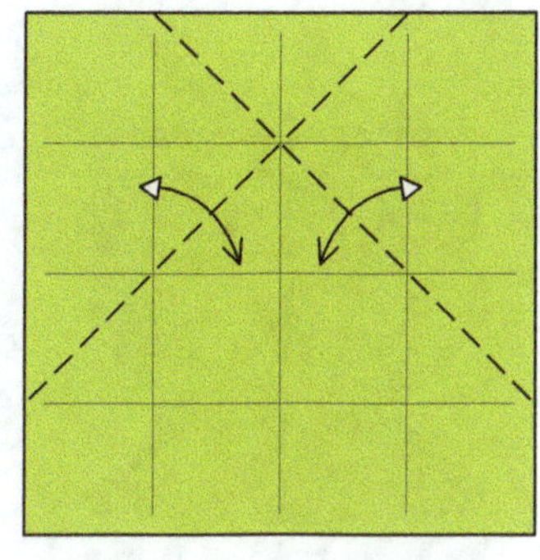

2. Precrease along the indicated diagonals.

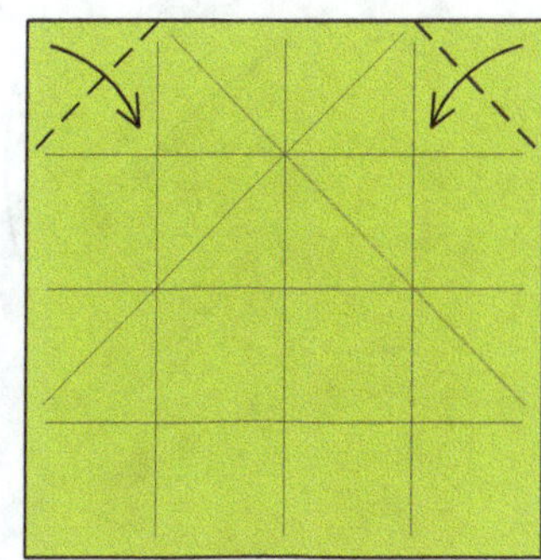

3. Valley in the top corners.

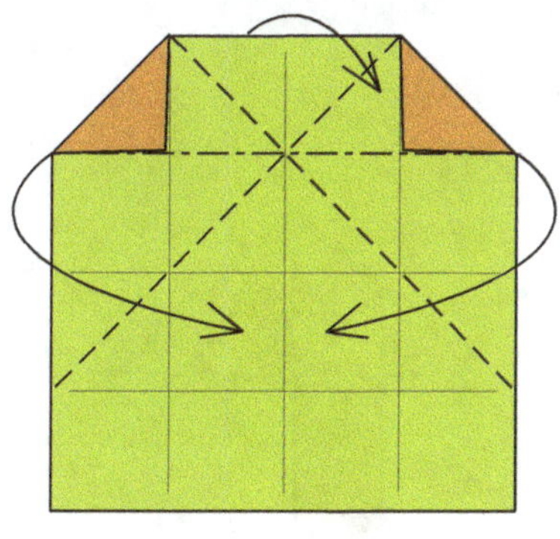

4. Collapse (like a waterbomb base).

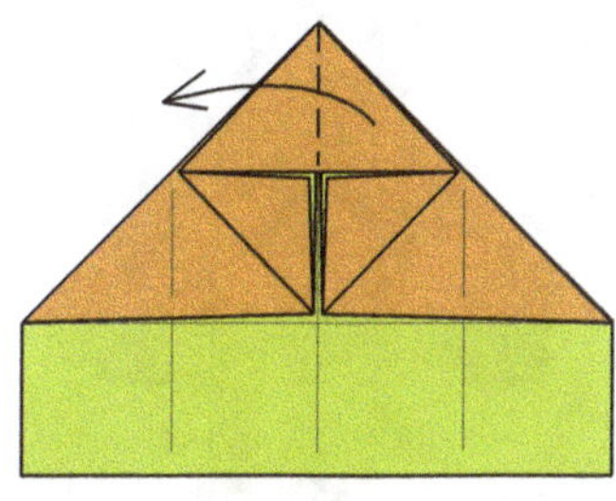

5. Swing over one flap.

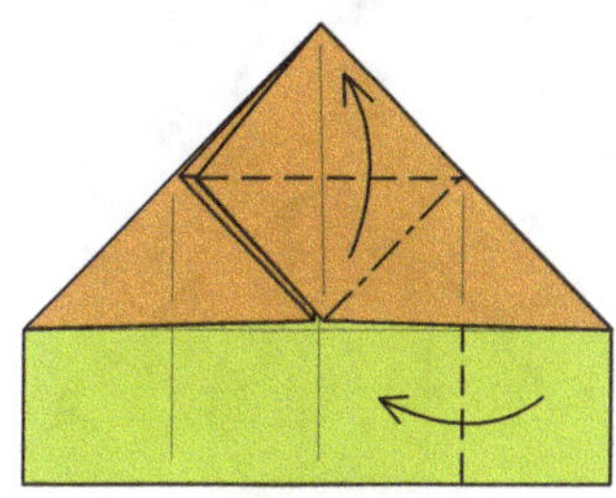

6. Swivel up.

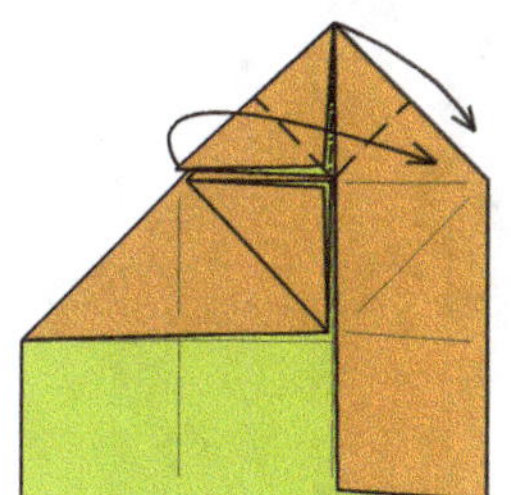

7. Swing over, while incorporating a reverse fold.

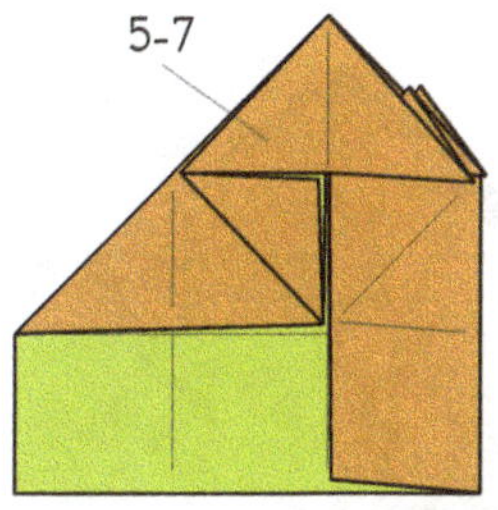

8. Repeat steps 5-7 in mirror image.

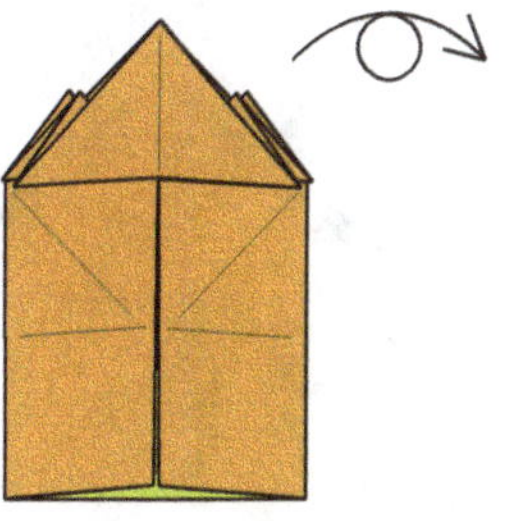

9. Turn over.

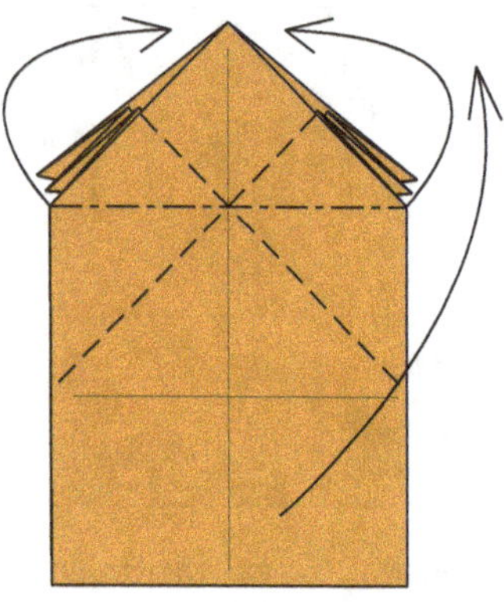

10. Collapse upwards (like a waterbomb base).

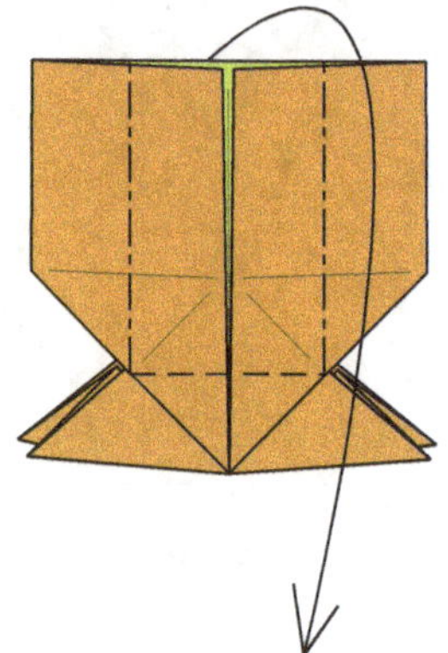

11. Petal fold down.

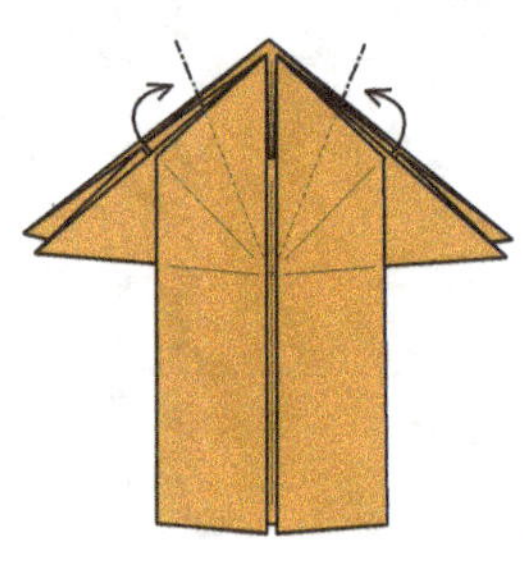

12. Reverse fold the inner flaps.

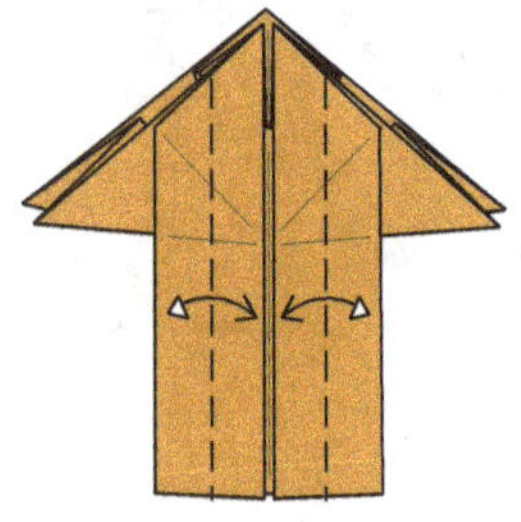

13. Precrease.

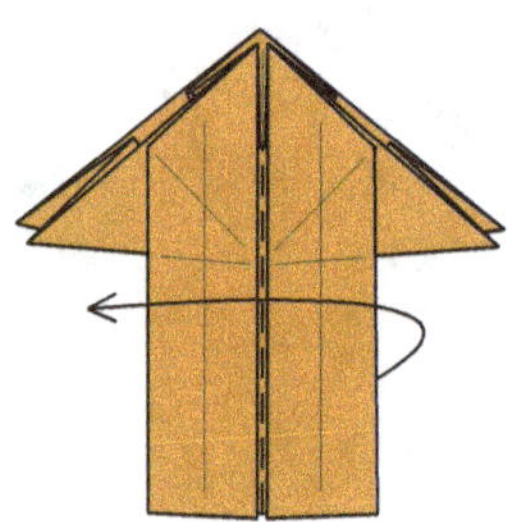

14. Swing over.

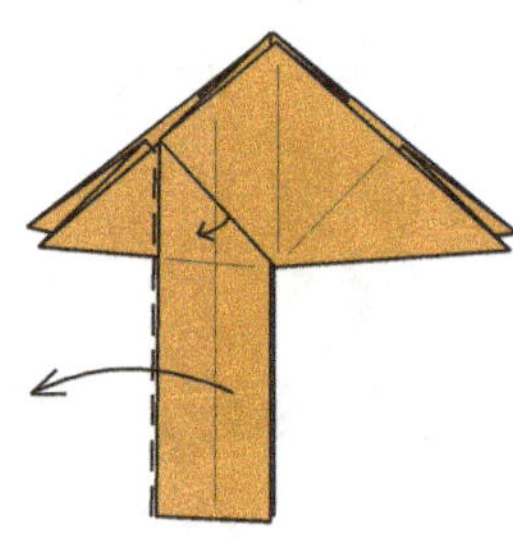

15. Pull out the single layer.

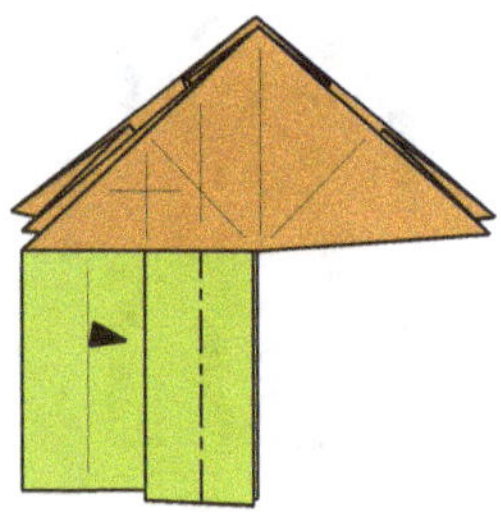

16. Closed reverse fold.

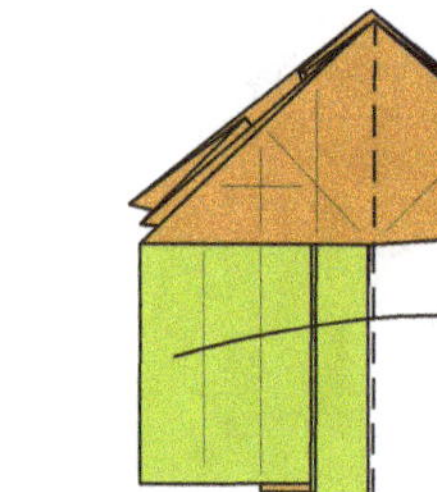

17. Swing back.

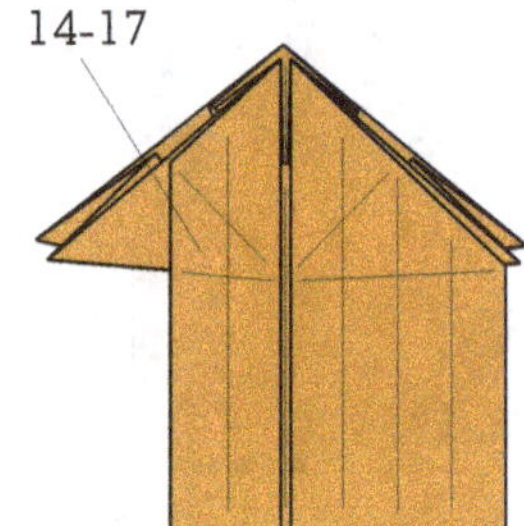

18. Repeat steps 14-17 in mirror image.

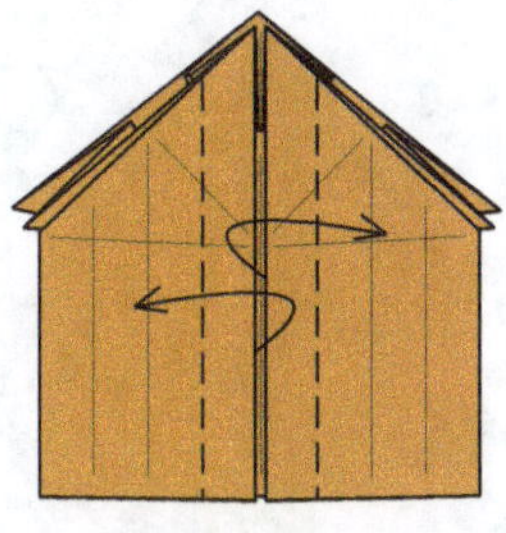

19. Open out two layers at each side. Model will not lie flat.

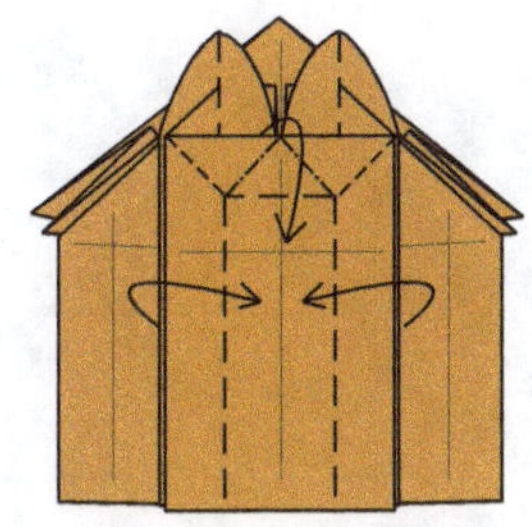

20. Close back up while petal folding down.

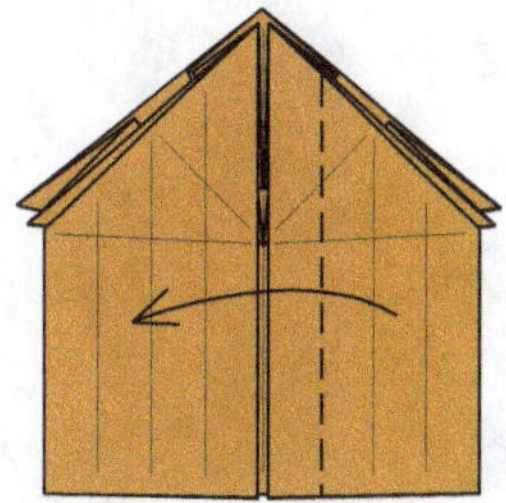

21. Valley over along the existing crease.

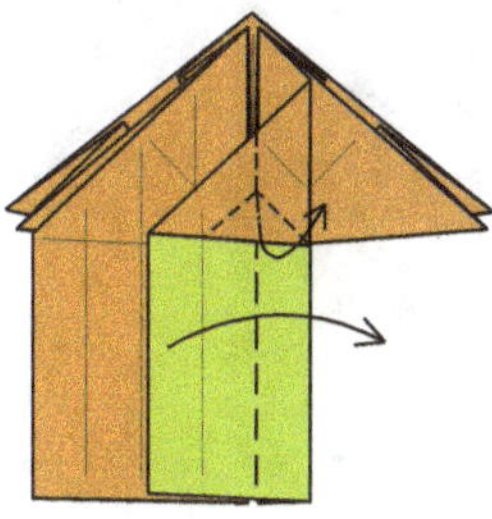

22. Valley over while incorporating a reverse fold.

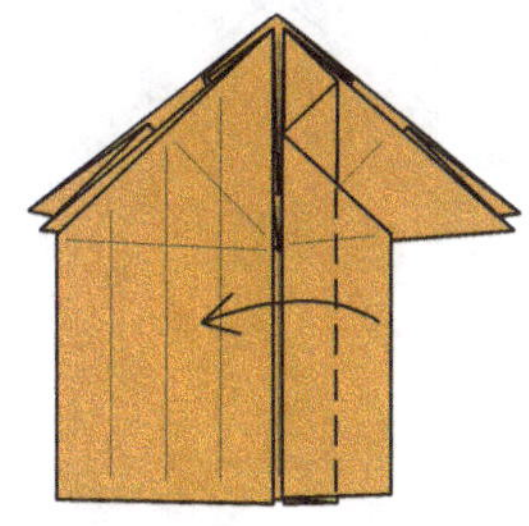

23. Valley along the existing crease.

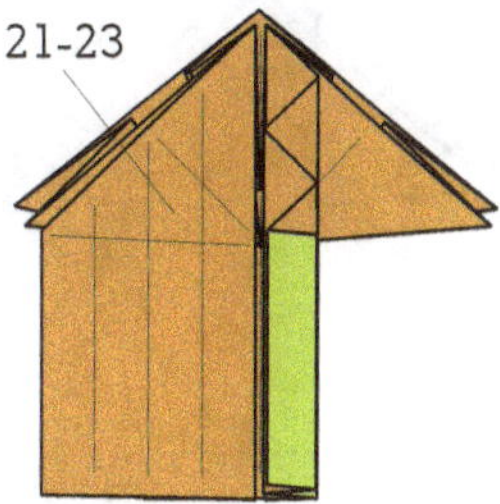

24. Repeat steps 21-23 in mirror image.

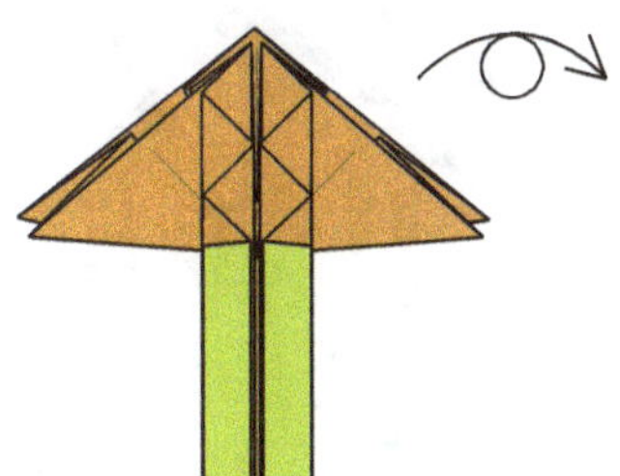

25. Turn over.

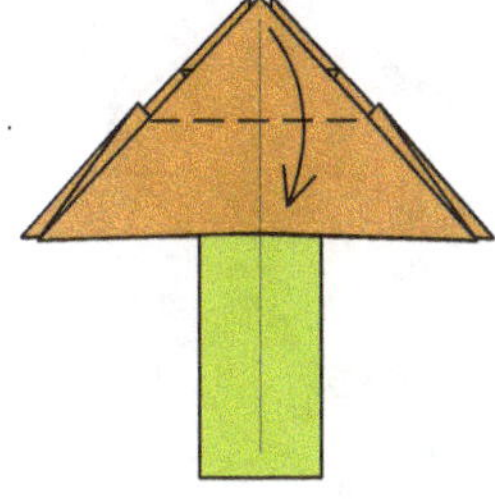

26. Valley down lightly, allowing squashes to form.

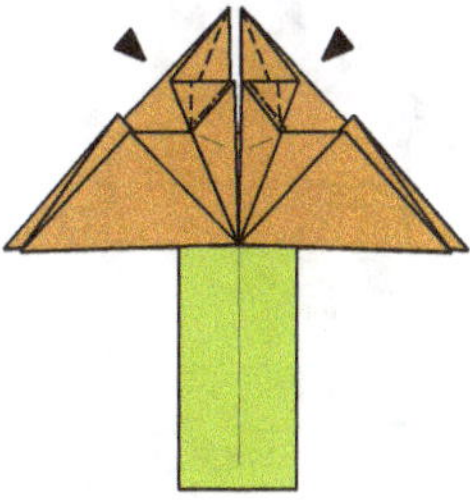

27. Reverse fold at the top.

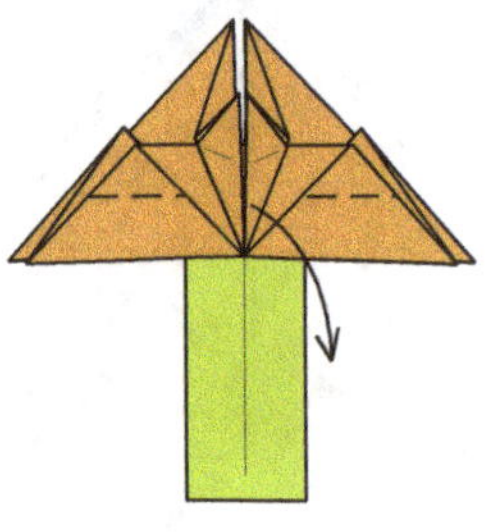

28. Stretch downwards.

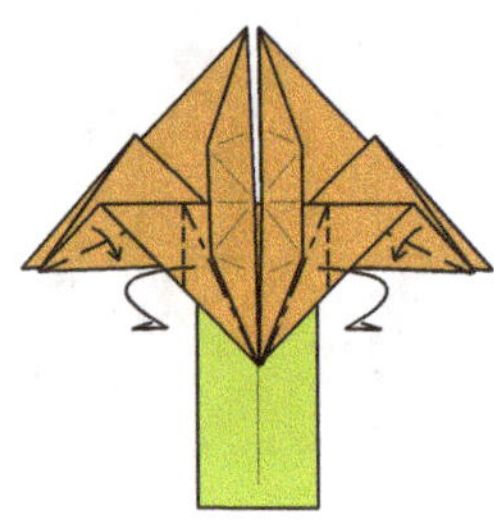

29. Swivel in along the angle bisectors.

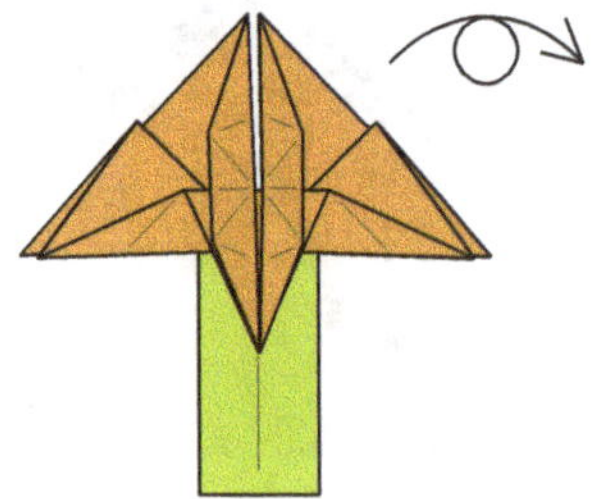

30. Turn over.

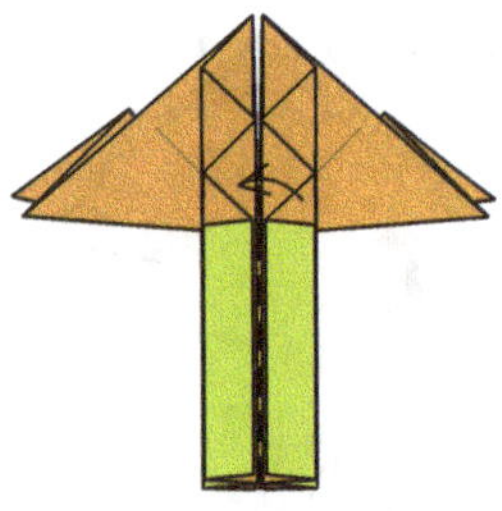

31. Swing over one pleat, allowing the tiny reverse fold to come undone.

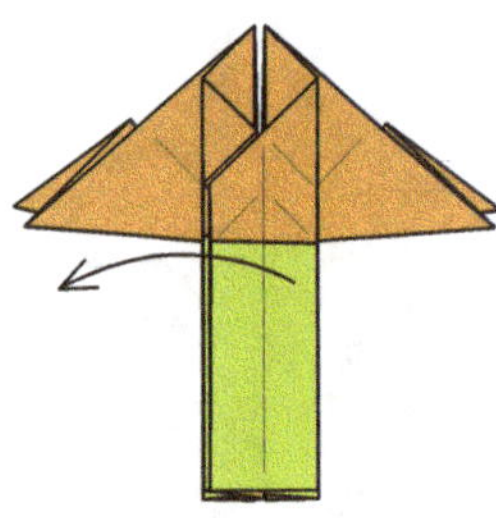

32. Pull out, undoing another pleat.

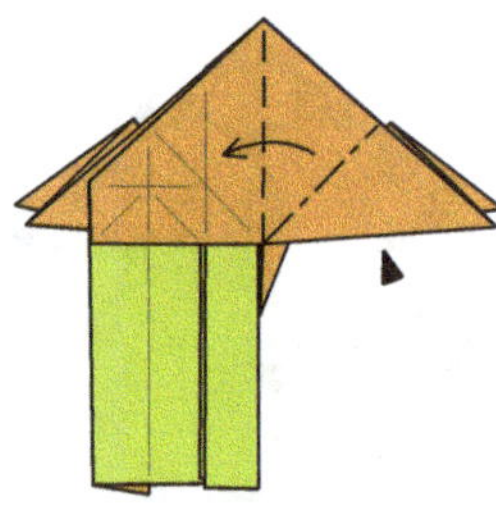

33. Squash upwards.

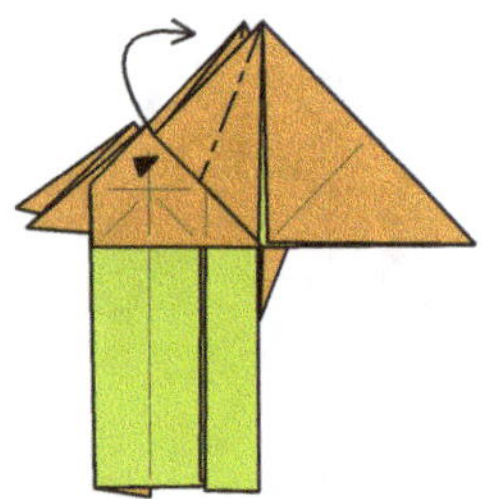

34. Reverse fold.

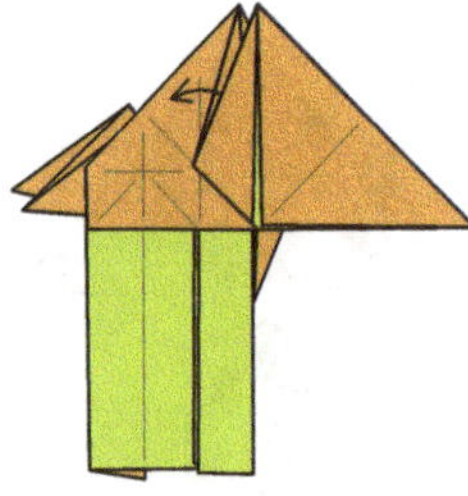

35. Undo the reverse fold.

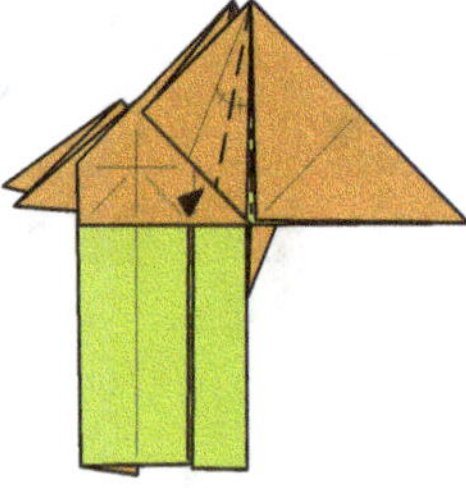

36. Reverse in and then out again, along the indicated angle bisector.

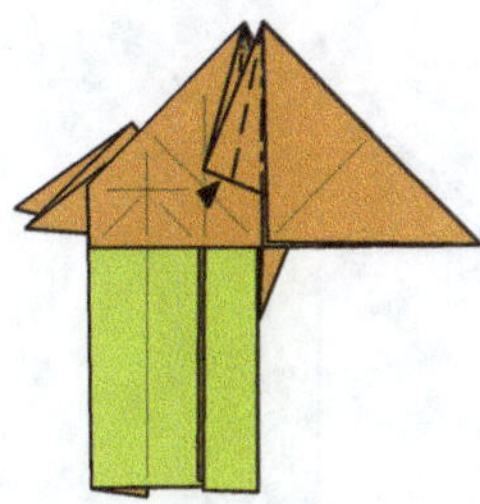

37. Reverse in and then out along the angle bisector.

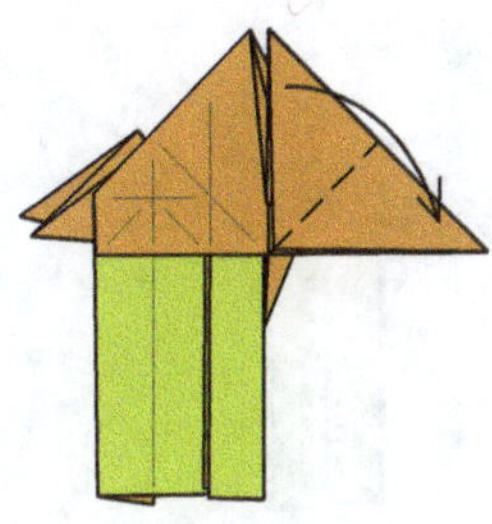

38. Valley down, allowing the reverse folds to come undone.

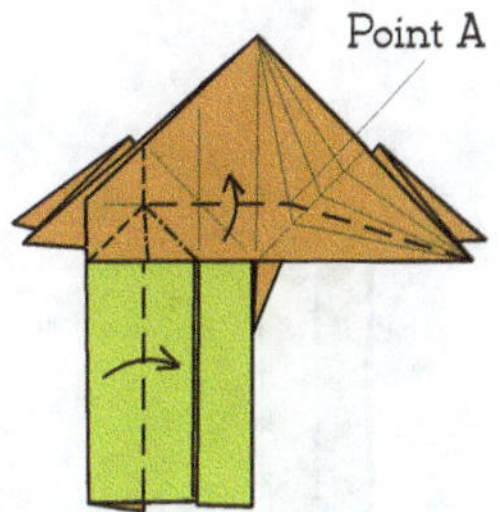

39. Swivel upwards, keeping the valley fold straight until it hits point A. The model will not lie flat.

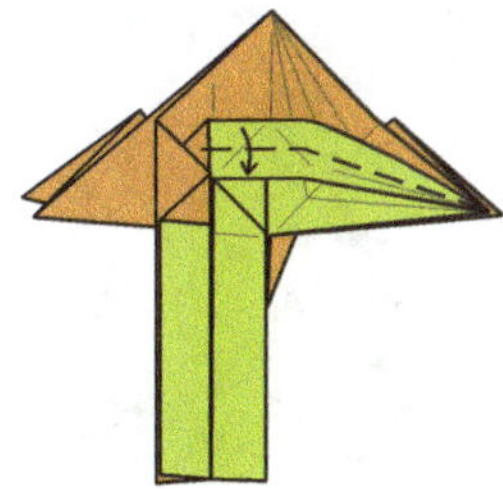

40. Valley down the raw edge.

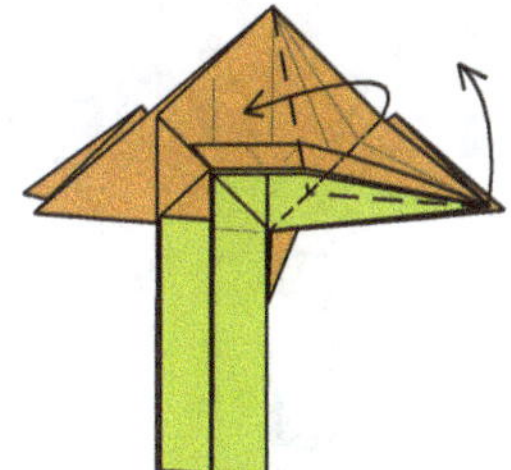

41. Swing back up, incorporating a reverse fold along the existing crease.

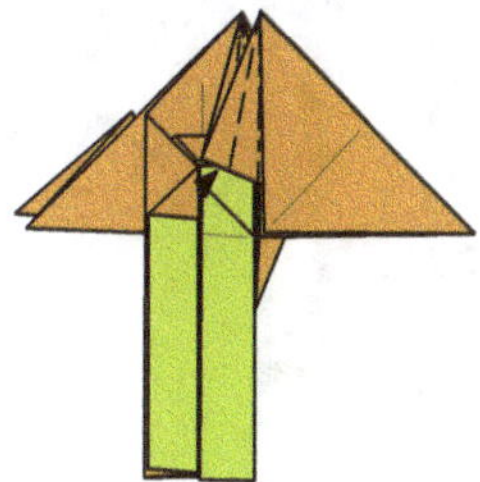

42. Replace the remaining reverse folds.

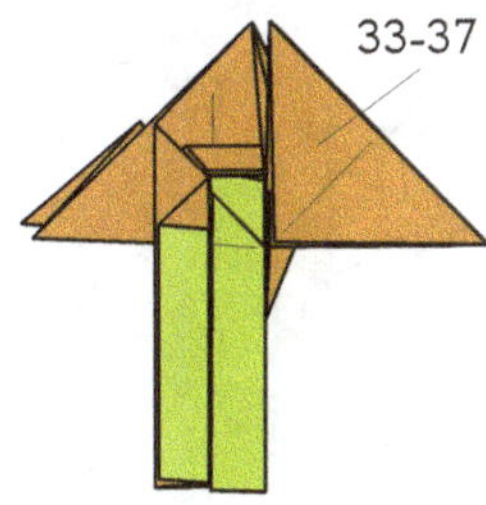

43. Repeat steps 33-37 on the indicated flap.

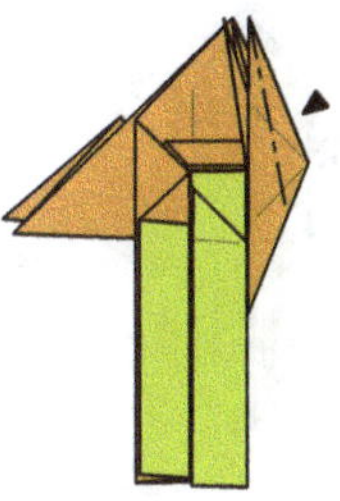

44. Closed sink along the angle bisector.

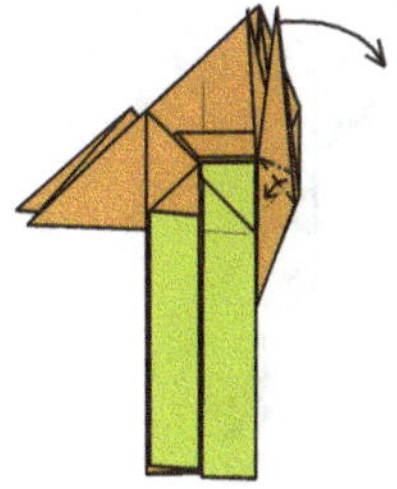

45. Squash the upper leg outwards.

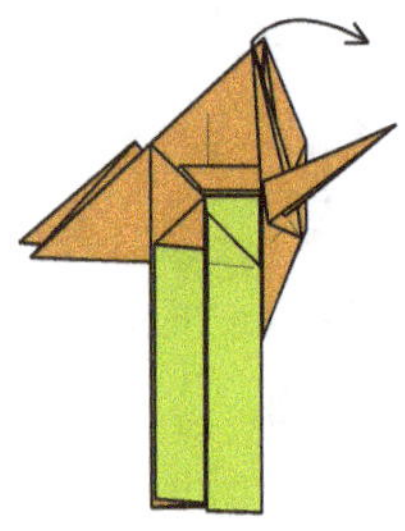

46. Pull the lower leg out slighly.

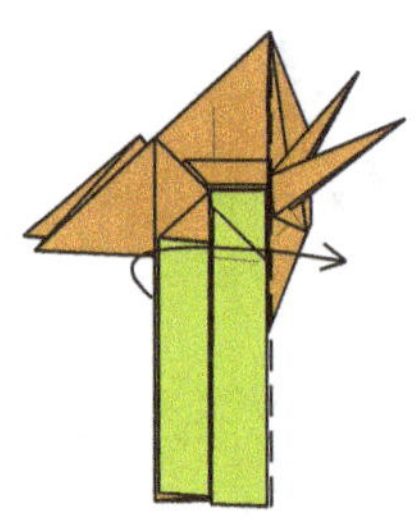

47. Swing over.

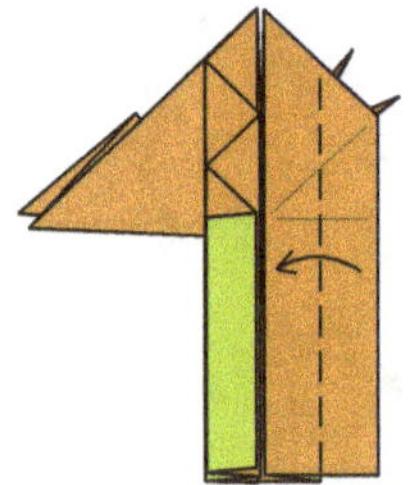

48. Valley along the existing crease.

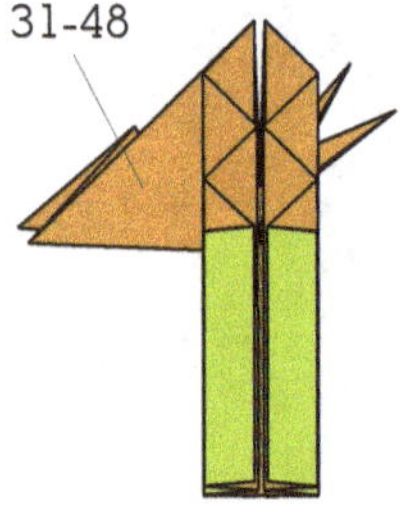

49. Repeat steps 31-48 in mirror image.

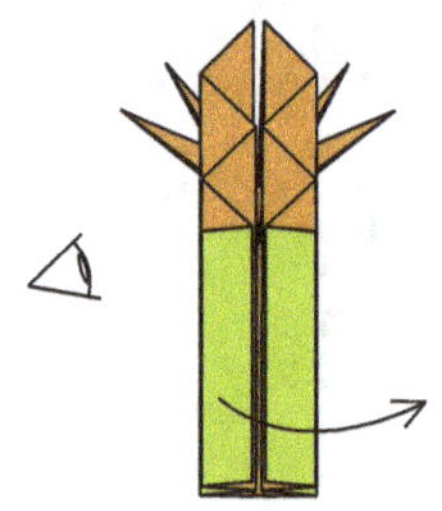

50. Spread apart one set of pleats.

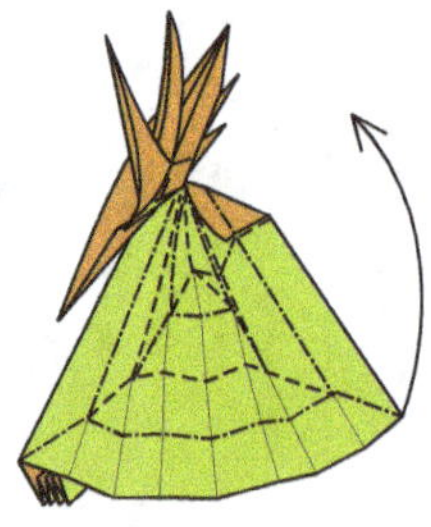

51. Stretch the corner while pleating the bottom edge up.

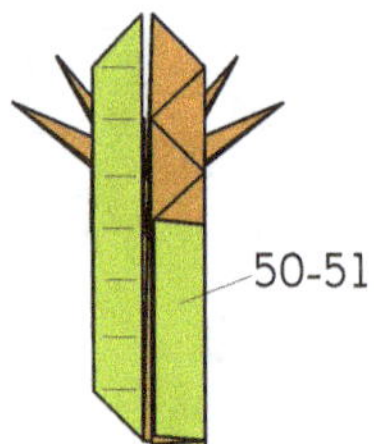

52. Repeat steps 50-51 on the other side.

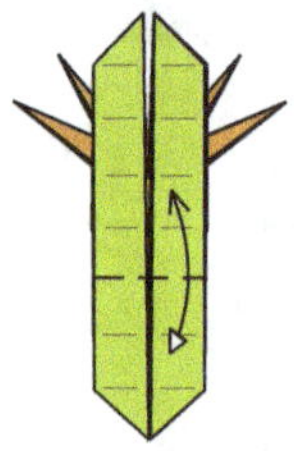

53. Precrease through all layers.

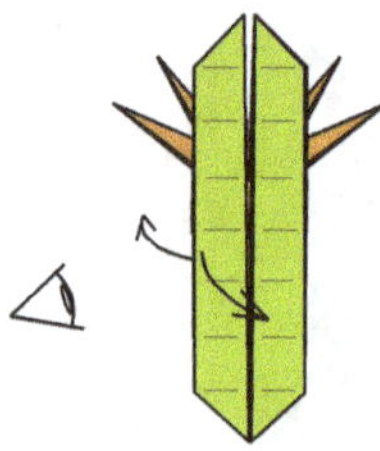

54. Spread apart the side layers.

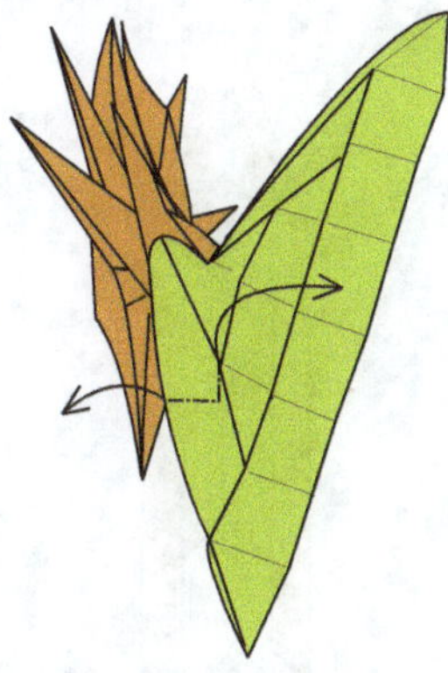

55. Stretch apart the indicated area, forming a ridge.

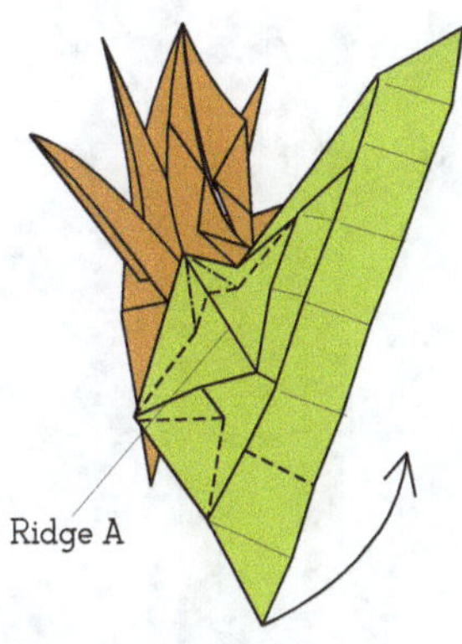

Ridge A

56. Flatten ridge A, while stretching the flaps upwards.

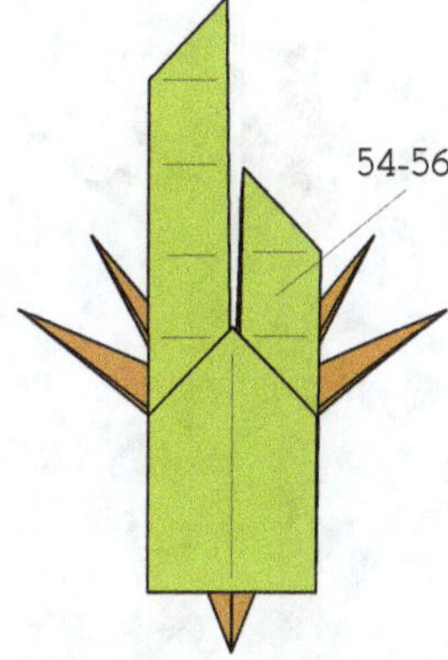

54-56

57. Repeat steps 54-56 in mirror image.

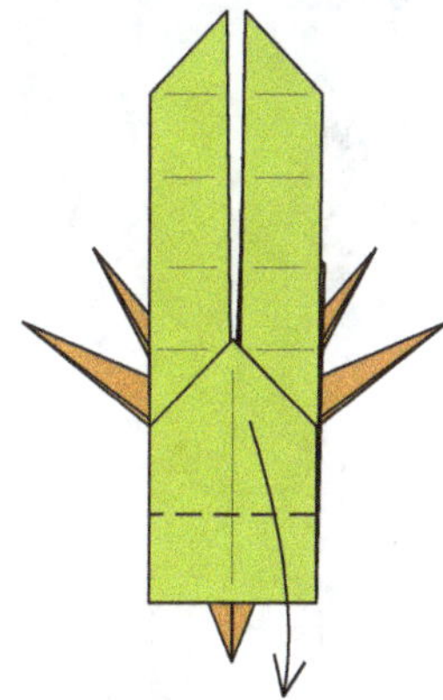

58. Swing down the bottom flap.

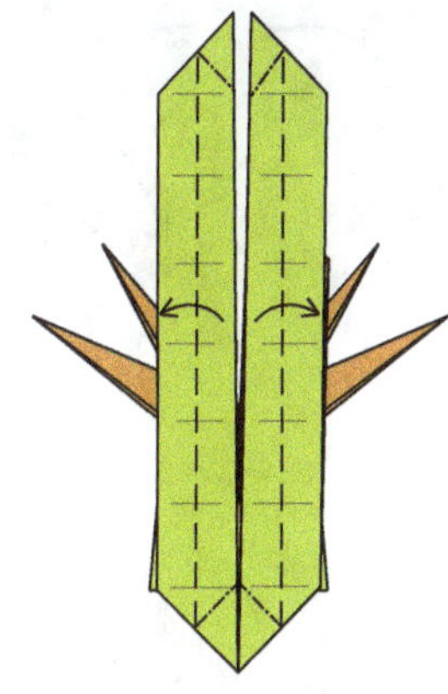

59. Valley out the single layers, allowing squashes to form at the top points and at the bottom.

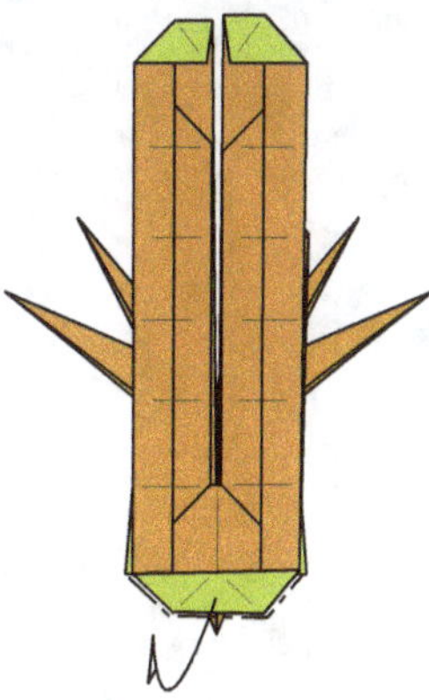

60. Wrap around the single layer.

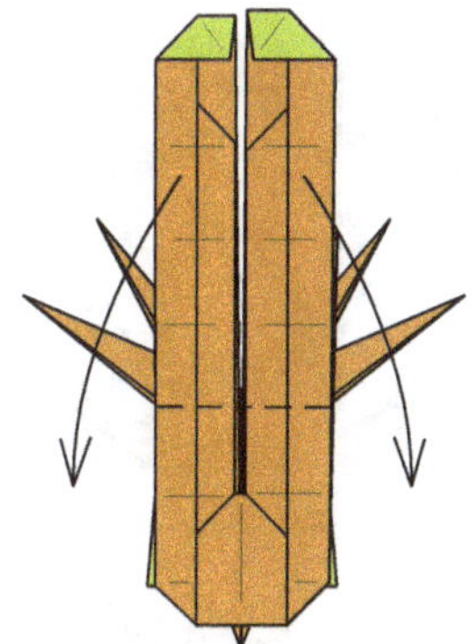

61. Swing down as far as possible.

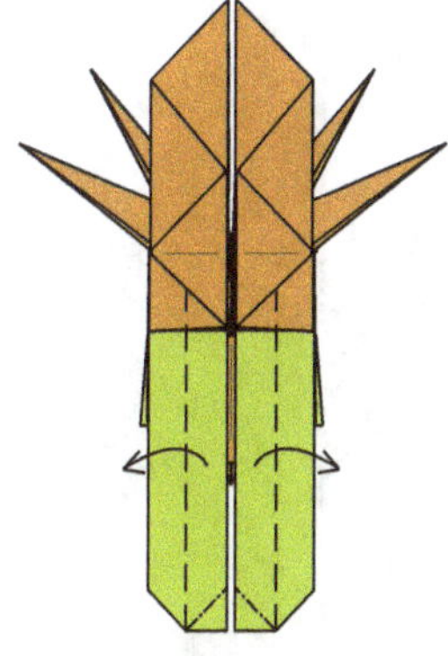

62. Valley the top layers outwards, allowing squashes to form at the bottom.

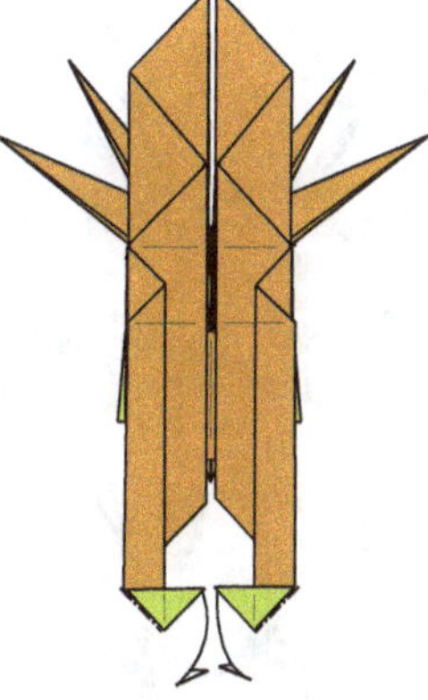

63. Outside reverse fold the bottom points.

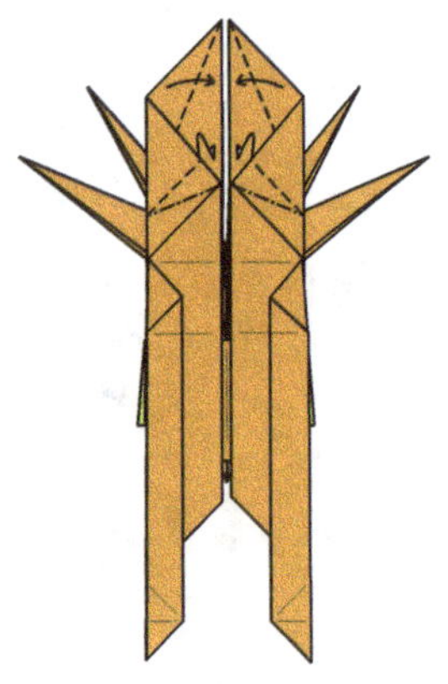

64. Swivel in at the top.

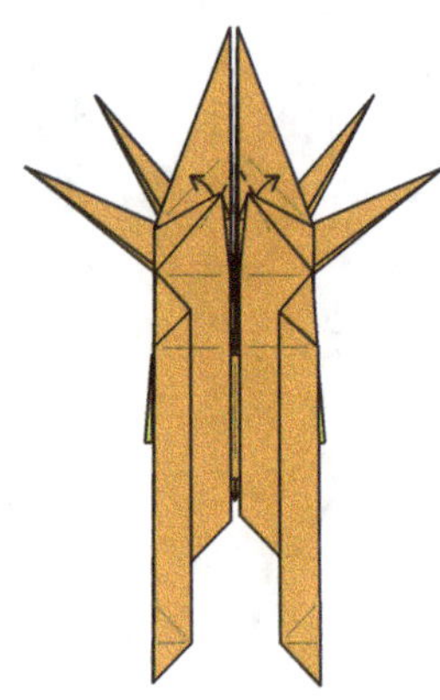

65. Form tiny reverse folds.

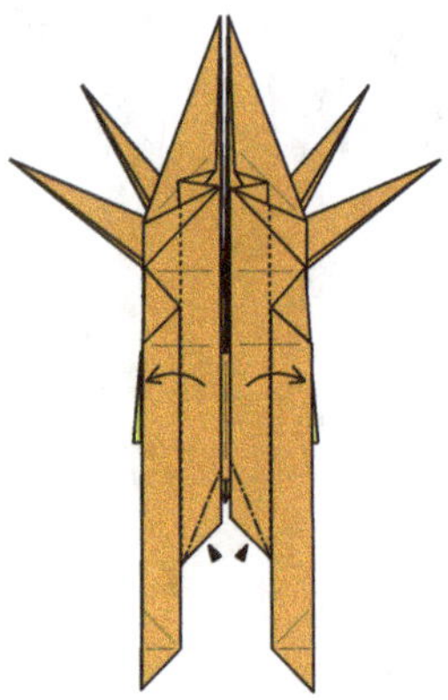

66. Valley outwards, allowing spread squashes t oform at the bottom.

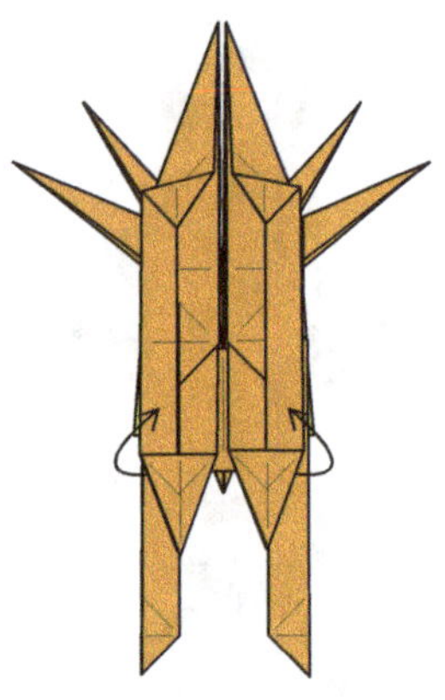

67. Pull a single layer around from each side to the surface.

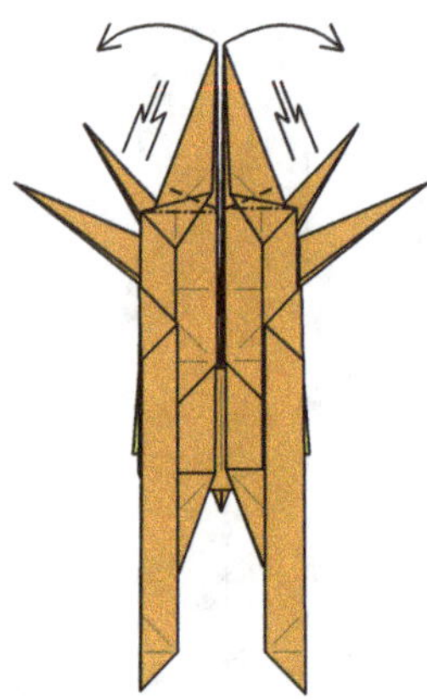

68. Crimp the top legs outwards.

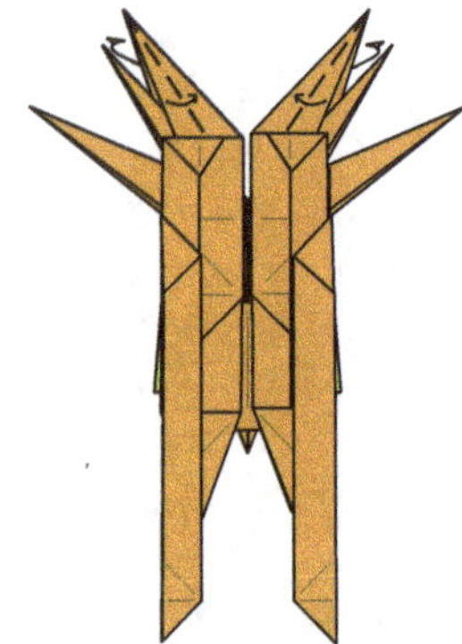

69. Thin the top legs at each side, allowing a swivel to form at the base of each leg.

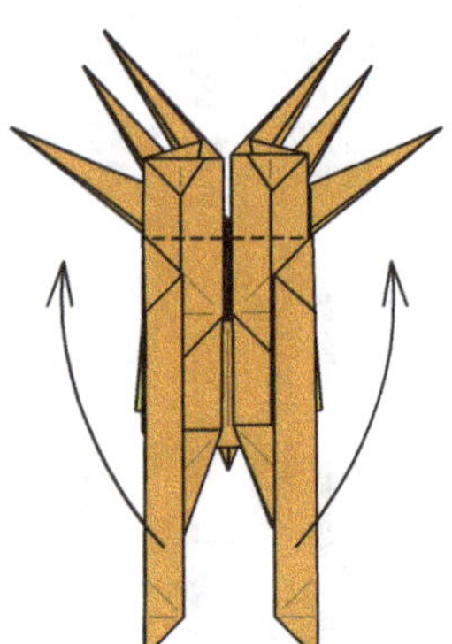

70. Swing the antennae up as far as possible.

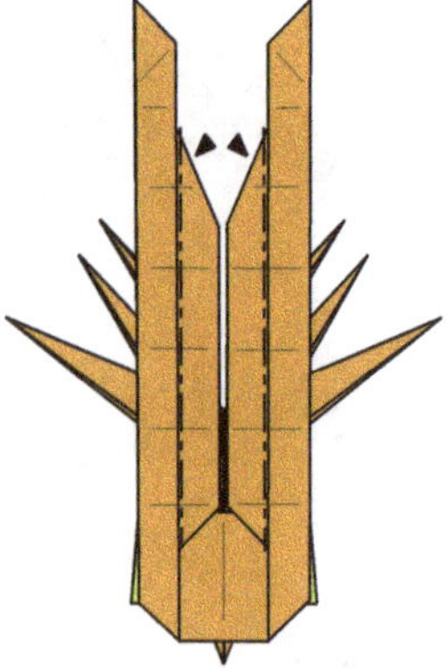

71. Sink the inner edges triangularly.

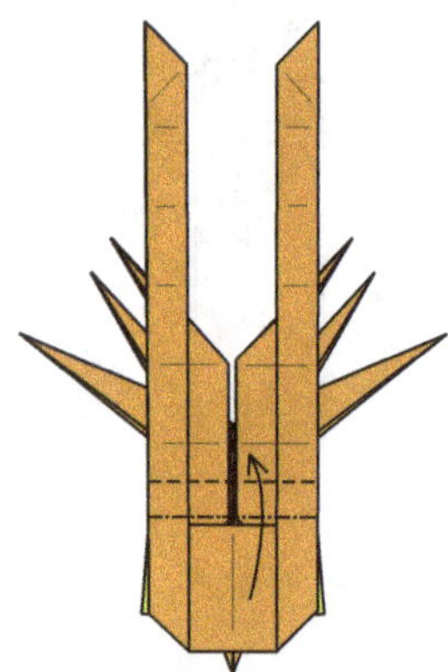

72. Pleat the top flap upwards.

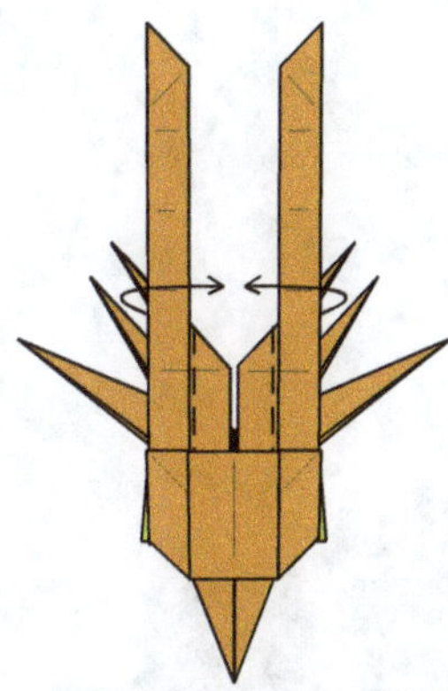

73. Swivel in the entire thickness. It is okay if the layers overlap each other.

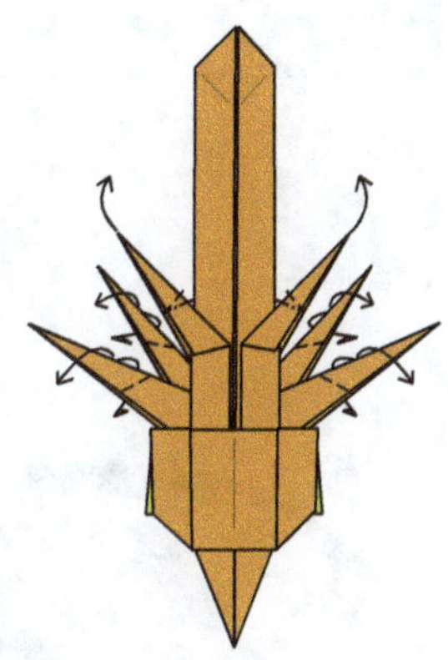

74. Crimp the front legs and outside reverse fold the lower sets of legs.

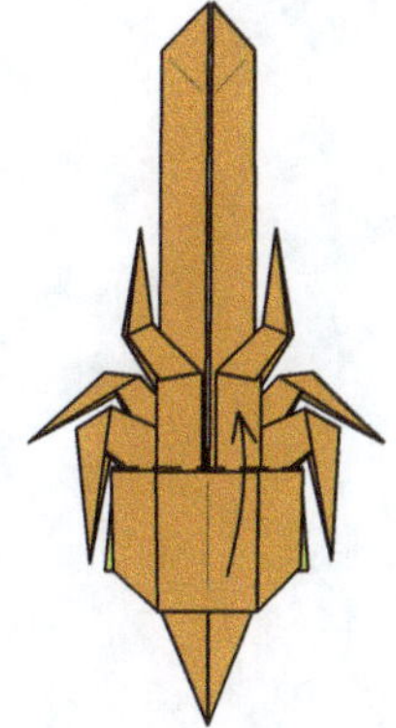

75. Swing the top layer of the body up.

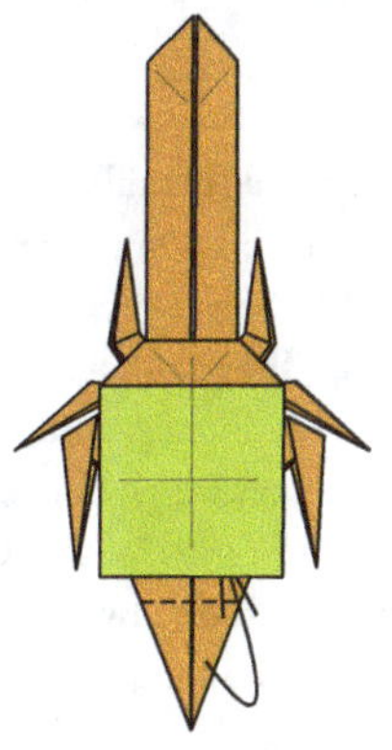

76. Tuck the bottom flap into the body.

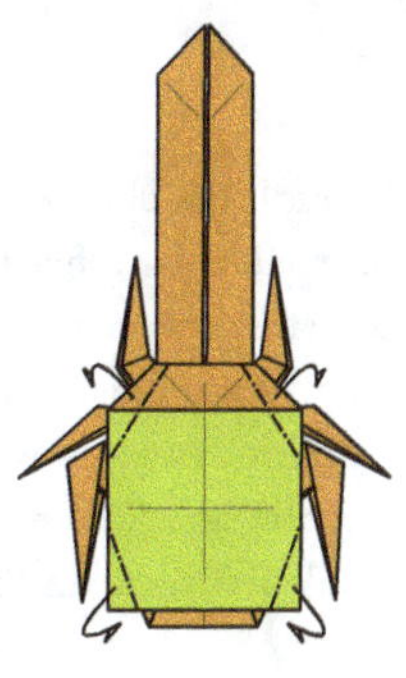

77. Trim the body with mountain folds.

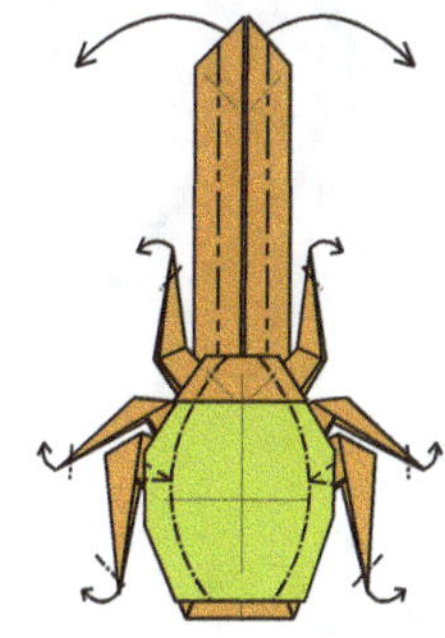

78. Flare the tips of the legs outwards. Rabbit ear the antennae outwards. Shape the body and legs.

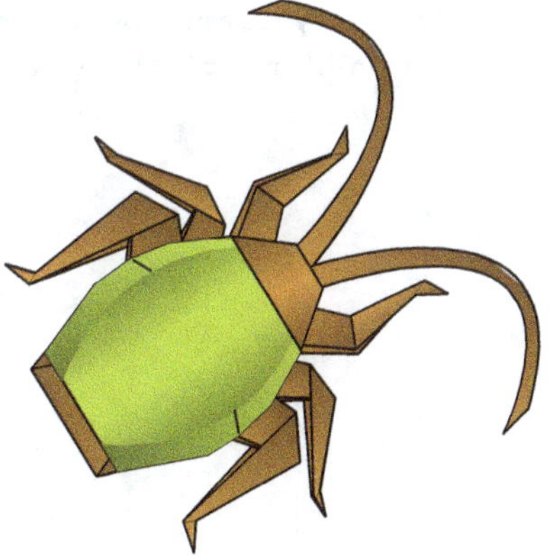

79. Completed *Cockroach*.

Black Pine Sawyer

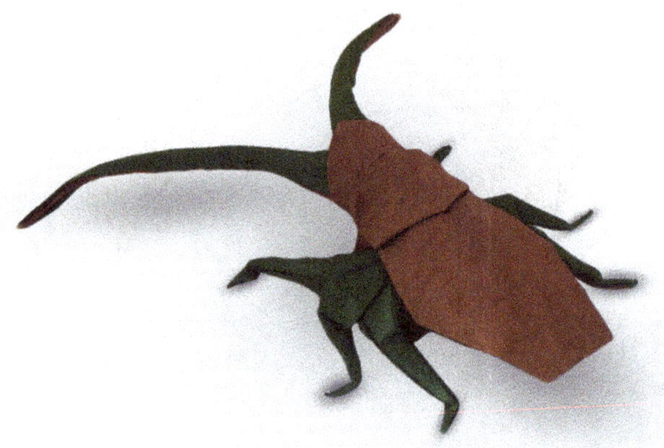

About

Although the shape and coloring of this model is similar to the *Cockroach*, the efficiency of this piece seems to be much greater. On closer inspection, the legs on this *Black Pine Sawyer* are a bit shorter, and give the illusion of length with the way they are formed. The design of this piece was the result of a doodle (hence, could be called a doodlebug). After arriving at the basic shape, I simply flipped though a book of insects and found the species that fit the closest. Given the variety of insects, it is pretty hard not to design one by accident, although finding the right name could be a challenge.

Tips

Most of this model is straightforward until you reach step forty-seven. When faced with a step that requires a lot of unfolding, I always try to see if I can trace my way back to the previous step (if things go wrong). By releasing the paper gradually, it should become apparent how the body section becomes flattened.

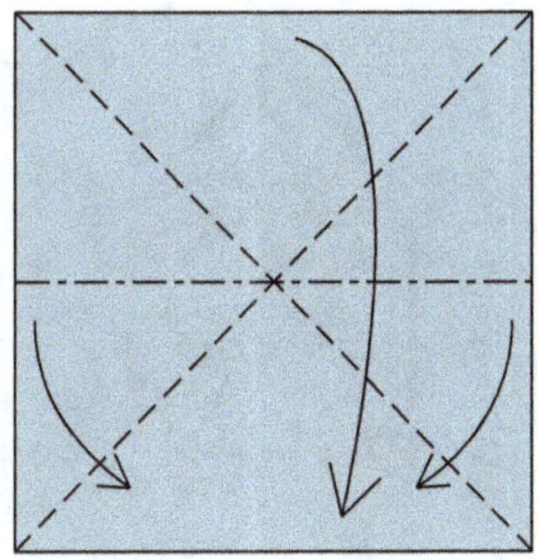

1. Collapse down (Waterbomb Base).

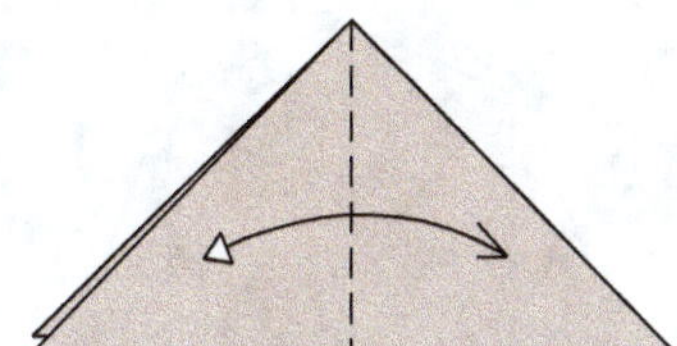

2. Precrease by swinging the flap back and forth.

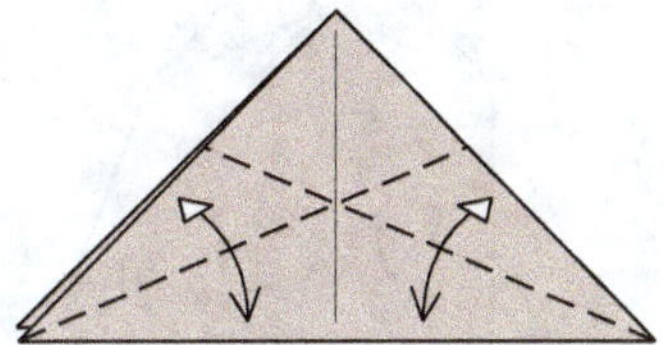

3. Precrease along the angle bisectors.

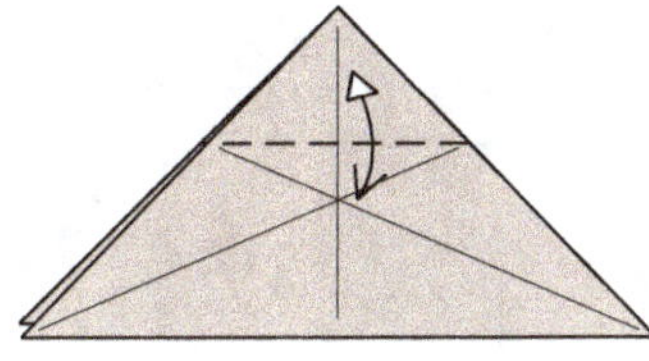

4. Precrease, noting where the creases hit the edges.

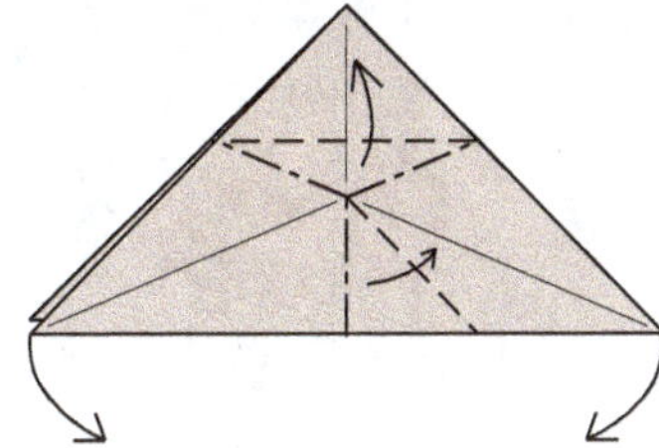

5. Collapse upwards.

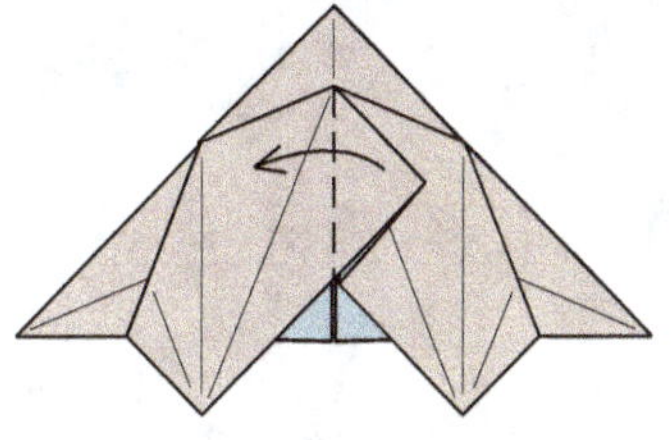

6. Swing over the center flap.

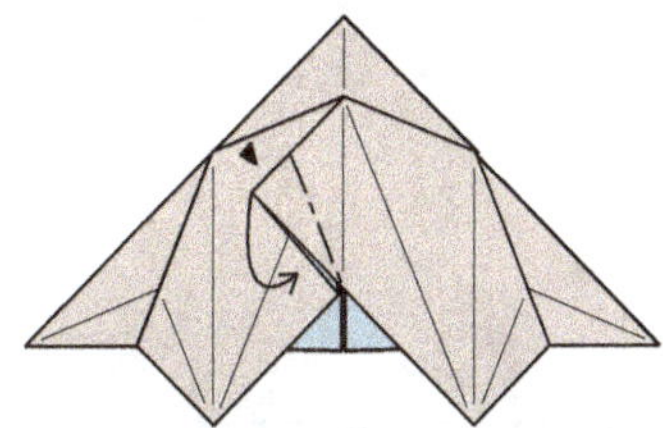

7. Reverse fold.

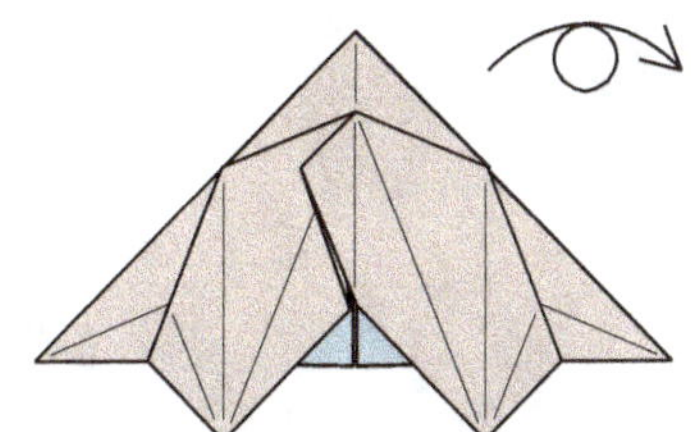

8. Turn over.

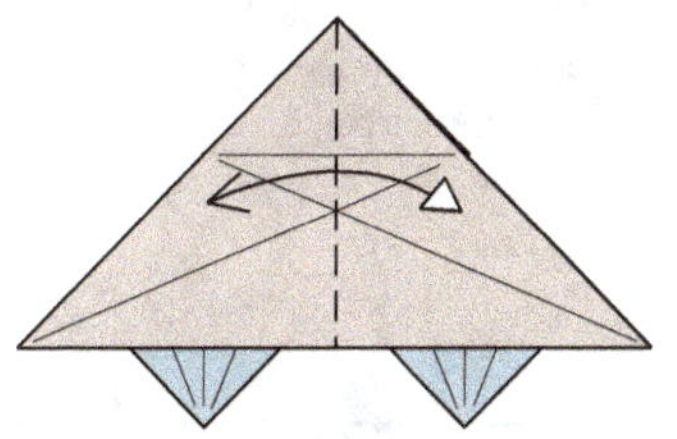

9. Precrease by swinging the flap back and forth.

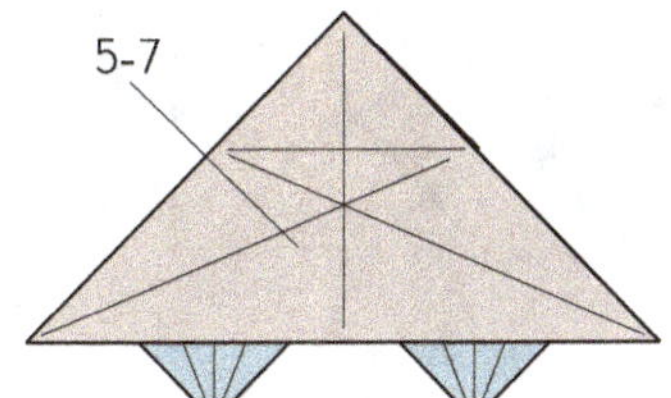

10. Repeat steps 5-7.

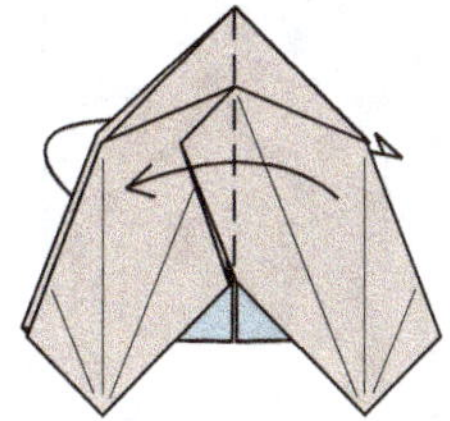

11. Swing over a flap at each side.

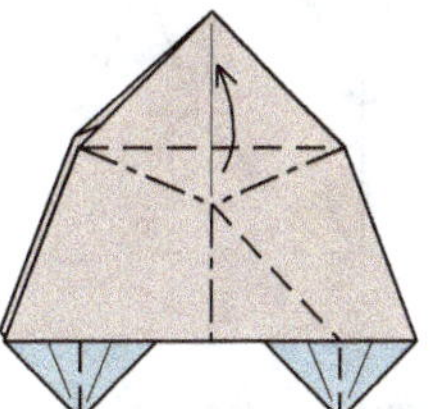

12. Collapse upwards.

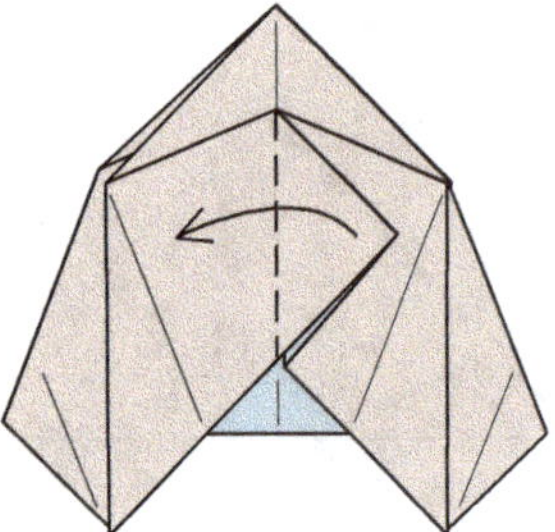

13. Swing over the center flap.

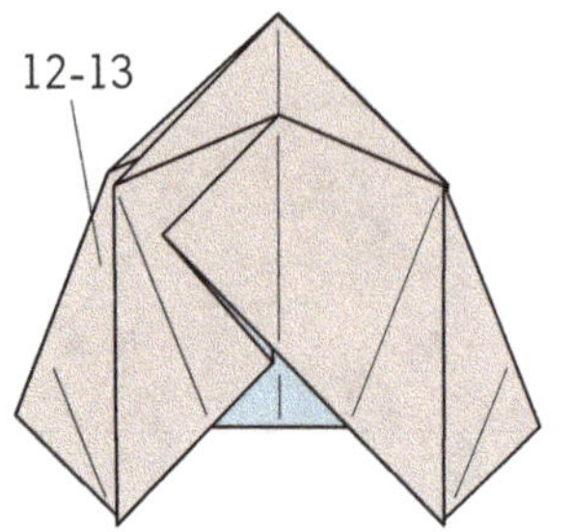

14. Repeat steps 12-13 behind.

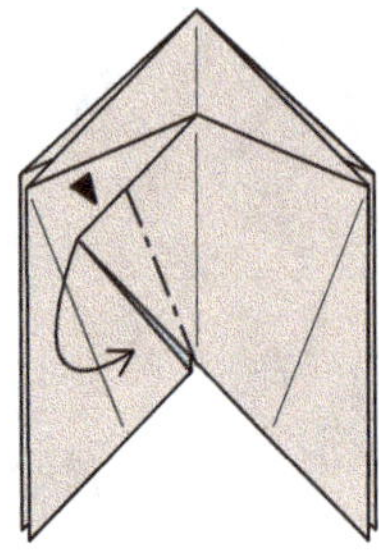

15. Reverse fold.

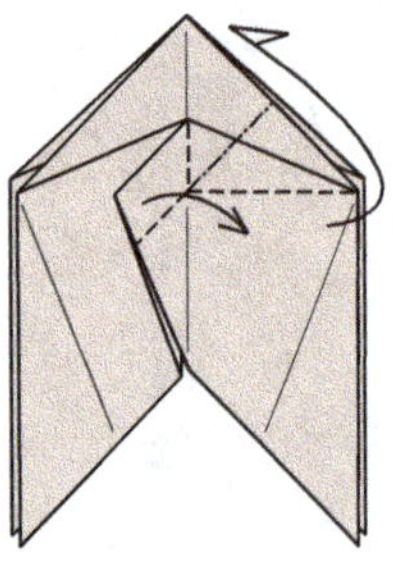

16. Pleat the large flap upwards while swinging over the center flap.

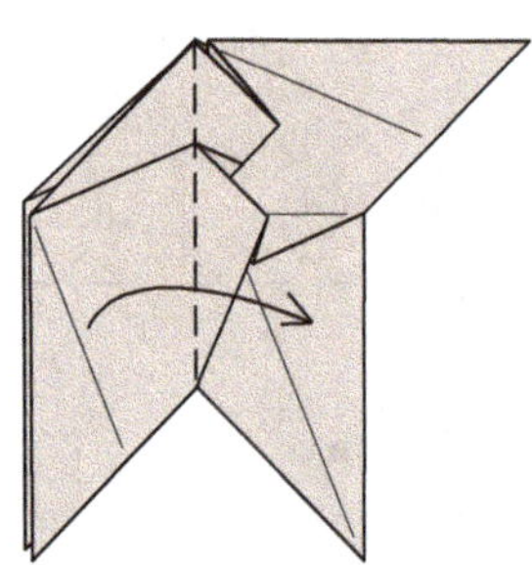

17. Swing over the large flap.

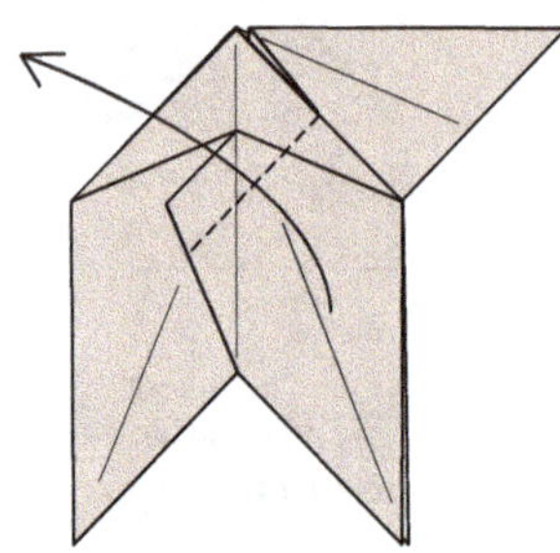

18. Valley fold the large flap up.

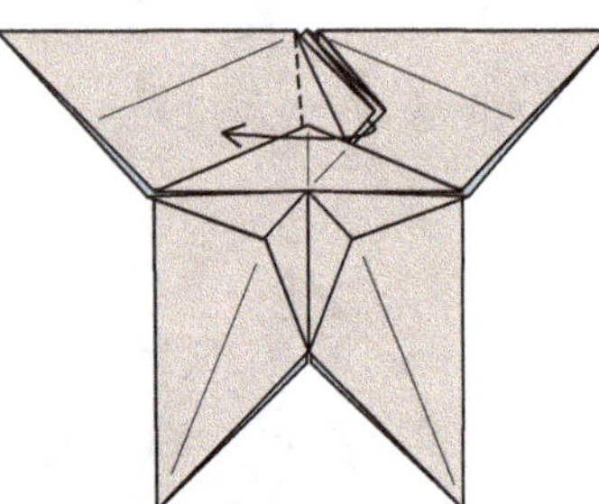

19. Swing over the center flap.

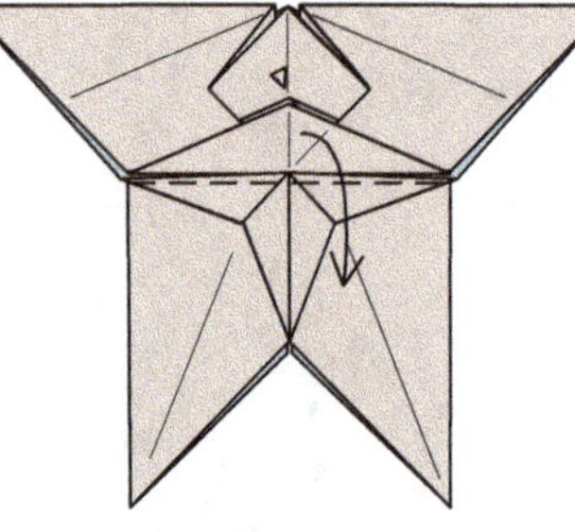

20. Swing the flap down, allowing a spread squash to form.

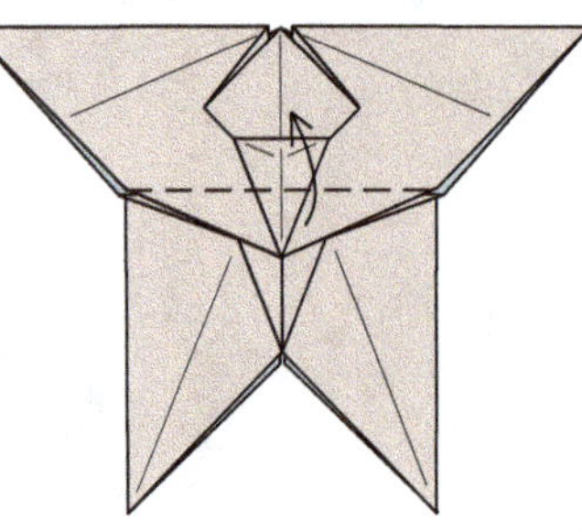

21. Valley fold the flap back up.

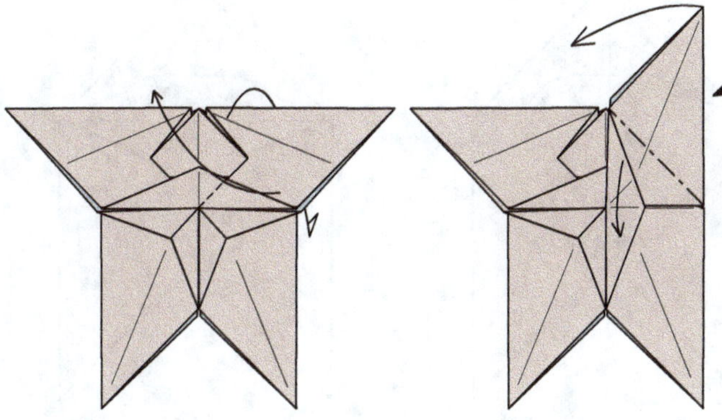

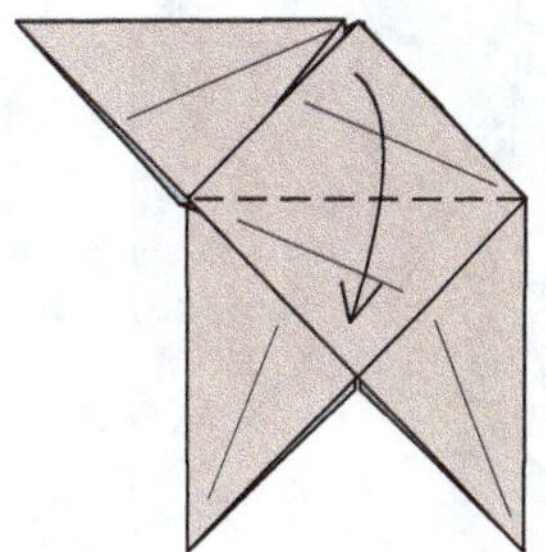

22. Twist the flap upwards.

23. Squash fold.

24. Valley fold the flap in half.

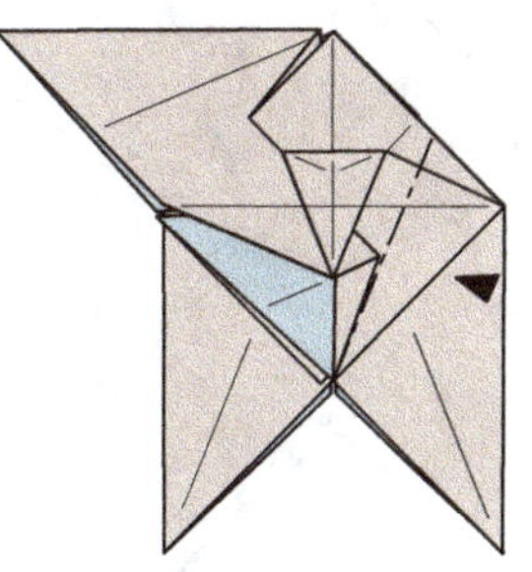

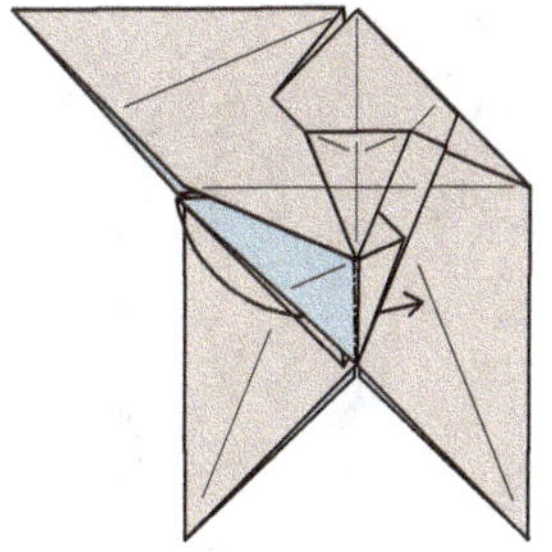

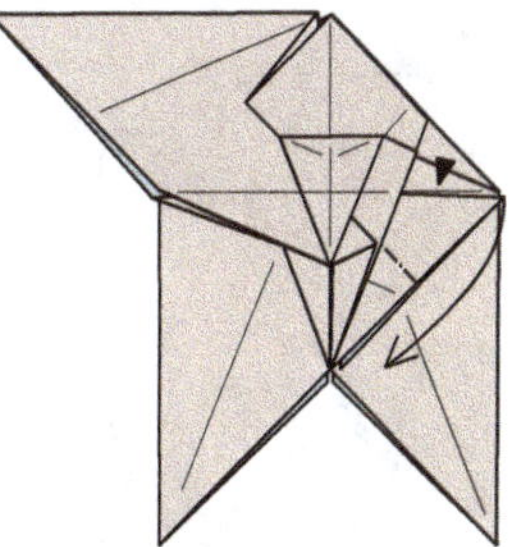

25. Sink along the angle bisector.

26. Reverse fold the flap though.

27. Reverse fold the flap down.

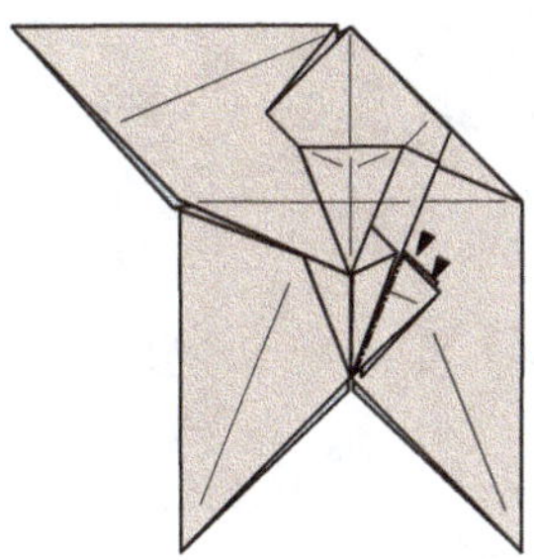

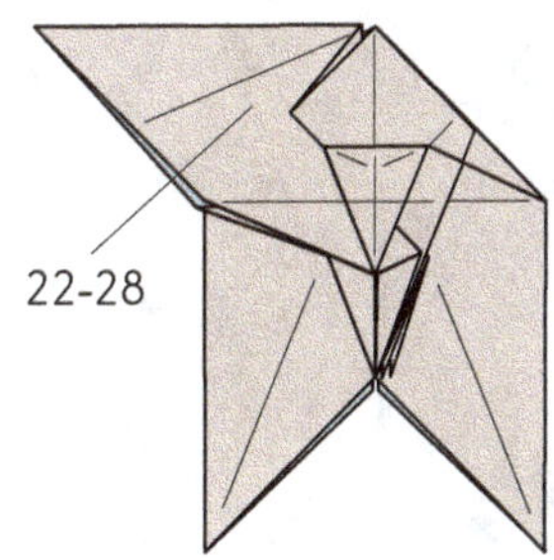

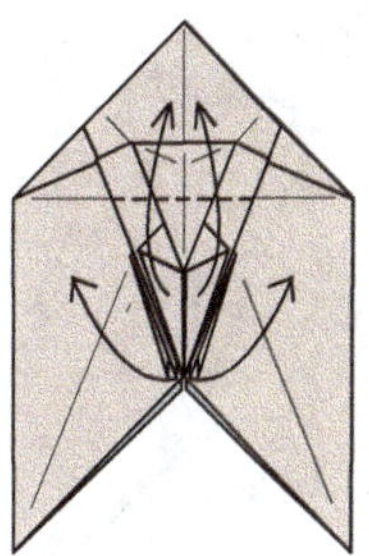

28. Reverse fold the two flaps.

29. Repeat steps 22-28 in mirror image.

30. Open out the clusters of flaps.

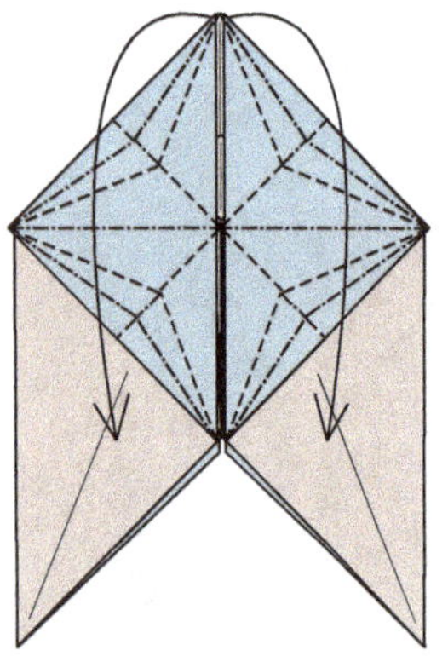

31. Close back up, adding additional reverse folds near the raw edges.

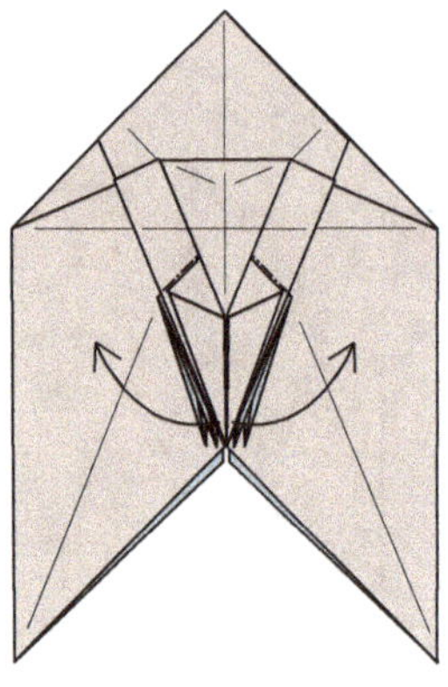

32. Reverse fold the clusters of flaps outwards, distributing the layers evenly.

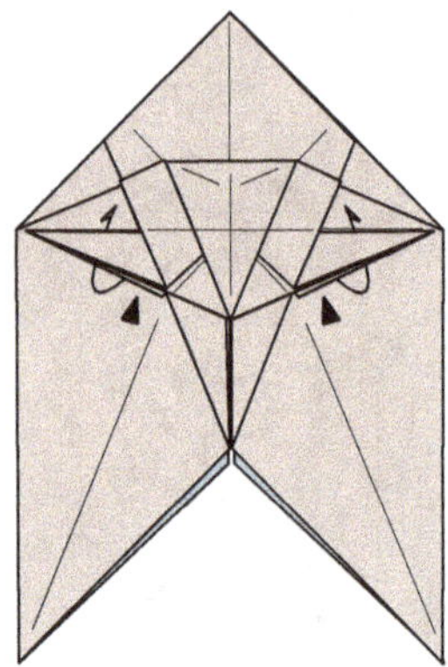

33. Reverse fold the bottom flaps through.

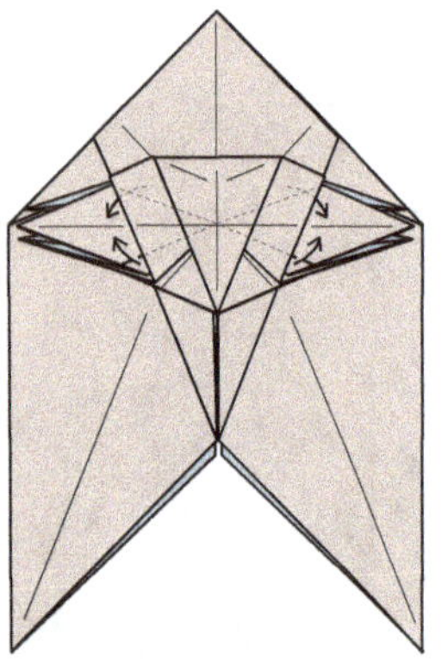

34. Valley fold the hidden layers to the center.

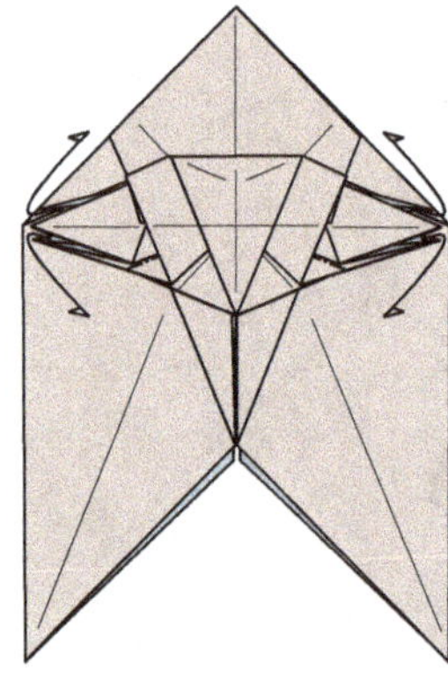

35. Mountain fold the flaps outwards.

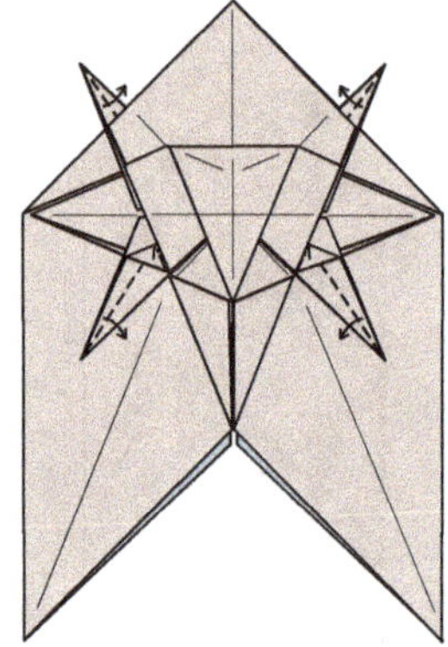

36. Valley fold the top layers over, swiveling in at the flaps base.

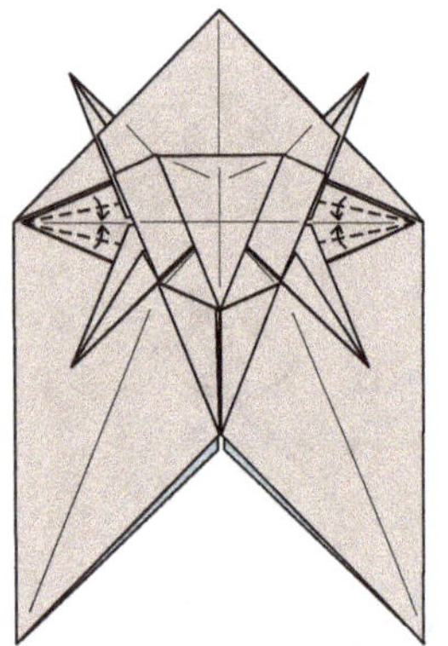

37. Valley fold the sides to the center, swiveling in at the flaps base.

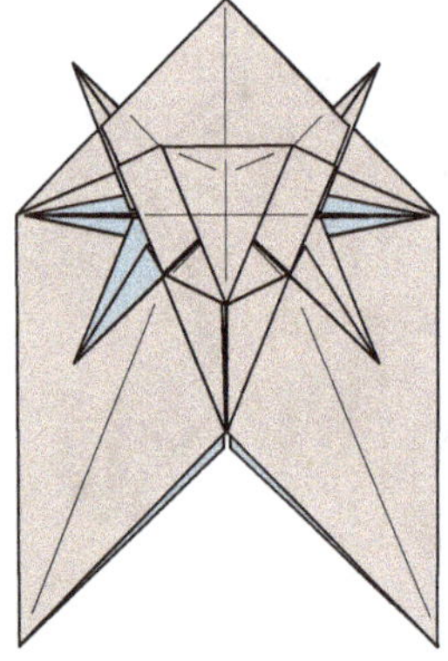

38. Turn over.

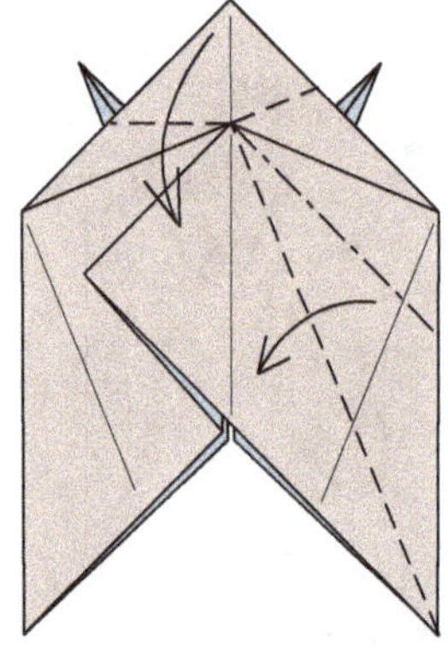

39. Pleat the large flap, allowing the top flap to fold down.

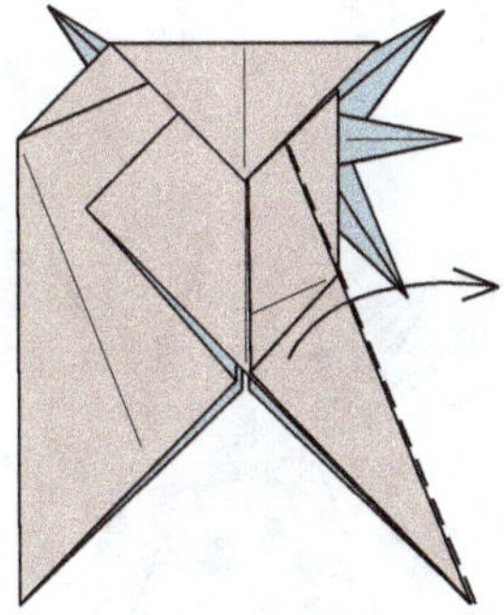

40. Valley fold the flap over.

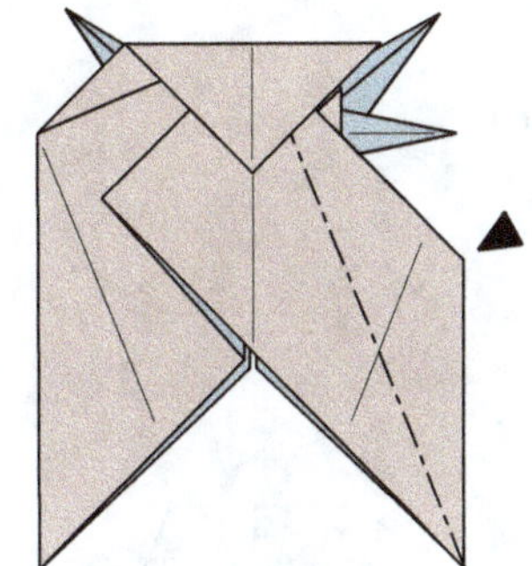

41. Closed sink.

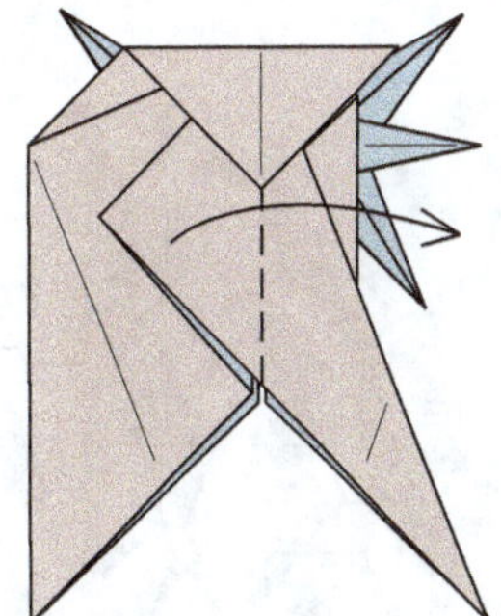

42. Swing the center flap over.

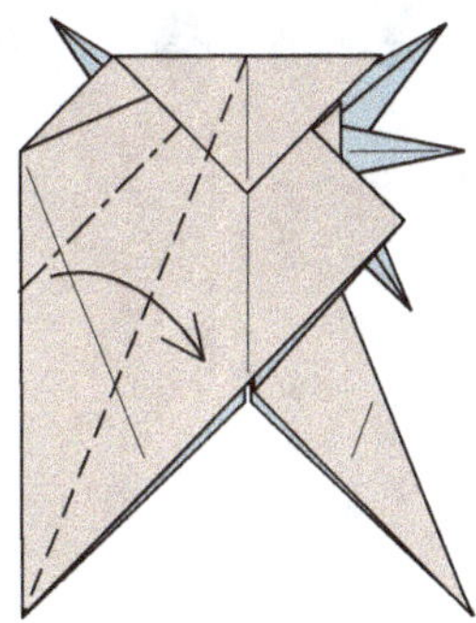

43. Pleat the top flap (similar to step 39).

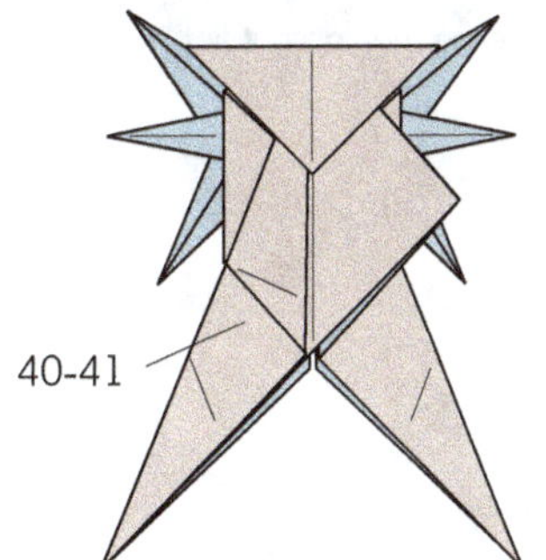

44. Repeat steps 40-41 in mirror image.

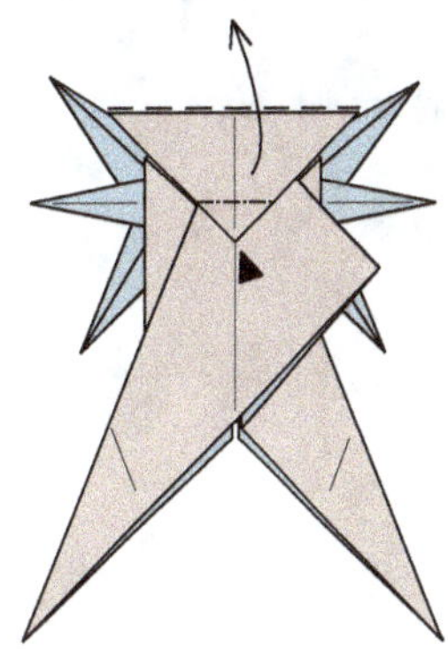

45. Spread squash the flap.

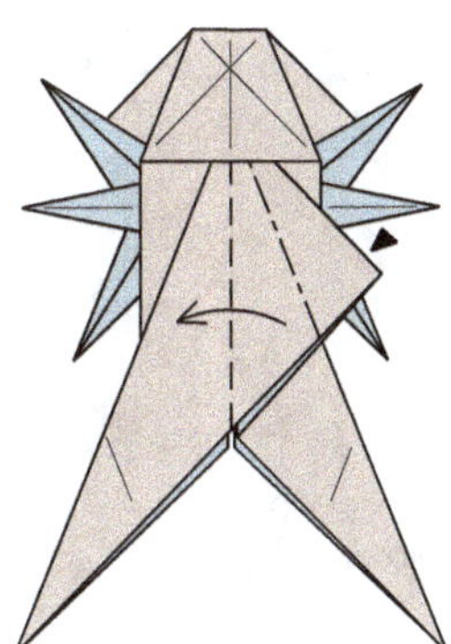

46. Squash fold the center flap.

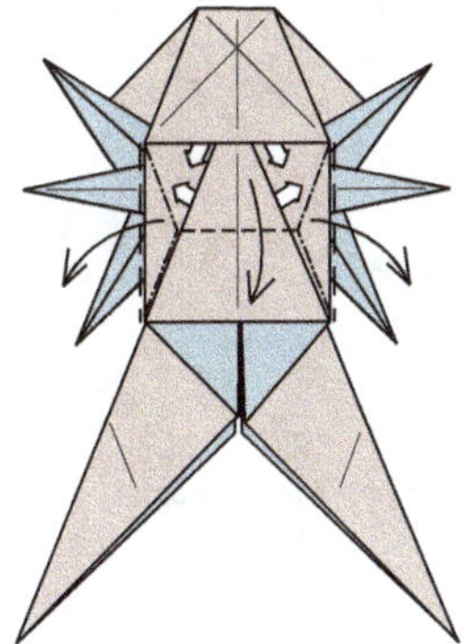

47. Pull out the trapped top layer, while untrapping the top flap and swinging it down.

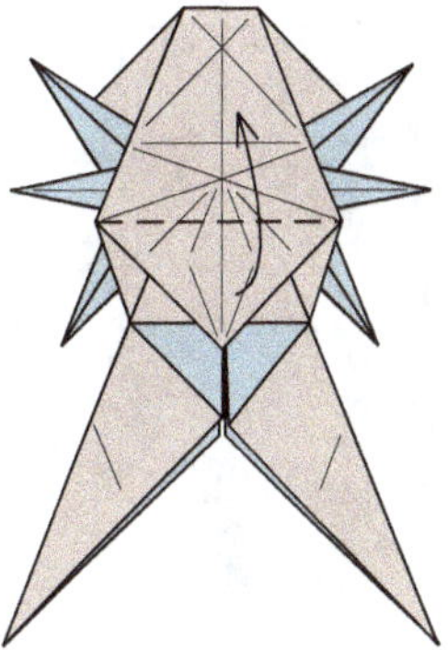

48. Swing the top flap up.

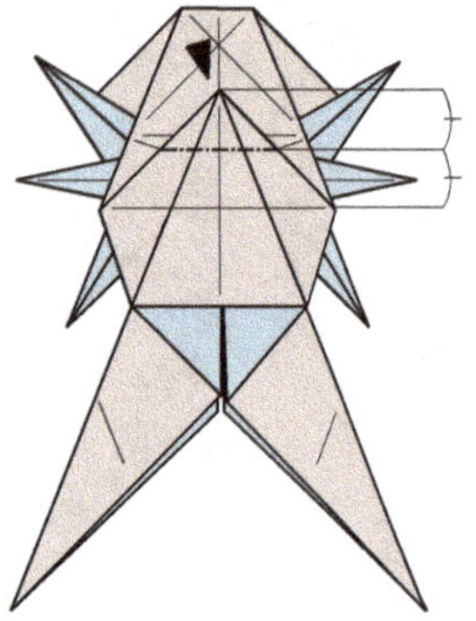

49. Sink the flap halfway.

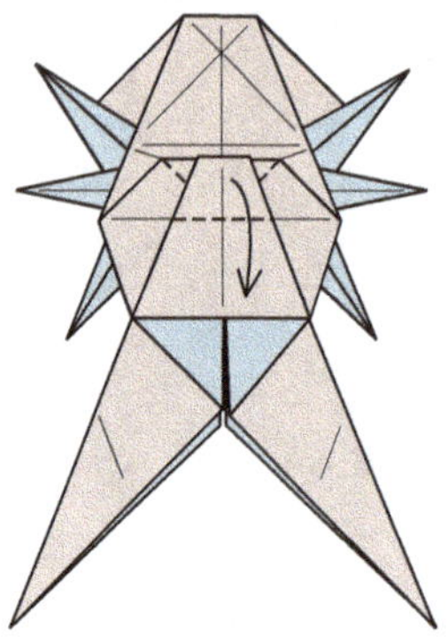

50. Spread the flap out flat.

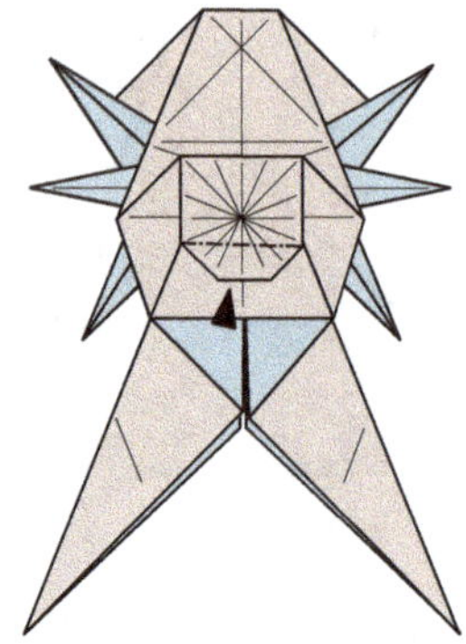

51. Closed sink the lower edge.

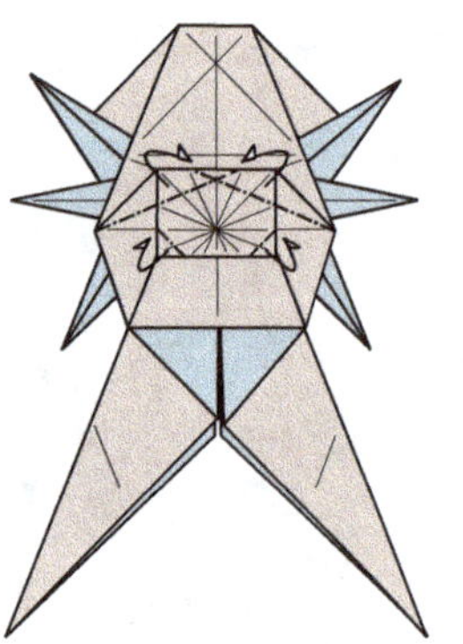

52. Mountain fold the corners.

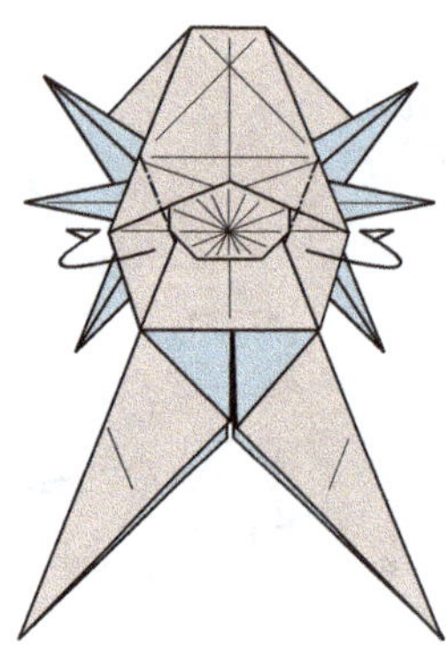

53. Mountain fold the sides.

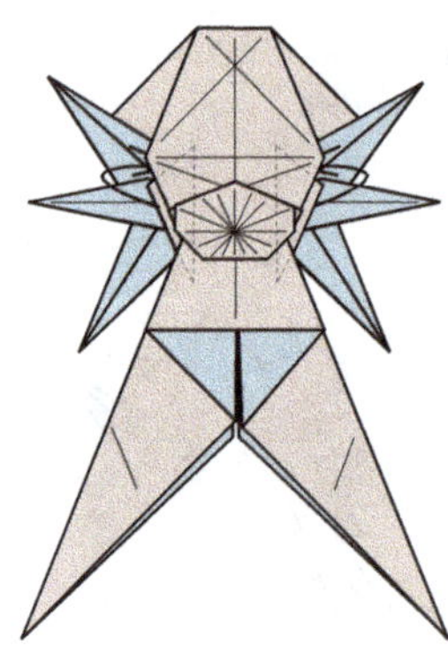

54. Valley fold the protruding flaps inside.

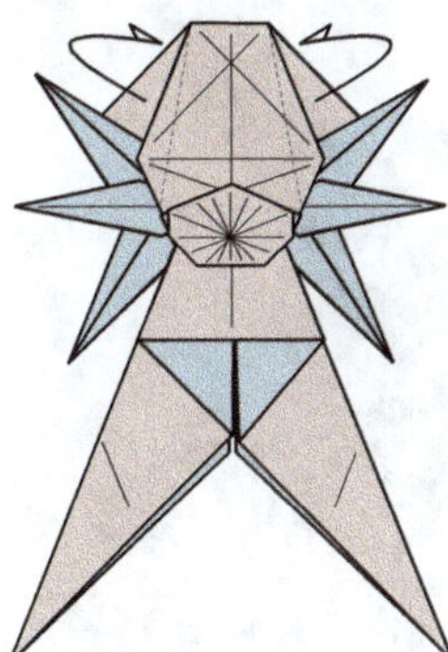

55. Mountain fold the flaps behind.

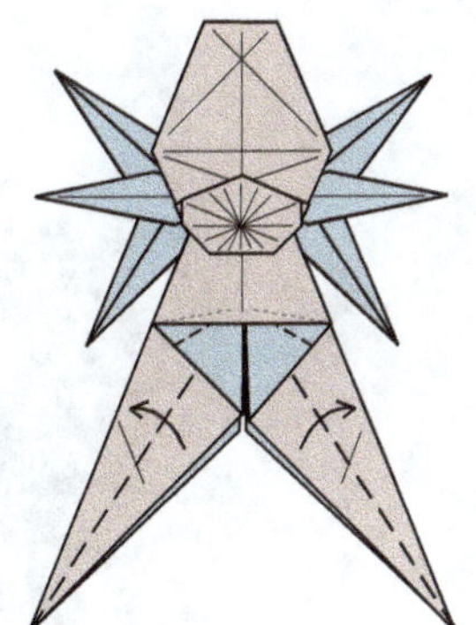

56. Valley fold the tip layer at each flap, swiveling under at the base.

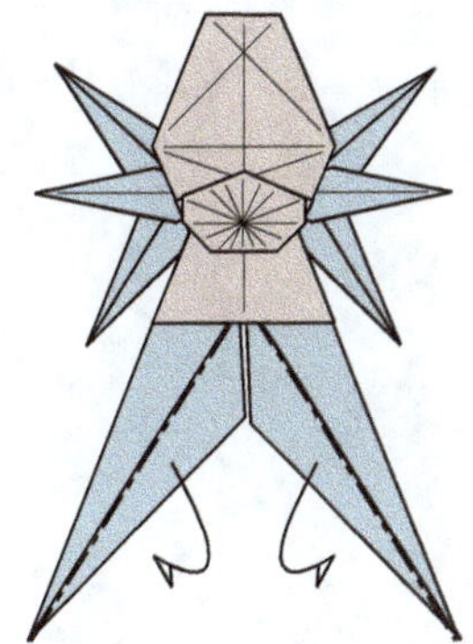

57. Mountain fold both flaps.

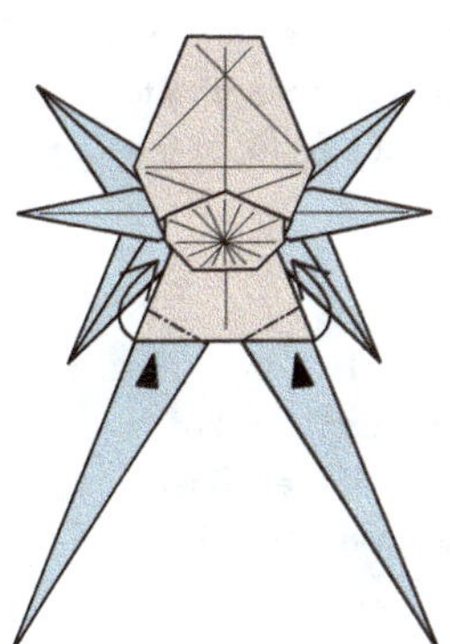

58. Reverse fold the corners.

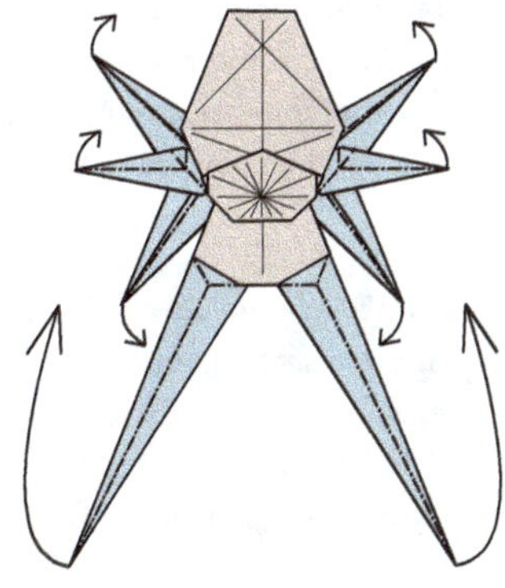

59. Mountain fold the antenna in half and curl them outwards. Shape the legs with rabbit ears and round the body.

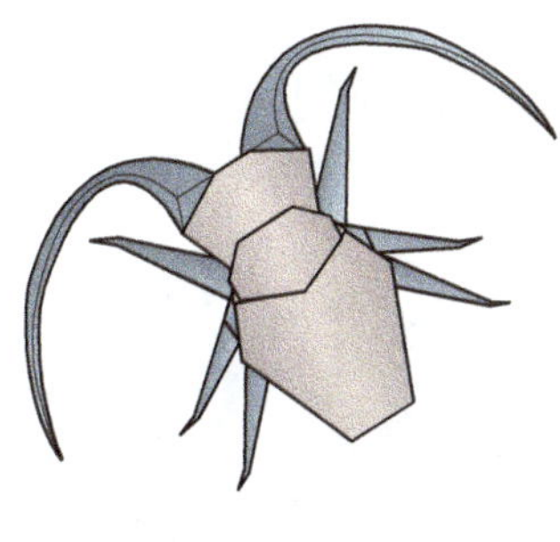

60. Completed *Black Pine Sawyer*.

Dragonfly

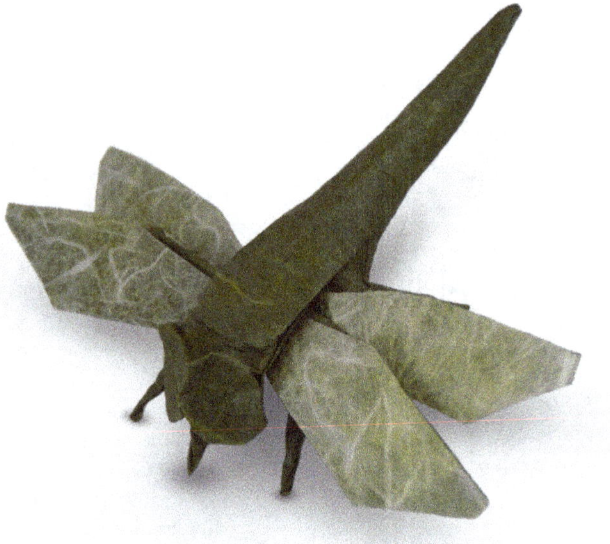

About

The highlight on this piece is the wings, so naturally that is what I focused on first in its design. I started with a square pleated in fourths, and then extracted the appendages from along the length of the resulting rectangle. To maximize the length of the legs I formed one set of legs from excess paper in the middle area of the model. The layers from the body go through a bit of rearranging to ensure they are the uppermost section. This adds to the feel that the appendages seem to be growing out from the body.

Tips

Step forty-one looks weird, but actually works. Simply focus on the side angle bisectors, and allow the center portion to collapse along the existing creases. Fortunately, this portion of the model is not visible in the end. Step sixty-three will require you to reach inside to spread apart the layers of the flap to be squashed.

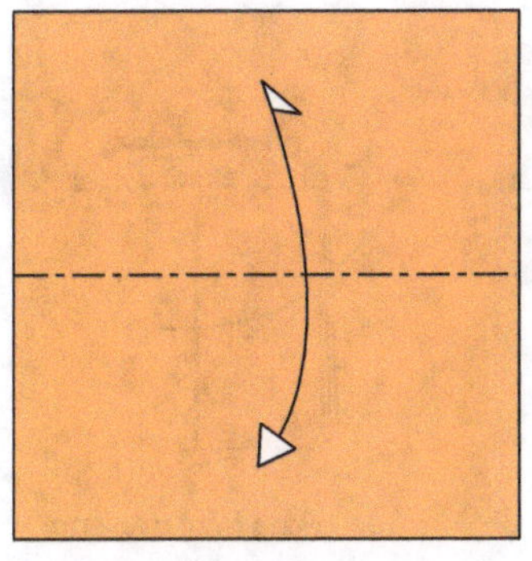

1. Precrease in half with a mountain fold.

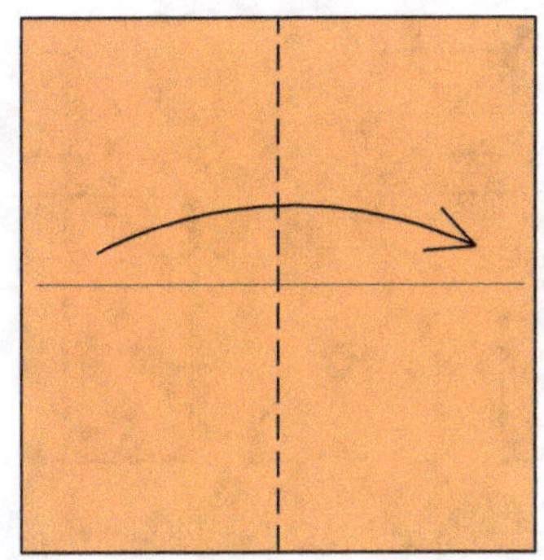

2. Valley fold in half.

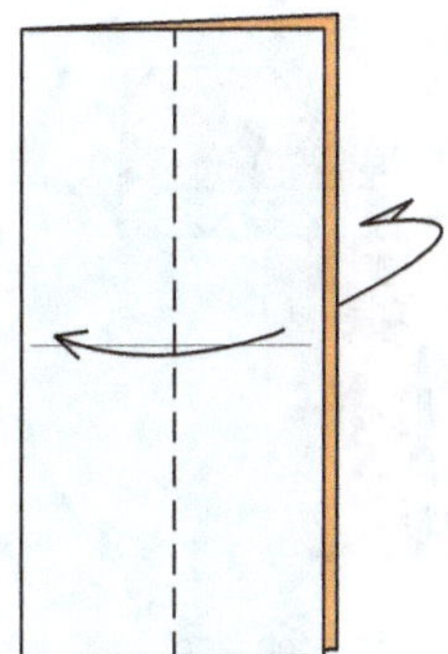

3. Valley fold both sides in half.

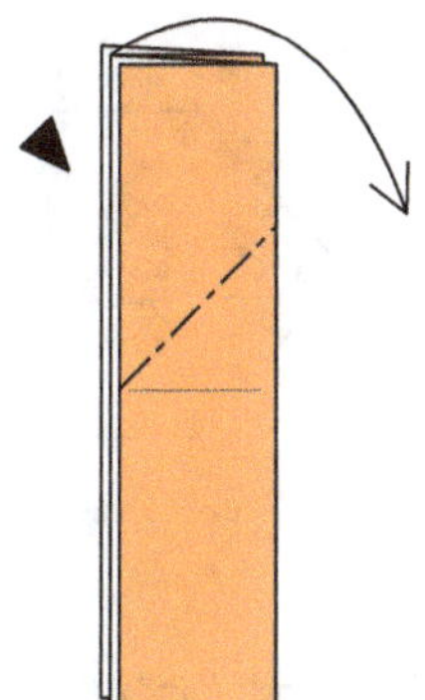

4. Reverse fold.

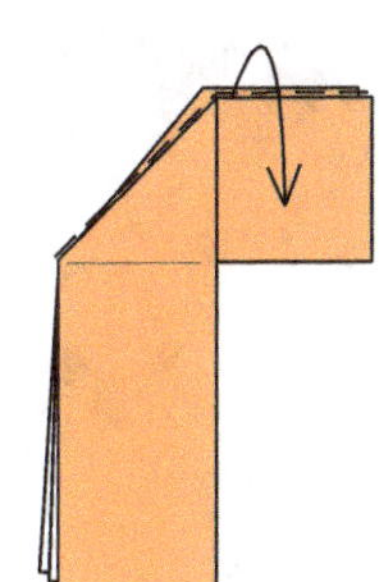

5. Wrap around a single layer.

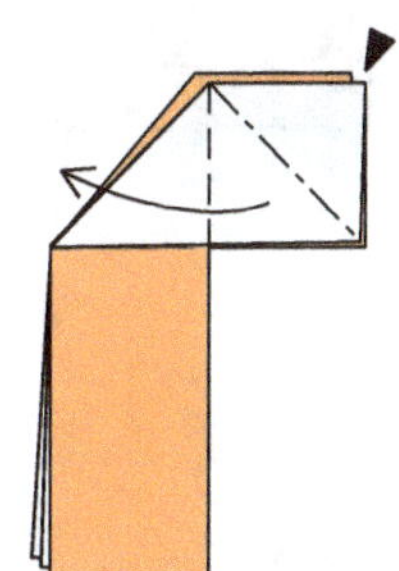

6. Squash fold.

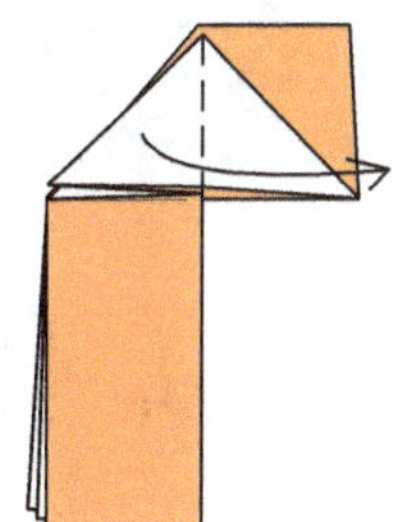

7. Valley fold the top flap over.

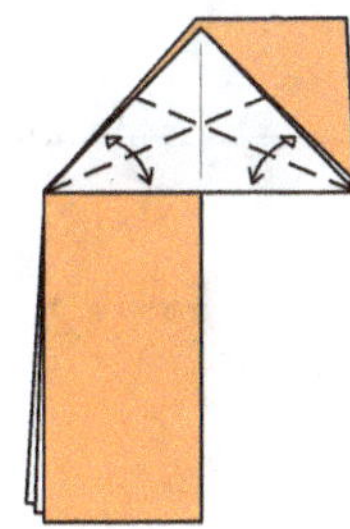

8. Precrease along the angle bisectors.

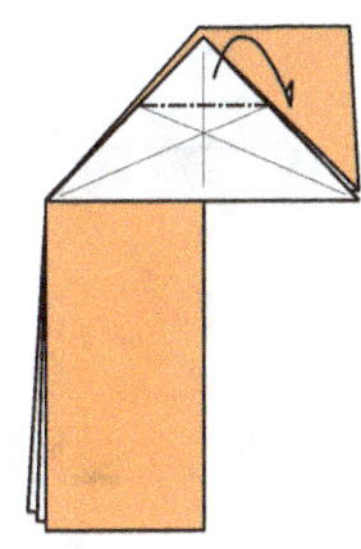

9. Mountain fold, using the creases as a guide.

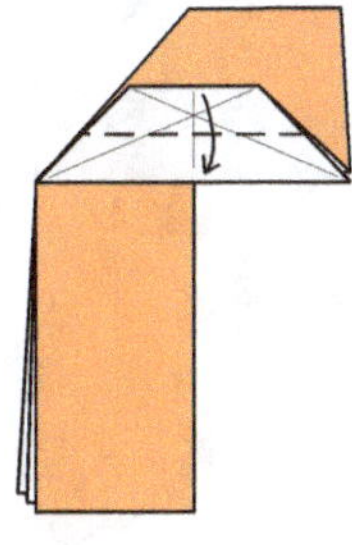

10. Valley fold in half, allowing the triangular flap from behind to swing forward.

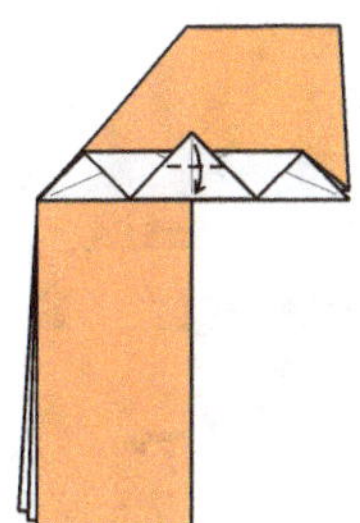

11. Valley fold the triangular flap in half.

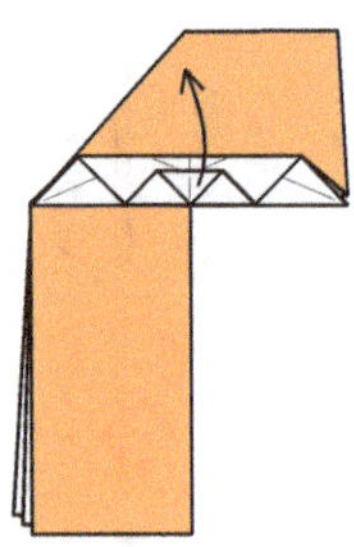

12. Unfold the pleat.

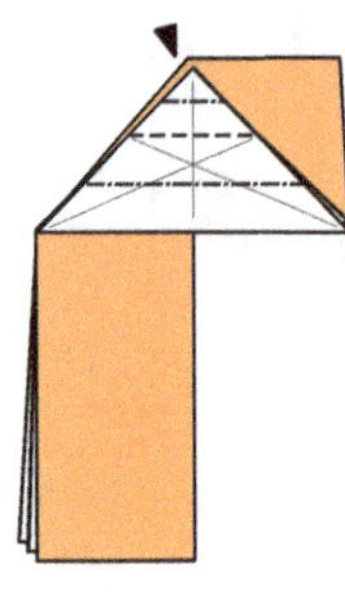

13. Sink the flap in and out, and then in again along the existing creases.

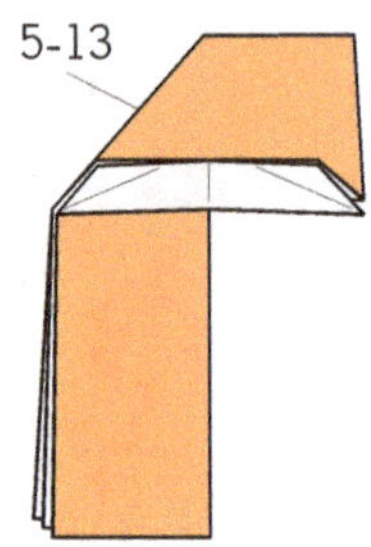

14. Repeat steps 5-13 behind.

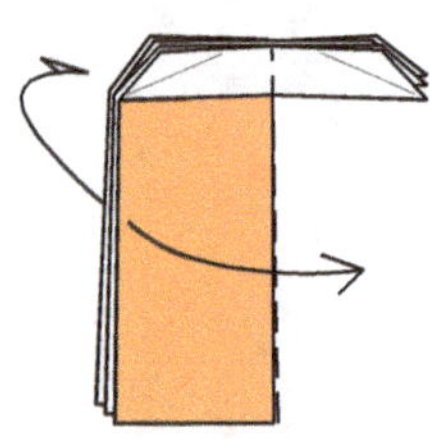

15. Swing over a layer at each side.

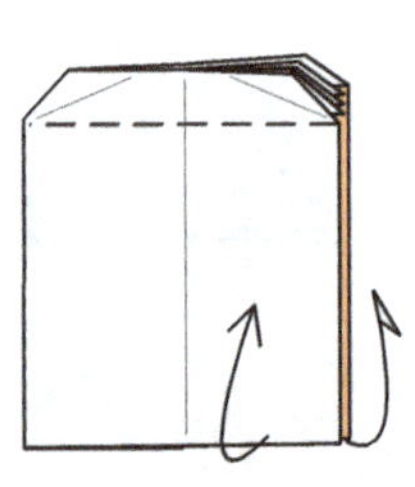

16. Wrap the outer layer around (outside reverse fold).

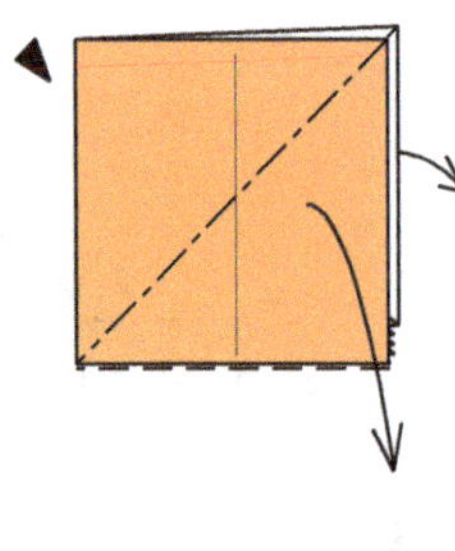

17. Spread squash, distributing the hidden inner flaps evenly.

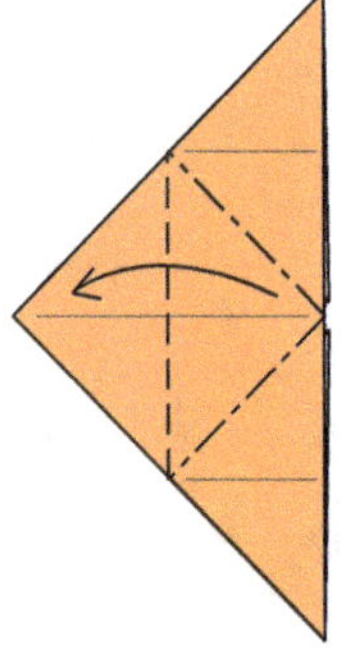

18. Petal fold.

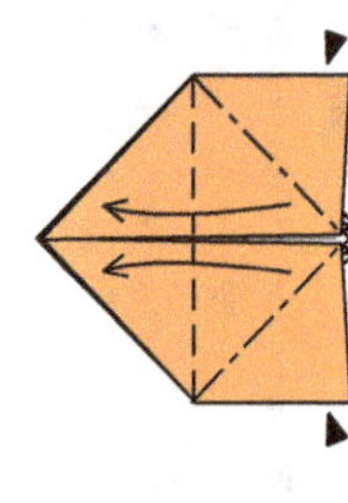

19. Squash fold both sides.

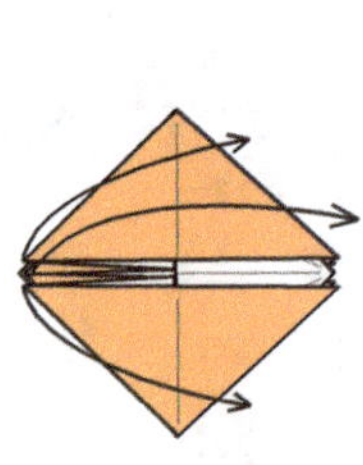

20. Open out the top section to the position of step 18.

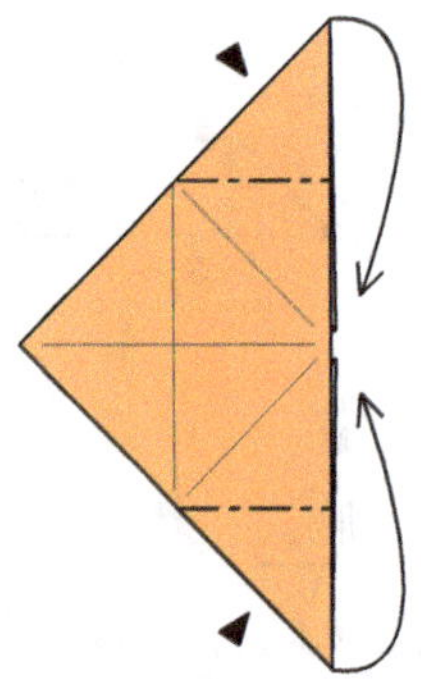

21. Reverse fold the two flaps.

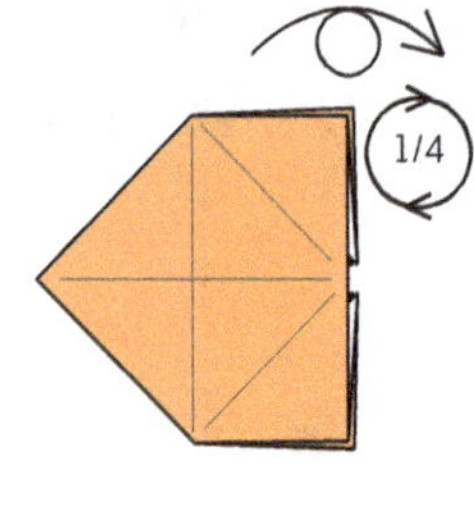

22. Turn the model over and rotate.

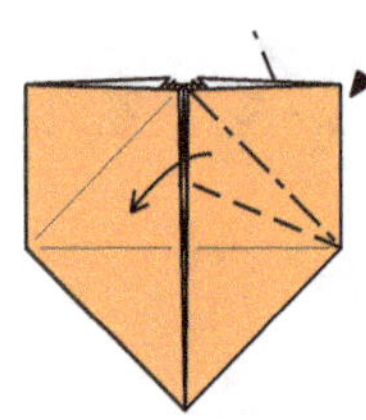

23. Form an asymmetrical squash.

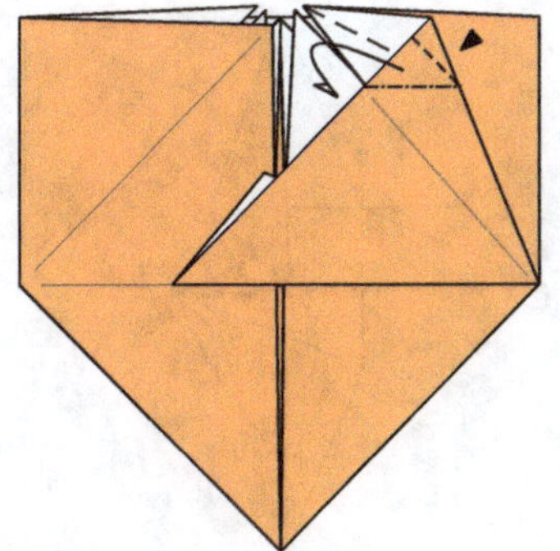

24. Reverse fold.

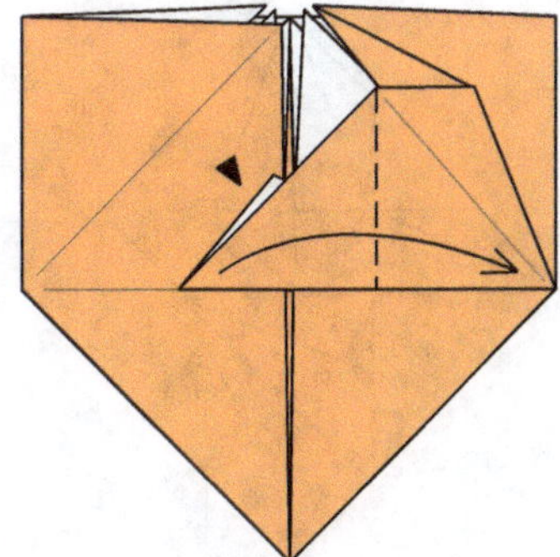

25. Valley fold the flap, allowing a squash to form.

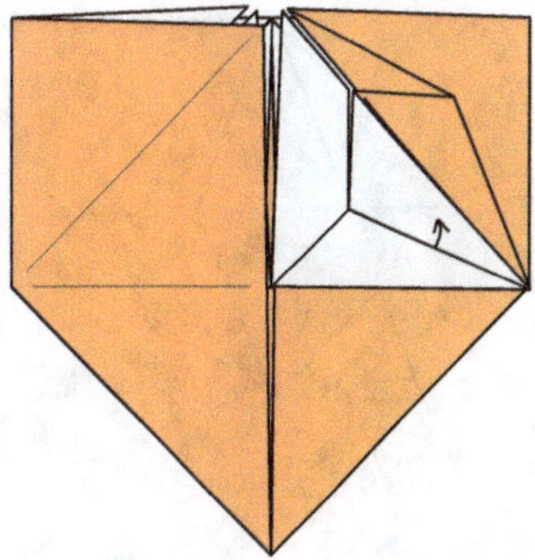

26. Pull out the trapped flap from the pocket.

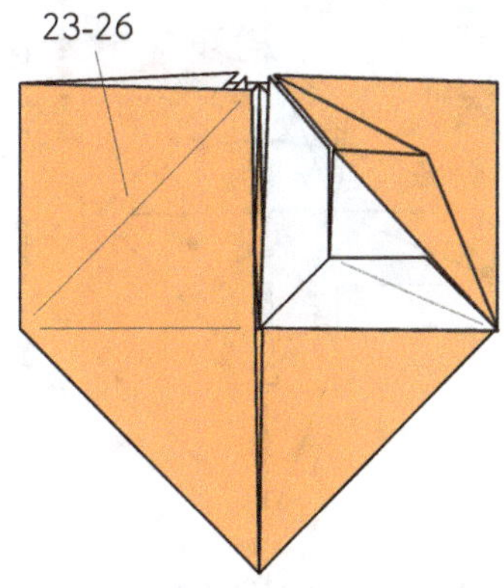

27. Repeat steps 23-26 in mirror image.

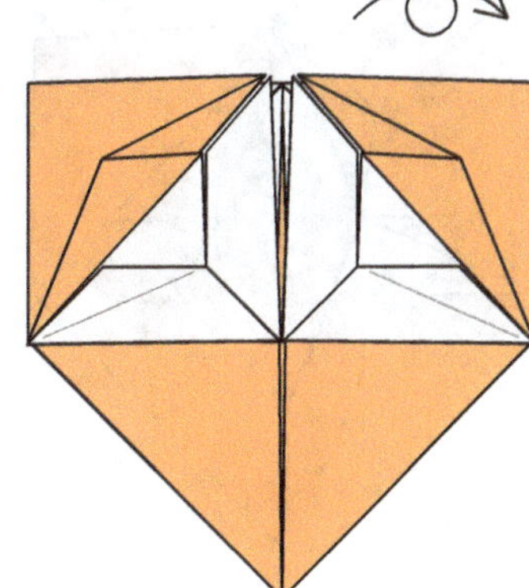

28. Turn over.

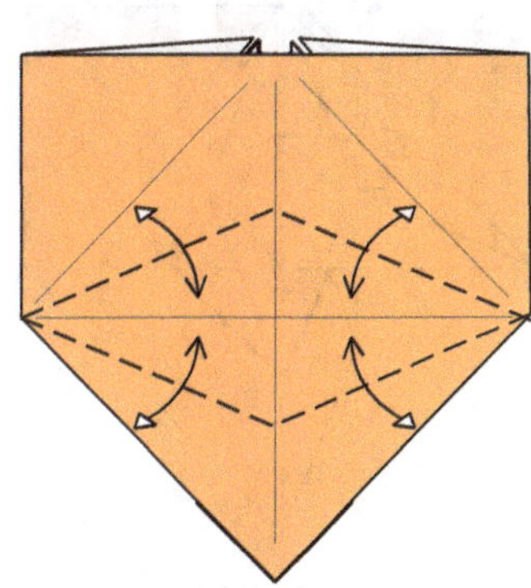

29. Precrease along the angle bisectors.

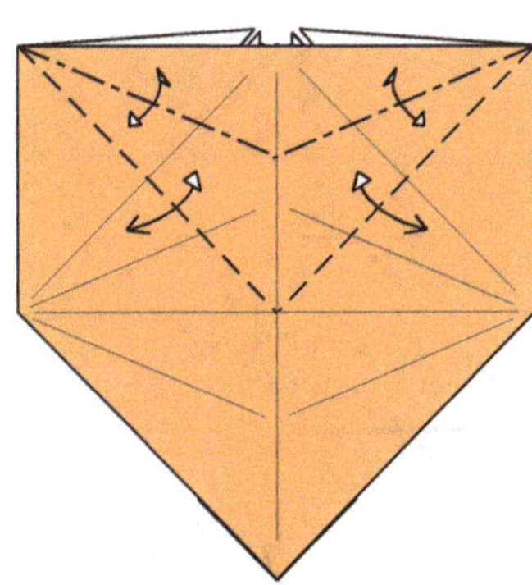

30. Precrease the top layer. This can be done by reverse folding the layer and unfolding.

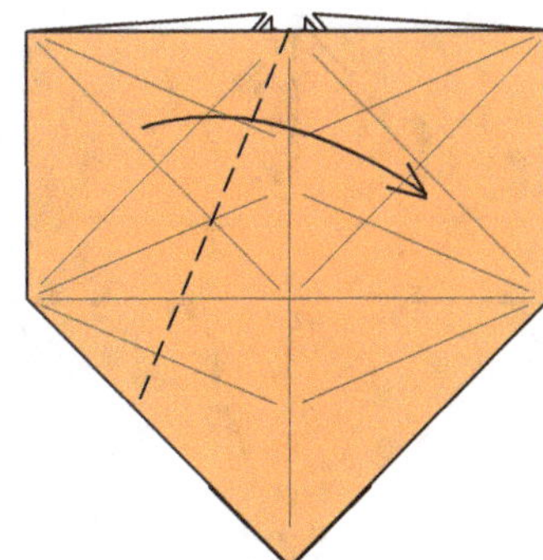

31. Valley fold.

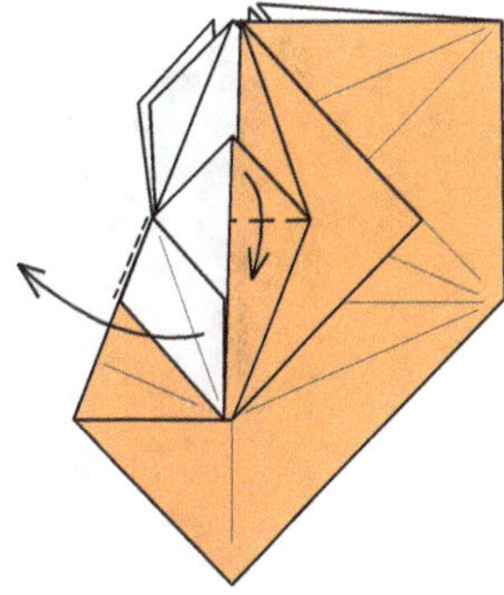

32. Swing the flap outwards, allowing a layer to swivel.

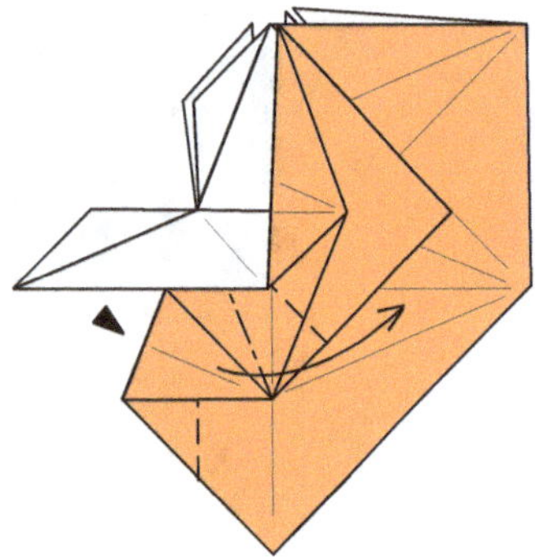

33. Swivel the corner up.

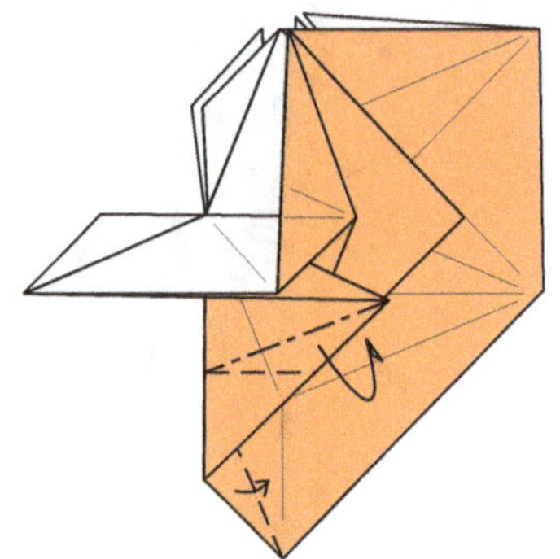

34. Swivel the edge under.

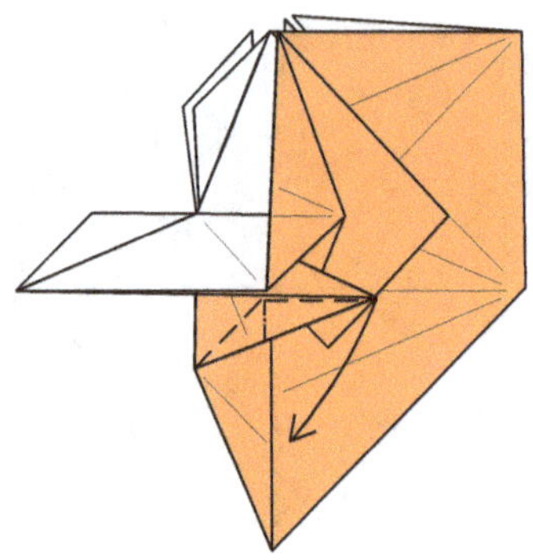

35. Rabbit ear the flap down.

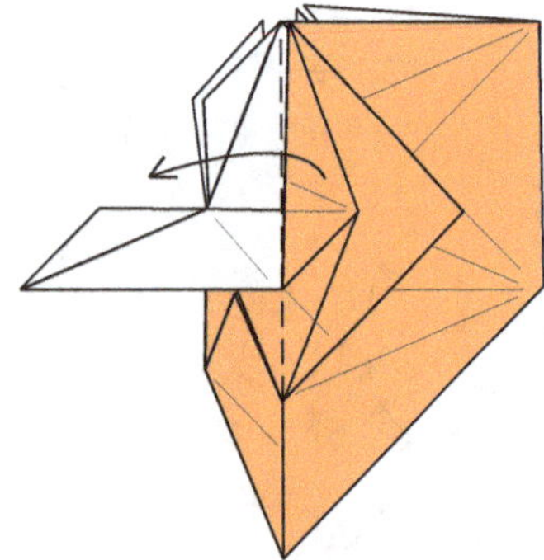

36. Valley fold over one layer.

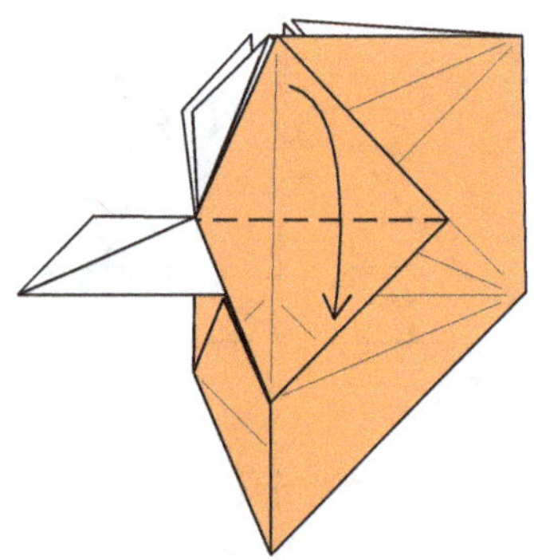

37. Valley fold the flap down.

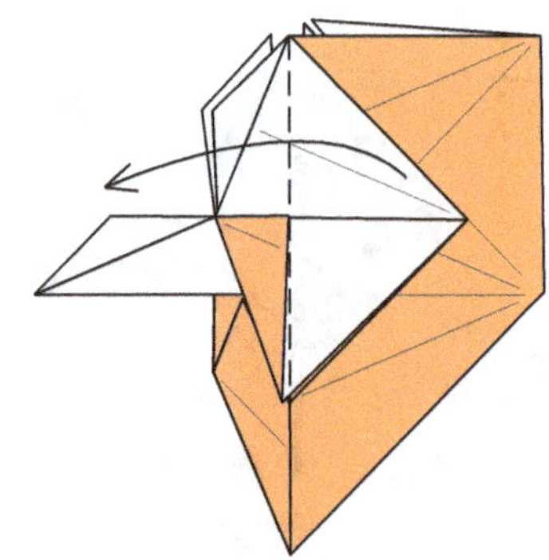

38. Valley fold the flap over.

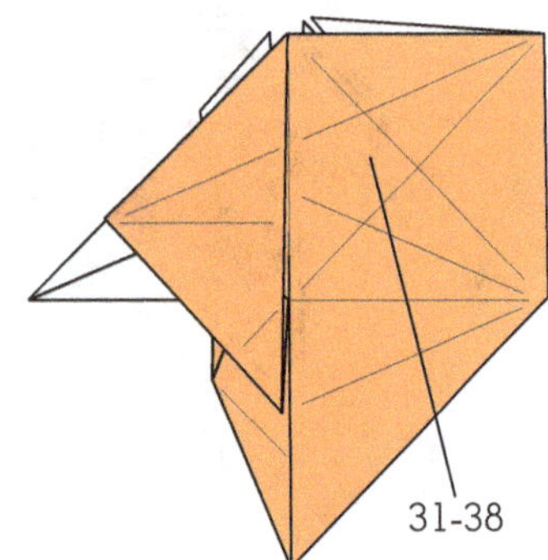

39. Repeat steps 31-38 in mirror image.

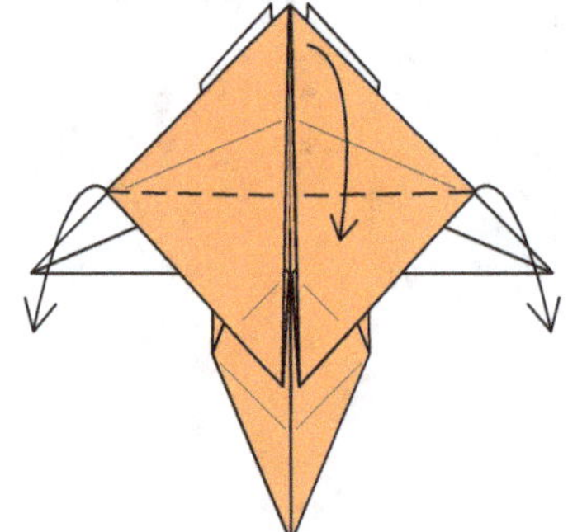

40. Pull the side points outwards, while bringing the top down.

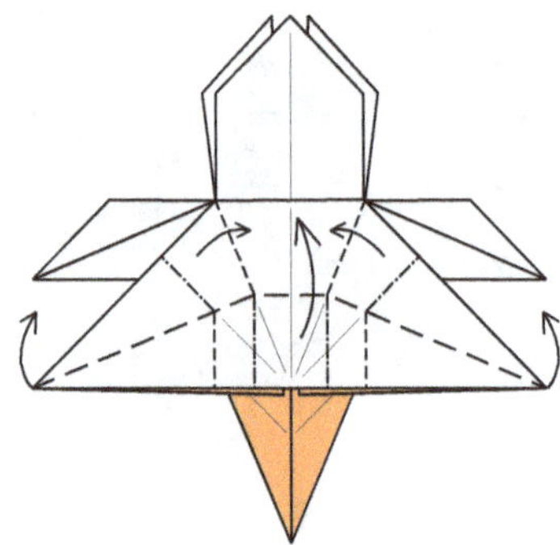

41. Valley fold up the single layer while crimping in the sides.

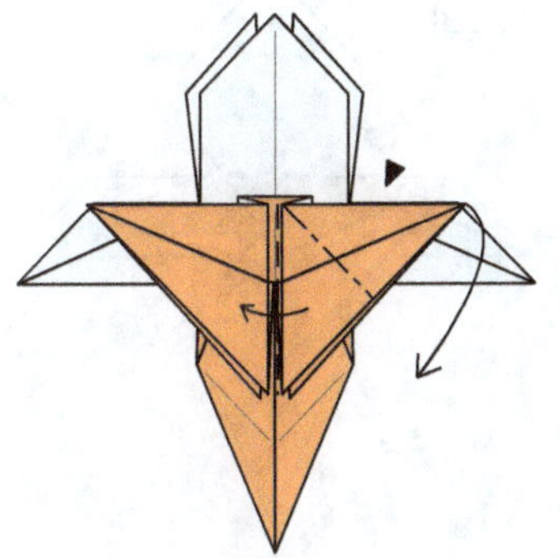

42. Squash fold.

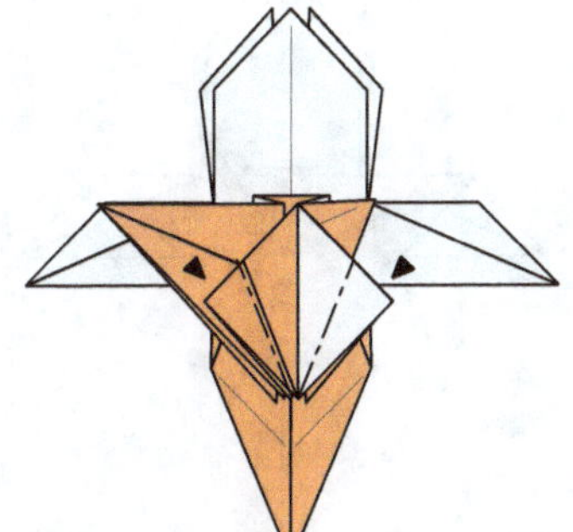

43. Reverse fold the sides.

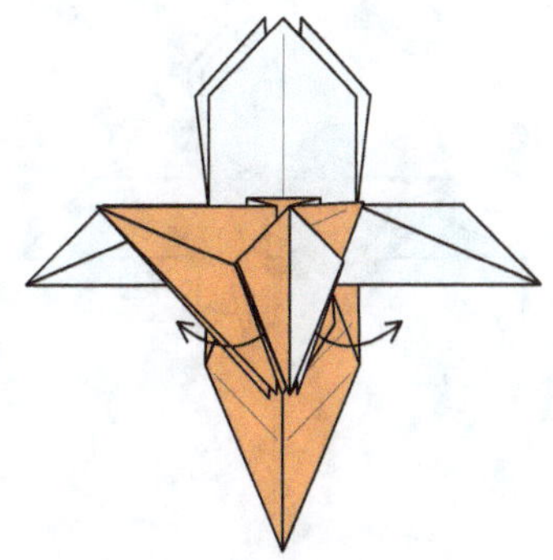

44. Undo the reverse folds.

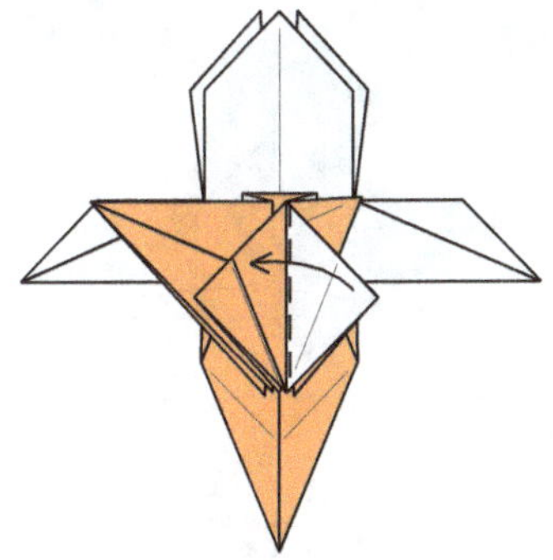

45. Swing over one flap.

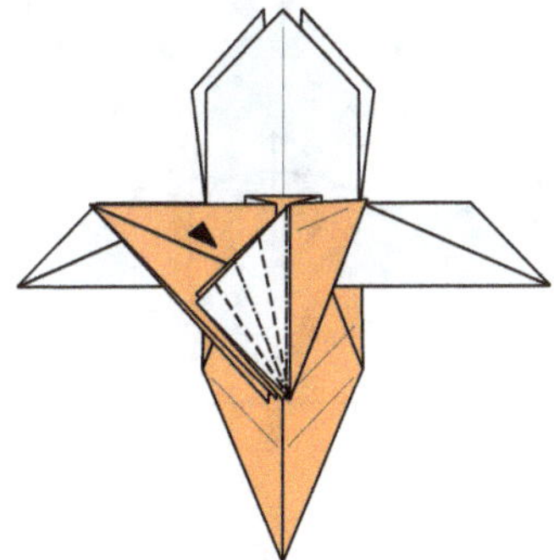

46. Reverse fold the top flap in and out along the angle quadsectors.

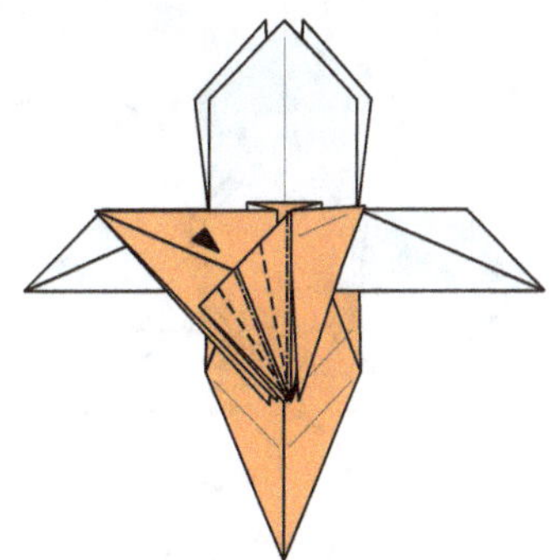

47. Reverse fold the other flap in and out along the angle quadsectors.

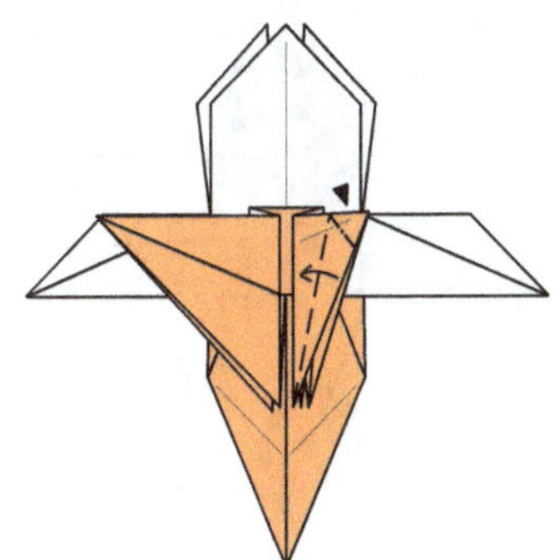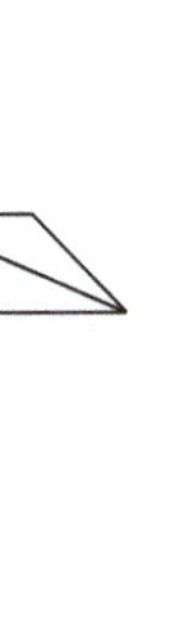

48. Squash fold.

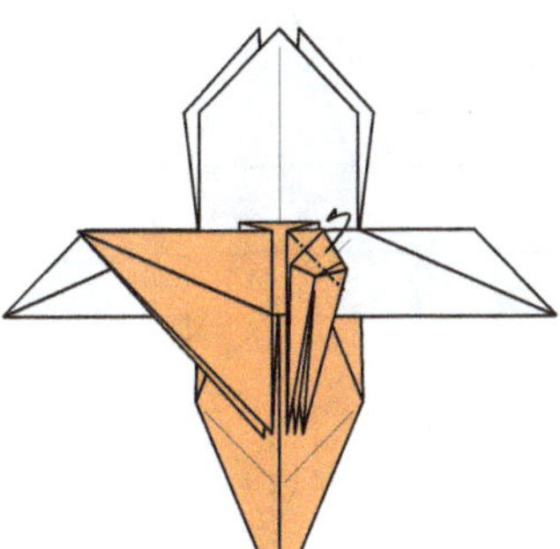

49. Mountain fold.

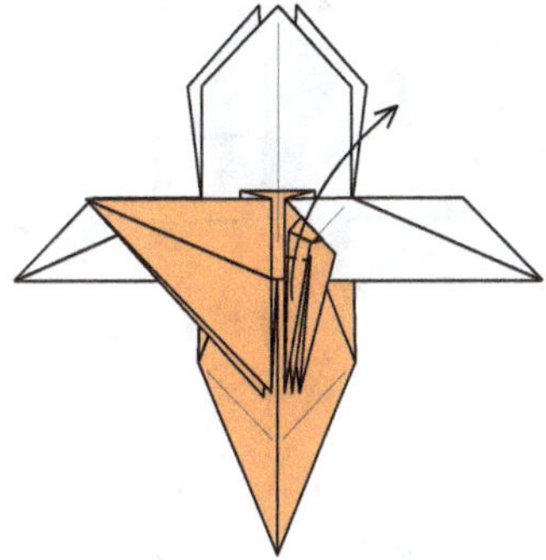

50. Valley fold the top flap up at a slight angle.

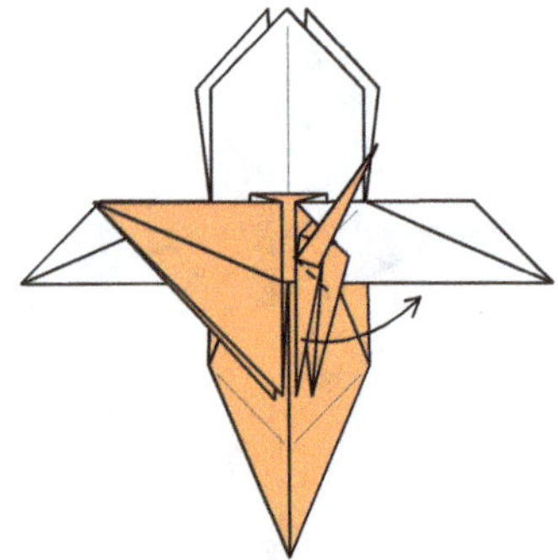

51. Valley fold the flap outwards.

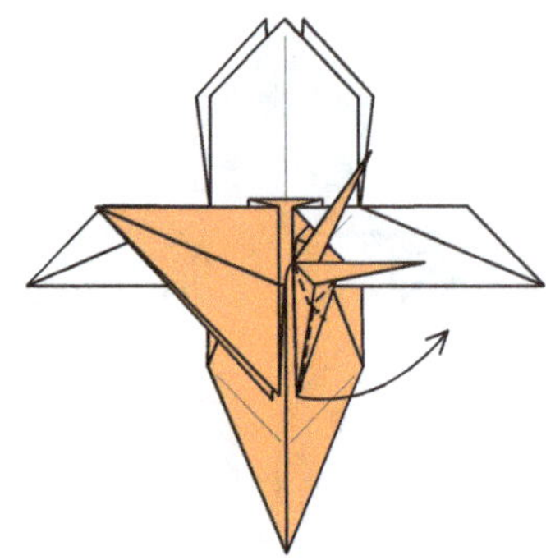

52. Rabbit ear the flap outwards, allowing squashes to form at its base.

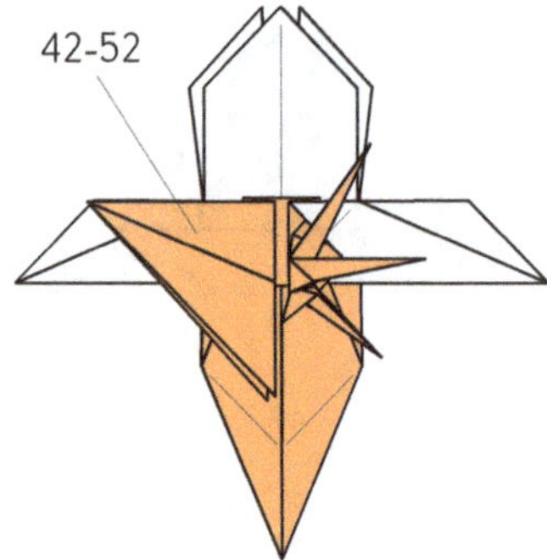

53. Repeat steps 42-52 in mirror image.

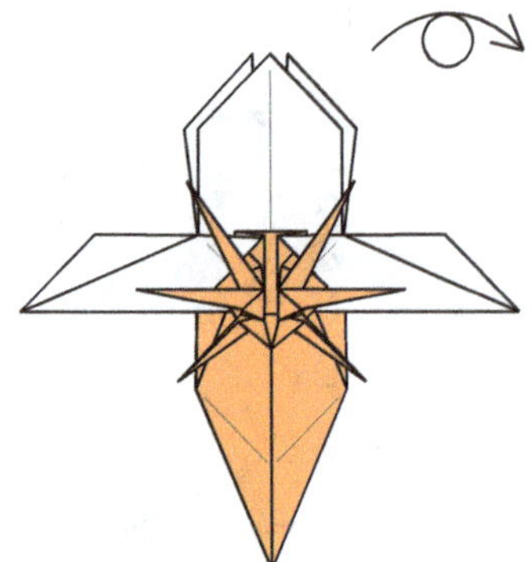

54. Turn over.

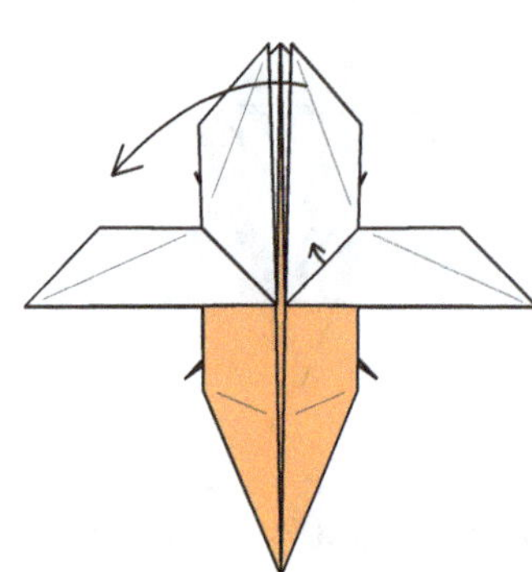

55. Pull the flap over, releasing the trapped layers.

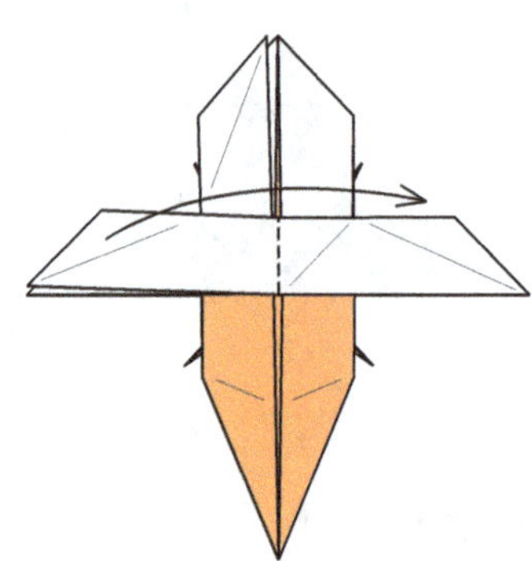

56. Swing the flap over.

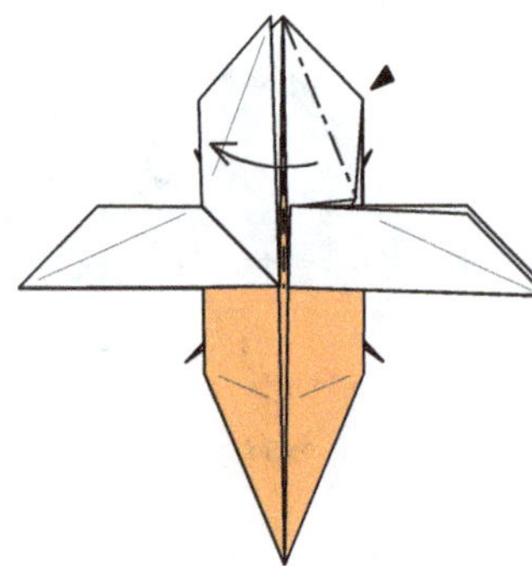

57. Pull one layer through, allowing the corner to spread squash flat.

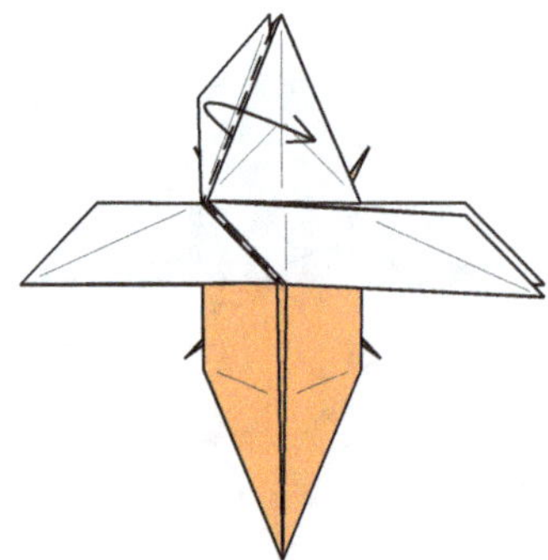

58. Wrap a single layer around.

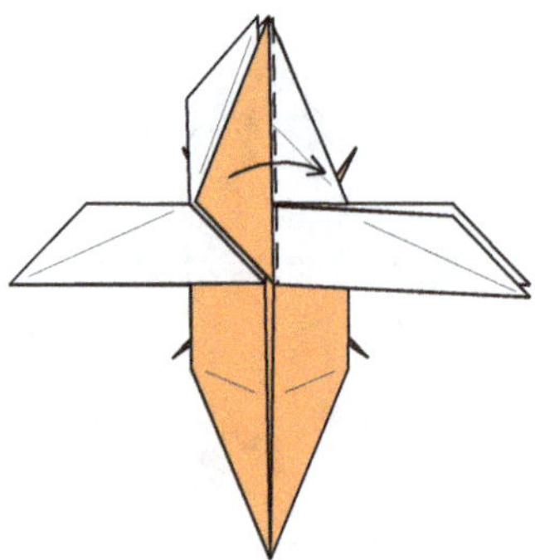

59. Swing the flap over.

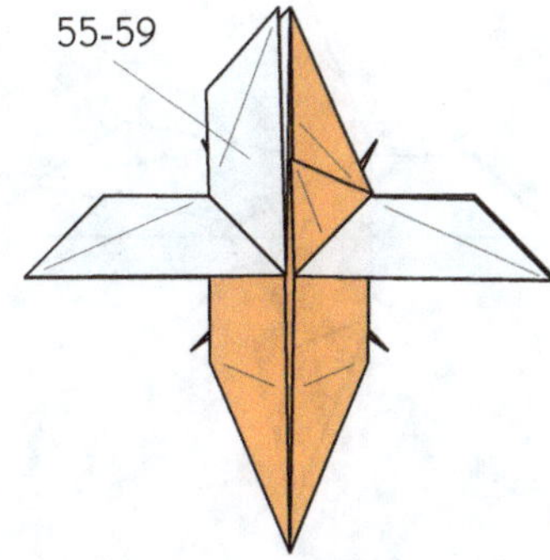

60. Repeat steps 55-59 in mirror image.

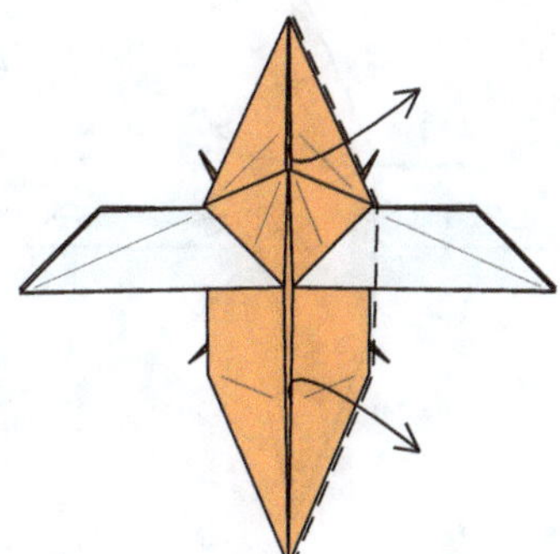

61. Open out the side layers. The model will not lie flat.

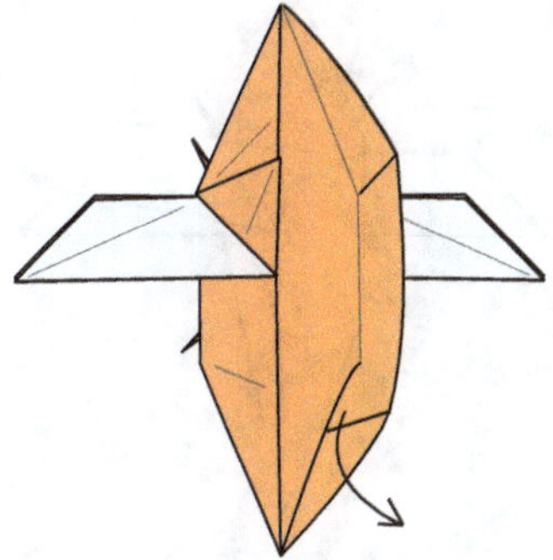

62. Pull out the flap, undoing a crimp.

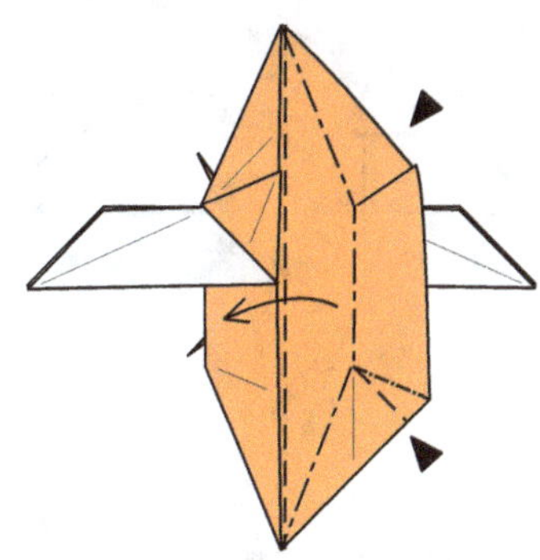

63. Squash the flap flat.

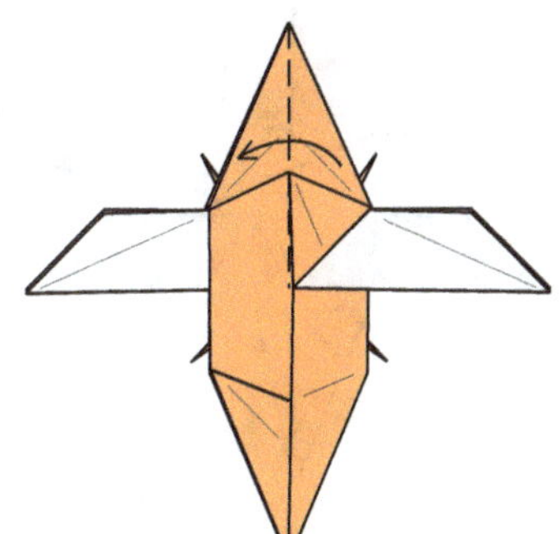

64. Swing over one flap.

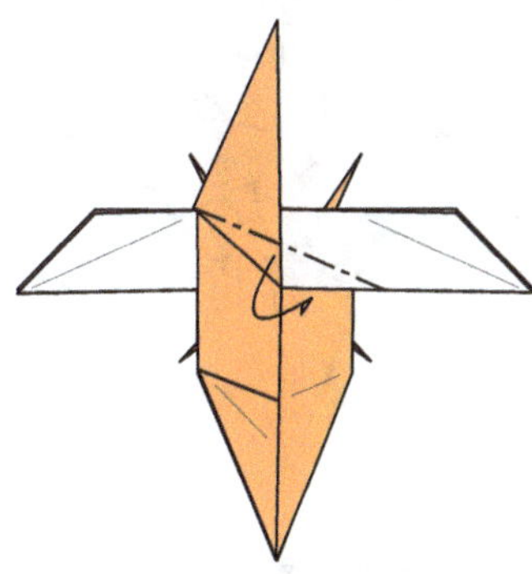

65. Mountain fold the top layer.

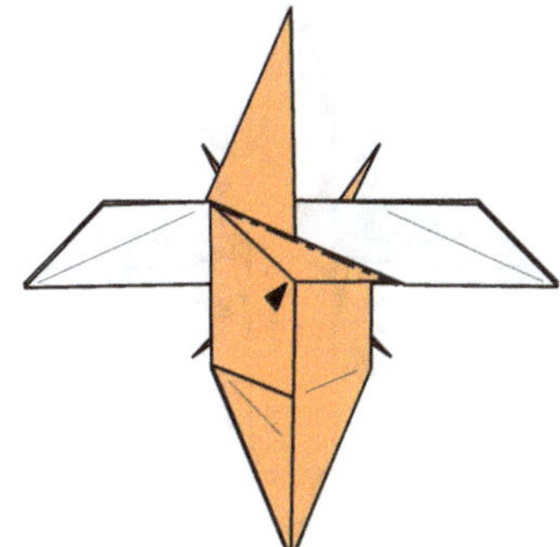

66. Sink the trapped corner.

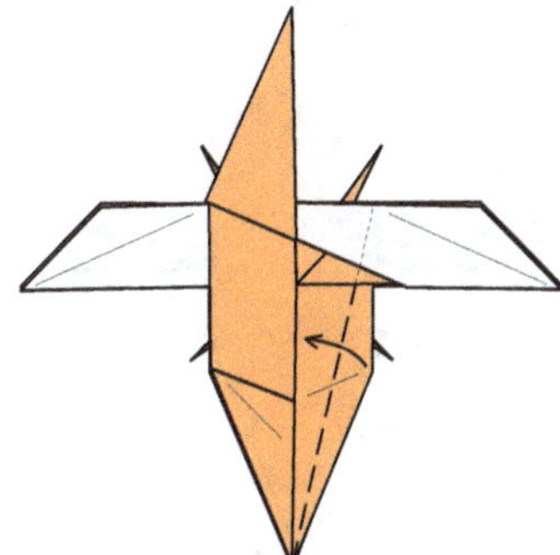

67. Valley fold over as far as possible.

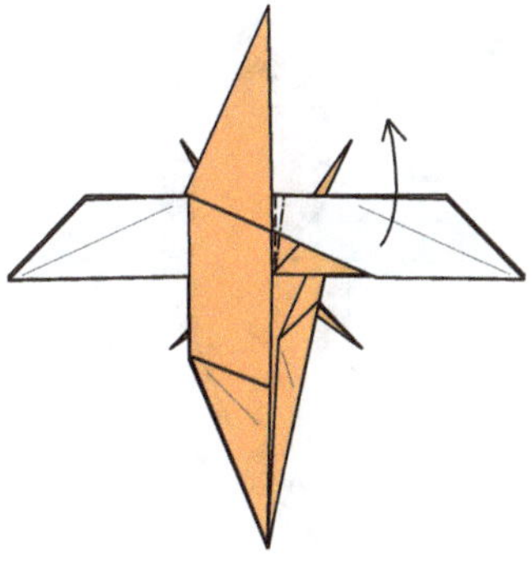

68. Pleat the flap up slightly.

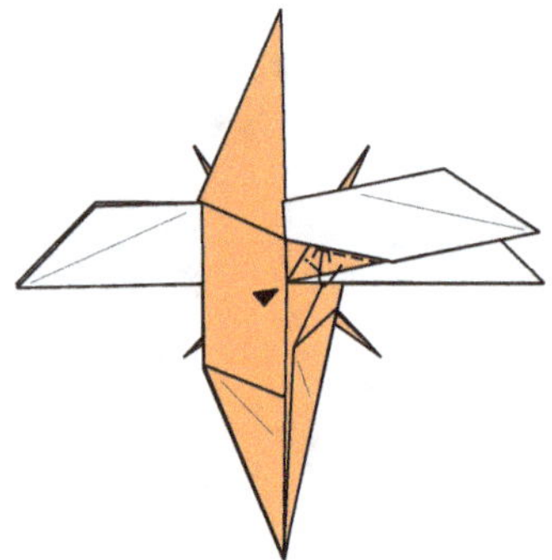

69. Squash fold, tucking in to the top flap.

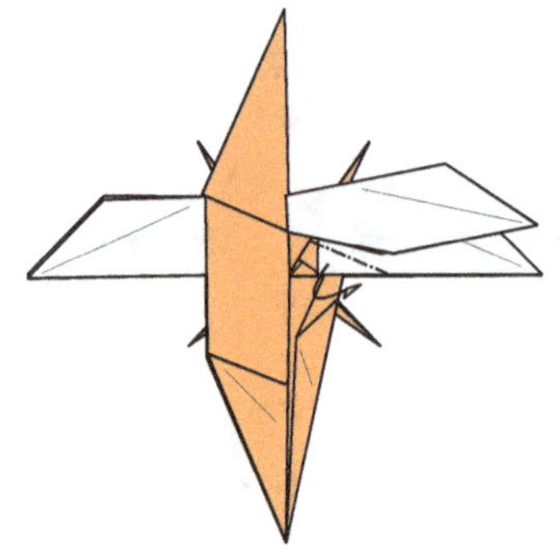

70. Mountain fold as far as possible.

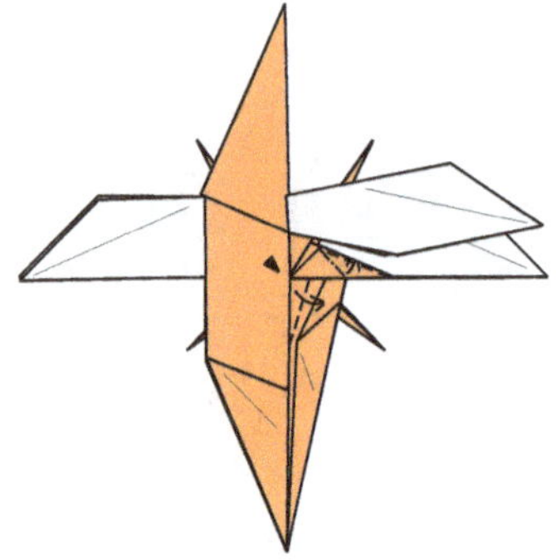

71. Swivel fold, tucking the layers in.

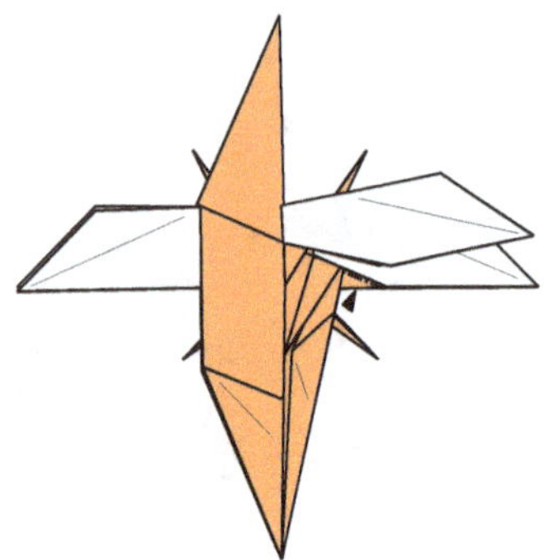

72. Sink the trapped corner.

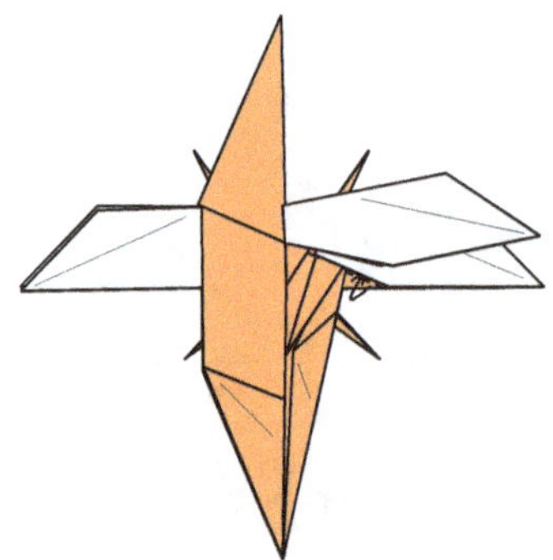

73. Tuck the remaining colored edge in.

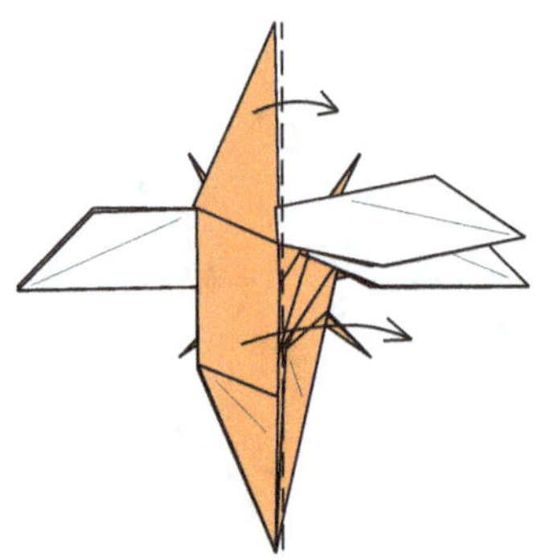

74. Swing over two flaps.

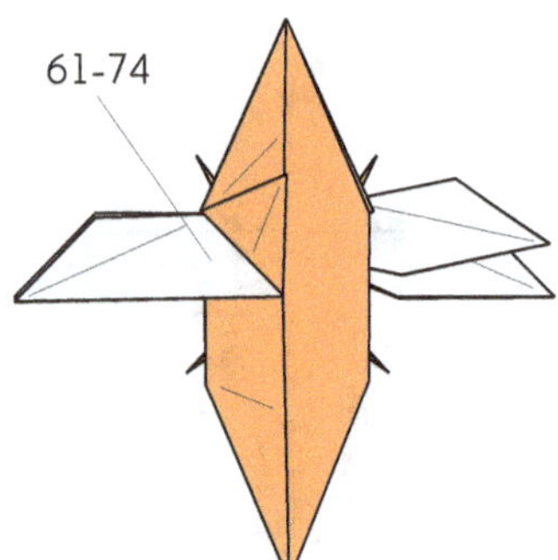

75. Repeat steps 61-74 in mirror image.

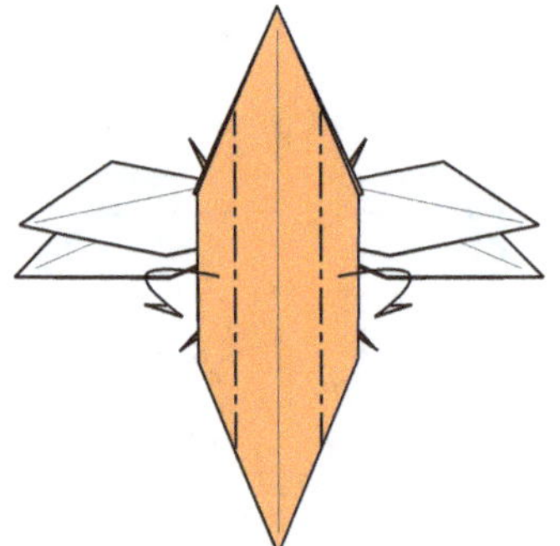

76. Mountain fold the sides.

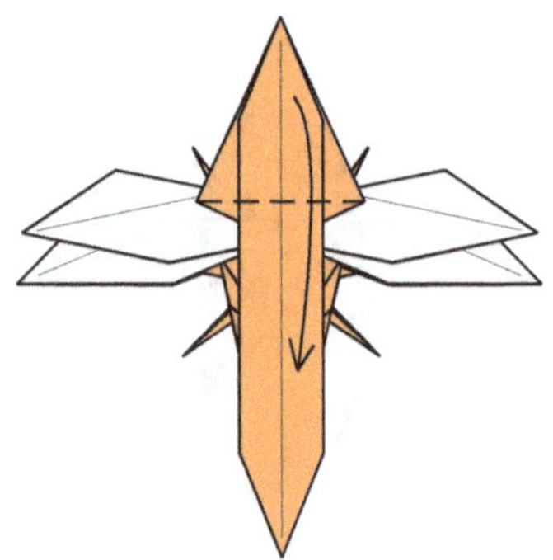

77. Valley fold the top flap down.

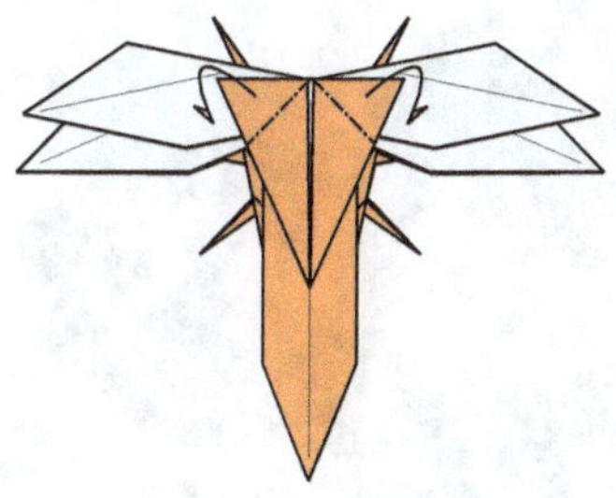 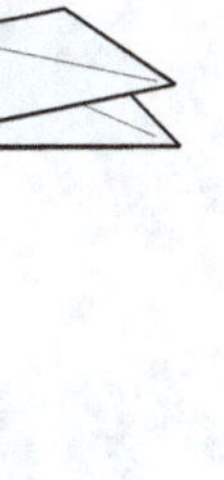 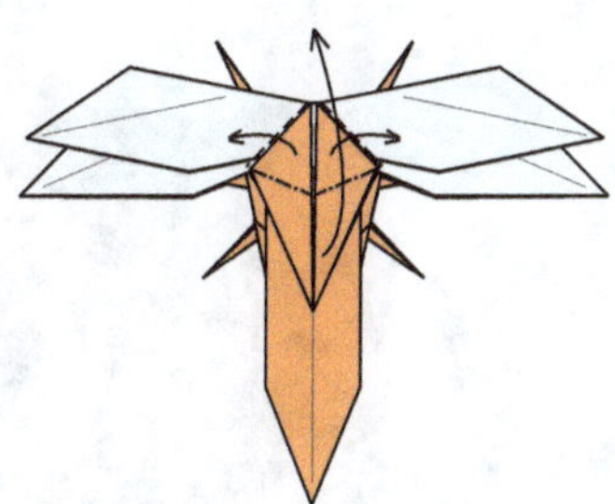 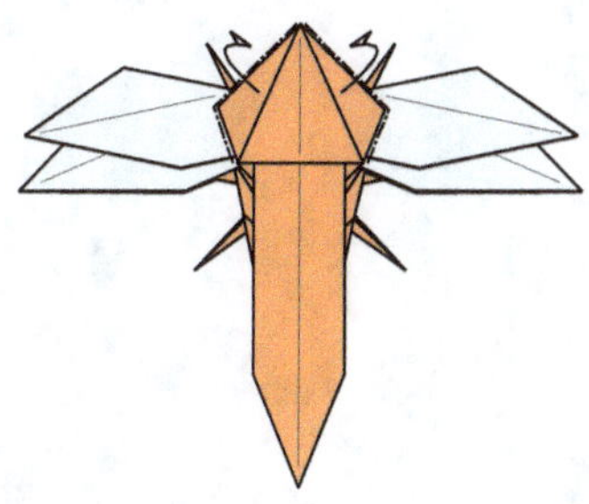

78. Mountain fold the corners.

79. Pull out the two side layers at each side and squash flat.

80. Wrap around a layer at each side.

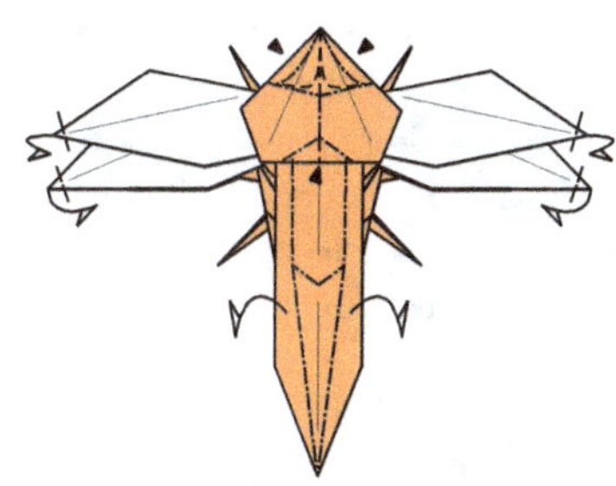

81. Reverse fold the tips of the wings. Pinch the top point and ad mountain folds to form the eyes. Shape the body and legs to taste.

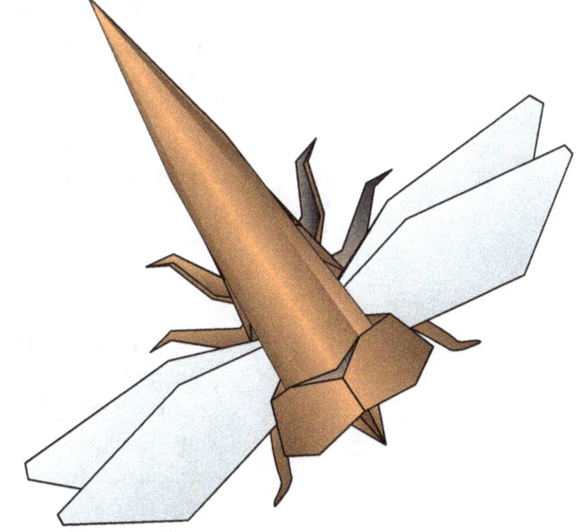

82. Completed *Dragonfly*.

Butterfly

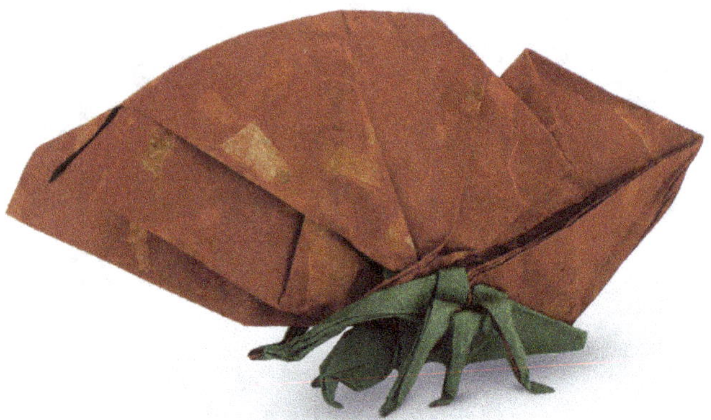

Although many butterflies in origami do not feature legs, I thought it would be a nice addition for my stab at the subject. When the wings are in the upright position, the body and legs are more prominent. The general feel for this model is based on a toy I vaguely remember from my childhood. Strangely enough, the design is loosely based on a lobster I had concocted years before. The claws and body were expanded to become wings, and one set of legs was converted to antennae. This is a model where you can really be creative and have fun with the paper choice for the wings.

Step forty-eight might look involved, but many of the folds should fall into place naturally. I first crease the long mountain folds, and then just press everything flat. Steps fifty-seven and fifty-eight are unusual, but it is important to realize that the exact way the wings flatten is not critical. It is more important that both wings look symmetrical.

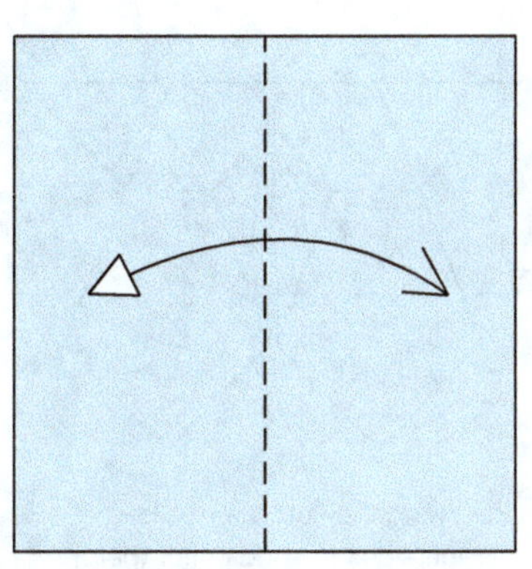

1. Precrease in half.

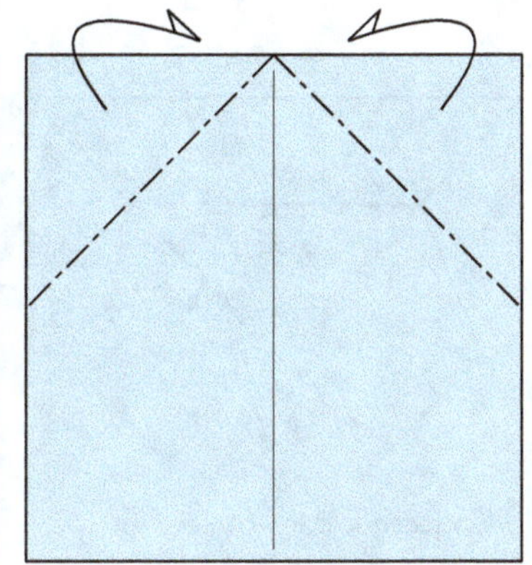

2. Mountain fold the corners behind.

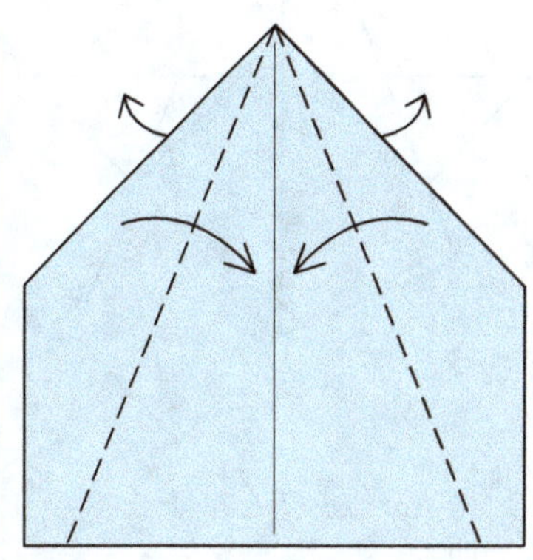

3. Valley fold the sides to the center, allowing the flaps from behind to flip outwards.

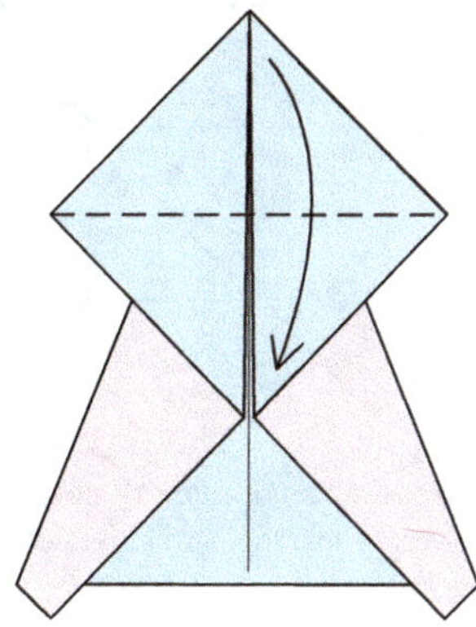

4. Valley fold the top section in half.

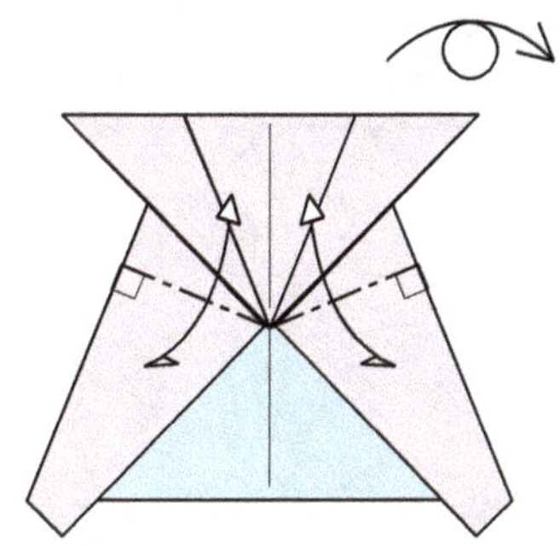

5. Precrease the sides with mountain folds and turn over.

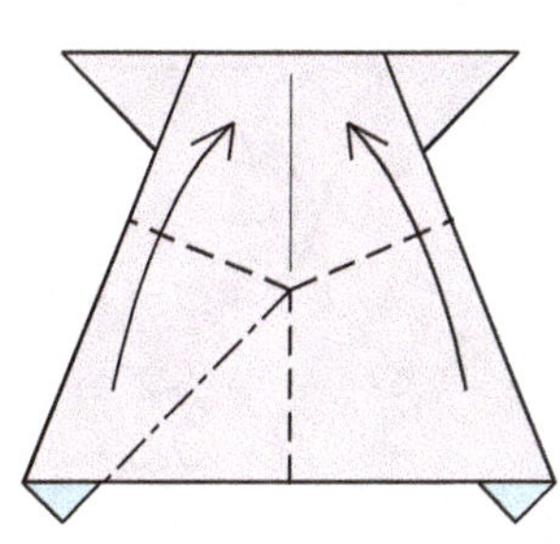

6. Rabbit ear the bottom section up.

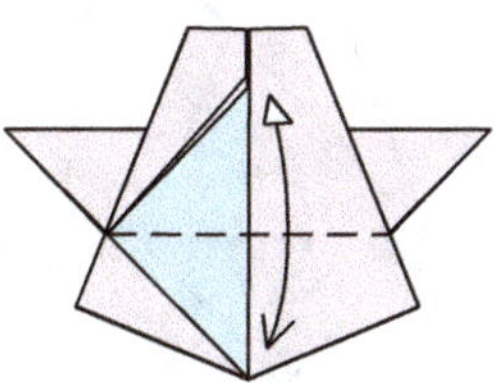

7. Precrease.

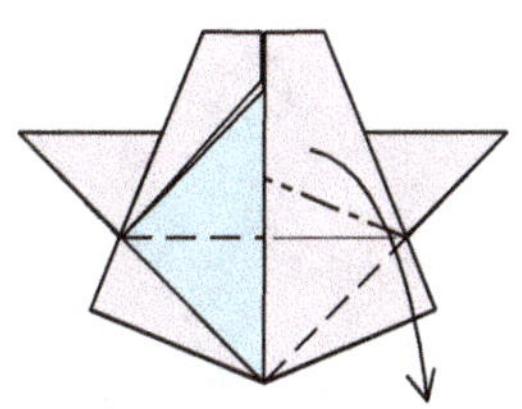

8. Form an asymmetrical squash.

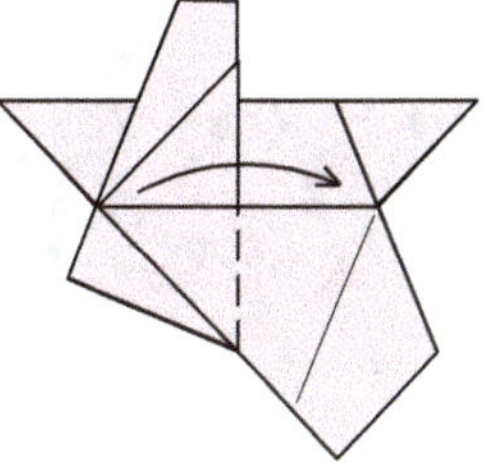

9. Swing over the center flap.

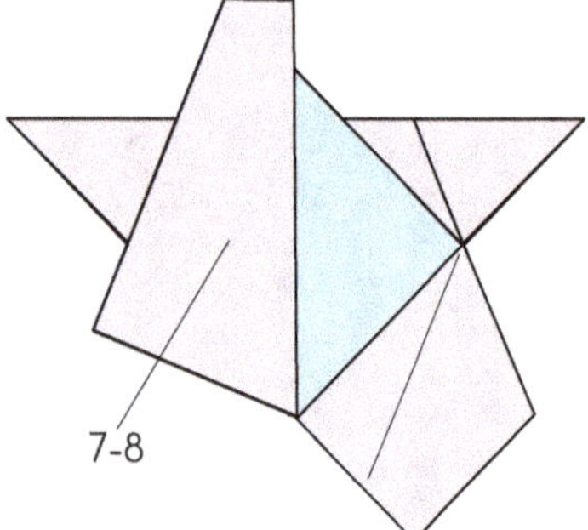

10. Repeat steps 7-8 in mirror image.

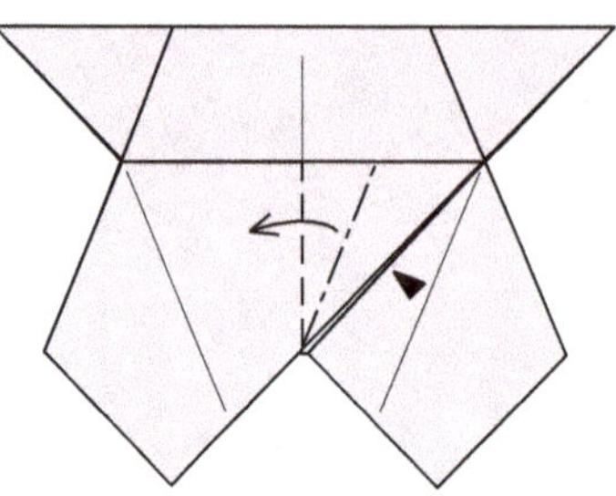

11. Squash fold the center flap.

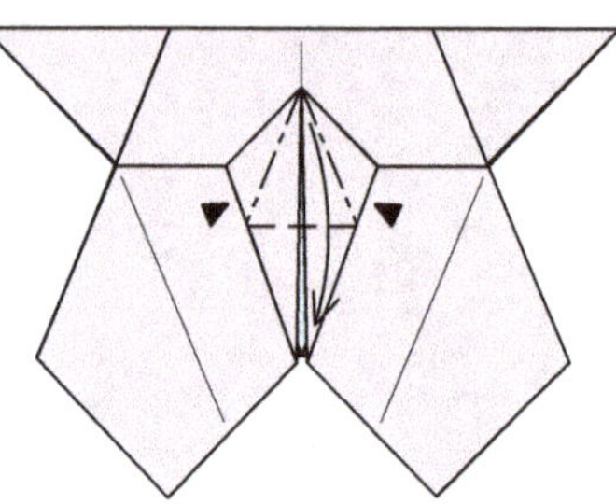

12. Swing the flap down, allowing the sides to squash flat (petal fold).

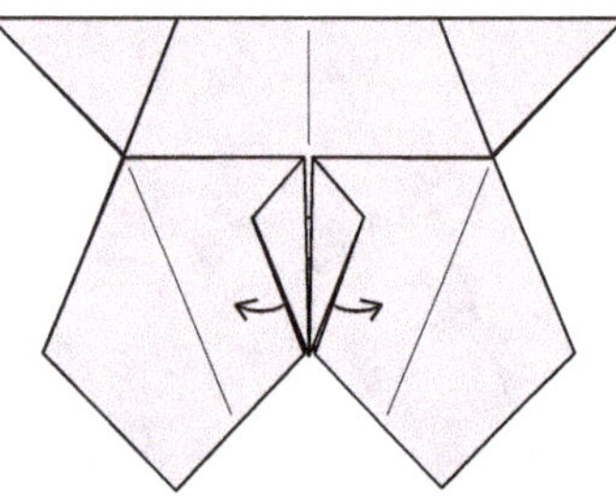

13. Pull out a single layer from each side.

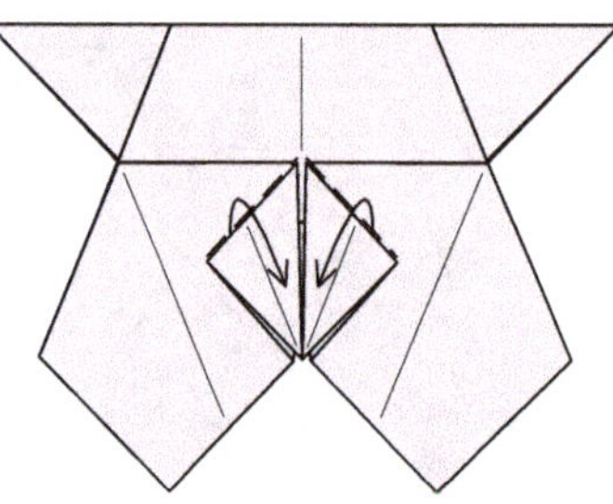

14. Wrap around a single layer at each side.

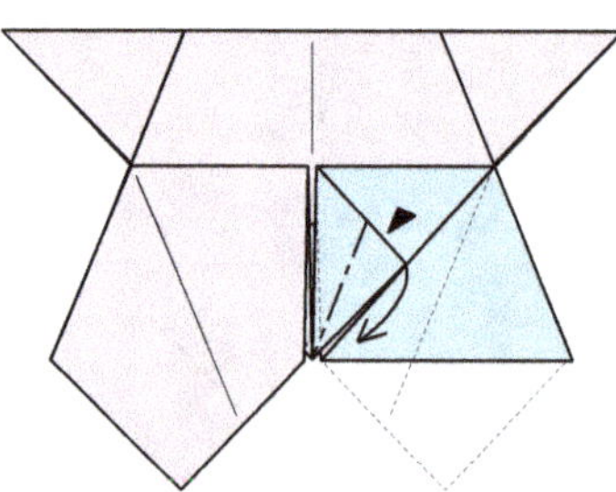

15. This is a partial cutaway view. Reverse fold the hidden flap at each side.

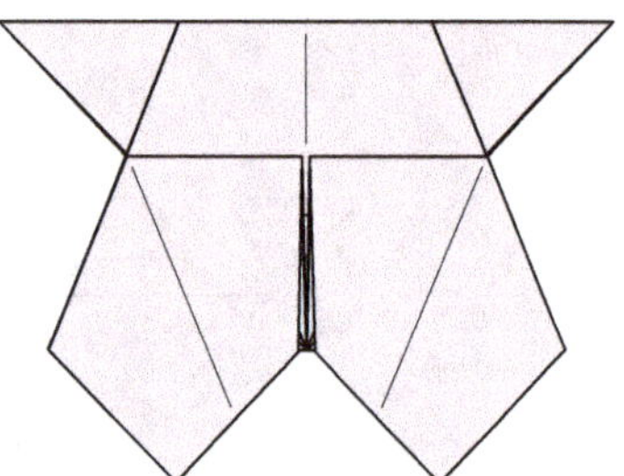

16. Turn over.

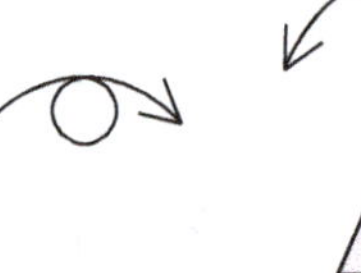

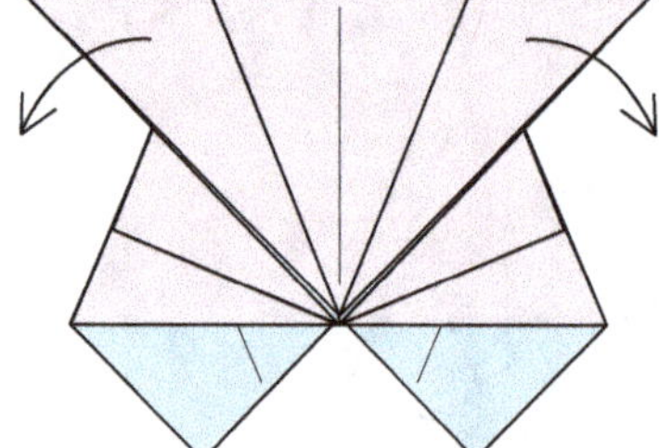

17. Pull out the side corners, undoing a crimp at each side.

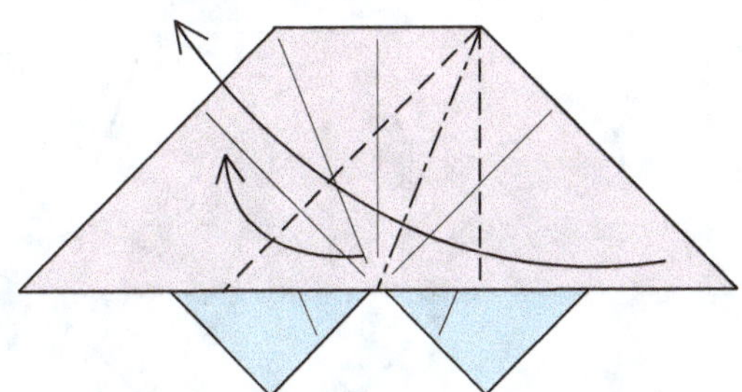

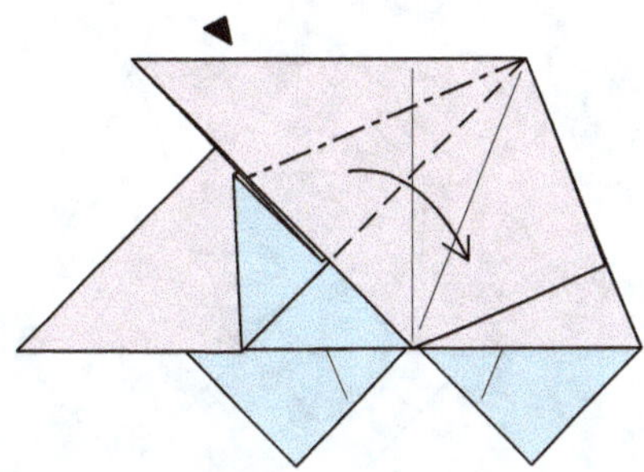

18. Bring the side flap up to meet the top edge while crimping.

19. Squash fold the flap.

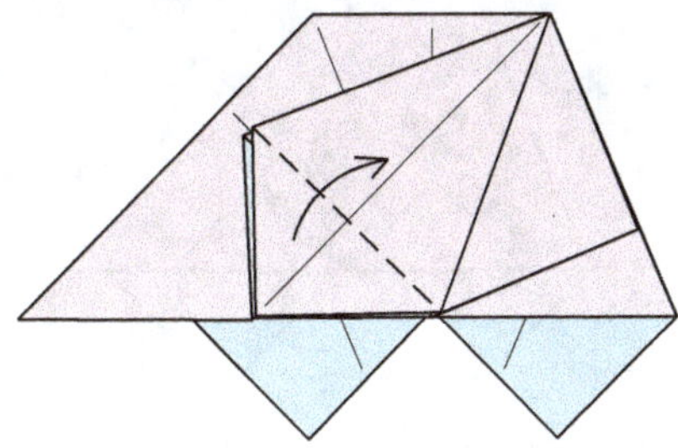

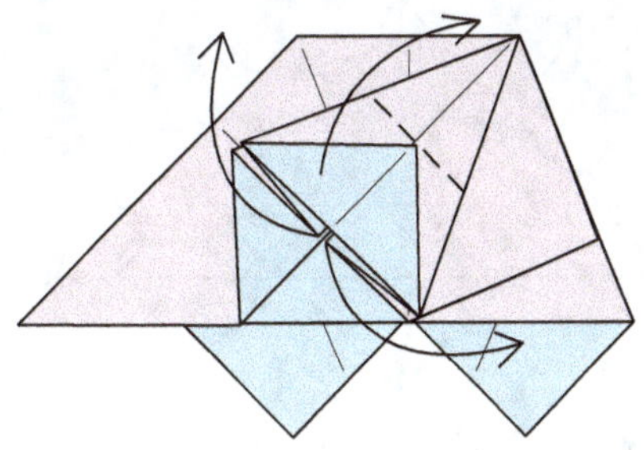

20. Valley fold up.

21. Valley fold up, allowing the inner layers to squash flat.

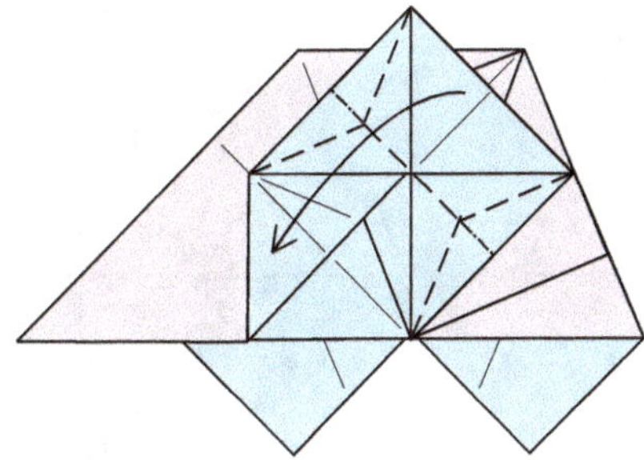

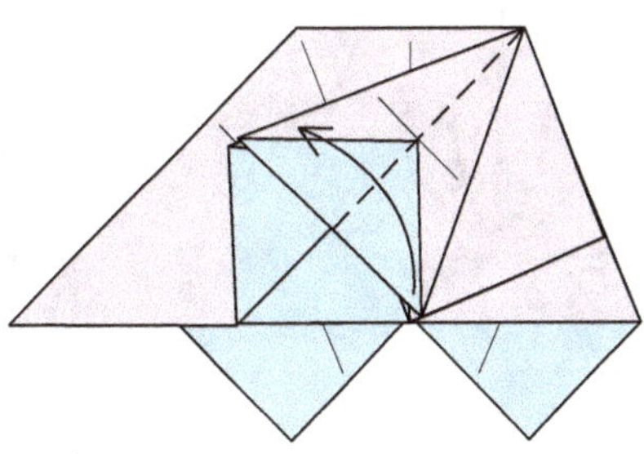

22. Valley fold back down, while reverse folding the sides.

23. Swing up one flap, undoing a set of reverse folds.

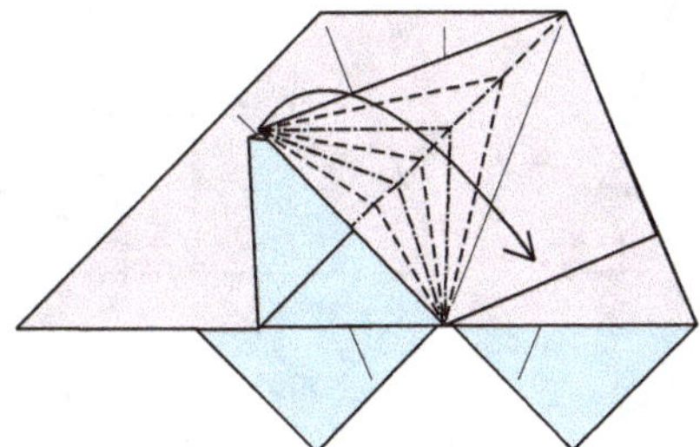

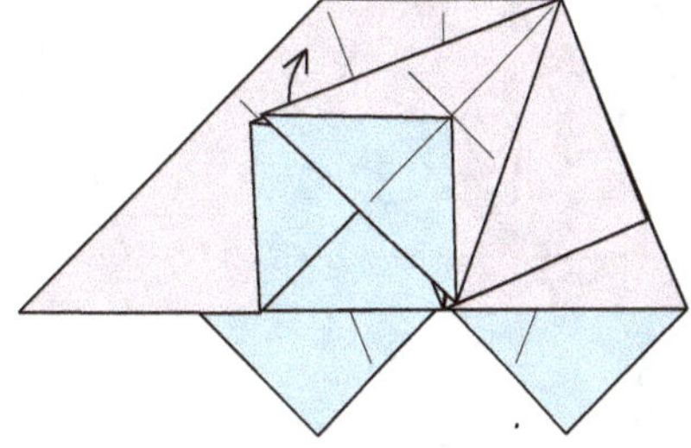

24. Swing the flap back down, inserting valley folds between the existing creases. Form the top sets of reverse folds first, working your way towards the outer edge.

25. Undo a reverse fold.

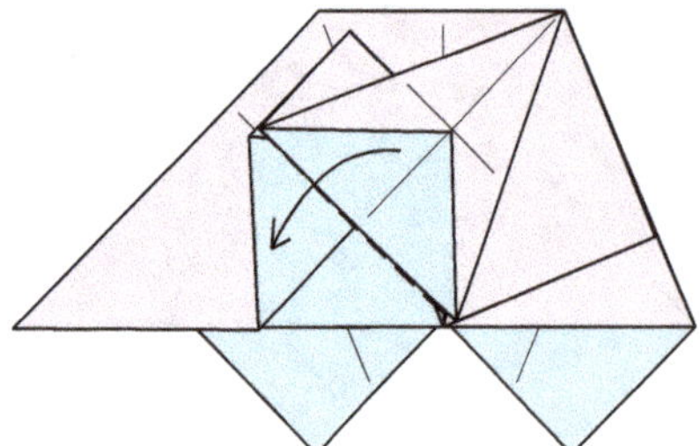

26. Swing the flap down.

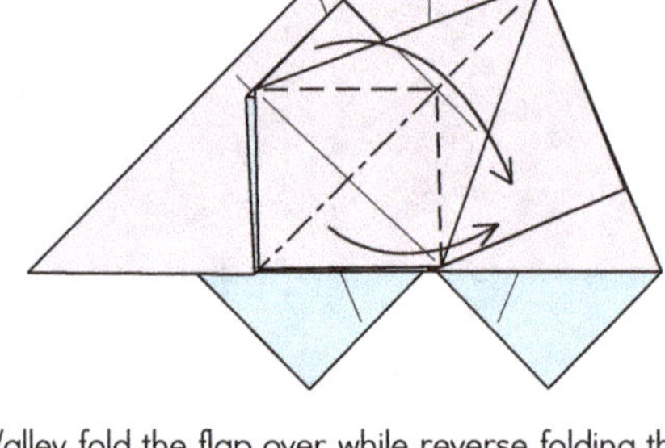

27. Valley fold the flap over while reverse folding the original corner outwards.

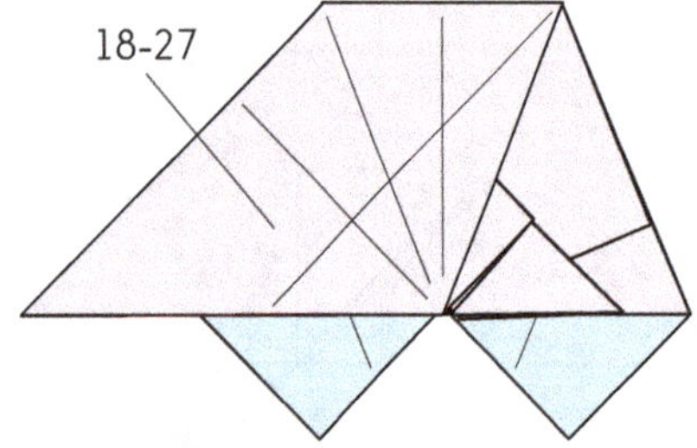

28. Repeat steps 18-27 in mirror image.

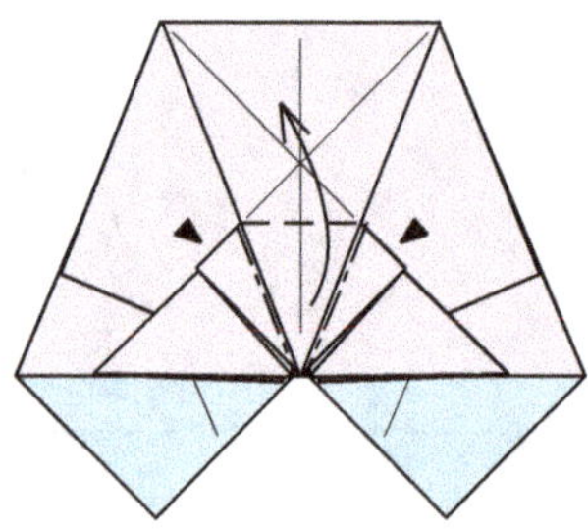

29. Valley fold the flap up while squash folding the sides (petal fold).

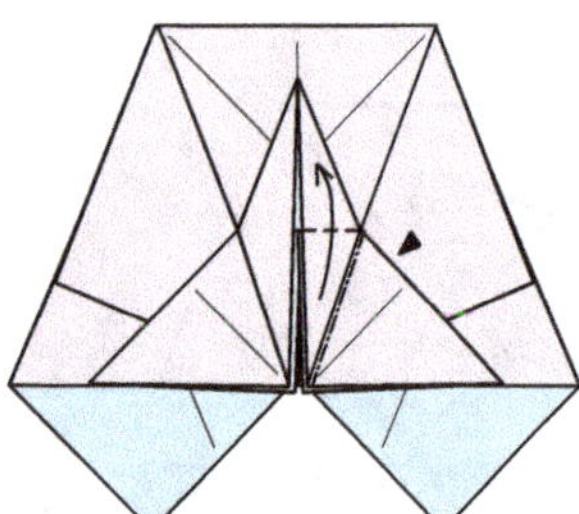

30. Squash fold the flap over.

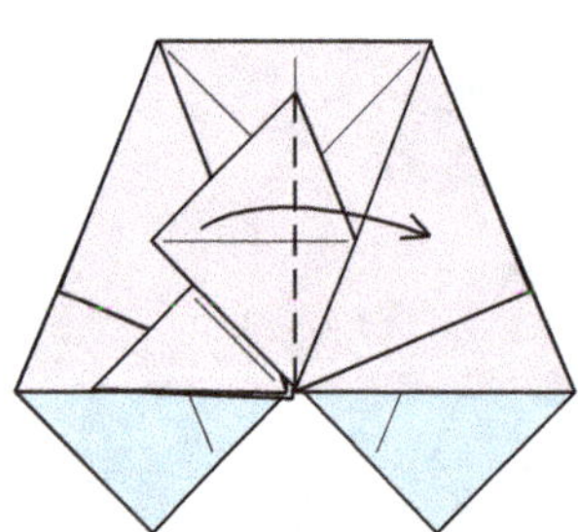

31. Valley fold the flap over.

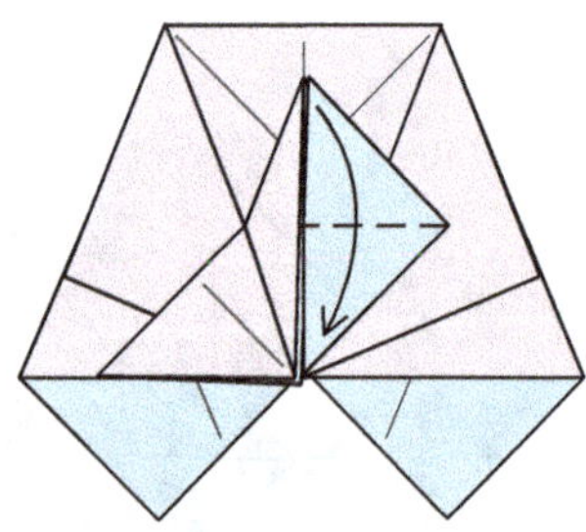

32. Valley fold the flap down.

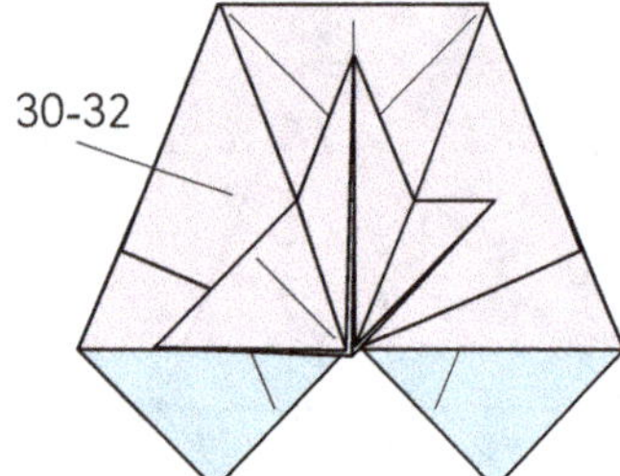

33. Repeat steps 30-32 in mirror image.

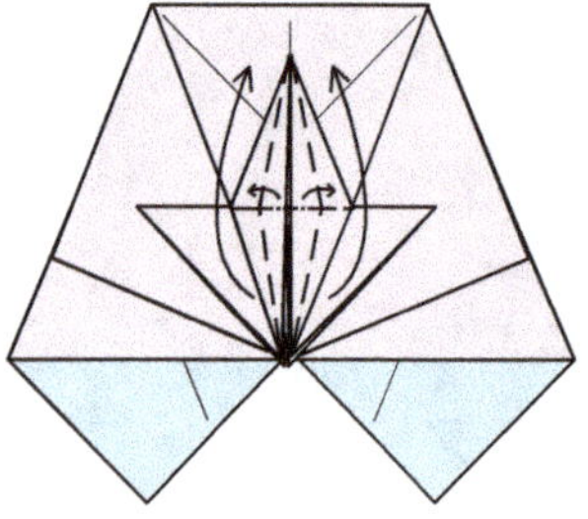

34. Valley fold the flaps up while reverse folding the top single layers outwards.

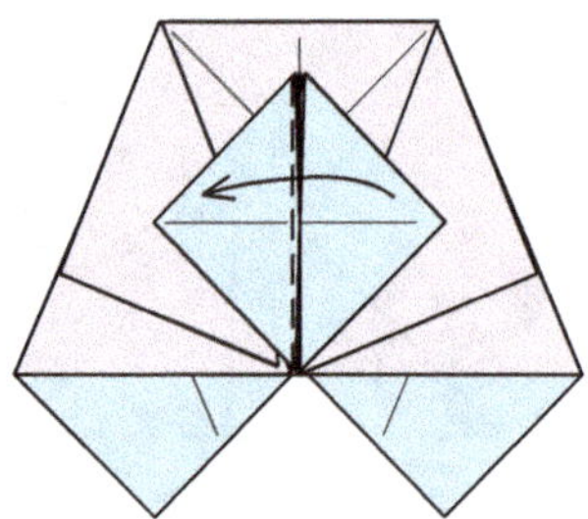

35. Swing the flap over.

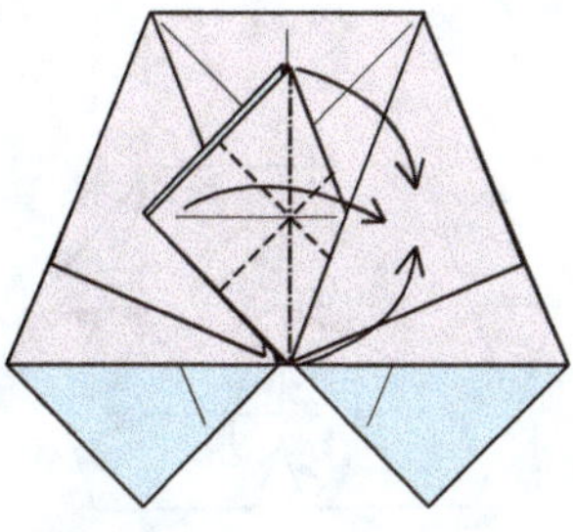

36. Fold the flap back while reverse folding.

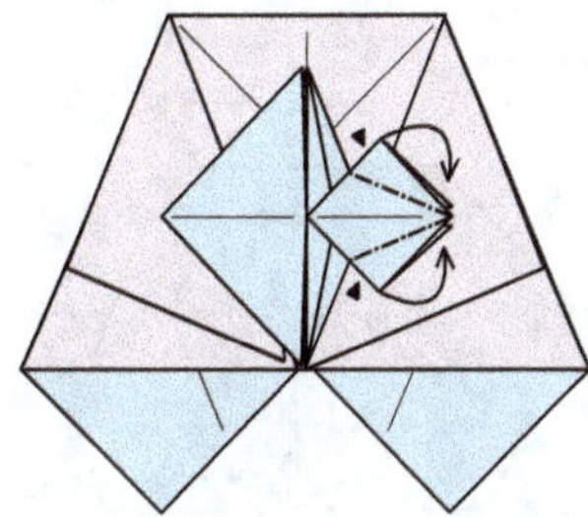

37. Reverse fold the sides.

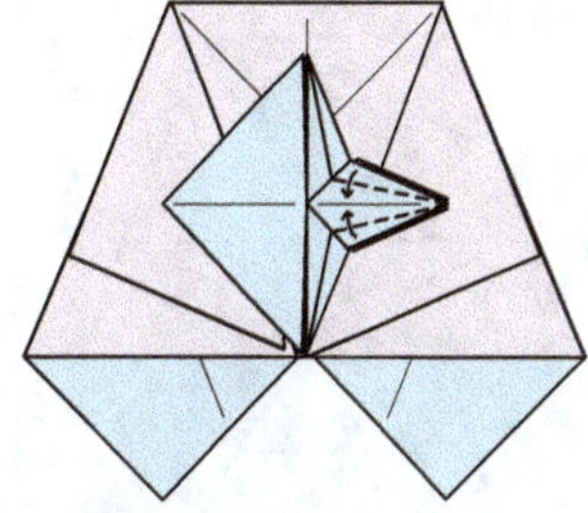

38. Valley fold the sides to the center.

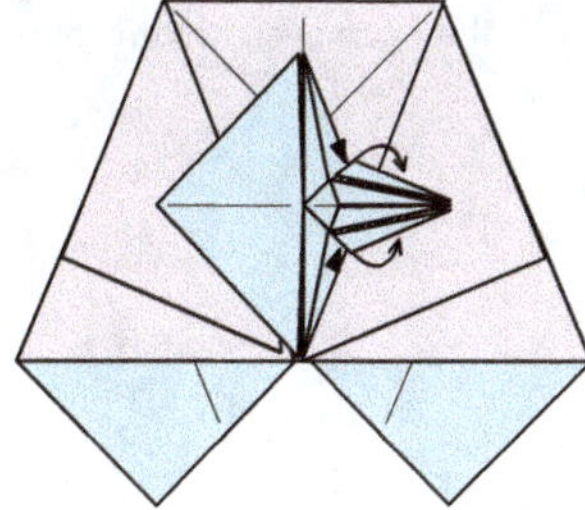

39. Reverse fold the sides.

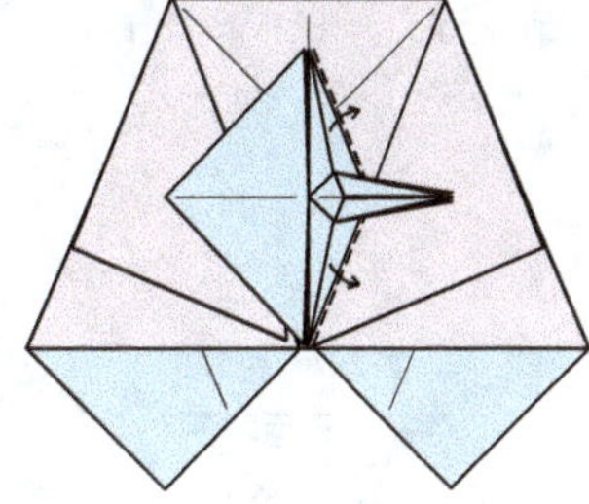

40. Carefully pull out the top layer from each side.

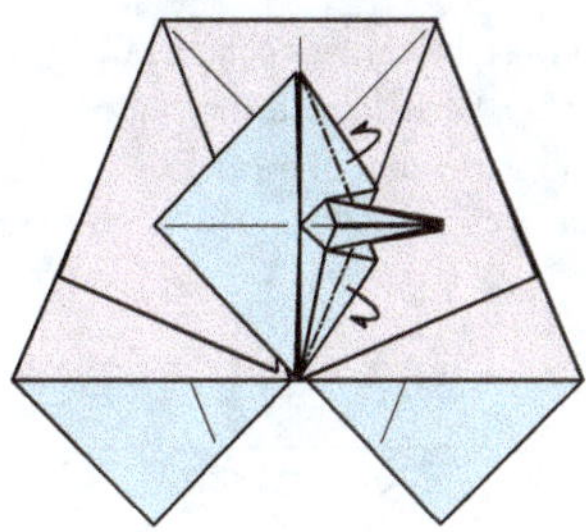

41. Mountain fold the edges around as many layers as possible.

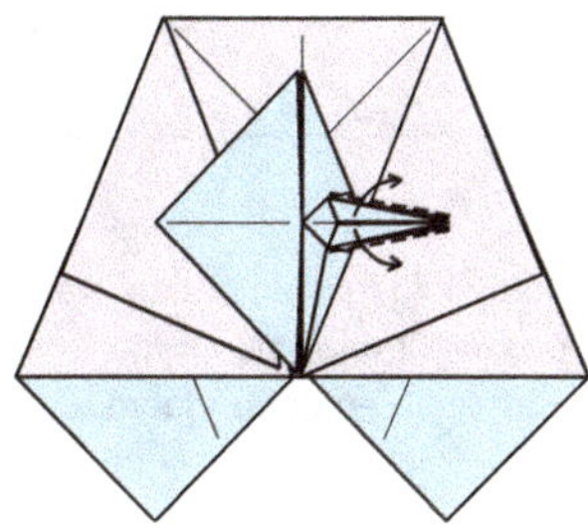

42. Open out the top flaps.

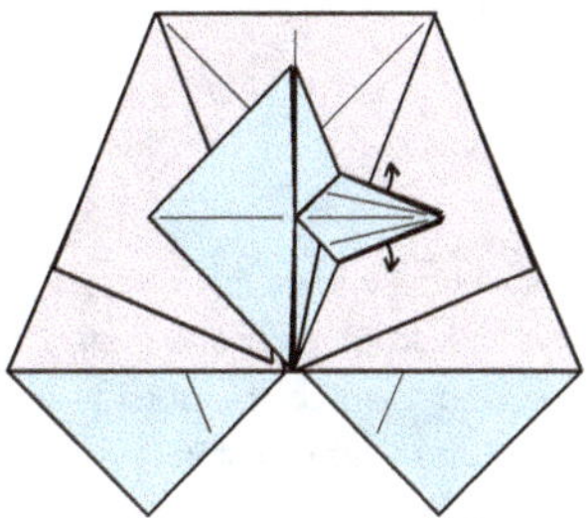

43. Undo the set of reverse folds.

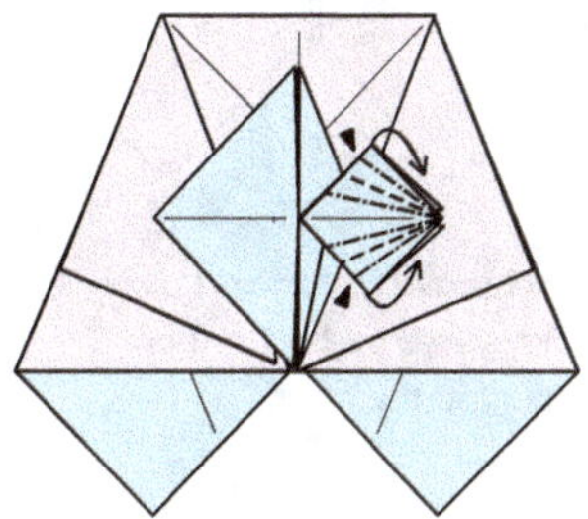

44. Reverse fold the sides in and out along the existing creases.

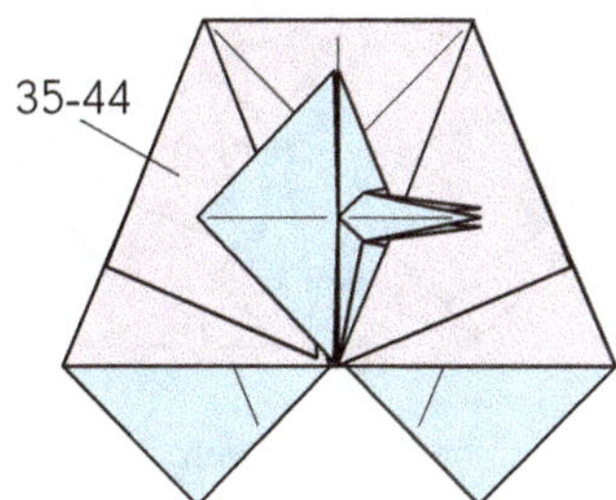

45. Repeat steps 35-44 in mirror image.

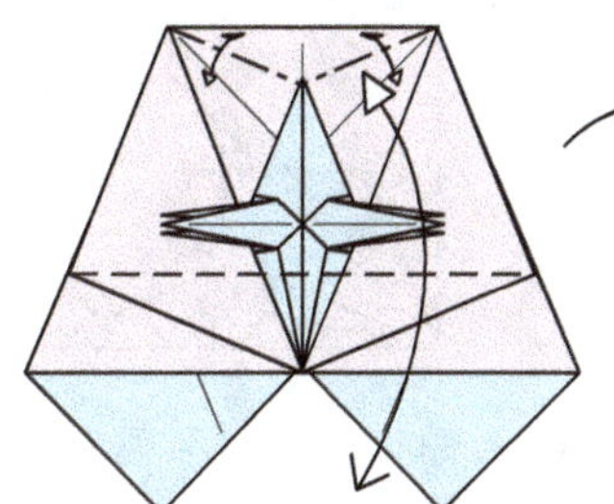

46. Precrease the top section and then turn over.

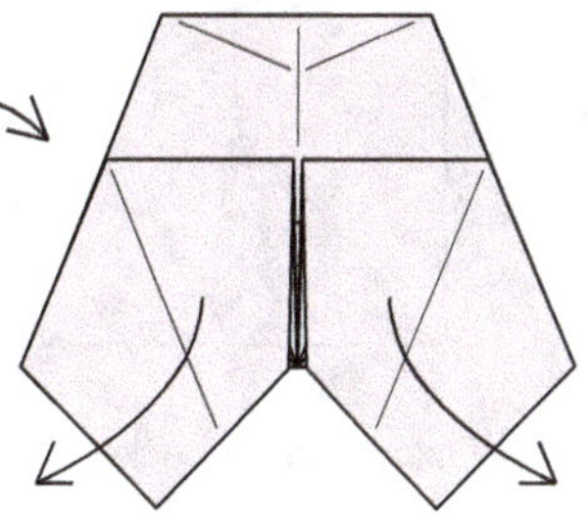

47. Open out the bottom section.

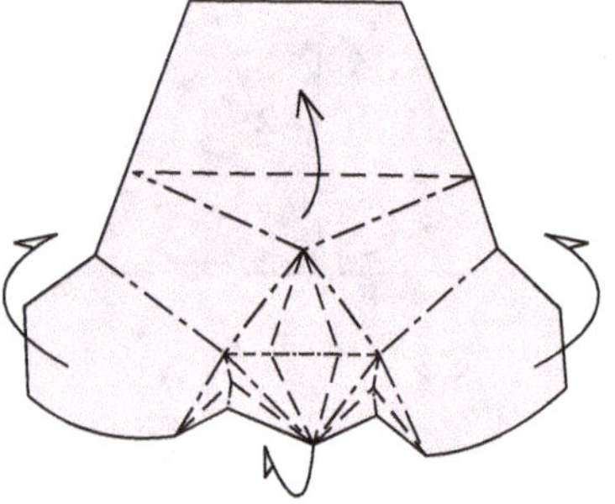

48. Invert the center section, pulling it up, while folding the bottom flaps towards the back.

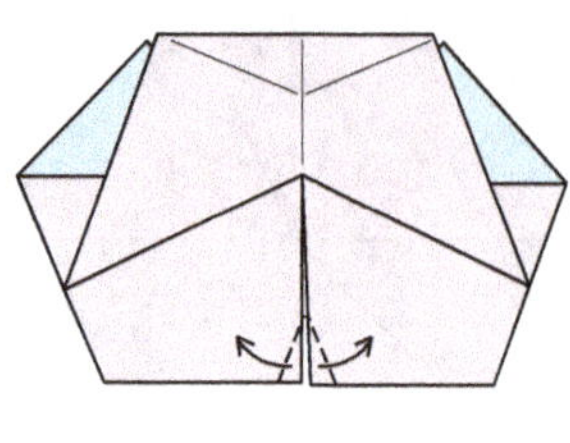

49. Valley fold the bottom corners outwards.

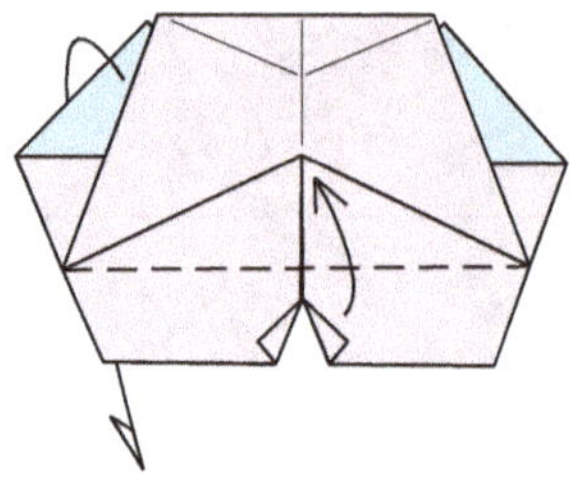

50. Flip the back section towards the surface.

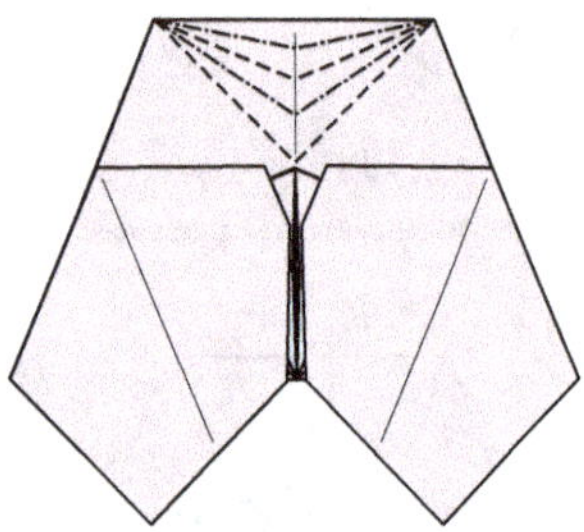

51. Precrease by forming a series of reverse folds and then opening them up.

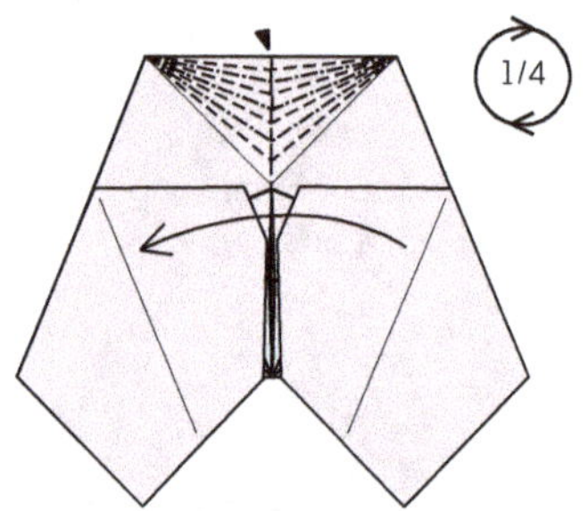

52. Insert valley folds in-between the folds from the previous step, working towards the outside (this is a series if nested reverse folds). Rotate the model.

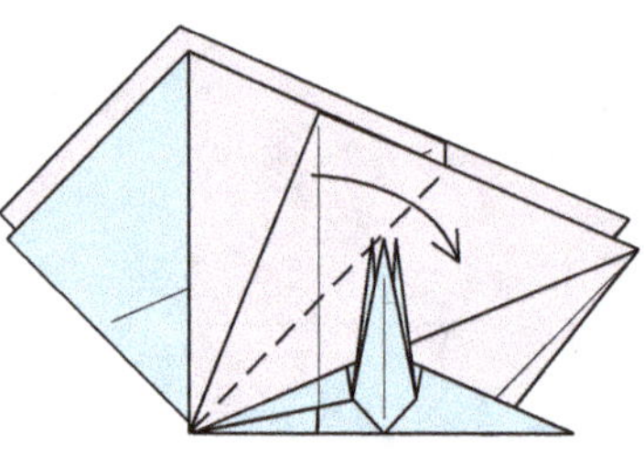

53. Valley fold the center flap over, passing it underneath the cluster of leg appendages.

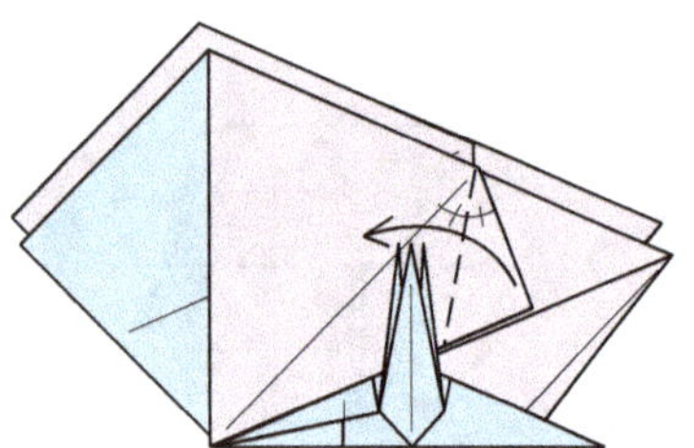

54. Valley fold along the angle bisector.

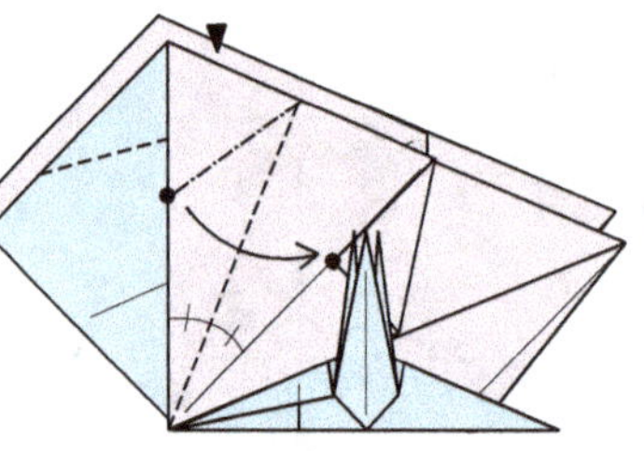

55. Valley fold along the angle bisector, allowing a squash to form at the top. Note how the edge should hit the flap.

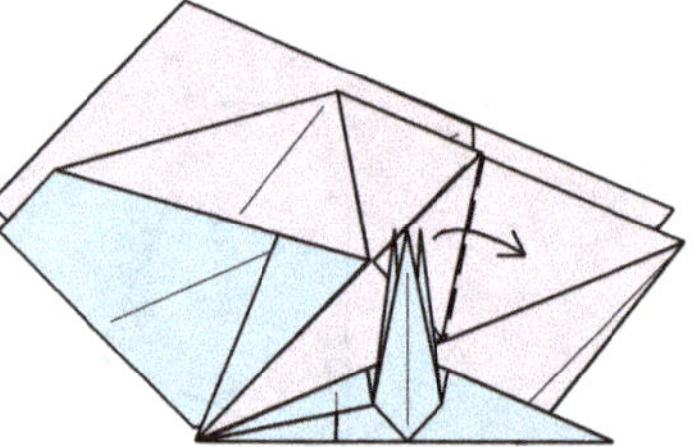

56. Swing the flap back over.

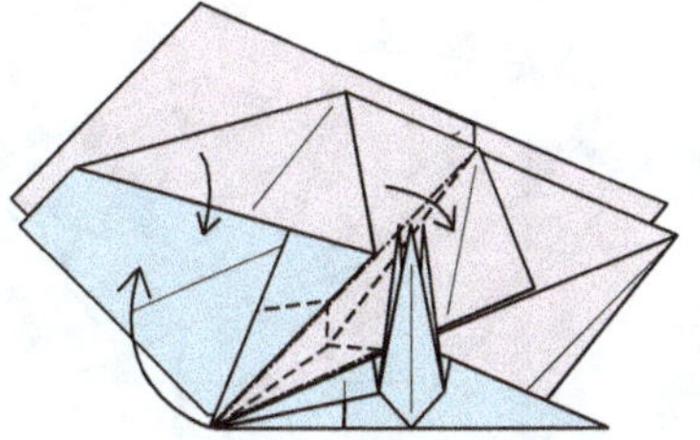

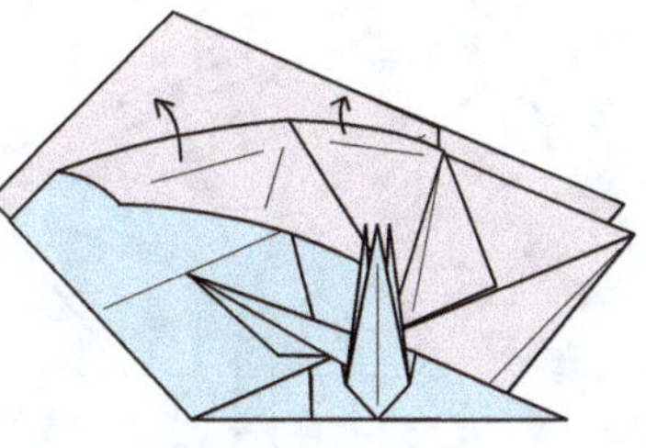

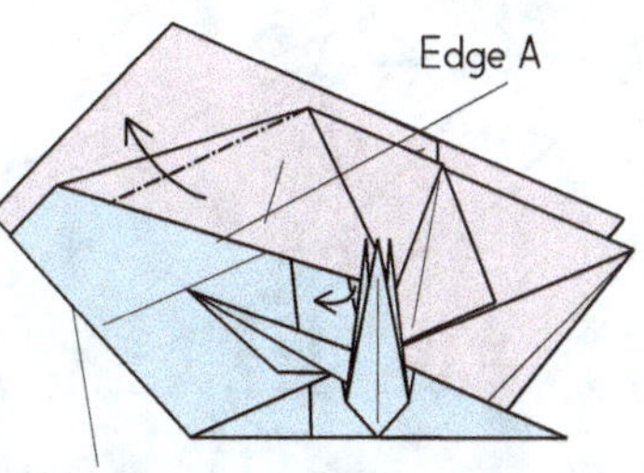

57. Collapse the top layer of the flap for the antennae while folding it upwards. This will cause the top of the wings to become convex.

58. Flatten the top edge of the wing, pressing in an upwards direction, creating a new outer edge.

59. Swivel the white section, such that edge A becomes parallel with edge B.

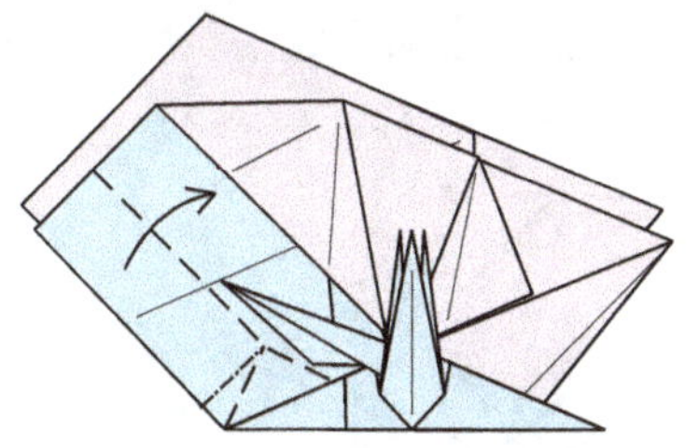

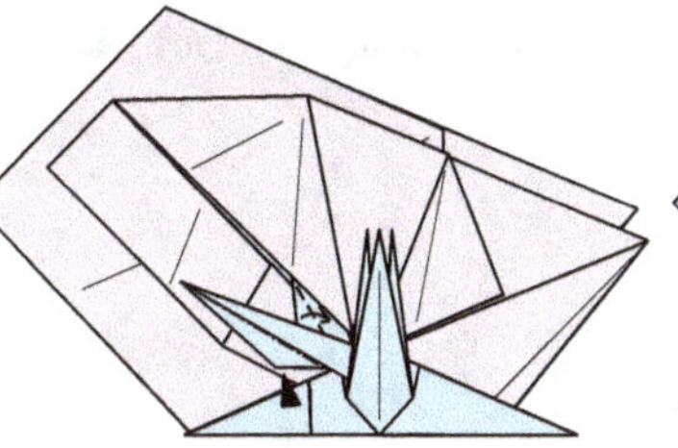

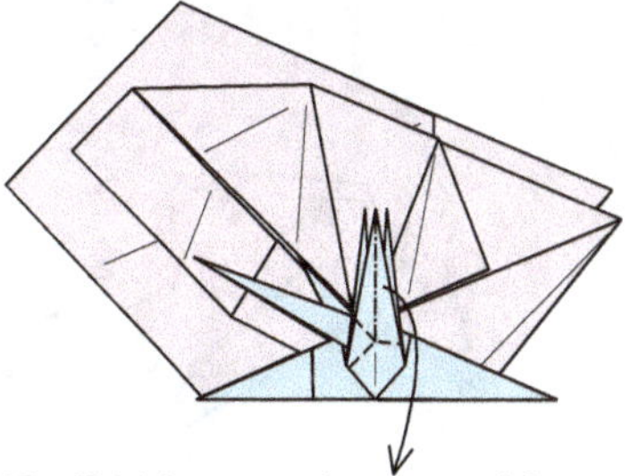

60. Valley fold the colored section in half, allowing a rabbit ear to form.

61. Reverse fold the flap in half, swiveling over paper where the wing is.

62. Fold the center leg down, while folding it in half.

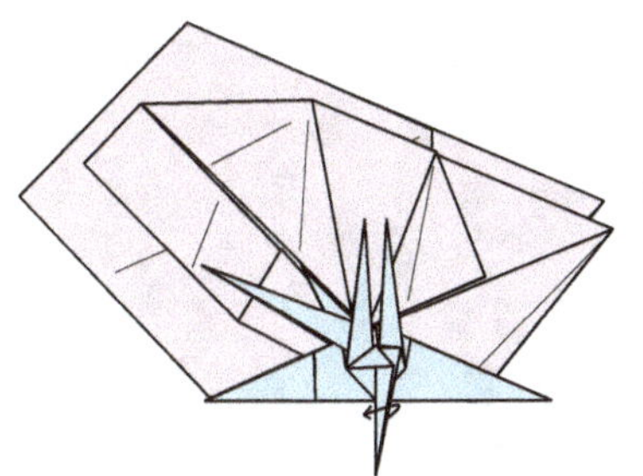

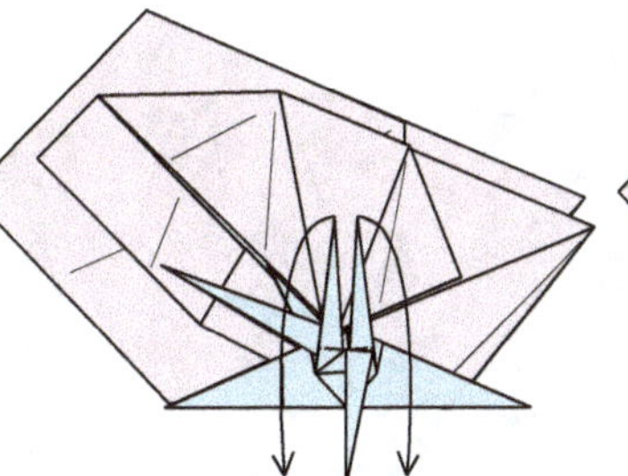

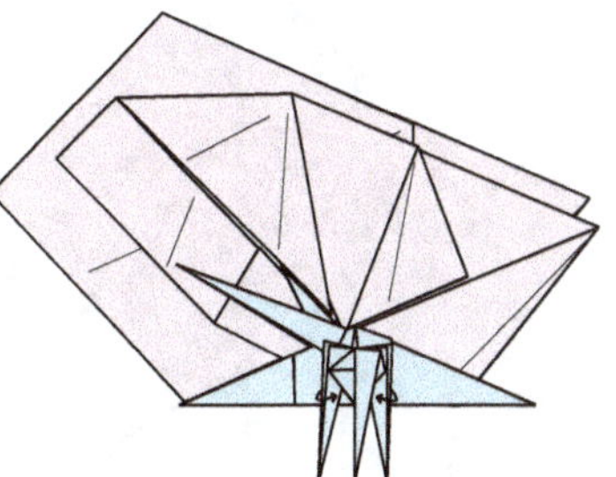

63. Tuck the top layer of the flap into the pocket below.

64. Reverse fold the side flaps down.

65. Tuck the top layers into the respective pockets below.

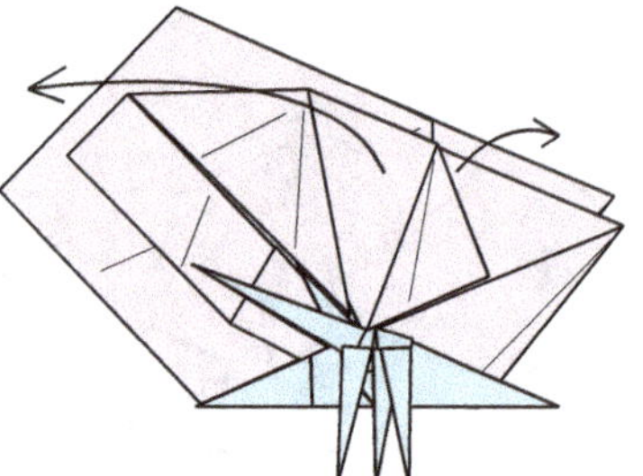

66. Pull apart the sections of the wing slightly.

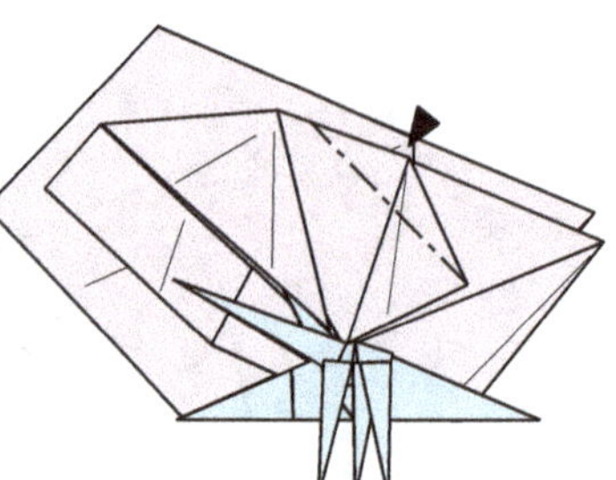

67. Closed sink the corner.

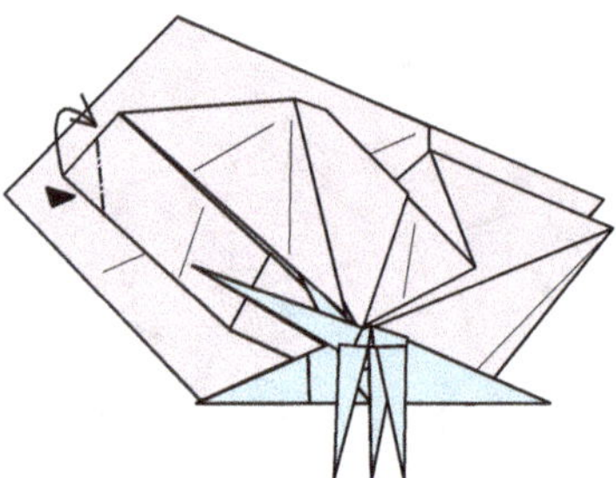

68. Reverse fold.

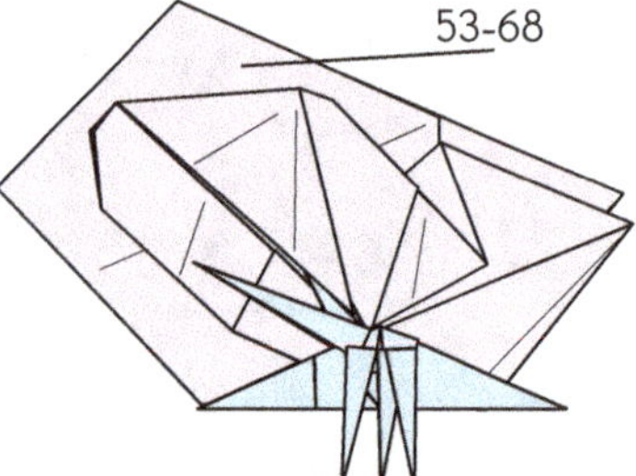

69. Repeat steps 53-68 behind.

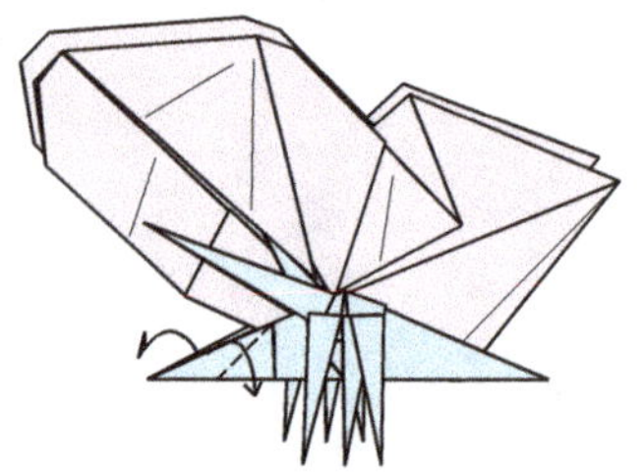

70. Outside reverse fold the head.

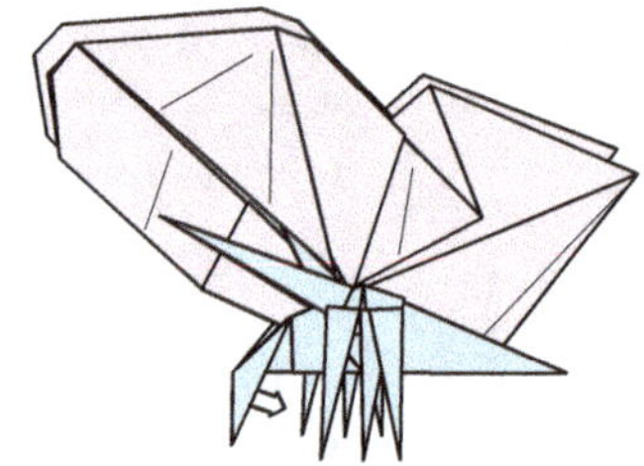

71. Unsink a single layer.

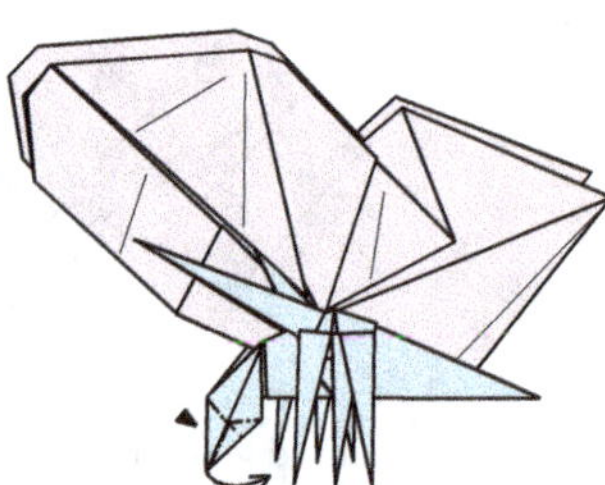

72. Pinch the point, pull it back and flatten (double rabbit ear).

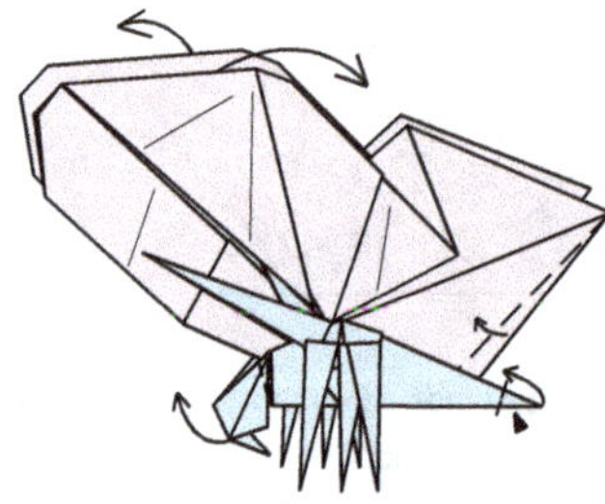

73. Crimp the head upwards. Reverse fold the tail. Fold the wings outwards slightly, and shape the model to taste.

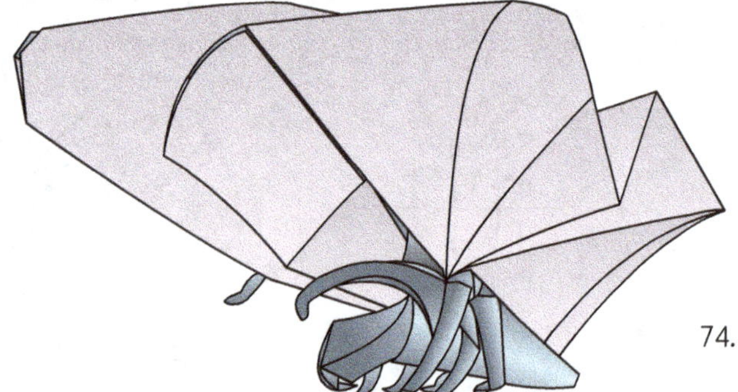

74. Completed *Butterfly*.

Bee

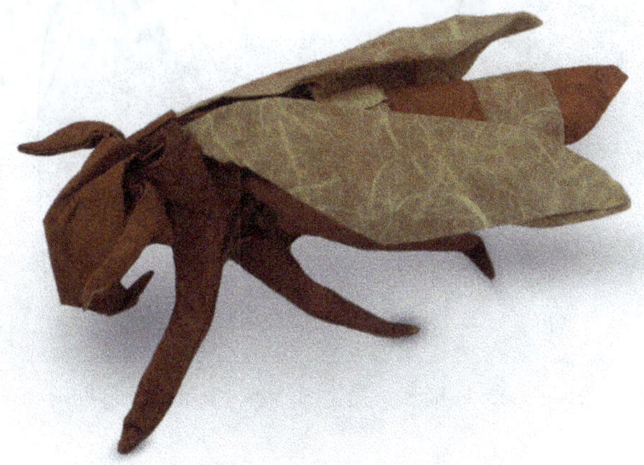

About

Shortly after devising an origami raccoon, I decided to leverage the technique used for the tail and add an extra set of legs and wings to make a bee. Although the folding sequence is somewhat normal, from a structural standpoint this is a strange model. The two sets of flaps coming from the middle portion of the paper (the wings and a set of legs) are colored differently, resulting in a model's center that was difficult to resolve (which in layman's terms would be to flatten neatly). It took a bit of effort to arrive at a set of steps that would be easy to follow. While some people might find the idea of a striped flap to be a novelty in origami, my favorite feature is the way the wings tuck into the head section. Feel free to enjoy the appendage of your own choosing.

Tips

There is a lot of flap flipping in this model, so careful attention to the directions is needed. In step thirty, you can prevent ripping by grasping the paper at the weak points (the top and bottom corners) while performing this inverting maneuver.

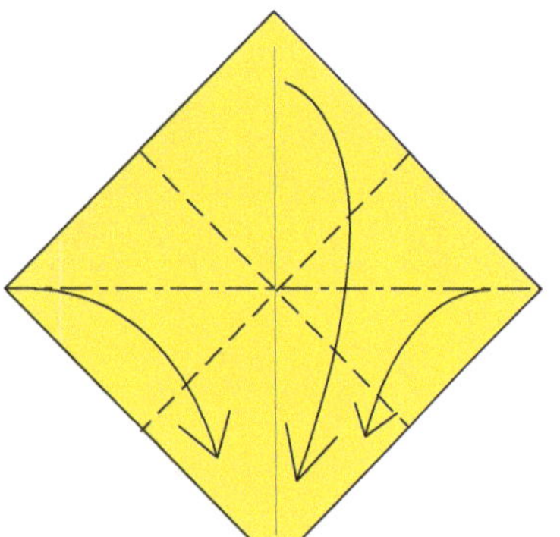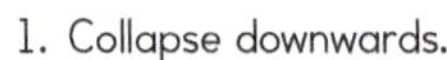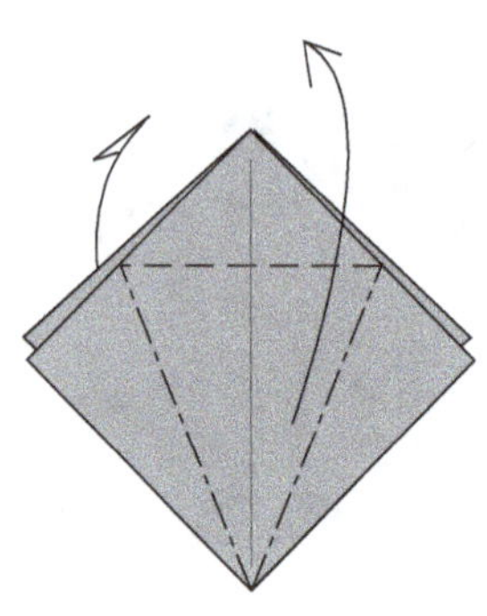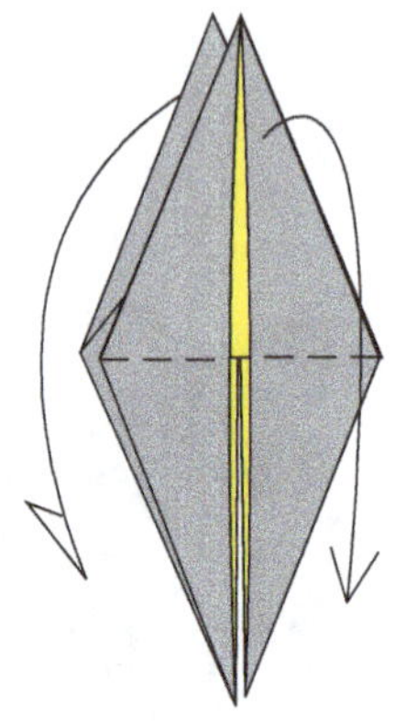

1. Collapse downwards.

2. Petal fold up. Repeat behind.

3. Valley fold the top flaps down.

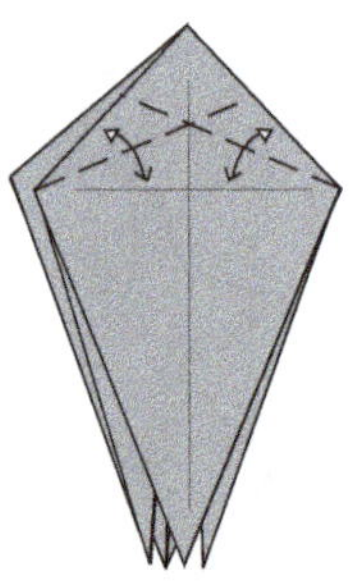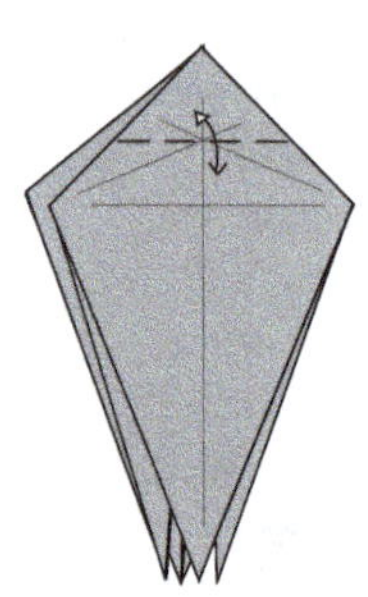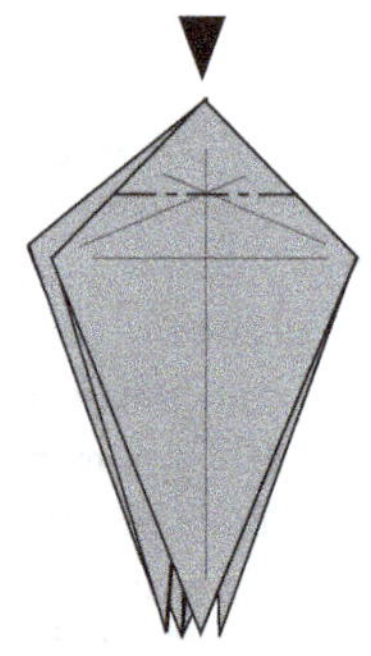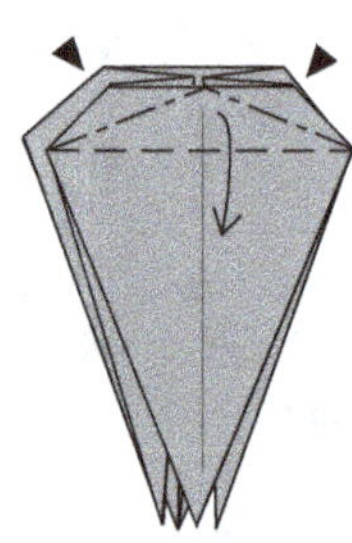

4. Precrease the top.

5. Precrease through the intersection of creases.

6. Sink the top point.

7. Spread squash.

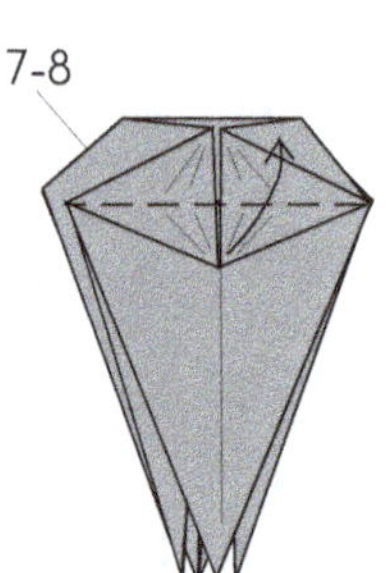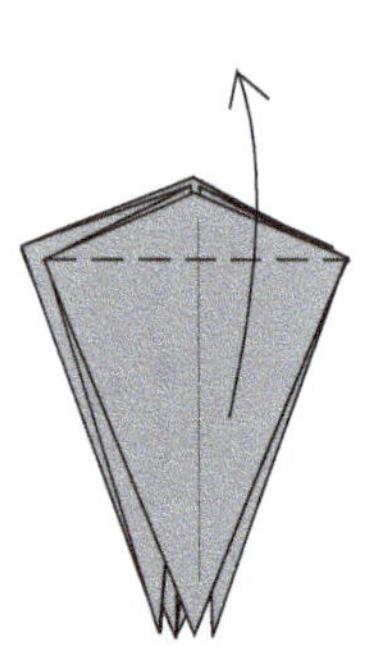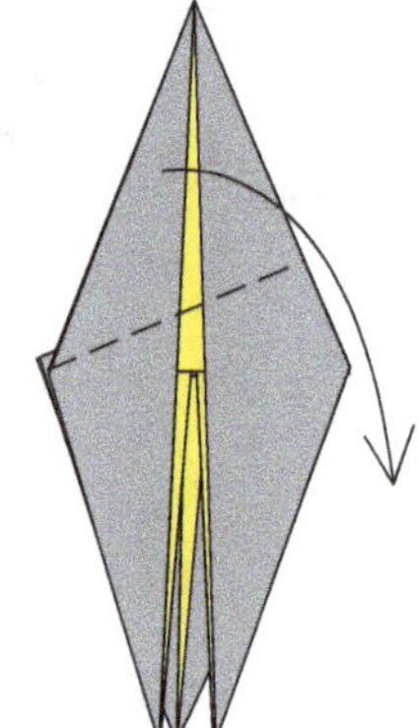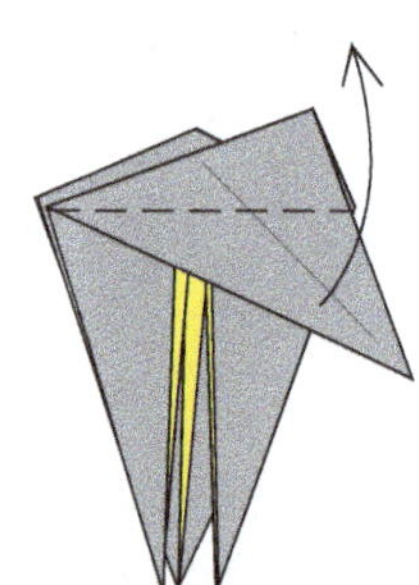

8. Flatten. Repeat steps 7-8 behind.

9. Swing the front flap up.

10. Valley fold down.

11. Valley fold up.

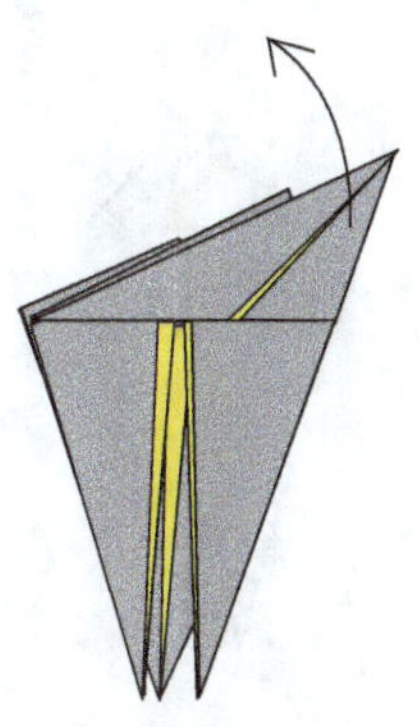

12. Unfold.

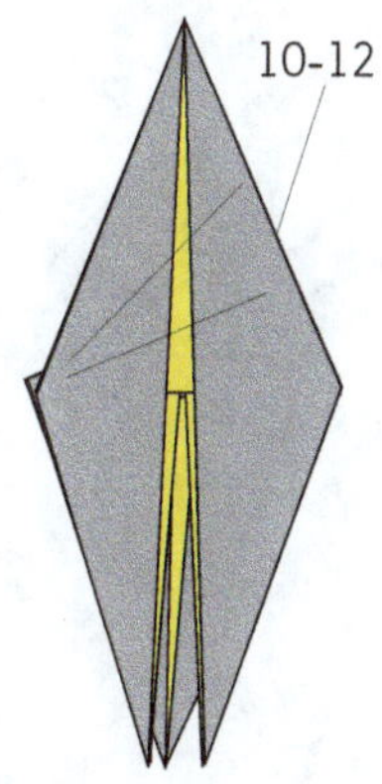

13. Repeat steps 10-12 in mirror image.

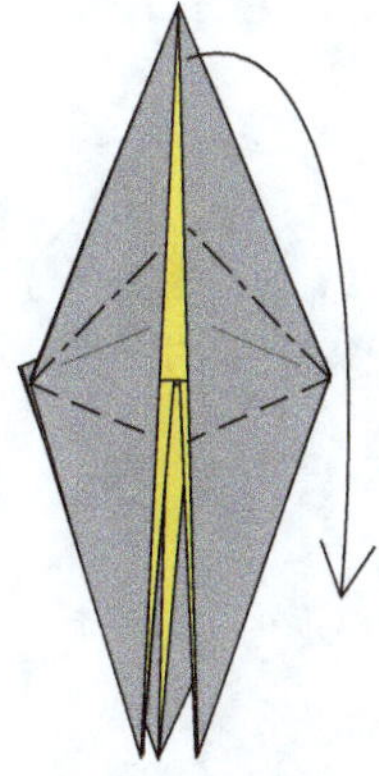

14. Swing down while spreading out the top layers.

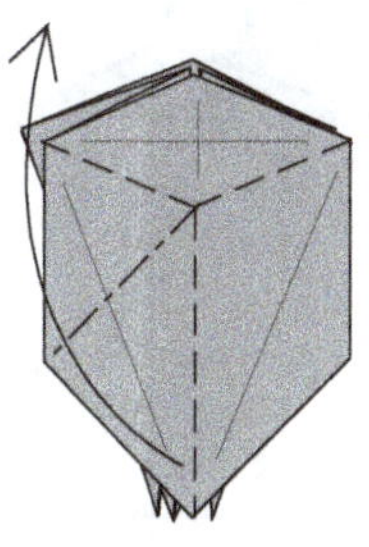

15. Rabbit ear.

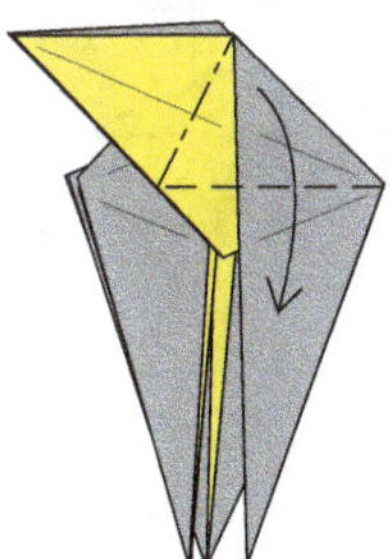

16. Squash fold.

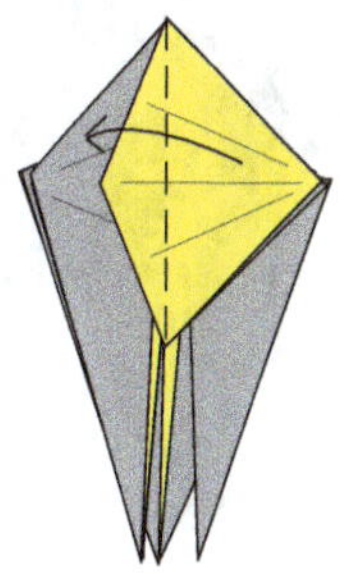

17. Valley fold over.

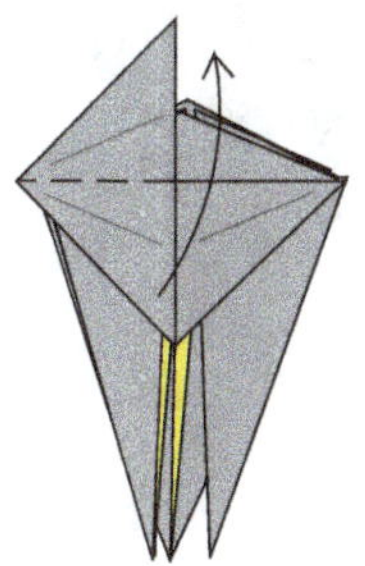

18. Swing up.

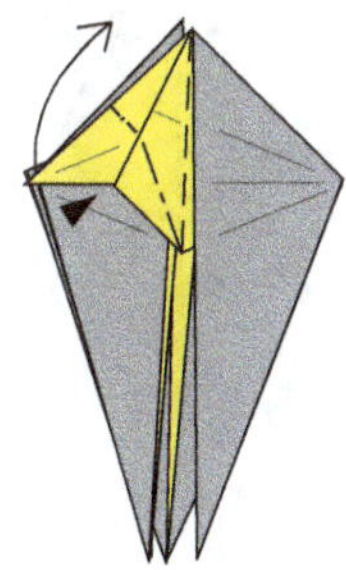

19. Spread squash.

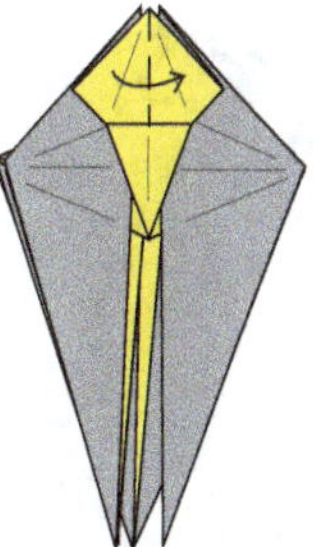

20. Swing over.

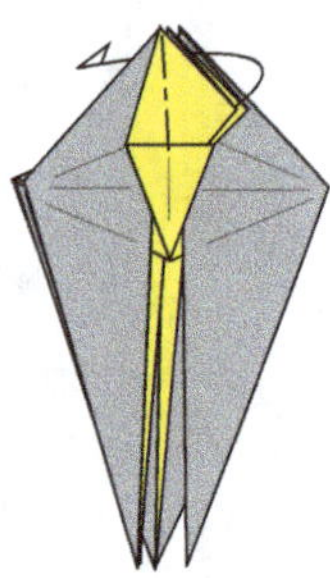

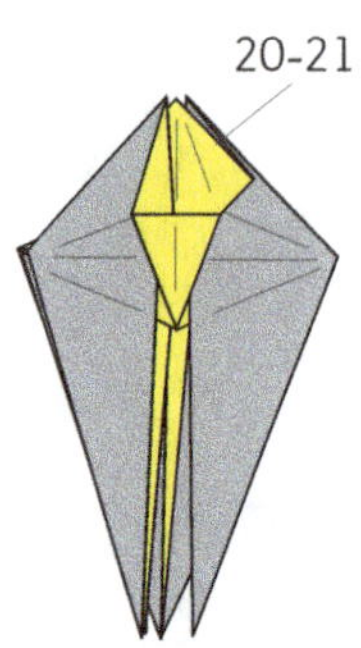

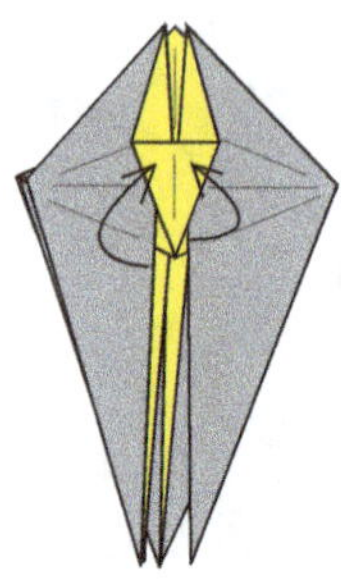

21. Pull the flap through.

22. Repeat steps 20-21 in mirror image.

23. Bring the colored layers to the surface.

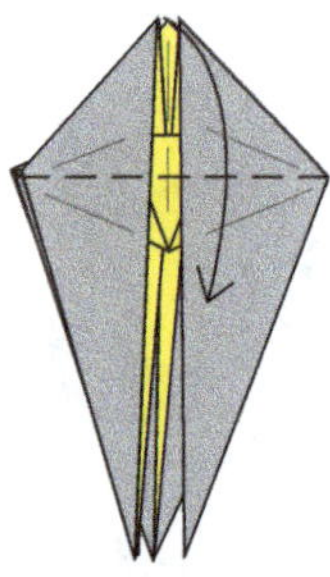

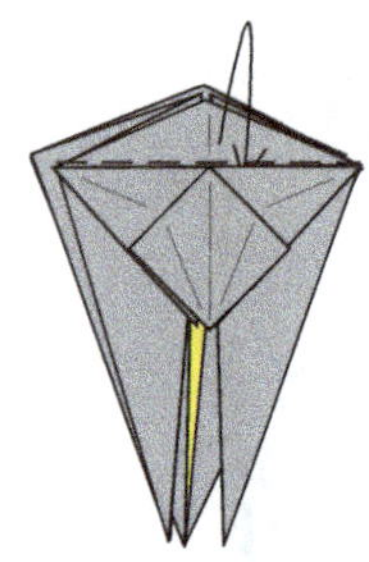

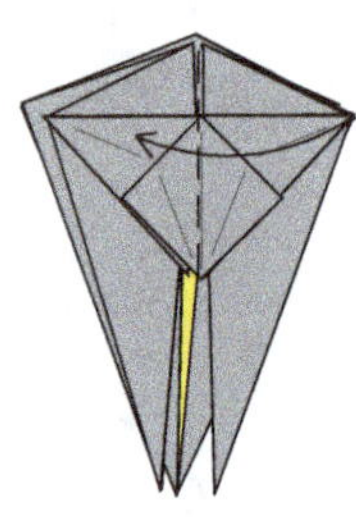

24. Swing down.

25. Tuck the flap into the pocket.

26. Swing the large flap over.

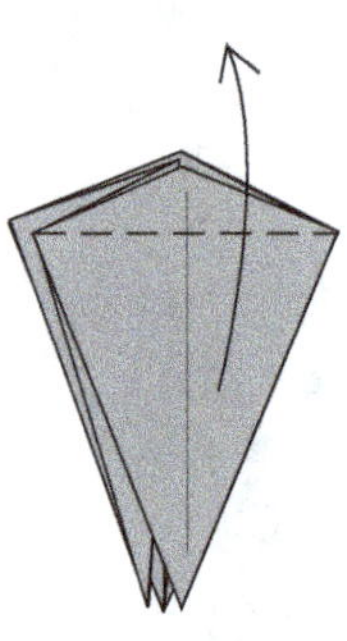

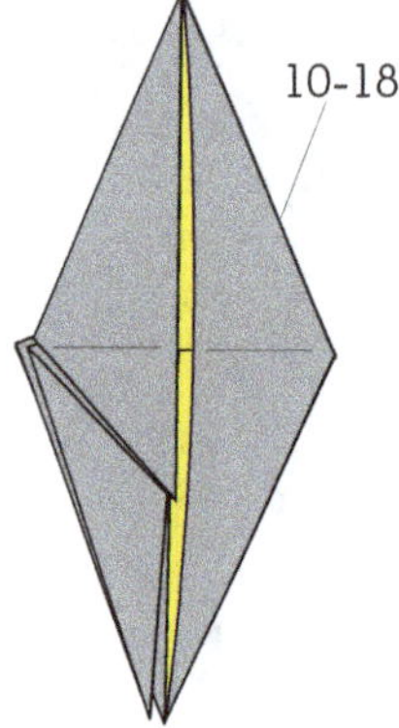

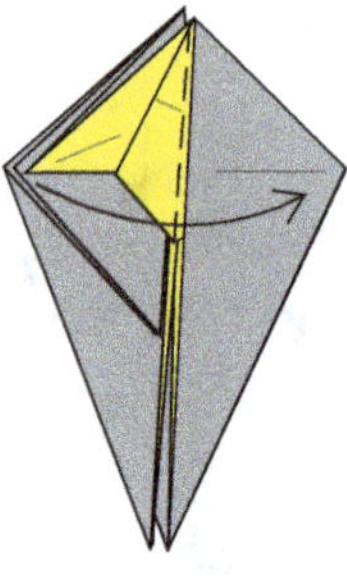

27. Carefully fold the flap up, releasing the trapped layer.

28. Repeat steps 10-18 on the indicated flap.

29. Swing over.

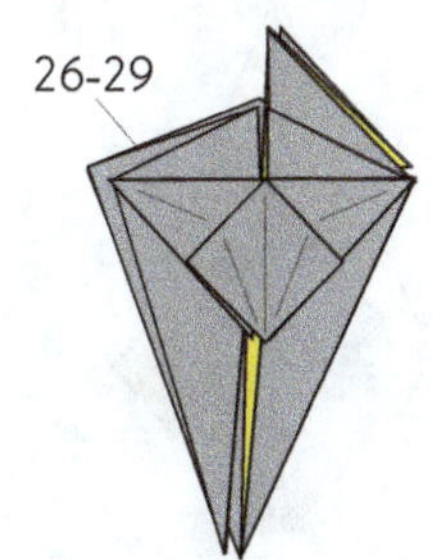
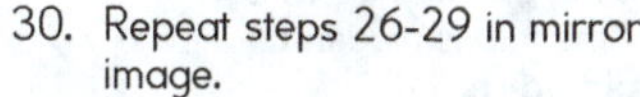

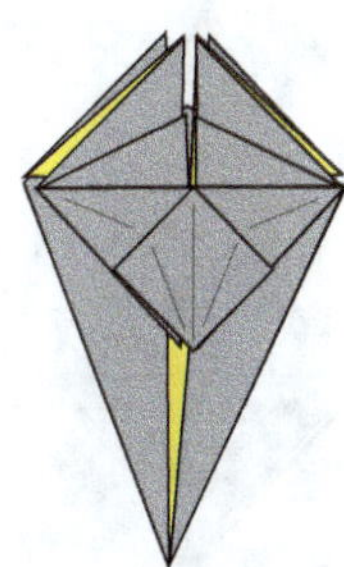

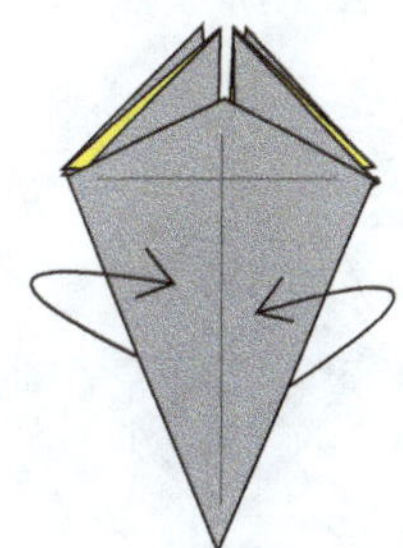

30. Repeat steps 26-29 in mirror image.

31. Turn over.

32. Wrap a single layer around each side.

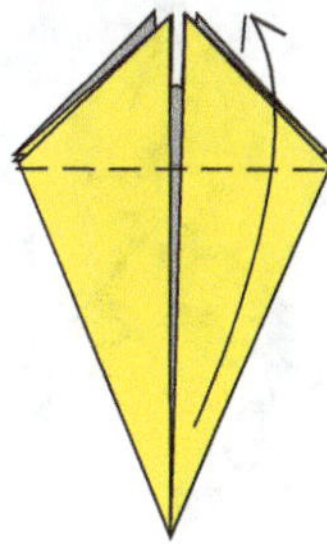

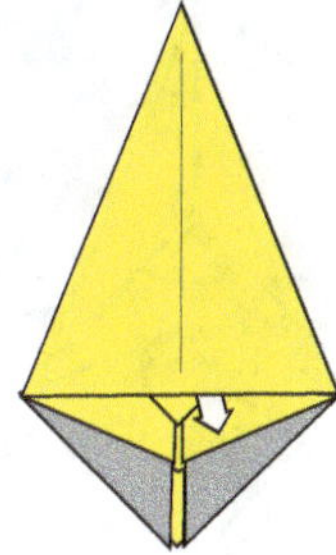

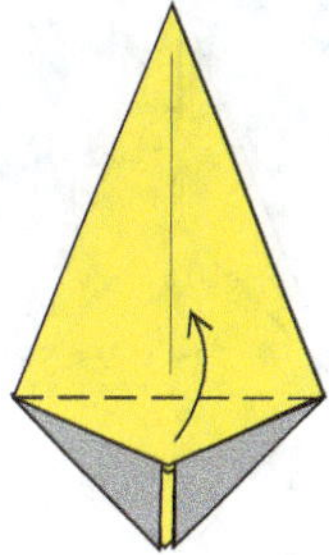

33. Valley fold up.

34. Unsink.

35. Valley fold up.

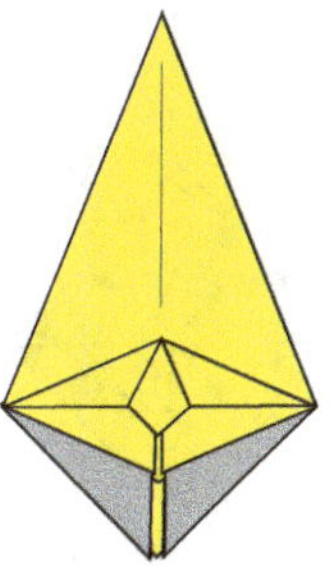

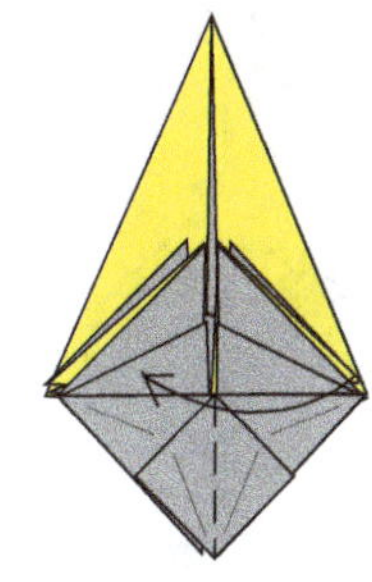

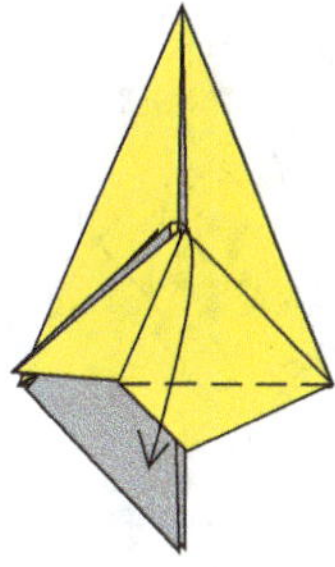

36. Turn over.

37. Swing everything over.

38. Swing down two flaps.

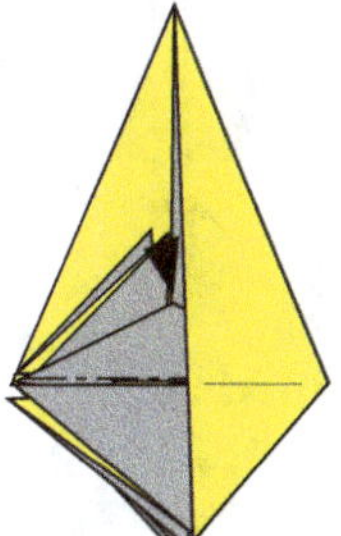

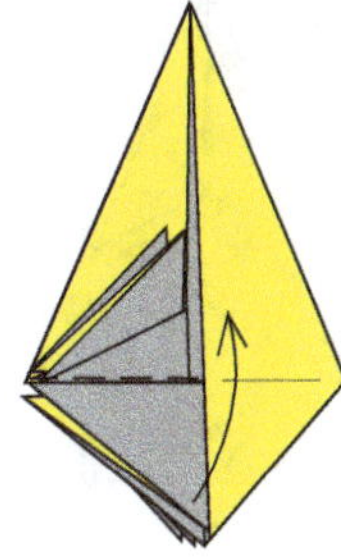

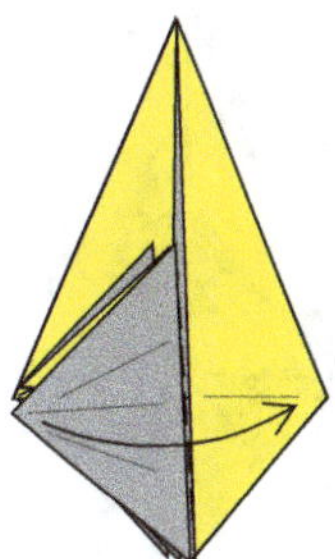

39. Closed sink.

40. Swing one flap up.

41. Swing the large flaps back.

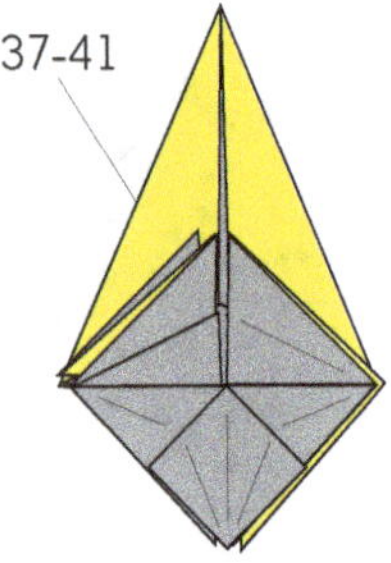

37-41

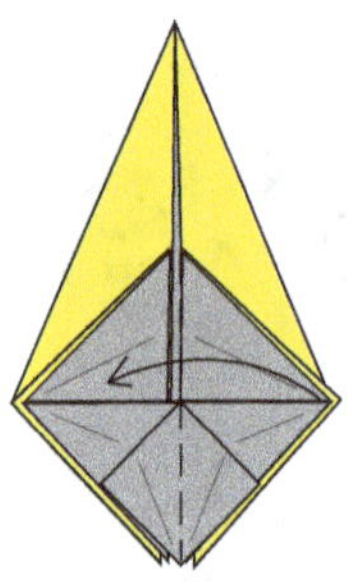

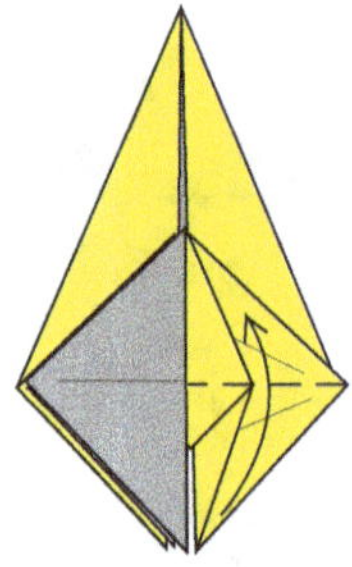

42. Repeat steps 37-41 in mirror image.

43. Swing one flap over.

44. Swing one flap up (a portion of the fold is hidden under the colored region).

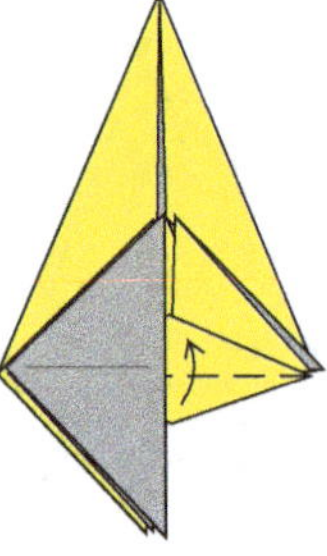

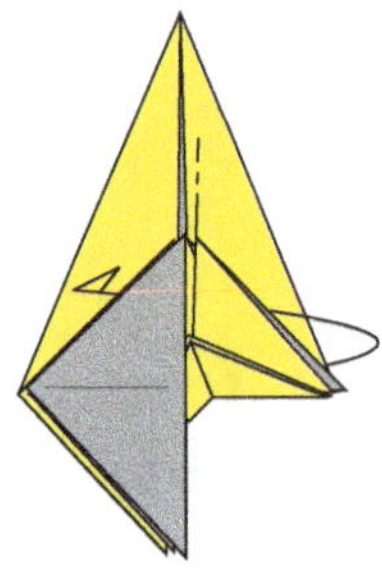

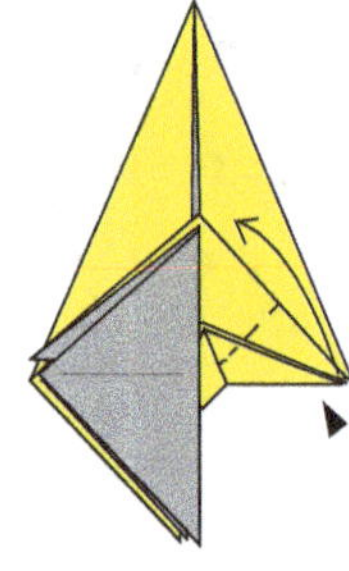

45. Swing up again.

46. Swing the flap through.

47. Reverse fold.

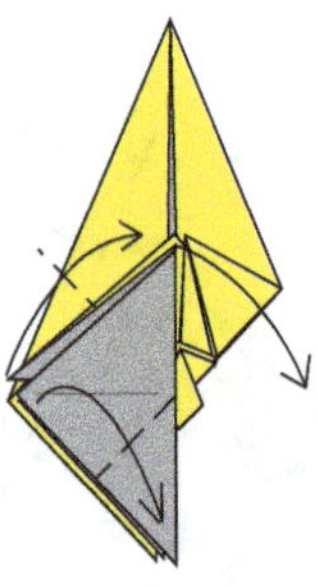

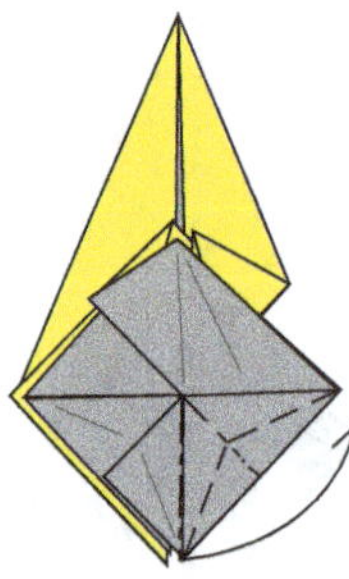

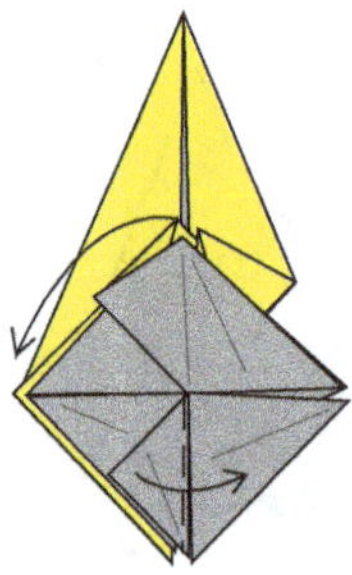

48. Rearrange the flaps as indicated.

49. Swing up, while incorporating a reverse fold.

50. Swing over the bottom flap. Stretch the top flap outwards

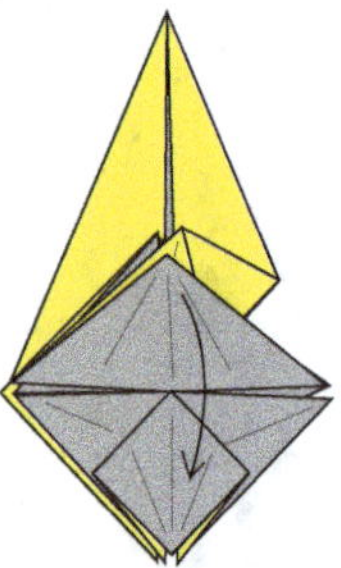

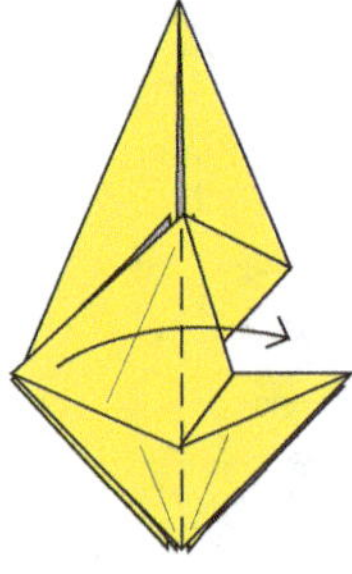

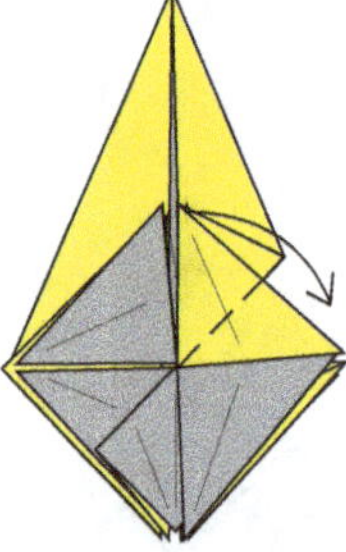

51. Swing down two flaps.

52. Swing over one flap.

53. Valley fold the corner down.

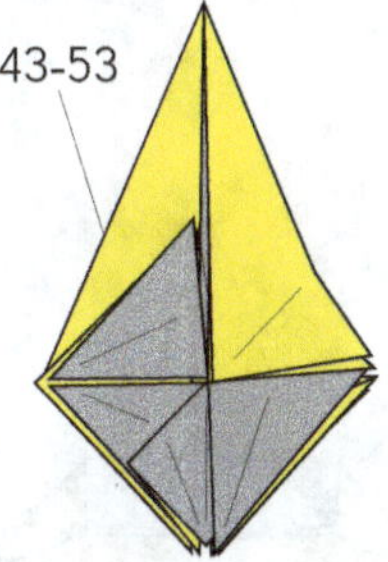

43-53

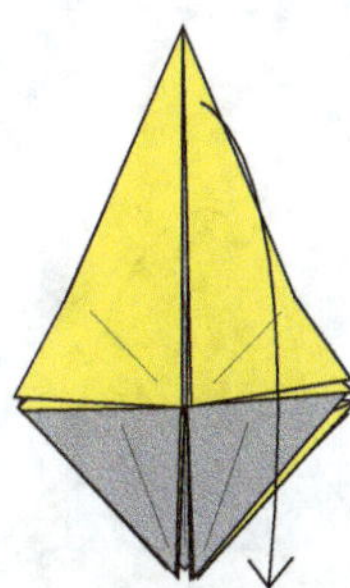

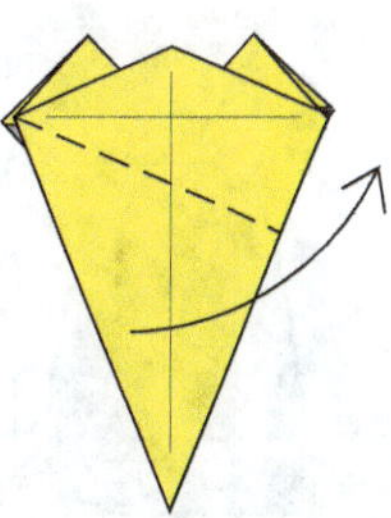

54. Repeat steps 43-53 in mirror image.

55. Swing the flap down.

56. Valley fold up.

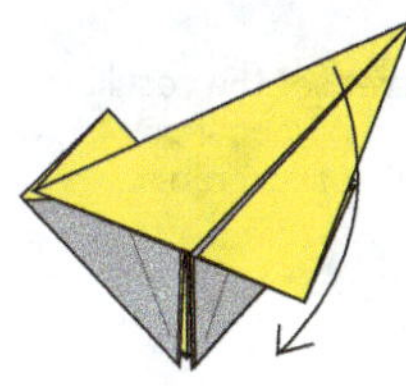

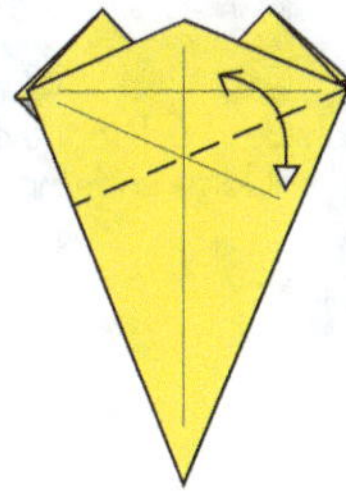

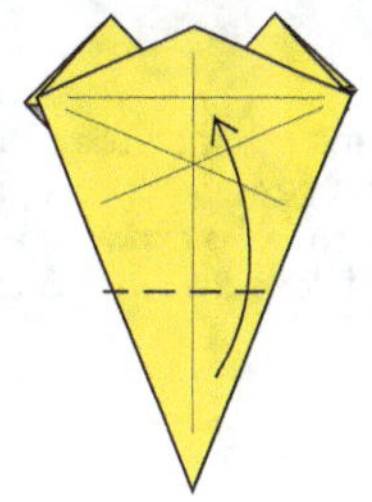

57. Swing the flap down.

58. Precrease in opposite direction.

59. Valley fold to the horizontal crease.

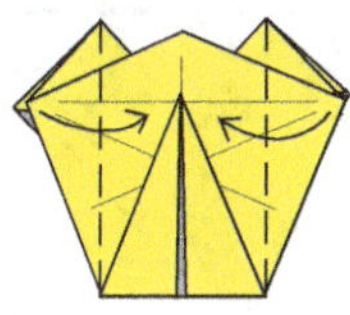

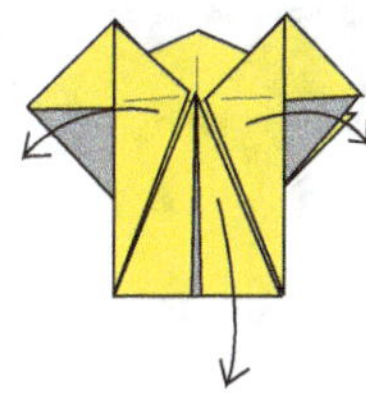

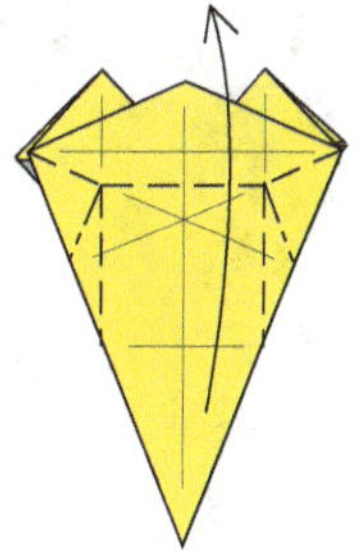

60. Valley fold the sides to the center.

61. Unfold.

62. Swing up while swiveling in the sides.

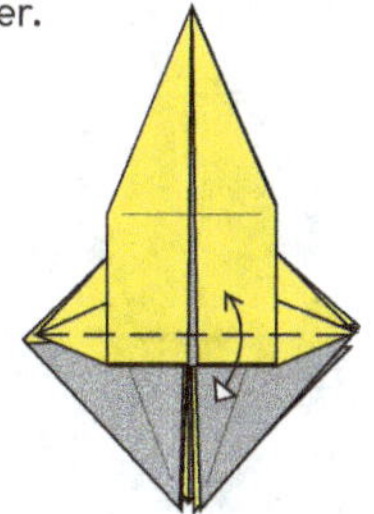

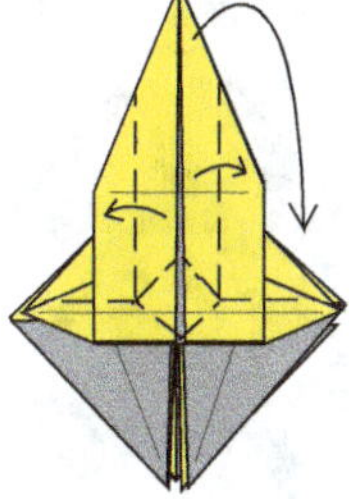

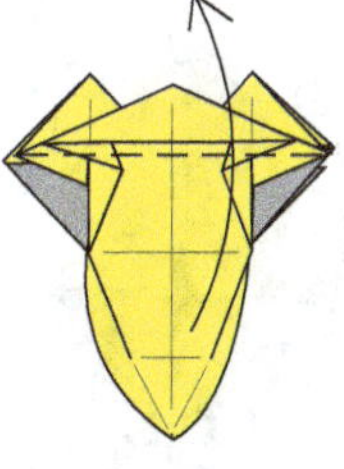

63. Precrease.

64. Valley fold the top single layers outwards while folding the tail upwards. The tail will not lie flat.

65. Valley fold the tail up.

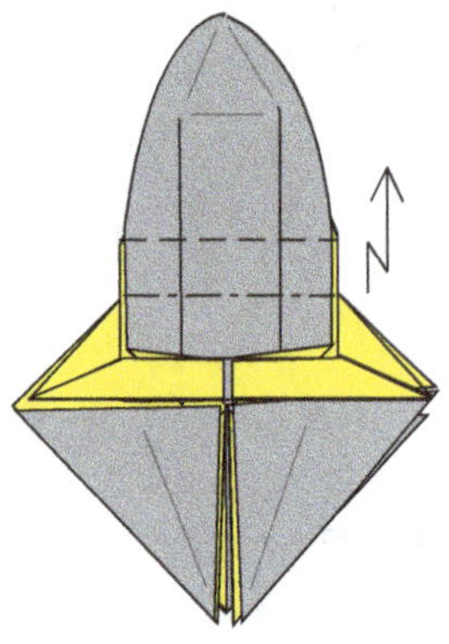

66. Pleat the tail. The valley fold lies along an existing crease. The mountain fold is midway from the valley fold to the white portion.

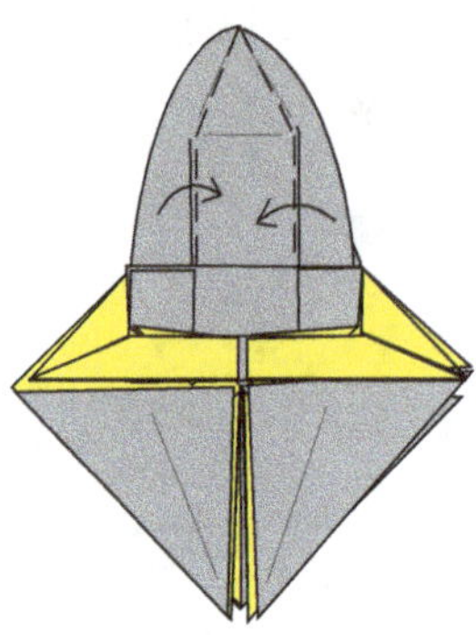

67. Fold the sides back to the center. A swivel will form underneath the pleat.

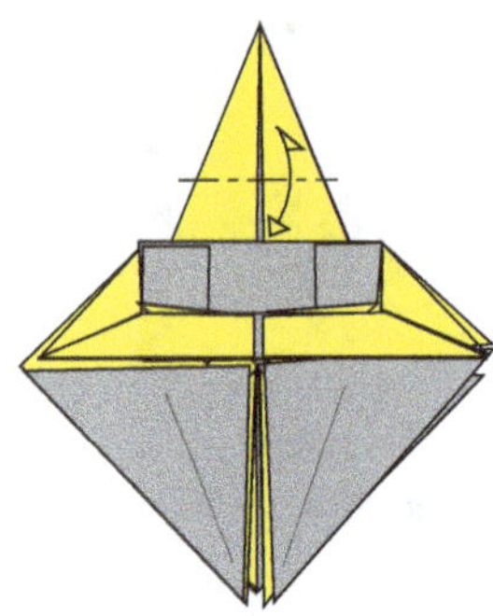

68. Precrease. The resulting width should be about as wide as the colored section below.

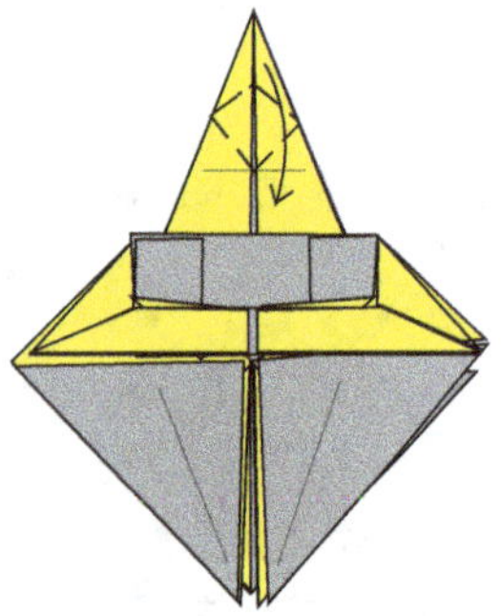

69. Squash the tip.

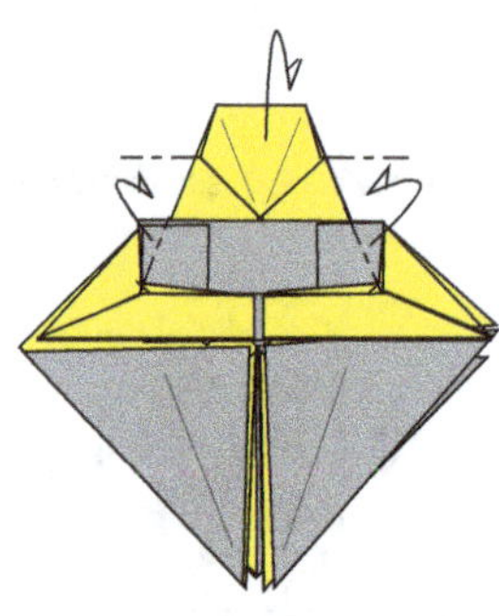

70. Swing the top back to reveal the colored triangle. Mountain fold the excess paper at the base ofthe tail.

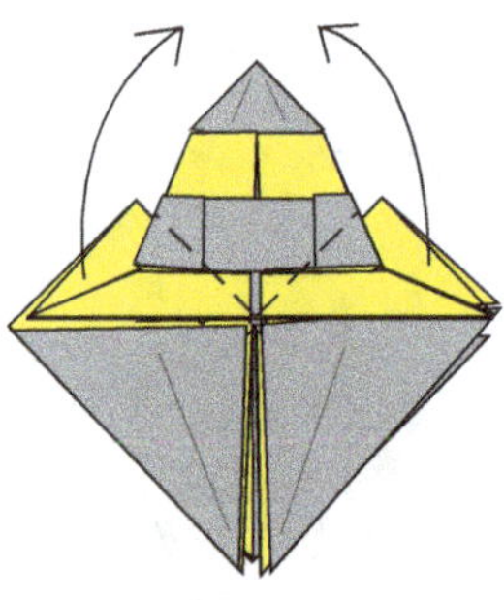

71. Valley fold upwards; do not crease sharply.

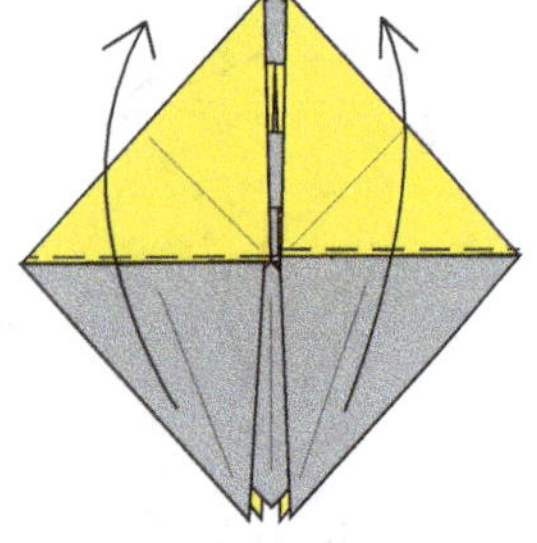

72. Swing the top flaps up.

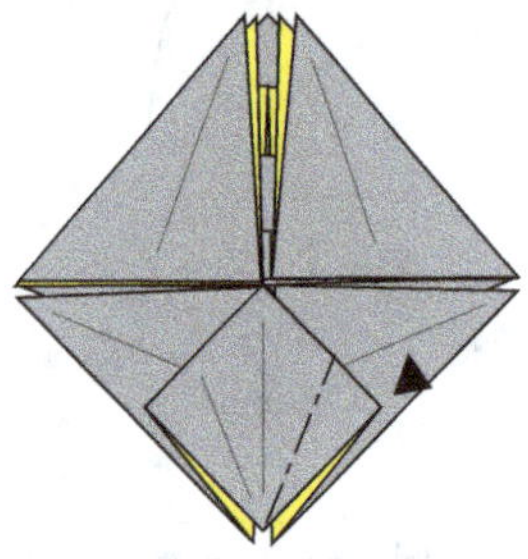

73. Reverse fold.

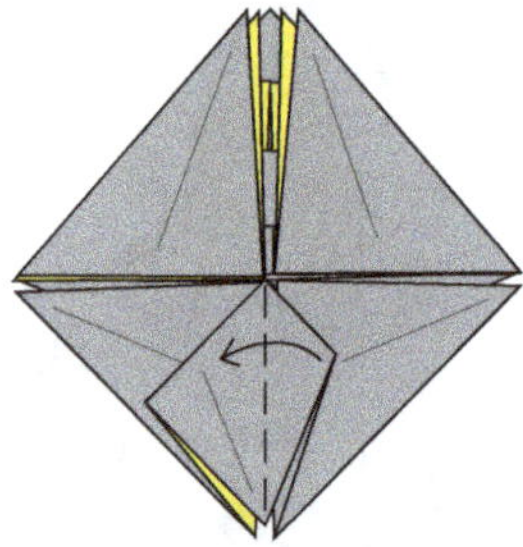

74. Swing over.

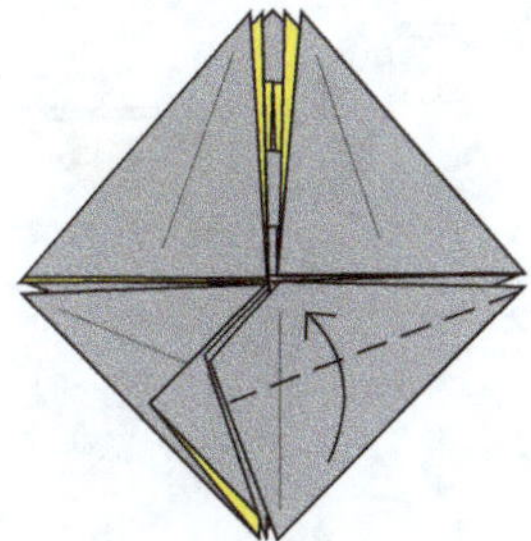

75. Valley fold up.

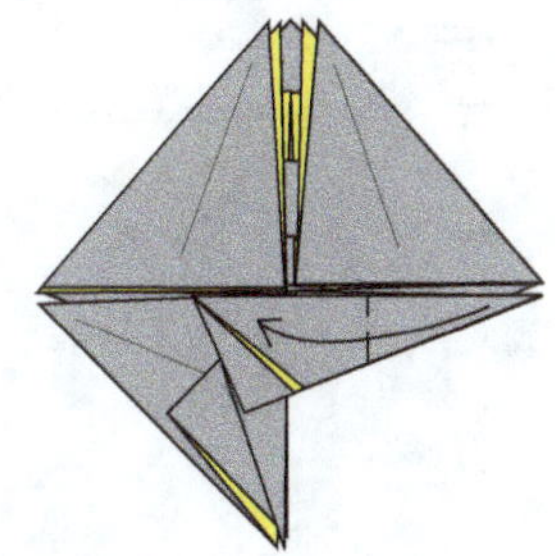

76. Swing over.

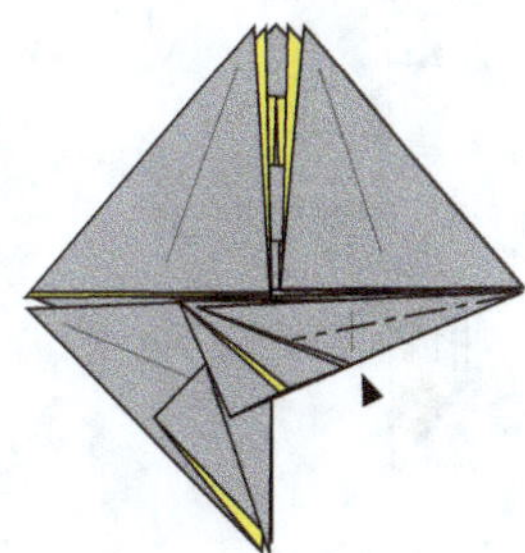

77. Sink.

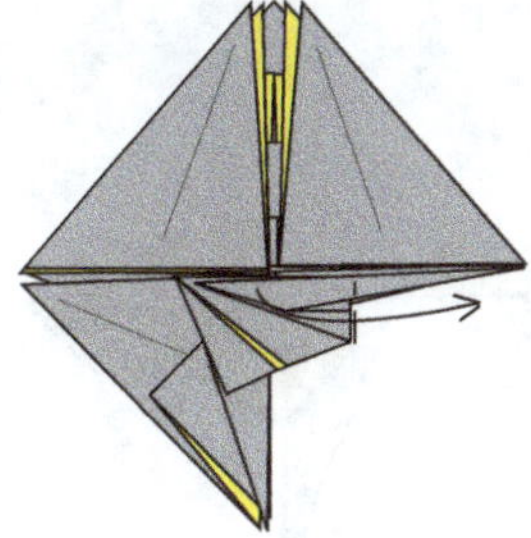

78. Swing back.

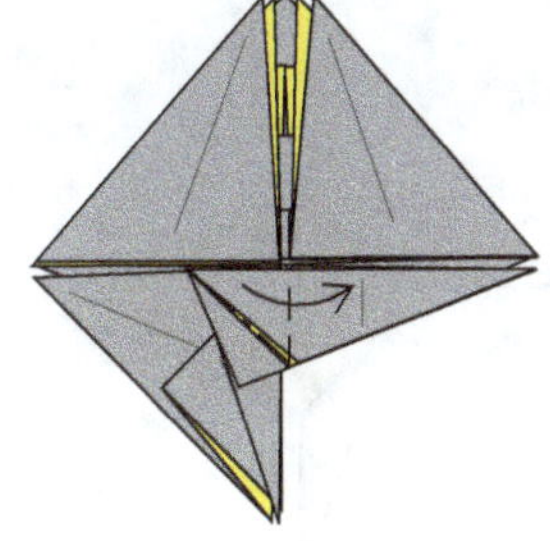

79. Swivel over.

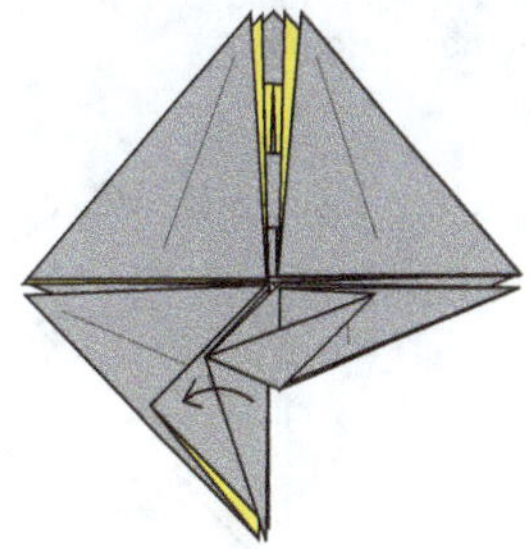

80. Pull out the top single layer.

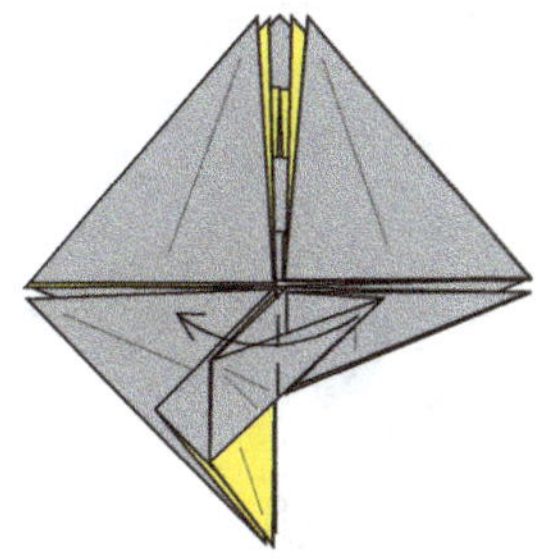

81. Swing over.

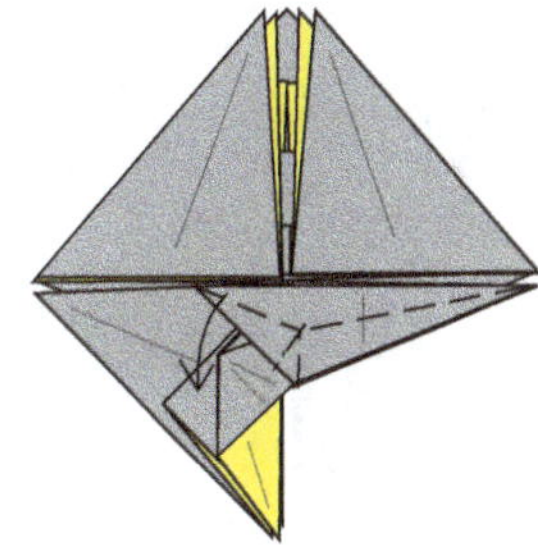

82. Rabbit ear.

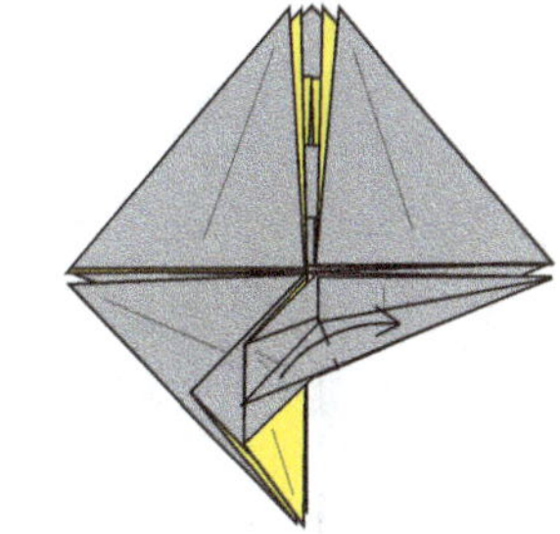

83. Swing over.

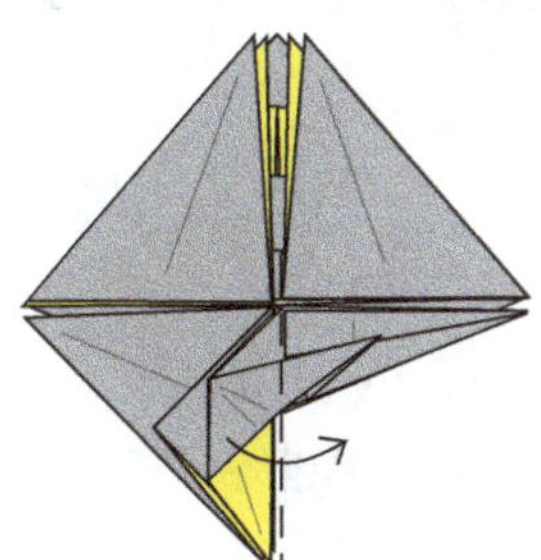

84. Swing over.

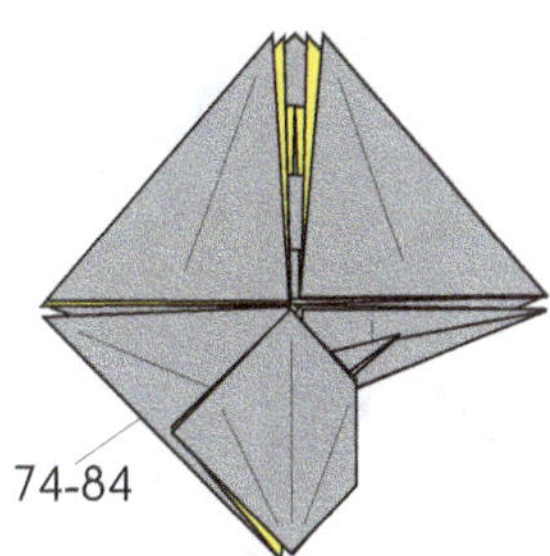

85. Repeat steps 74-84 in mirror image.

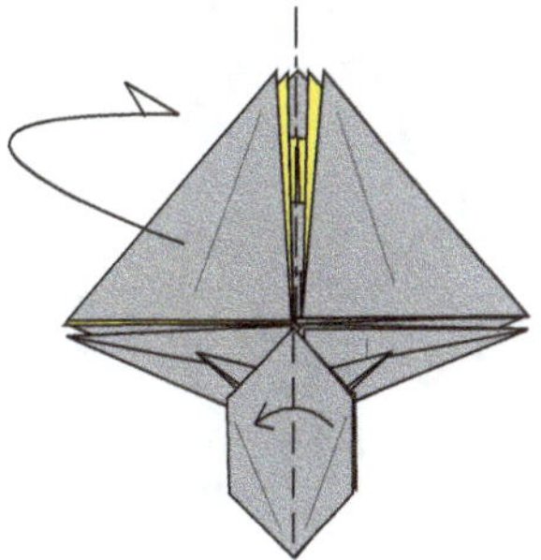

86. Lightly fold the model in half.

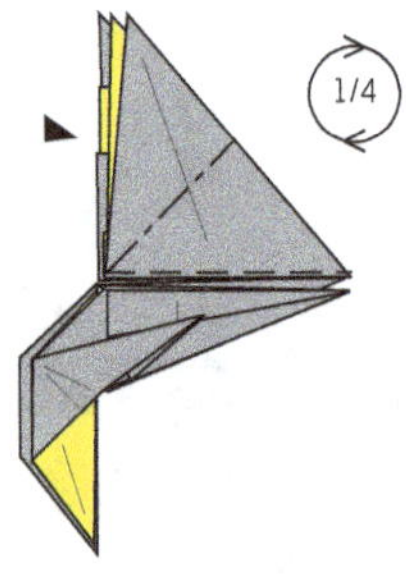

87. Squash fold flap, being sure to distribute the inner layers as evenly as possible. The tiny hidden flap should go towards the head. Rotate.

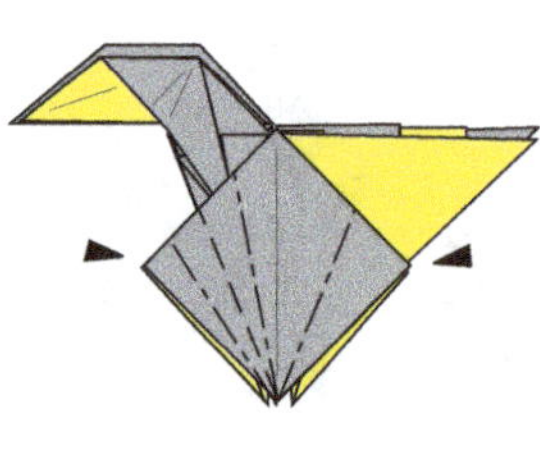

88. Reverse fold one half of the flap into angle quadsectors. Reverse fold the other half along the angle bisector.

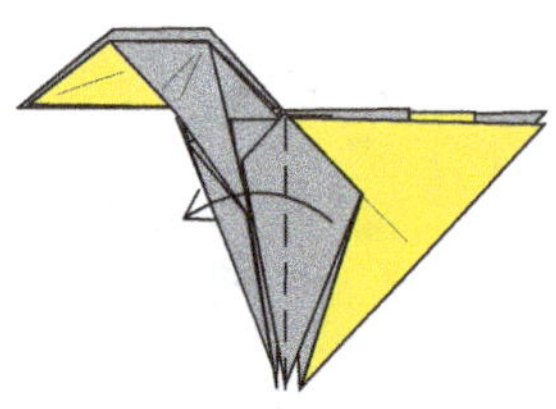

89. Swing over.

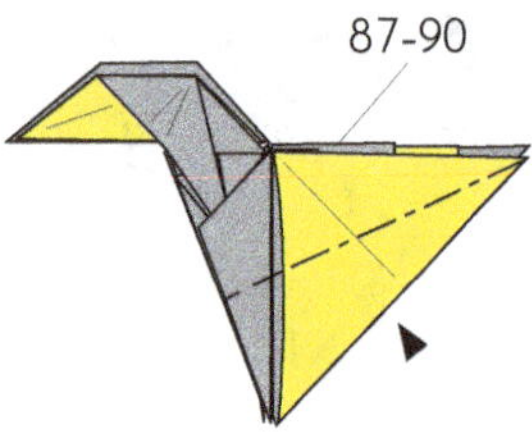

90. Squash fold. Repeat steps 87-90 behind.

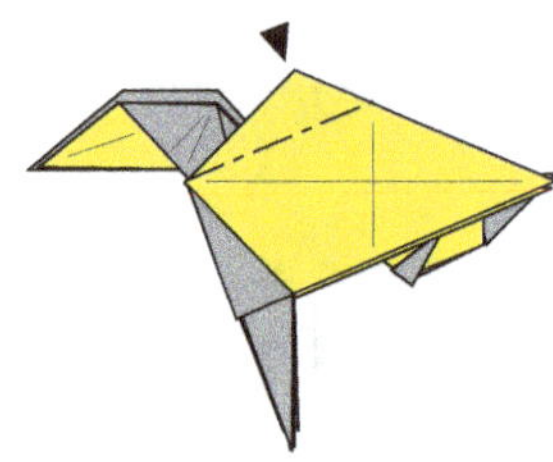

91. Reverse fold.

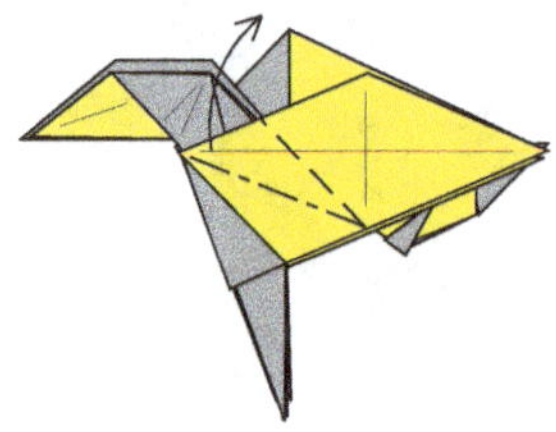

92. Swivel up. Make the valley fold as light as possible.

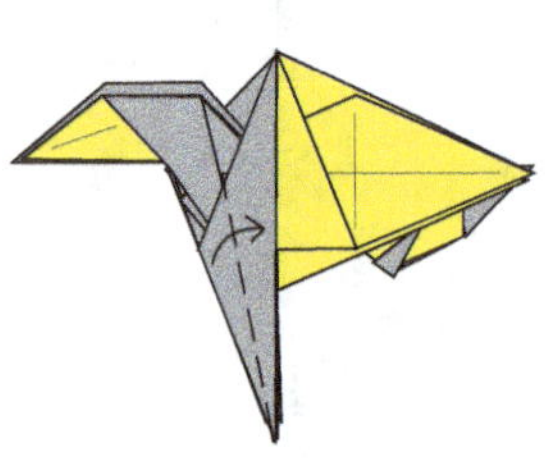

93. Valley fold.

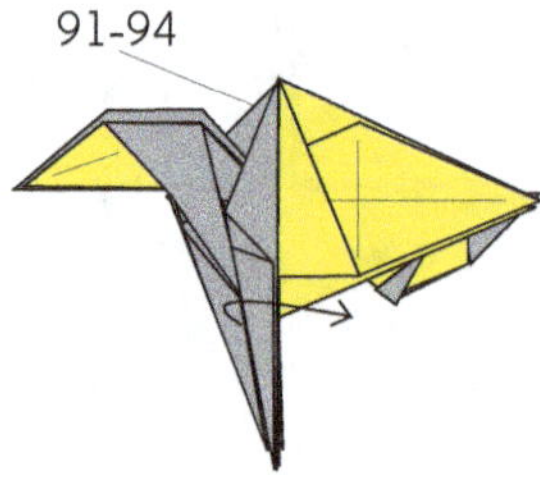

94. Swing over two flaps. Repeat steps 91-94 behind.

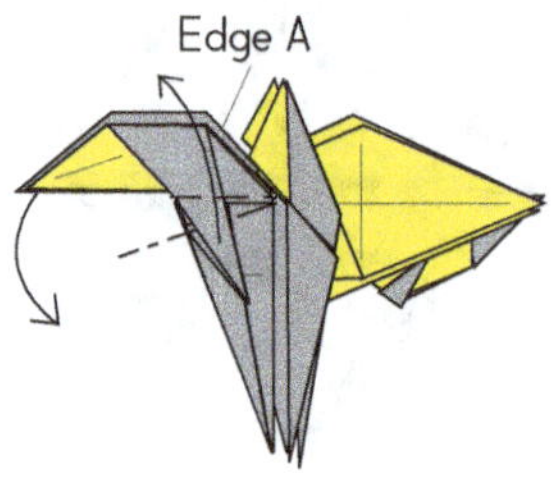

95. Crimp the head into the body, so that edge A lies straight. Alow the antennae to swing up.

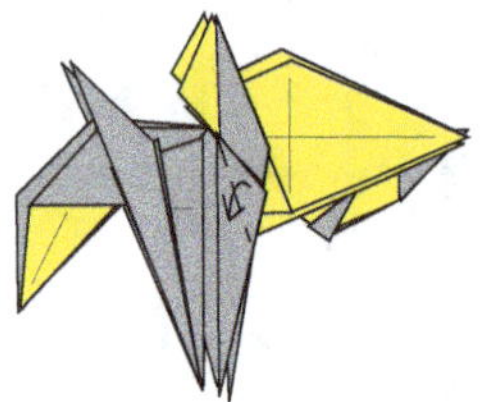

96. Valley fold.

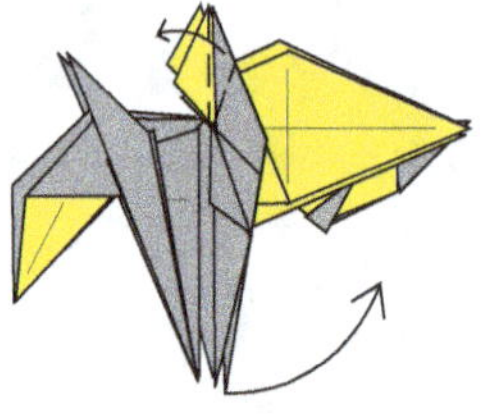

97. Pull out the back leg while swiveling at the top.

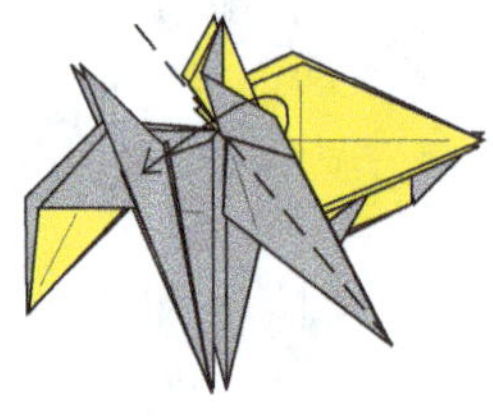

98. Valley fold down.

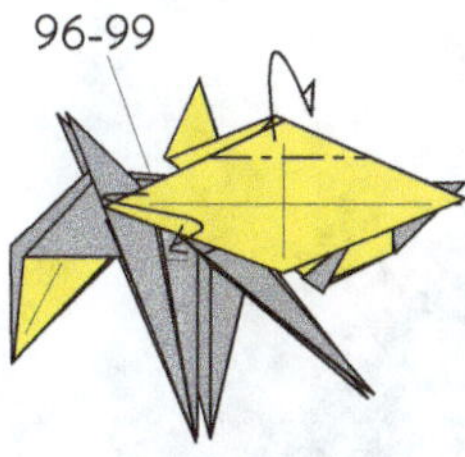

96-99

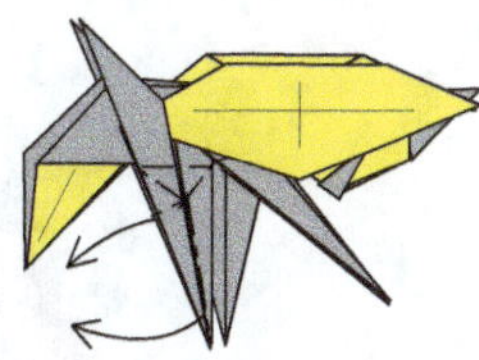

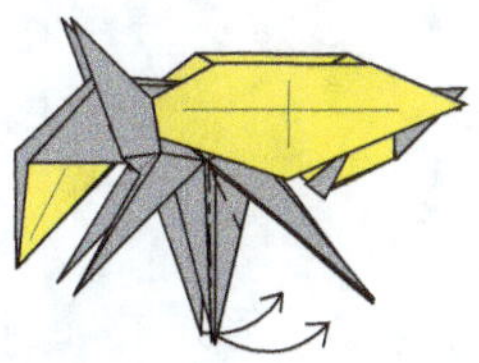

99. Tuck the tip of the wing into the pocket. Shape the wing. Repeat steps 96-99 behind.

100. Rabbit ear the front legs. Due to the thickness, they will stick out slightly.

101. Crimp the middle legs in half.

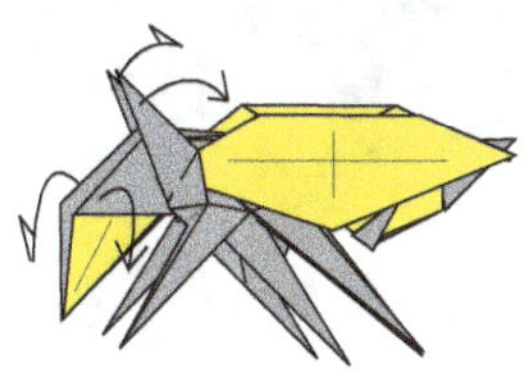

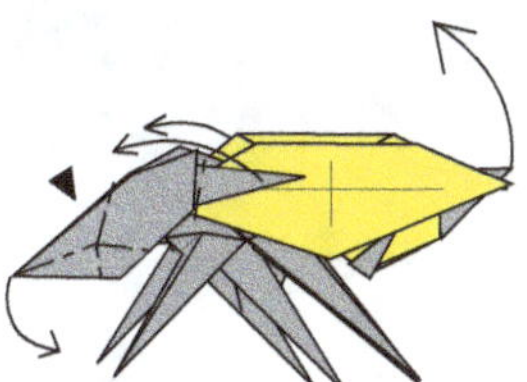

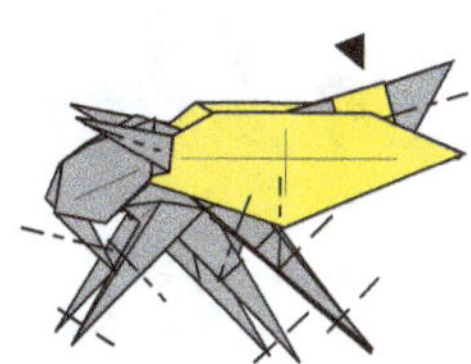

102. Pull the antennae back and outside reverse fold the head around them.

103. Curl the antennae around the head. Double rabbit ear the head. Pull tail upwards.

104. Crimp the legs. Curl the antennae and the tip of the head. Round out the abdomen, and curl the wings around it.

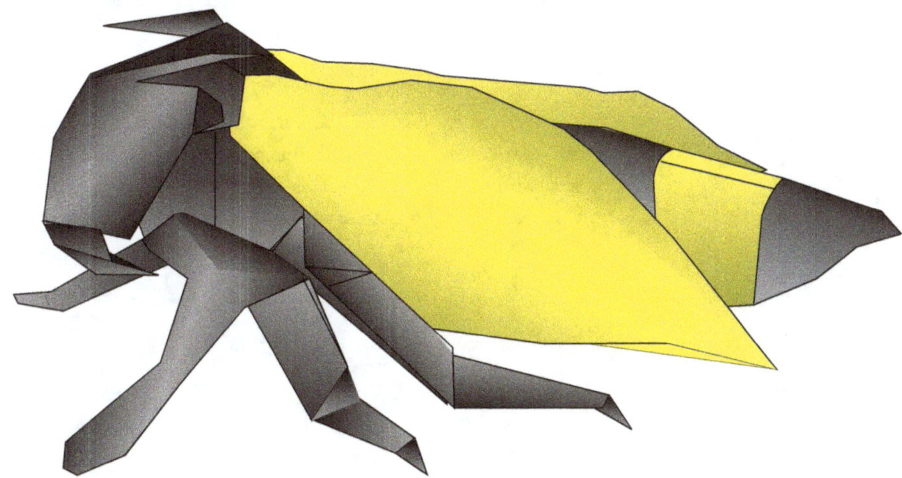

105. Completed *Bee*.

Ladybug

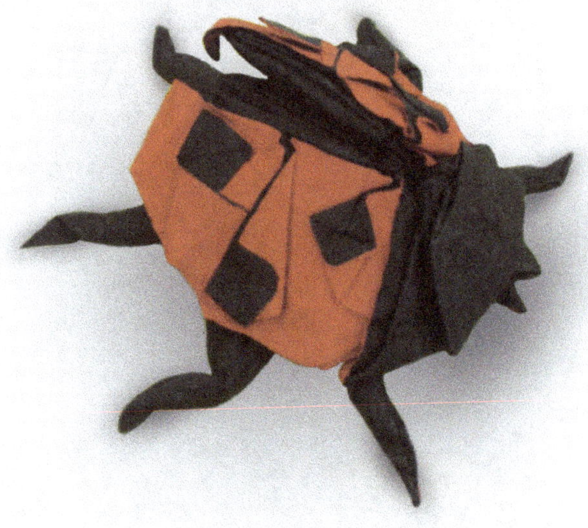

About

The ladybug is one of the few insects I actually like to look at in life (origami insects are less creepy to me). I was very particular about getting a specific pattern of dots on the wings, and to maintain maximum flexibility I treated each spot as an actual appendage. Luckily, it did not take too much effort to have a convex body, as a few crimps at the head section did the trick. Given the subject's near universal appeal (some regard its presence as good luck), it seemed like the perfect piece to showcase on this book's cover.

Tips

Step ninety involves coaxing various appendages into existence almost simultaneously. To cope with this complexity, locate the tips of the flaps first, and then extend the folds from those tips. It should become more apparent how the inner section should flatten.

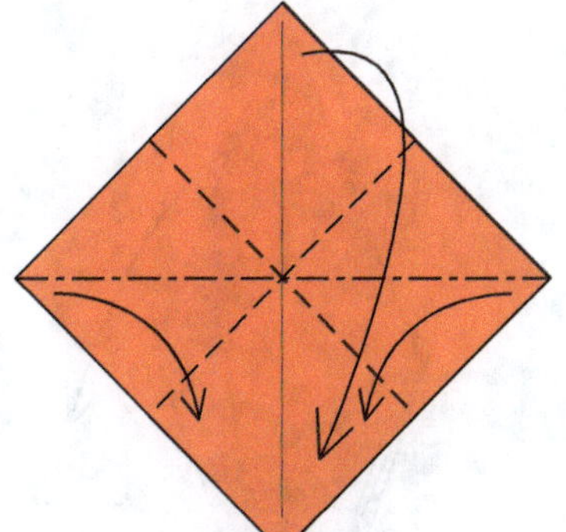

1. Form a preliminary base.

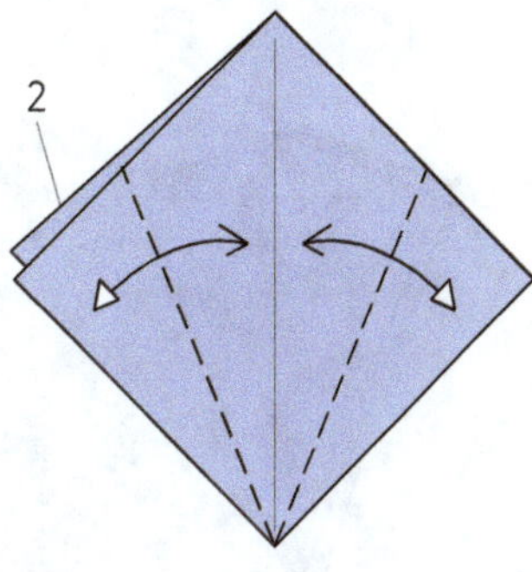

2. Precrease along the angle bisectors. Repeat behind.

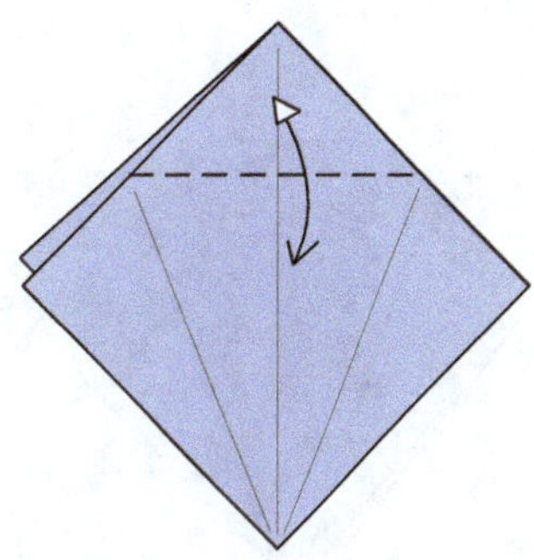

3. Precrease again.

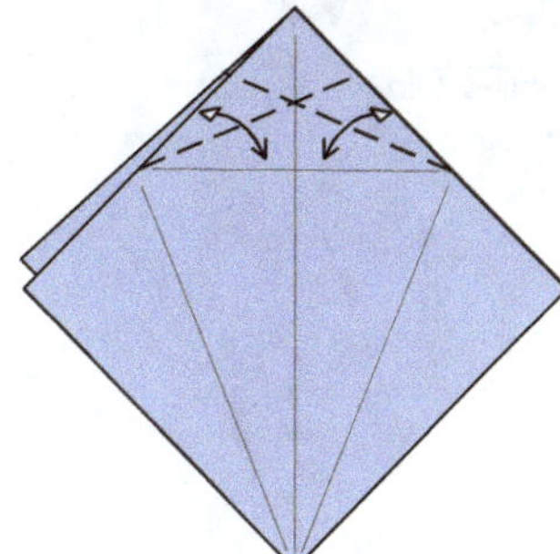

4. Precrease along the angle bisectors.

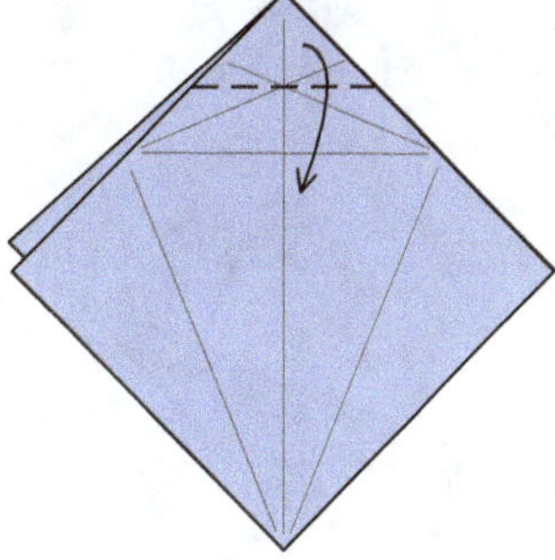

5. Valley through the intersection of creases.

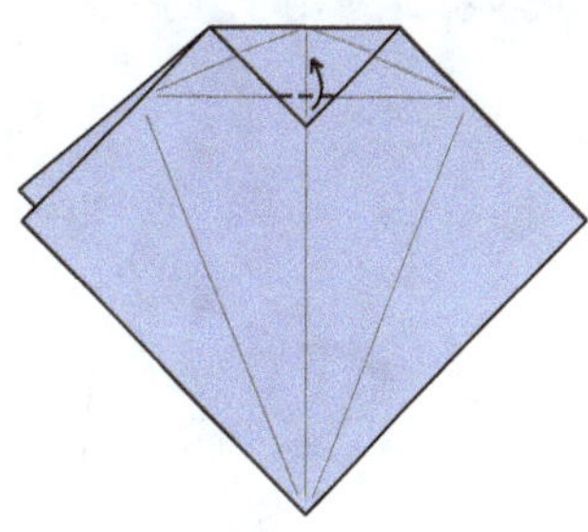

6. Valley up to align with crease below.

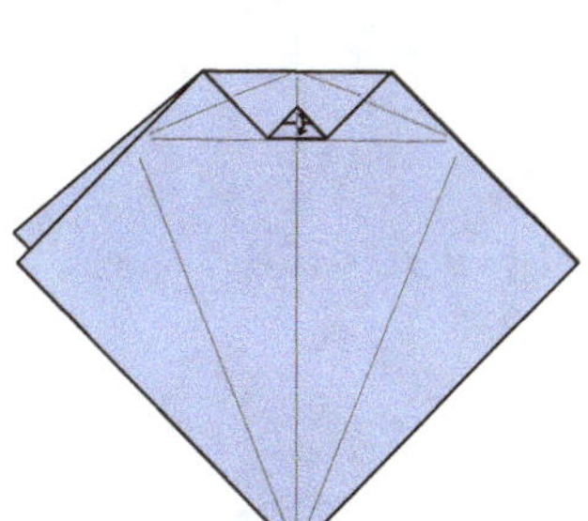

7. Valley down.

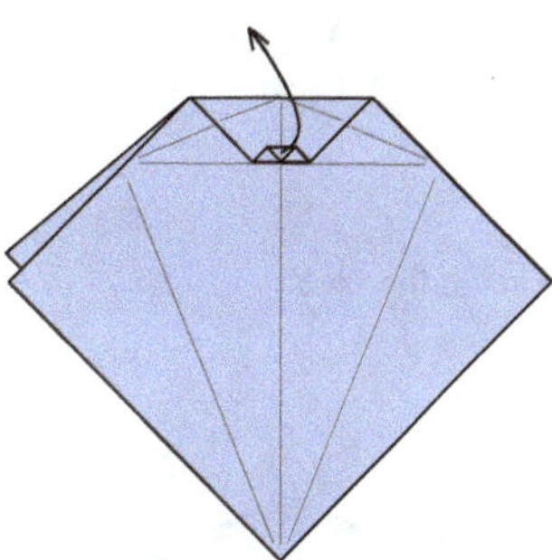

8. Unfold the pleat.

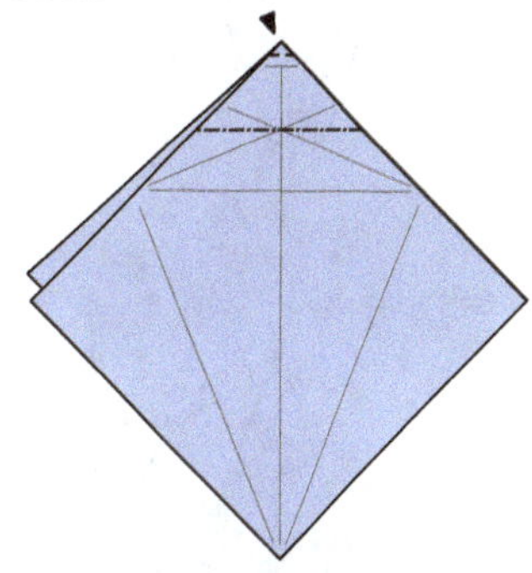

9. Sink down, and then up again.

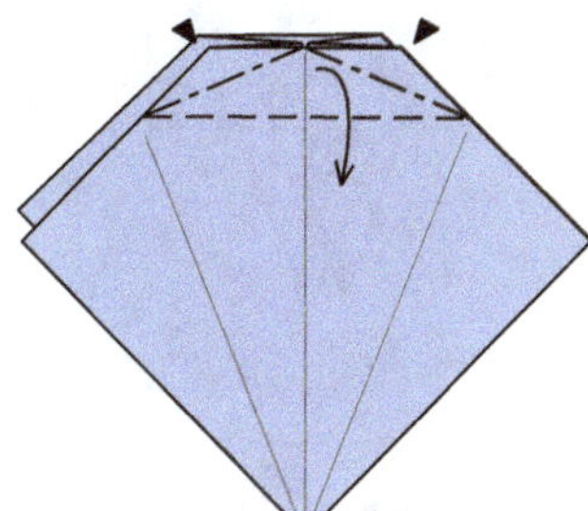

10. Valley down, spread squashing the sides.

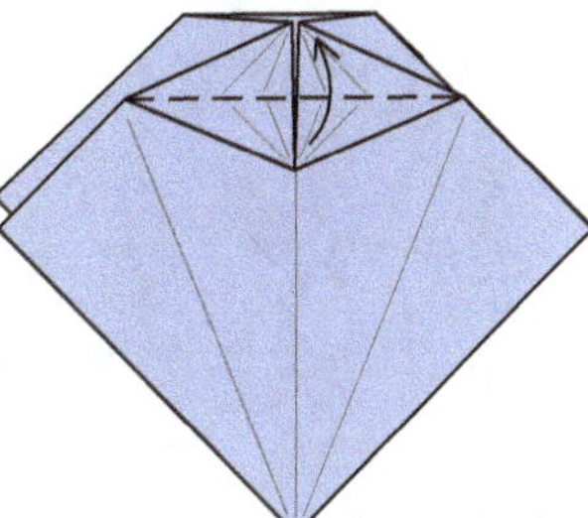

11. Valley up again.

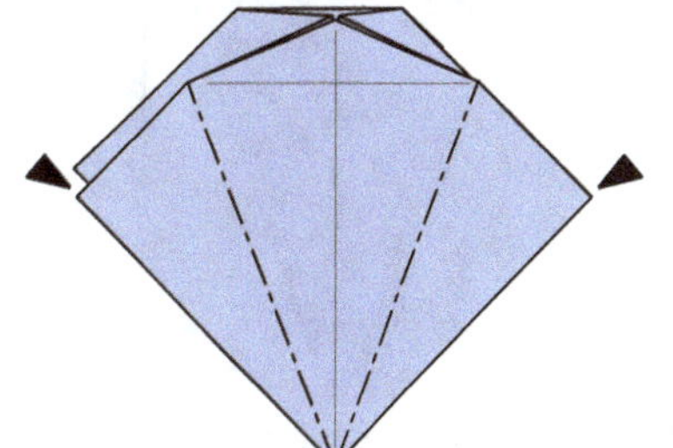

12. Reverse fold the sides.

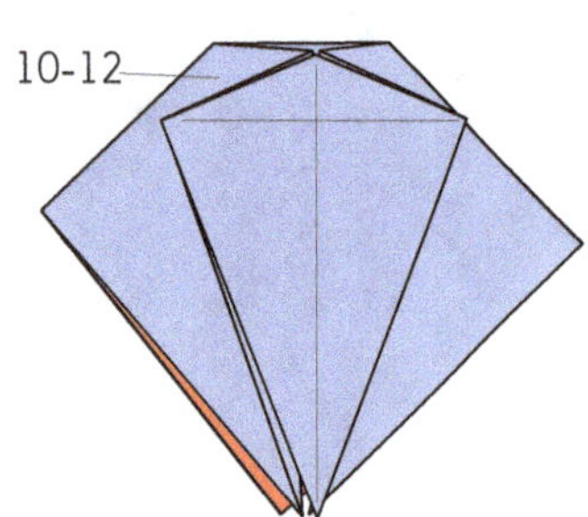

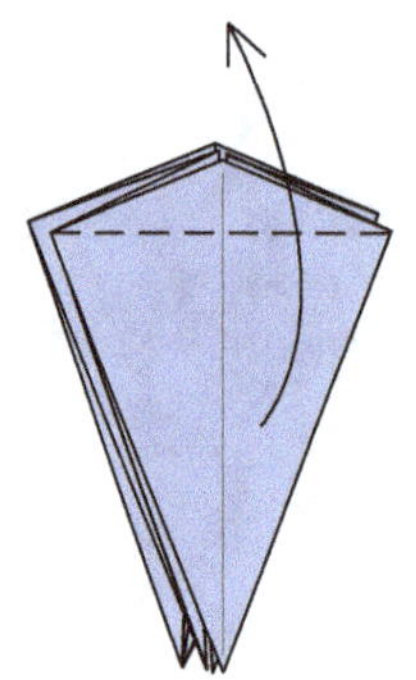

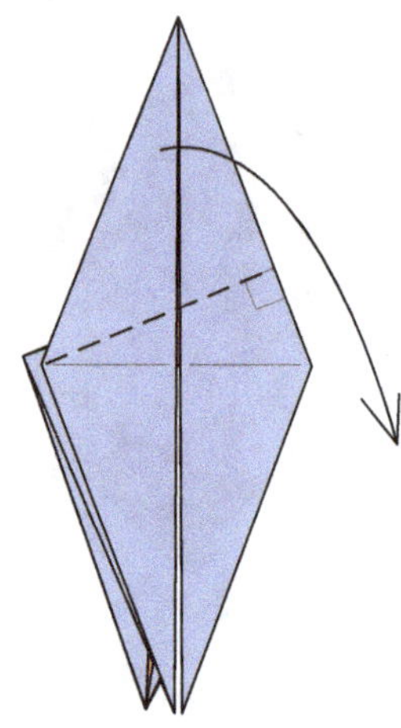

13. Repeat steps 10-12 behind.

14. Valley up the top flap.

15. Valley fold.

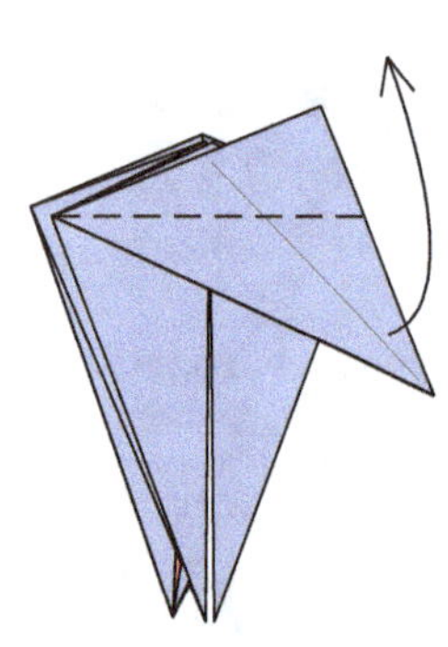

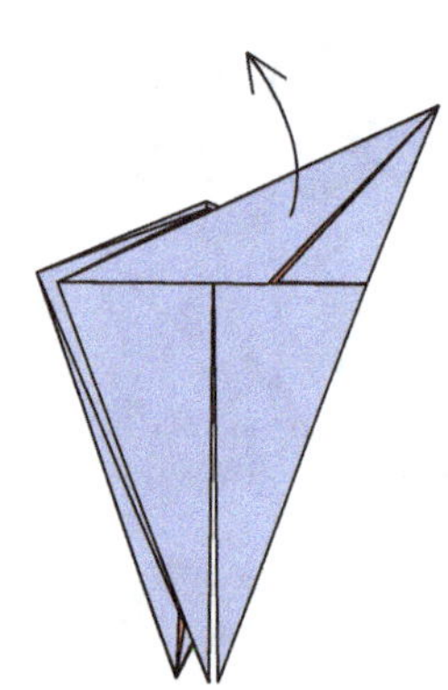

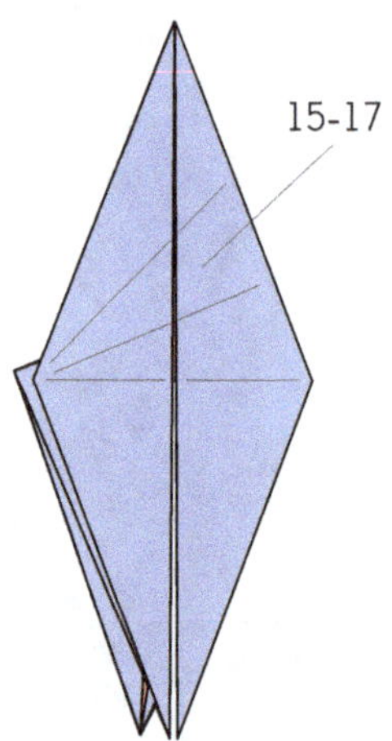

16. Valley up.

17. Unfold the pleat.

18. Repeat steps 15-17 in mirror image.

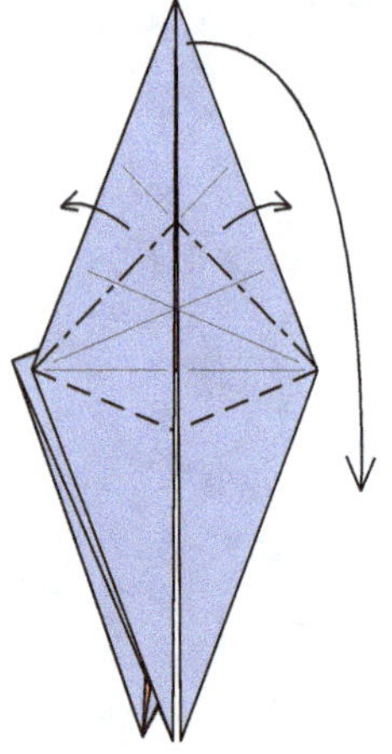

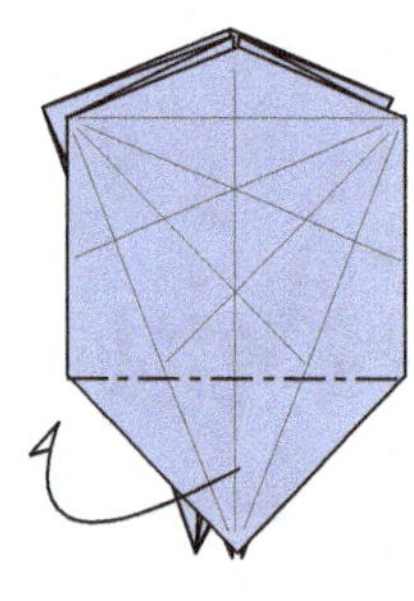

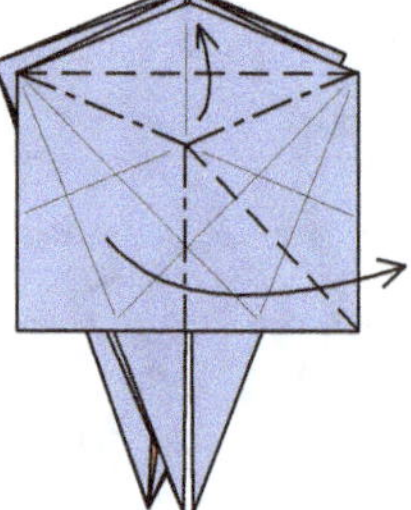

19. Spread apart the sides, squashing the top flap down.

20. Mountain fold.

21. Rabbit ear the top flap.

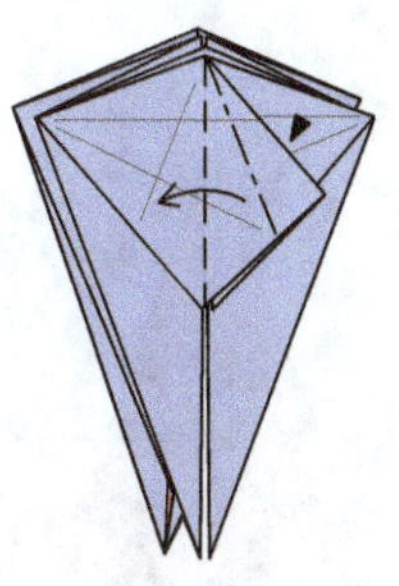

22. Squash the center flap.

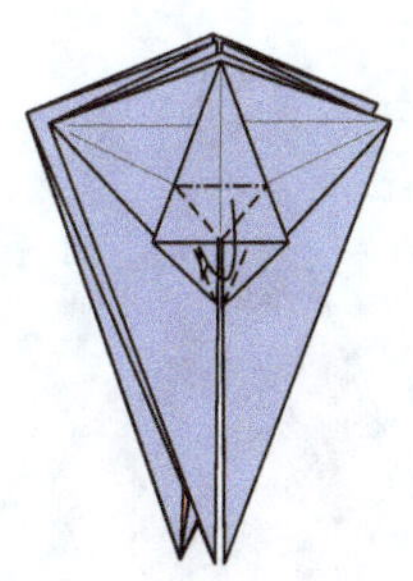

23. Petal fold under.

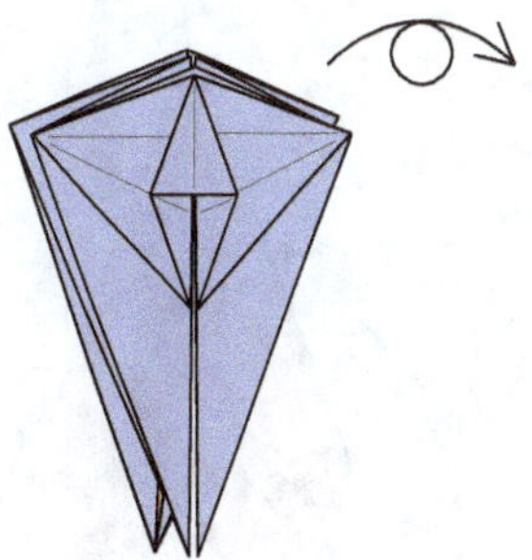

24. Turn over.

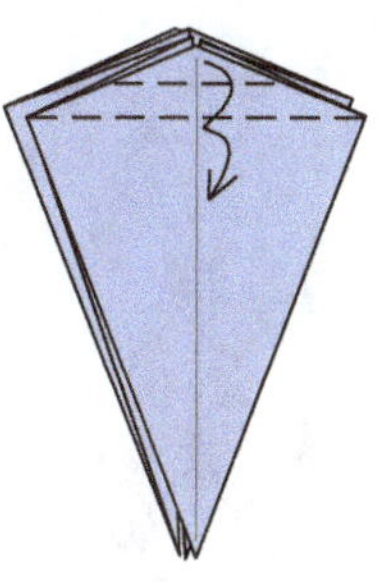

25. Valley the top flap over and over.

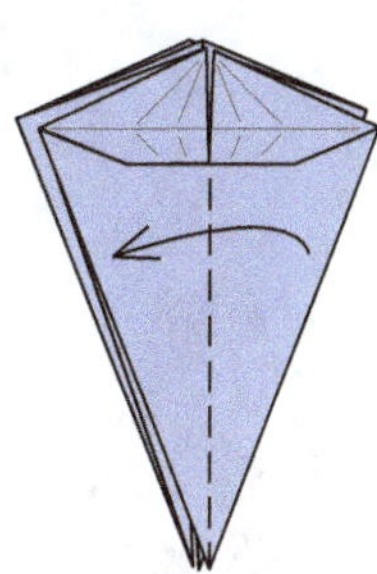

26. Swing over one flap.

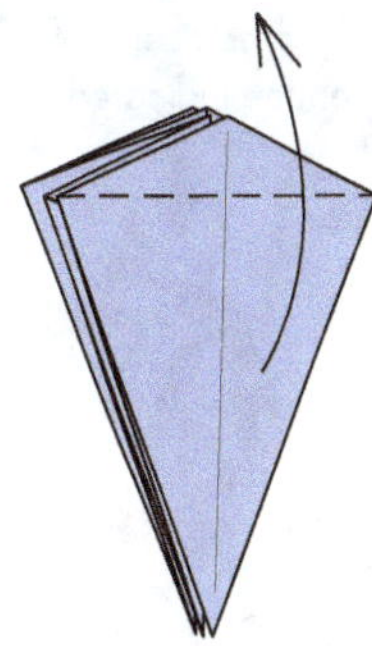

27. Valley up.

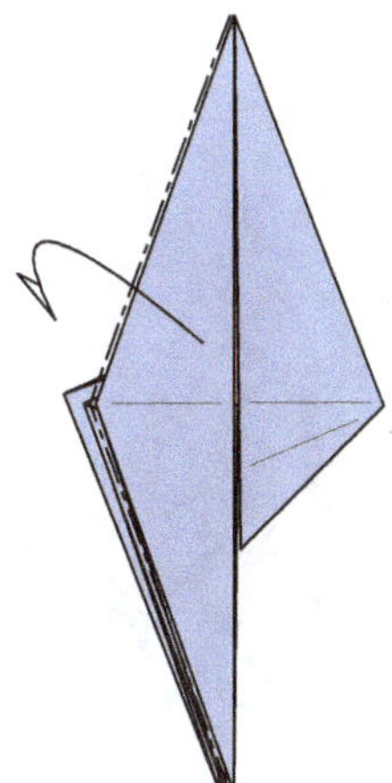

28. Wrap around one layer.

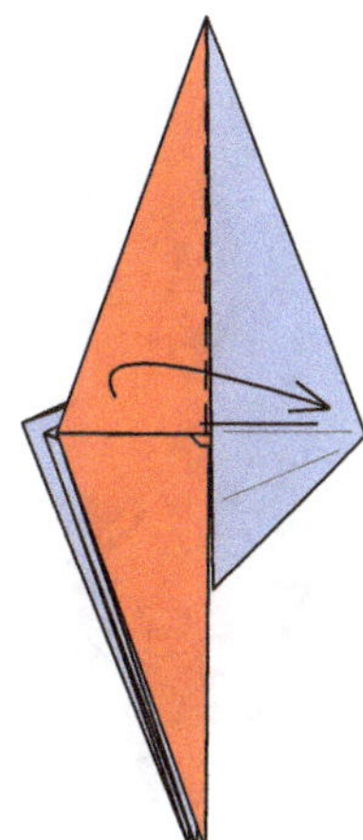

29. Swing the flap back.

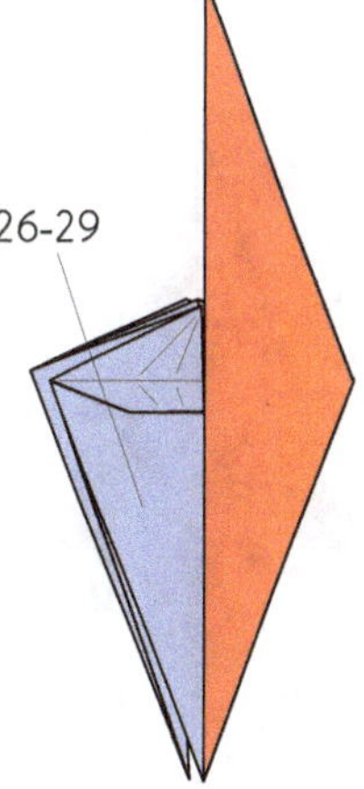

30. Repeat steps 26-29 in mirror image.

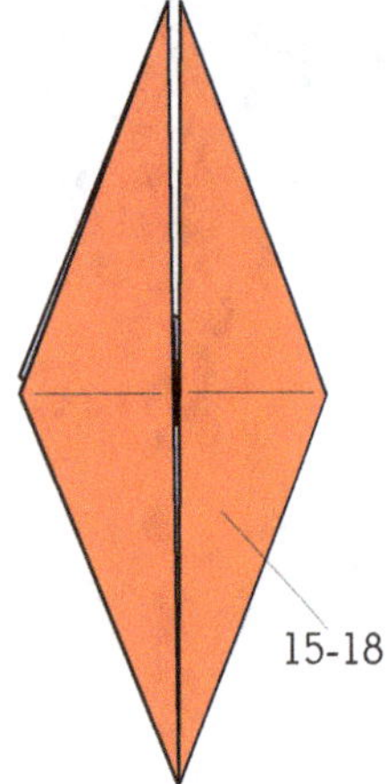

31. Repeat the precreasing of steps 15-18 on the indicated flap.

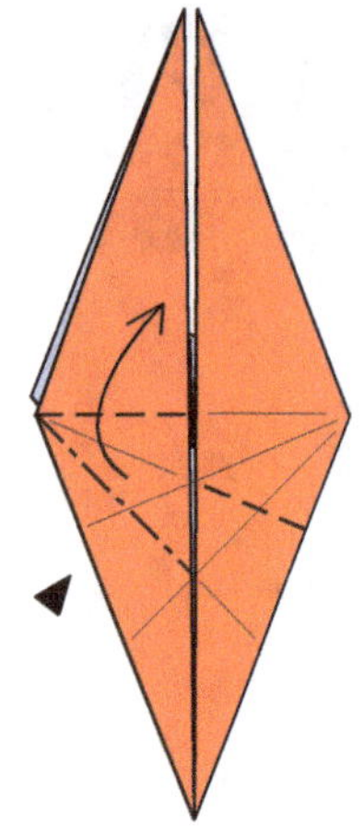

32. Squash fold.

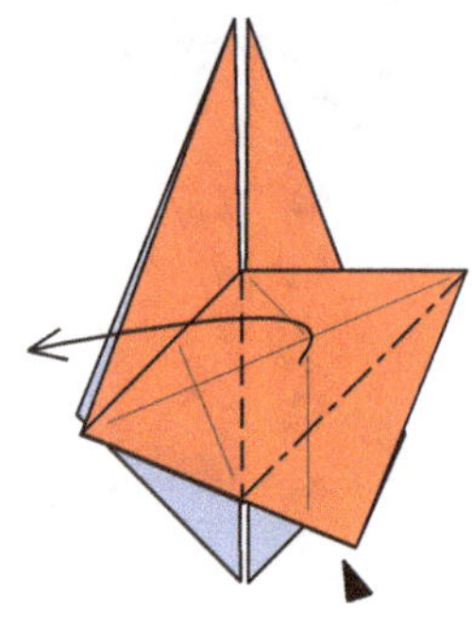

33. Squash again.

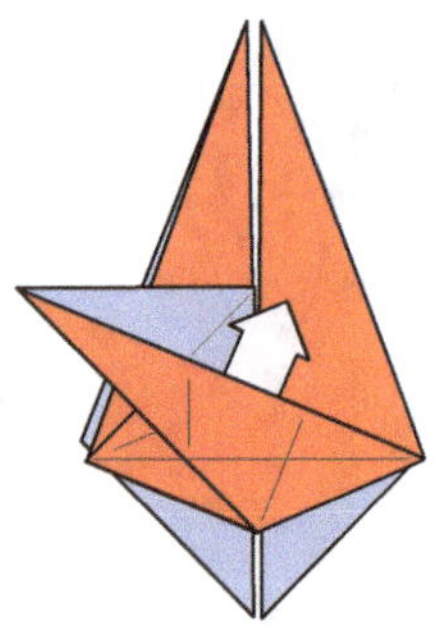

34. Pull out a single layer.

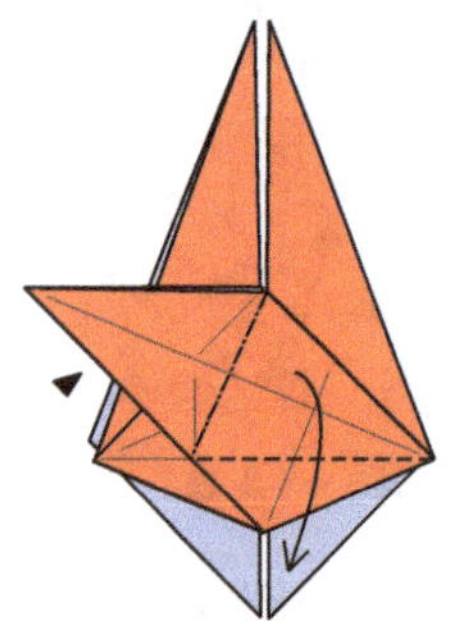

35. Squash fold.

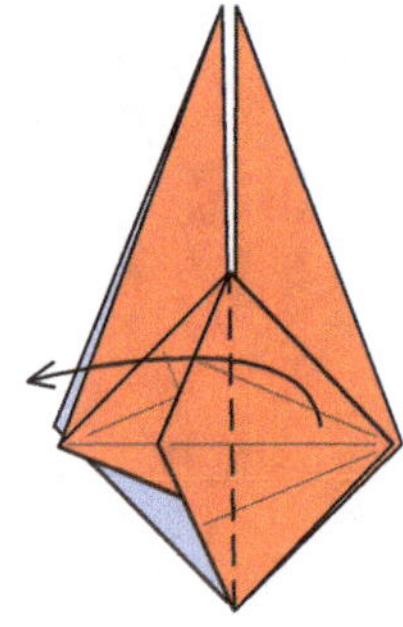

36. Valley over.

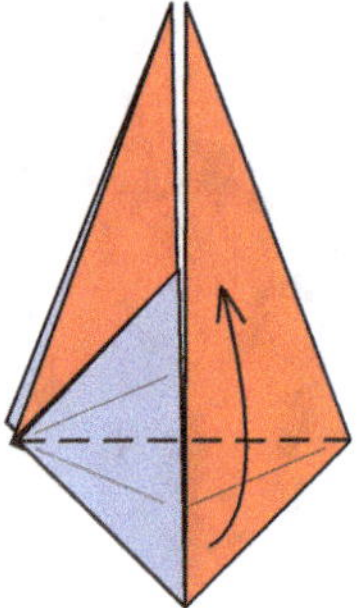

37. Valley up one flap.

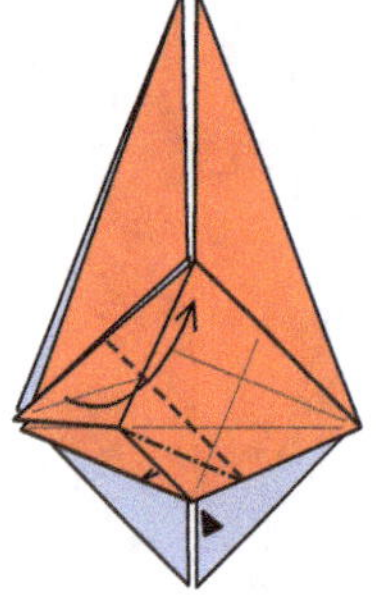

38. Valley up the side flap, allowing a spread squash to form at the bottom.

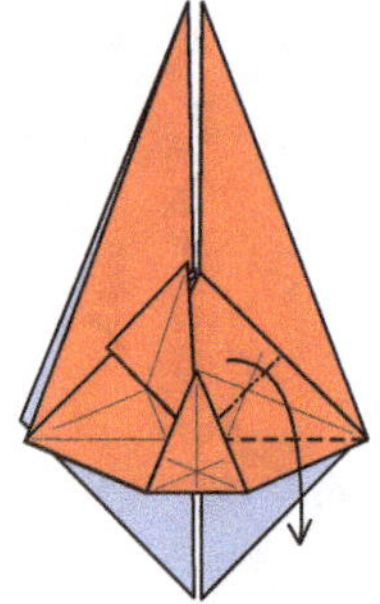

39. Swivel the side down.

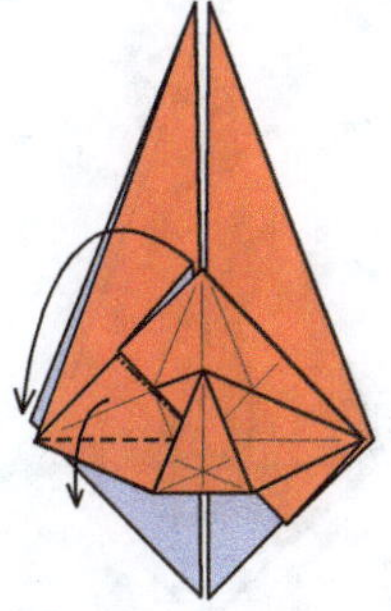

40. Pull the flap through to match the other side.

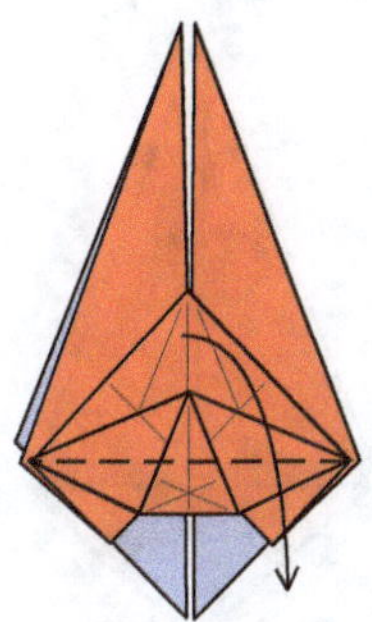

41. Valley down.

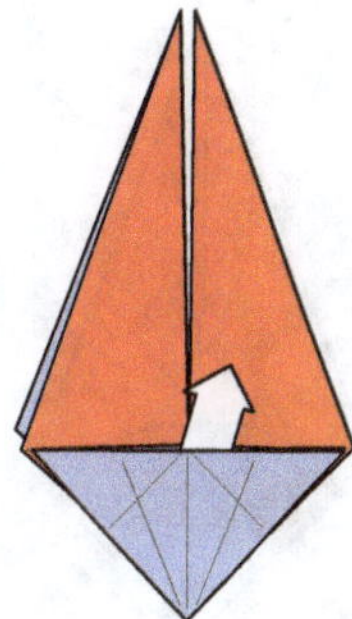

42. Unsink.

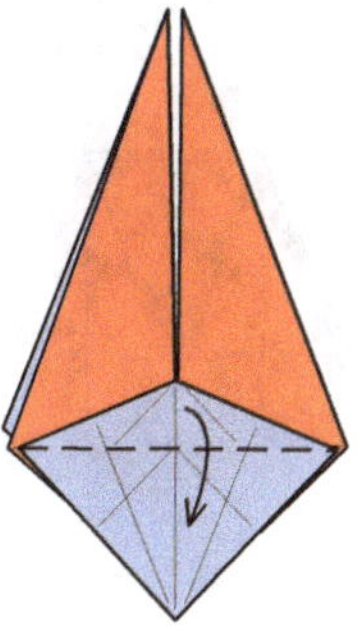

43. Valley down.

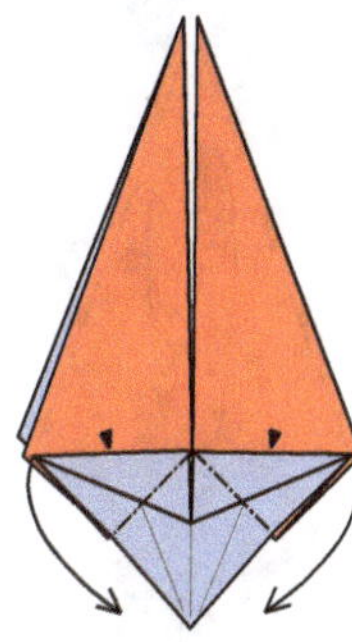

44. Reverse fold the side flaps down.

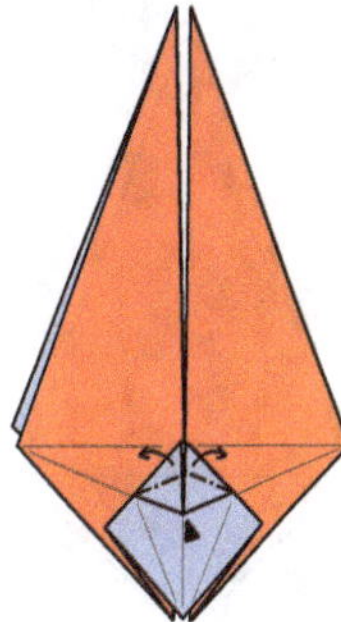

45. Spread squash by spreading apart the seam at the center.

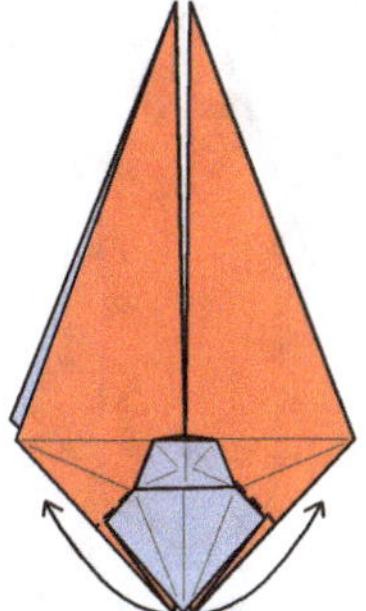

46. Reverse fold the flaps back up.

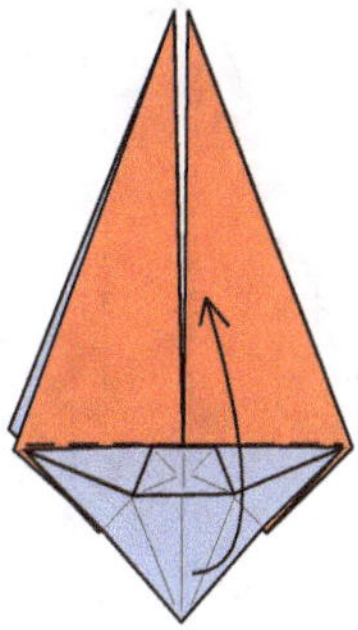

47. Valley back up.

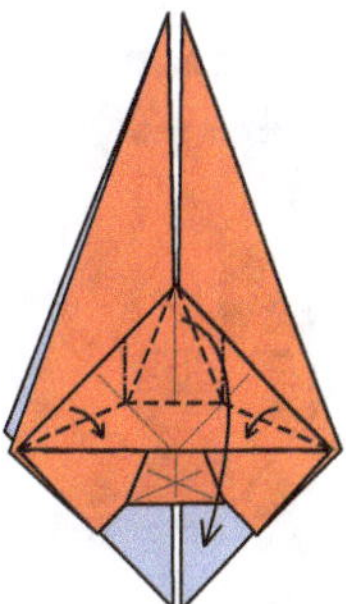

48. Valley down, while swiveling in the sides.

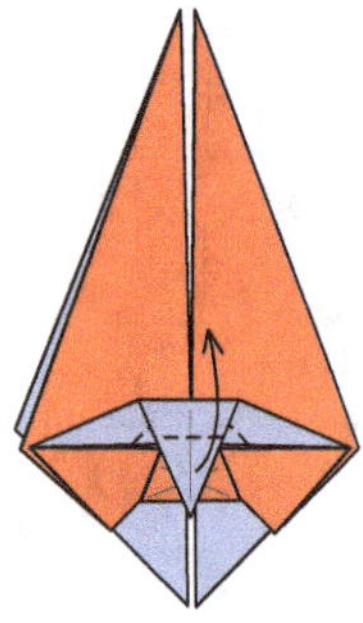

49. Valley up, allowing the sides to swivel outwards.

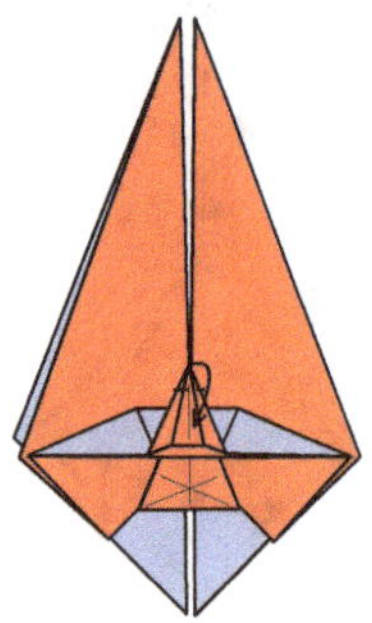

50. Valley the tip down.

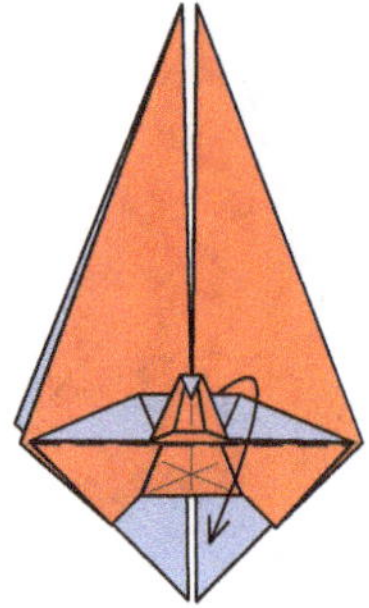

51. Swing two flaps down.

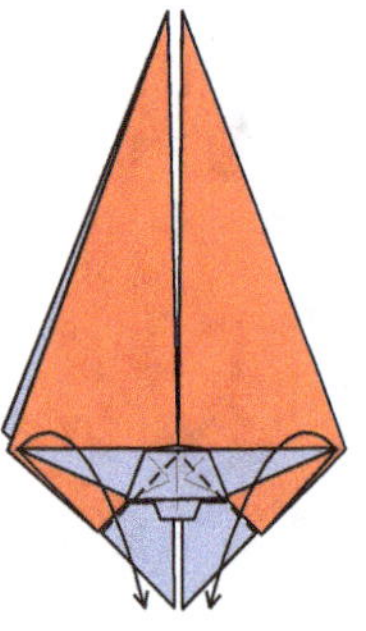

52. Valley the side flaps down.

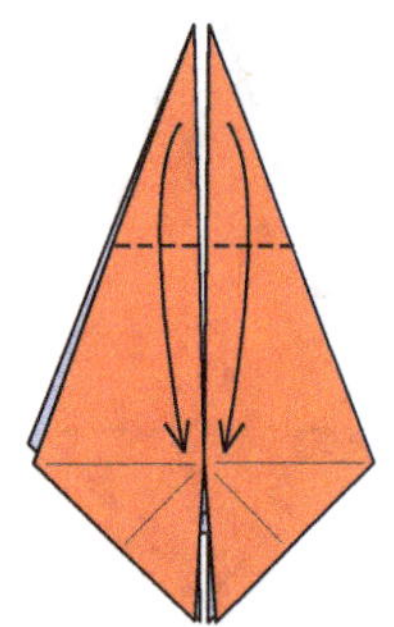

53. Valley the two flaps down.

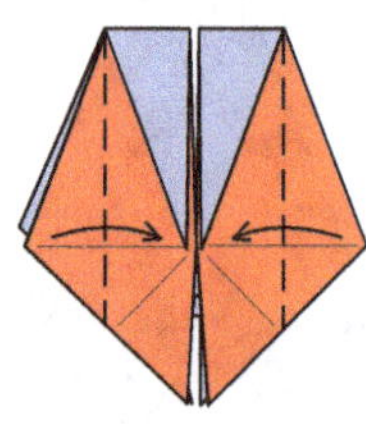

54. Valley the top flaps to the center.

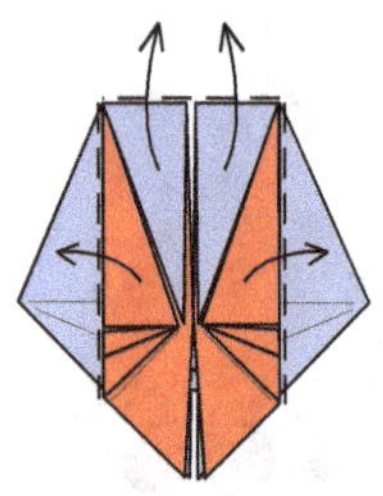

55. Unfold.

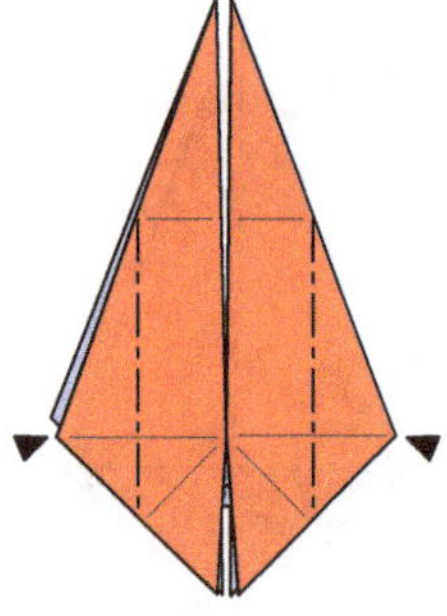

56. Open sink the sides (sinking triangularly).

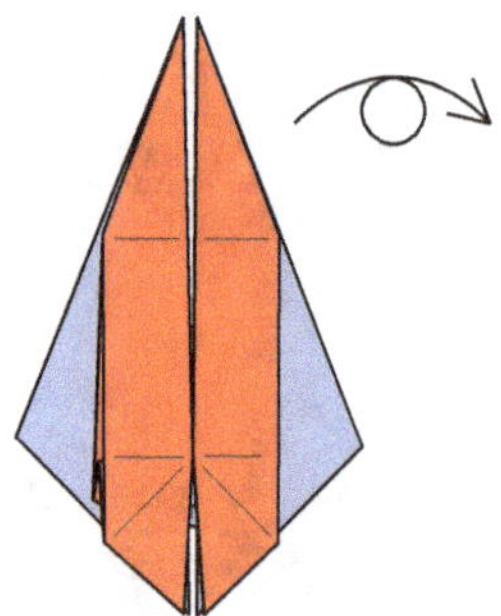

57. Turn over.

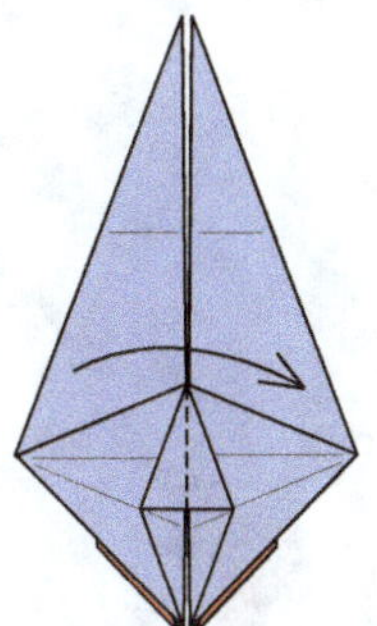

58. Swing over one flap.

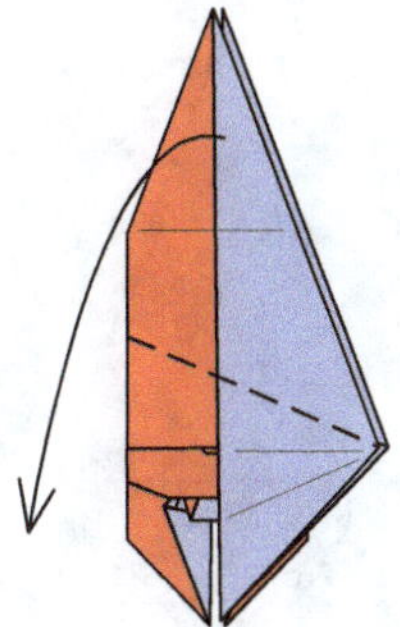

59. Valley down as far as possible.

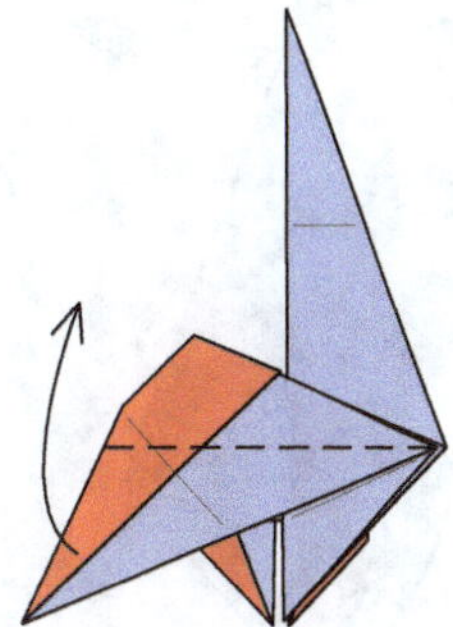

60. Valley up.

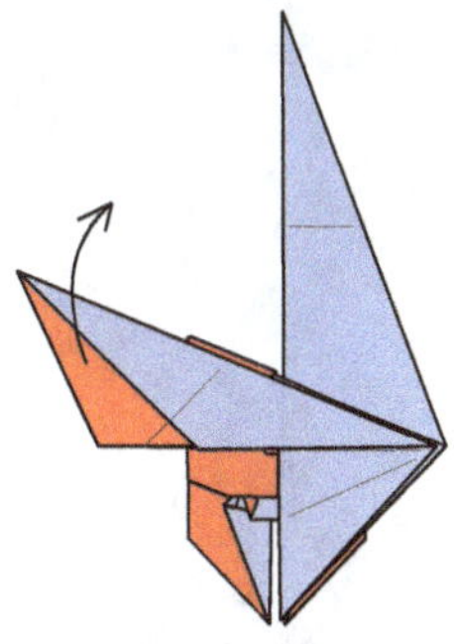

61. Unfold the pleat.

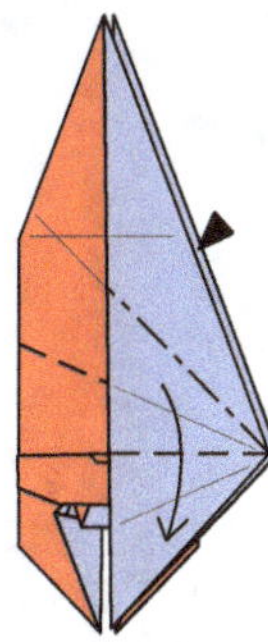

62. Squash fold.

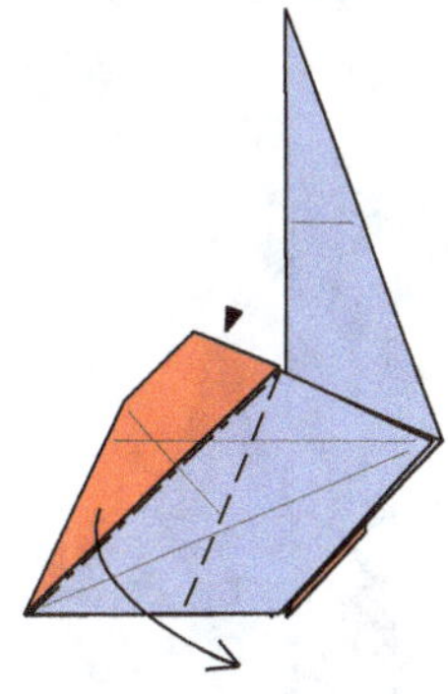

63. Swivel over the white edge to lie along the center.

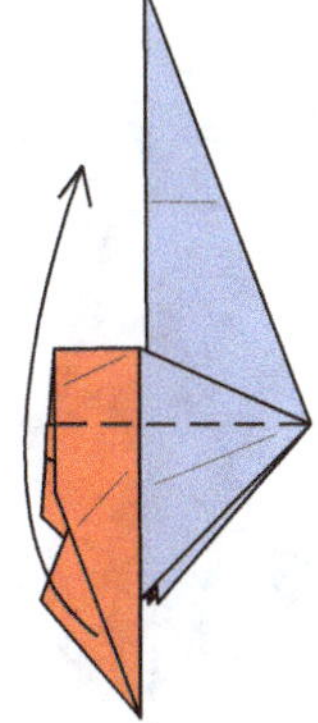

64. Valley up.

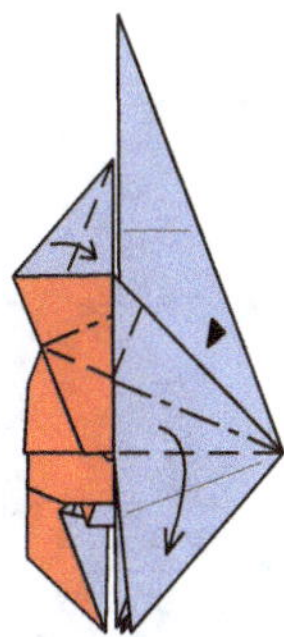

65. Form a squash at the right, allowing a squash at the left to form.

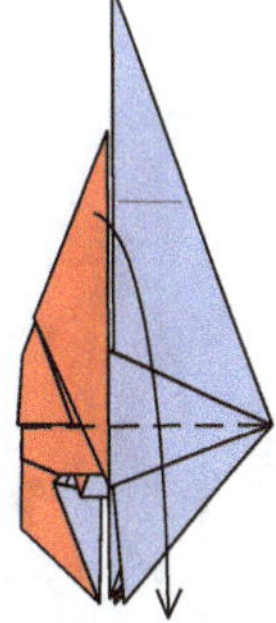

66. Swing back down.

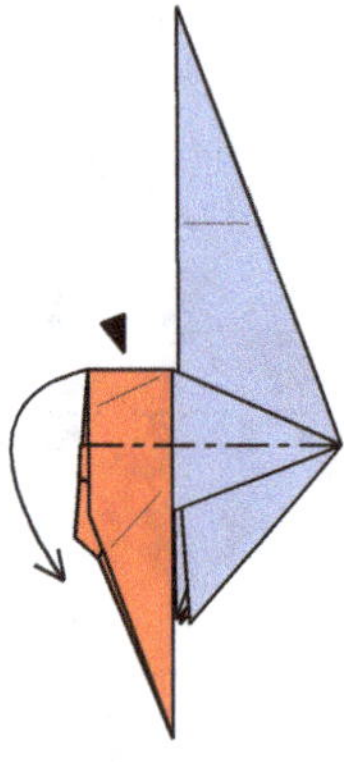

67. Sink (closed reverse fold) the flap.

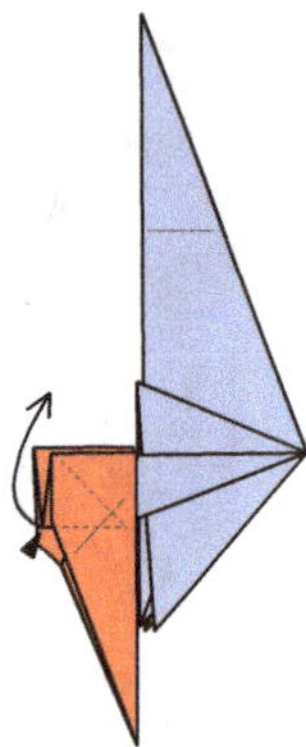

68. Reverse fold the hidden flap.

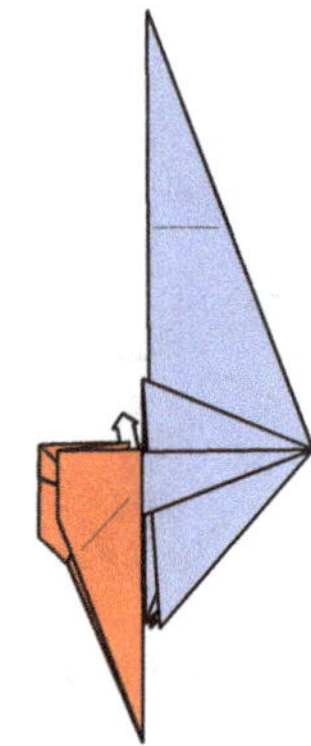

69. Unsink a single layer.

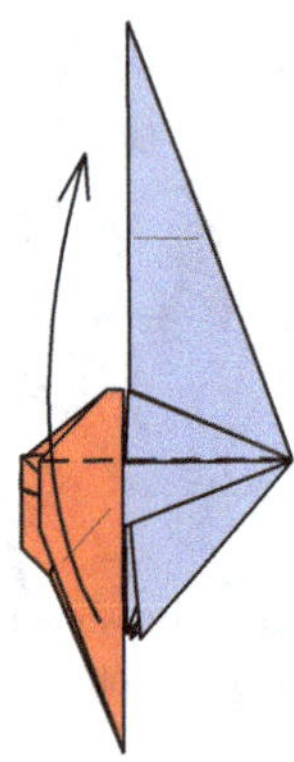

70. Swing up.

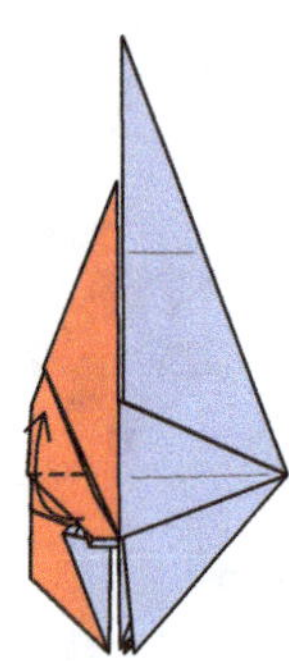

71. Valley the (partially hidden) thick flap up.

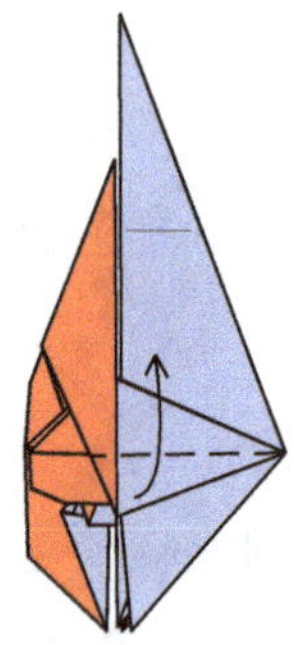

72. Valley the flap up.

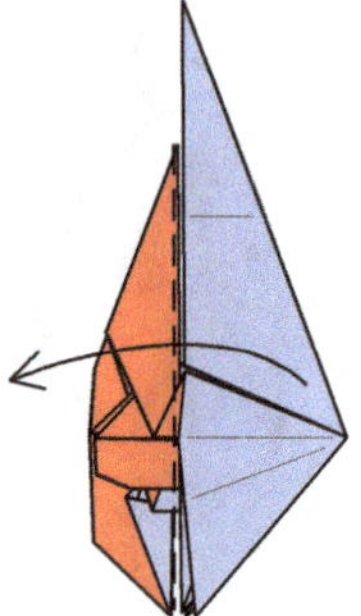

73. Swing over.

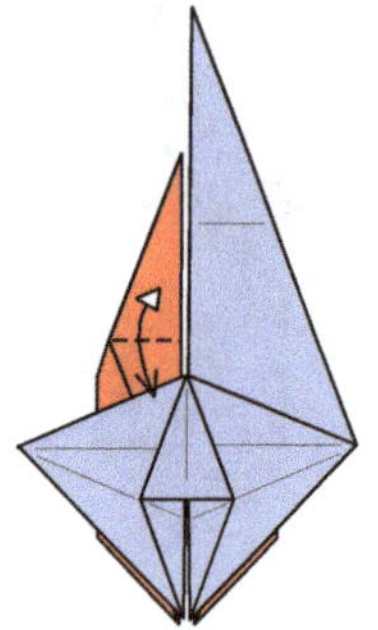

74. Precrease.

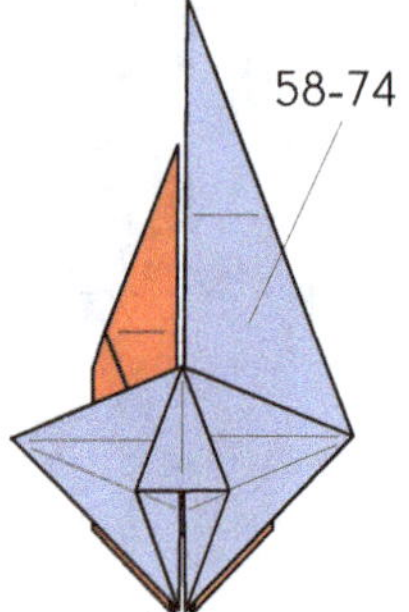

75. Repeat steps 58-74 in mirror image.

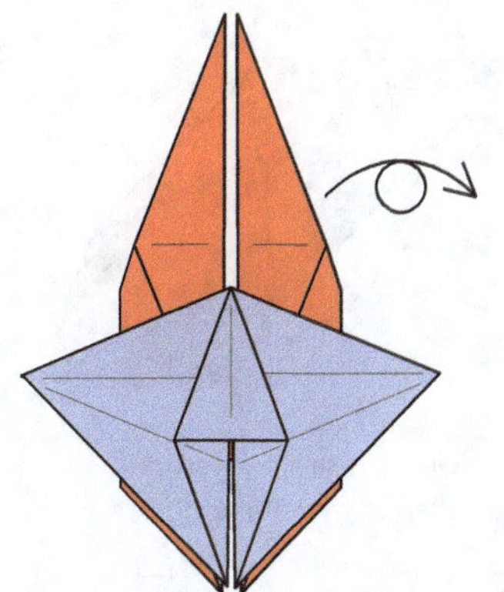

76. Turn over.

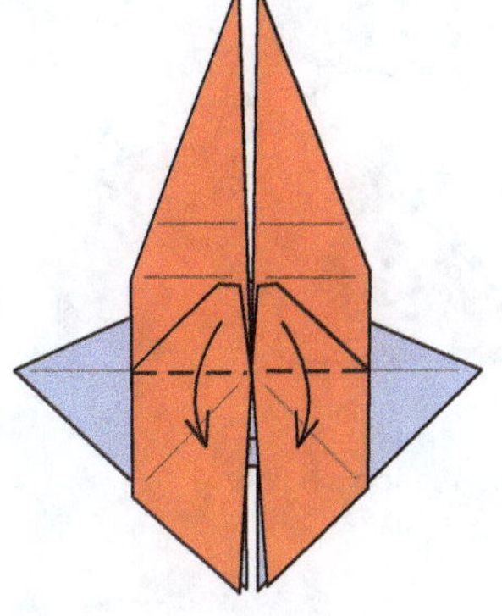

77. Swing down the small flaps.

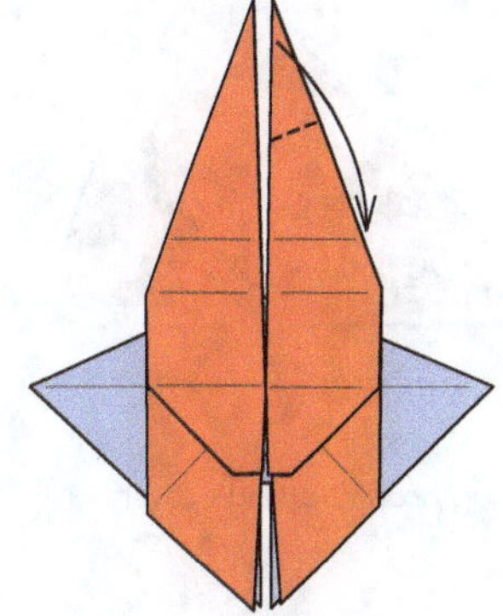

78. Valley to the top crease.

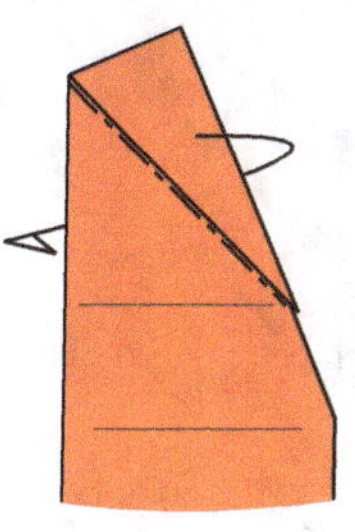

79. Mountain fold.

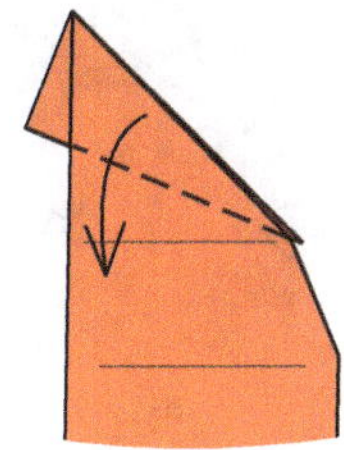

80. Valley fold.

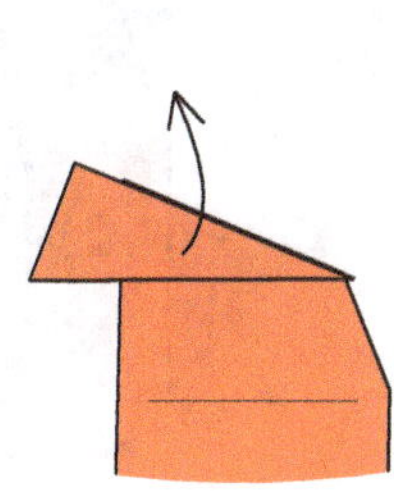

81. Unfold the pleat.

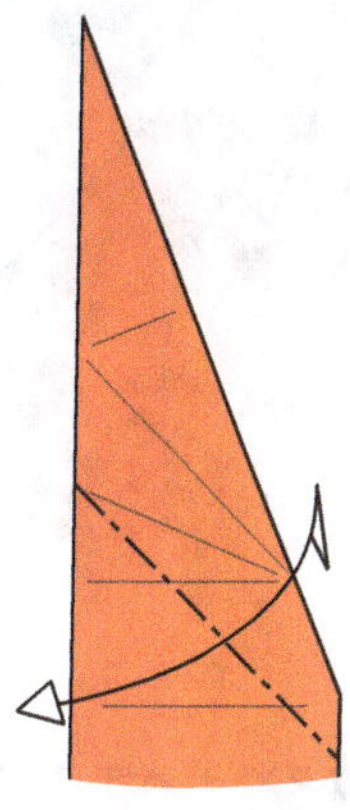

82. Precrease at a 45 degree angle, starting from the crease of step 80.

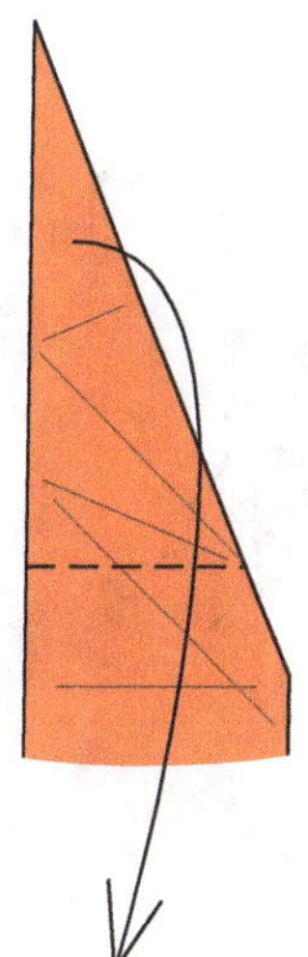

83. Valley down along the existing crease.

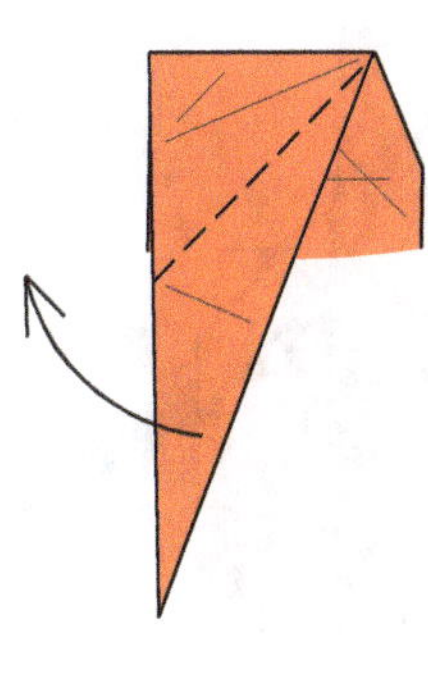

84. Valley along the existing crease.

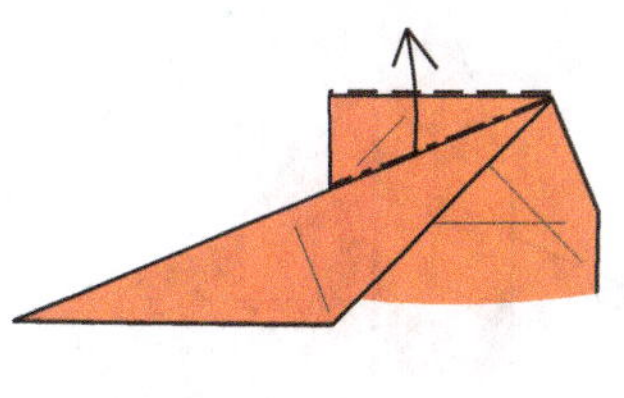

85. Slide out a single layer and flatten.

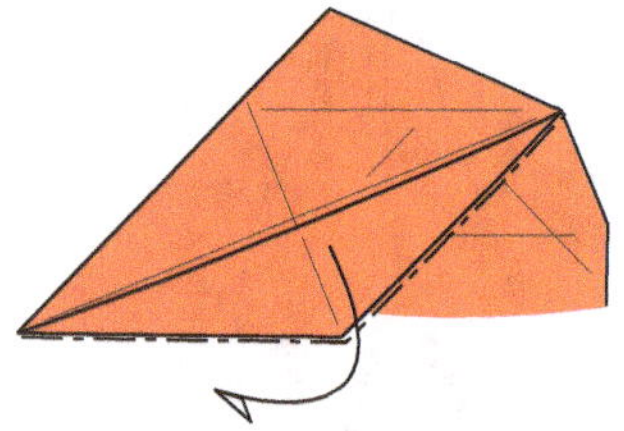

86. Wrap around a single layer.

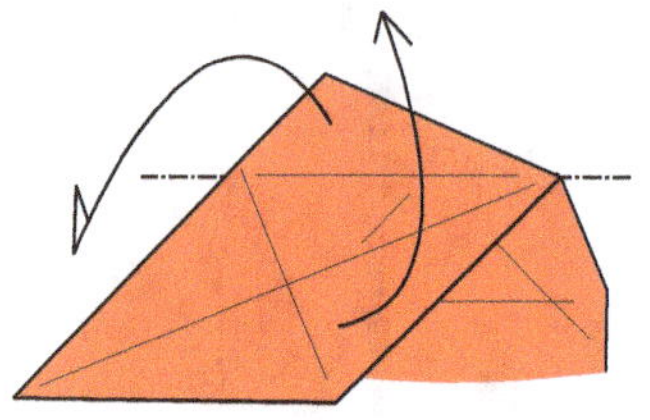

87. Flip the top section.

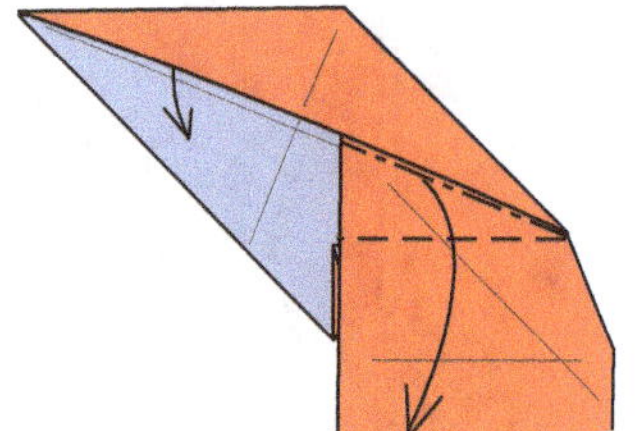

88. Pull out a single layer, and flatten to match the back.

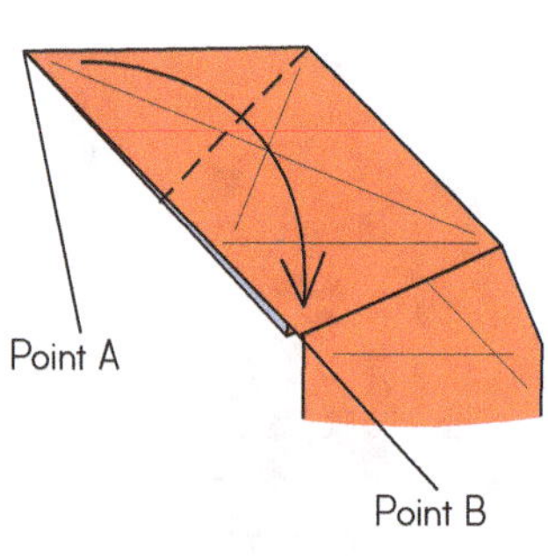

89. Valley point A over to point B.

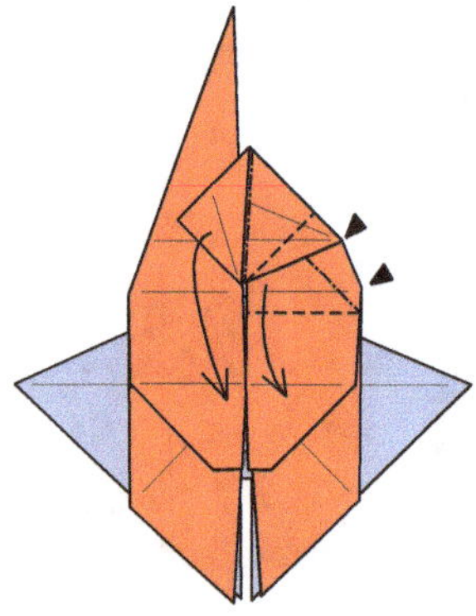

90. Spread squash the side, while stretching forward. The next step shows where points A and B land.

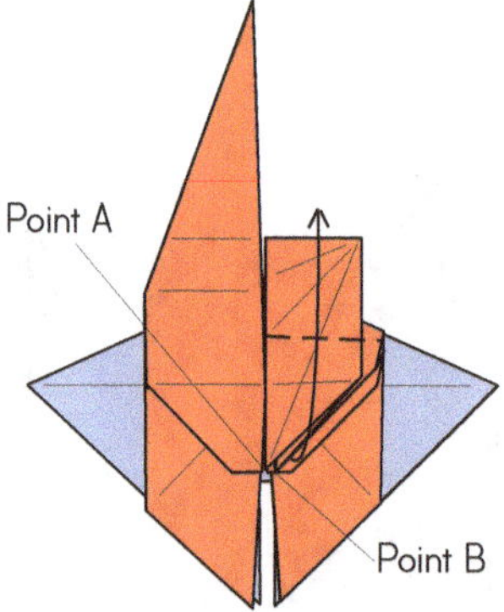

91. Swing up points A and B as far as possible.

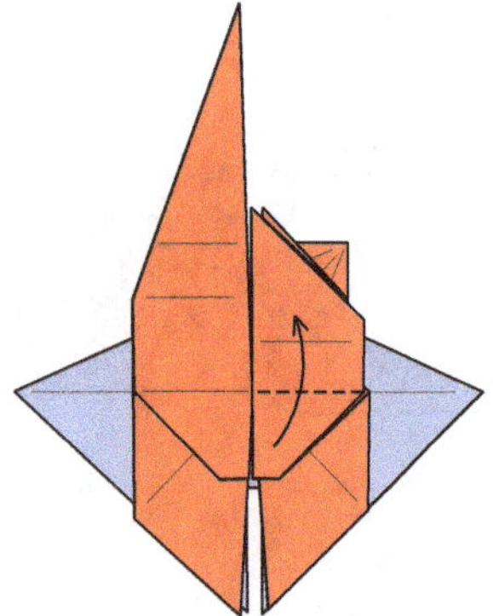

92. Swing up the next flap as far as possible.

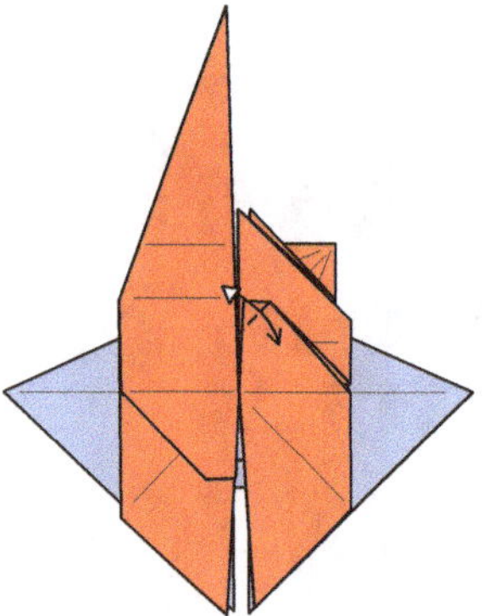

93. Precrease the top flap.

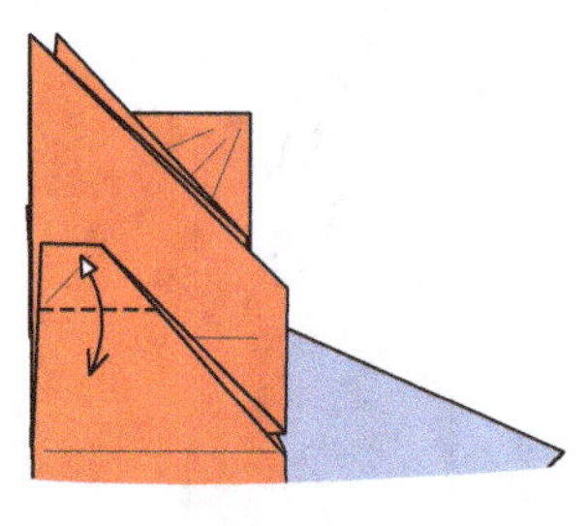

94. Precrease again.

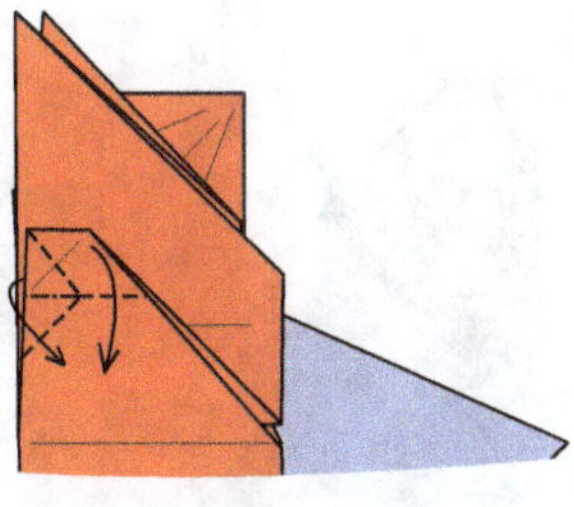

95. Valley down, while incorporating a reverse fold on the top layer.

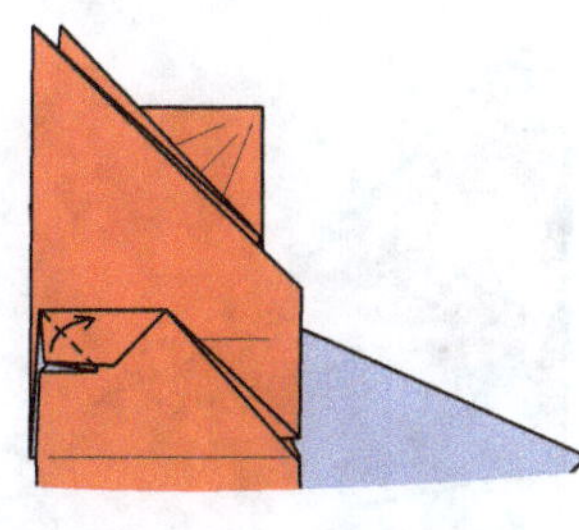

96. Valley fold up to reveal a colored square.

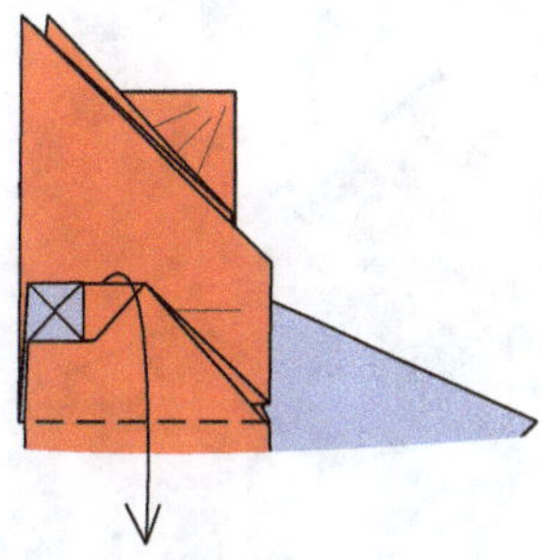

97. Swing the flap back down.

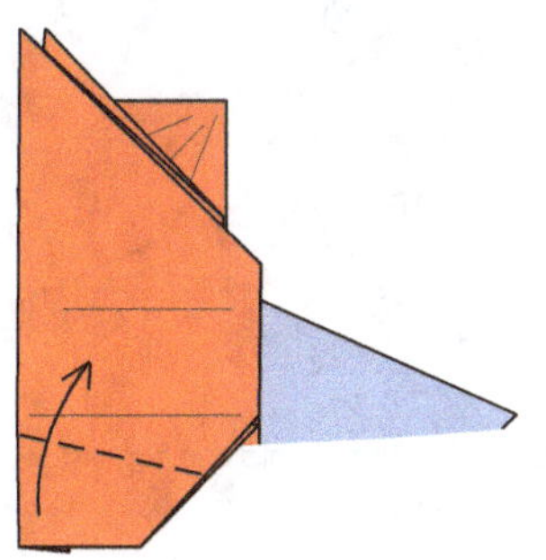

98. Valley fold the flap up. See the next step for approximate positioning.

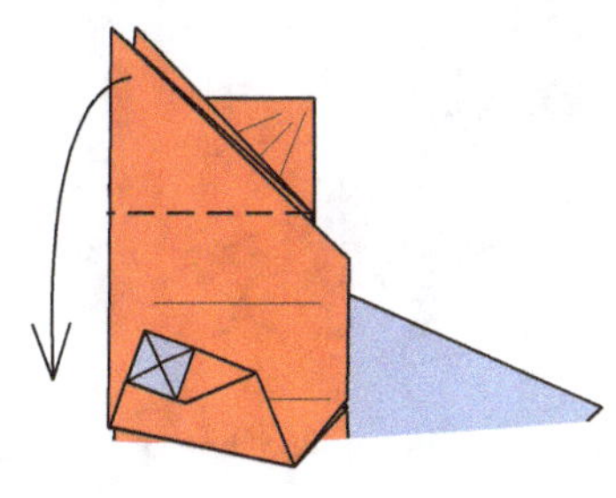

99. Swing down one flap.

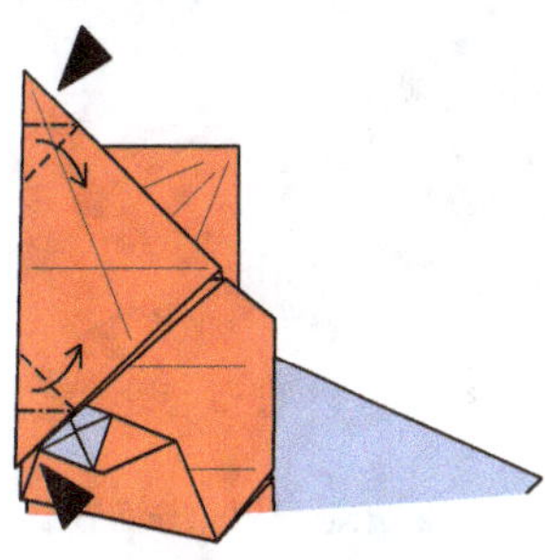

100. Squash fold the two flaps to create squares as large as the one made in step 96.

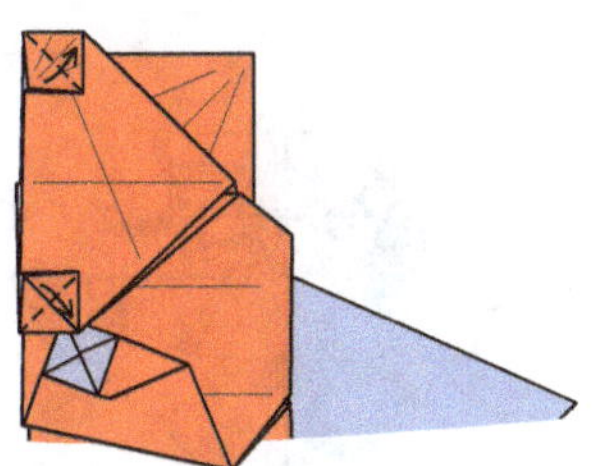

101. Valley fold to reveal the colored side.

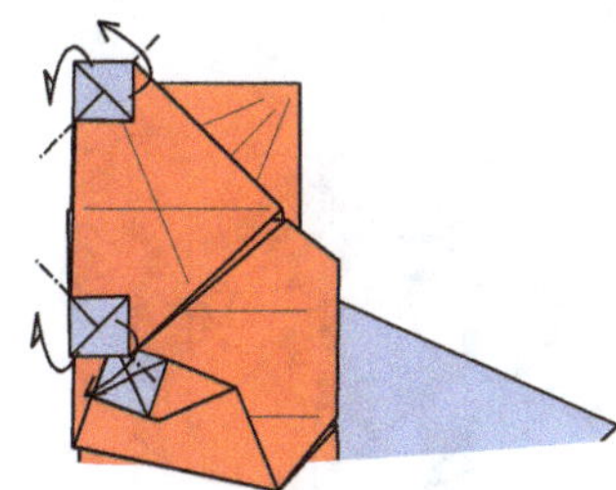

102. Flip the colored squares behind.

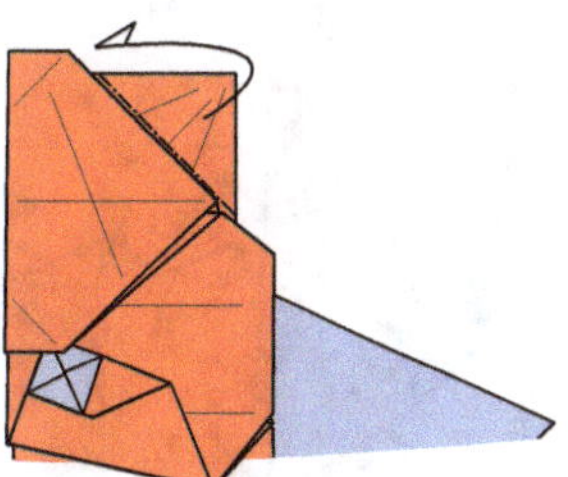

103. Mountain fold the corner to lie flush with the top edges.

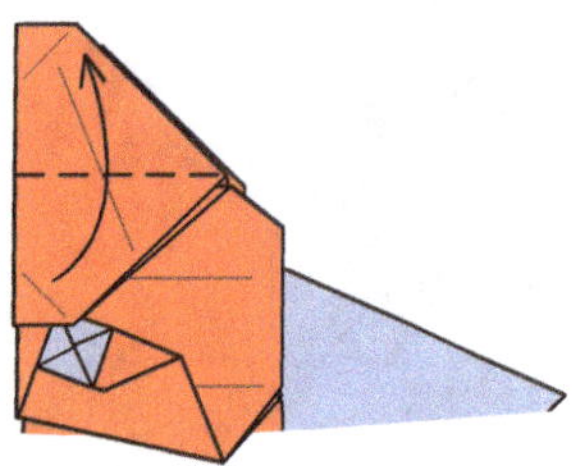

104. Swing one flap up.

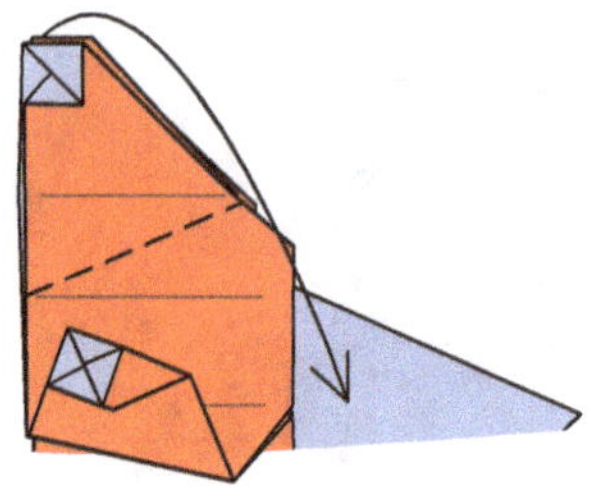

105. Valley down both flaps together.

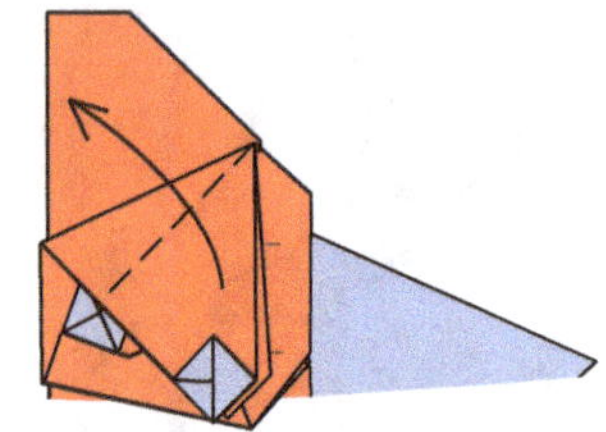

106. Raise one flap.

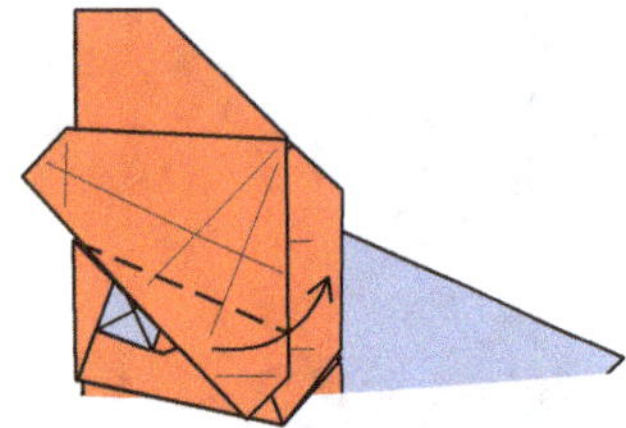

107. Valley fold the lower flap.

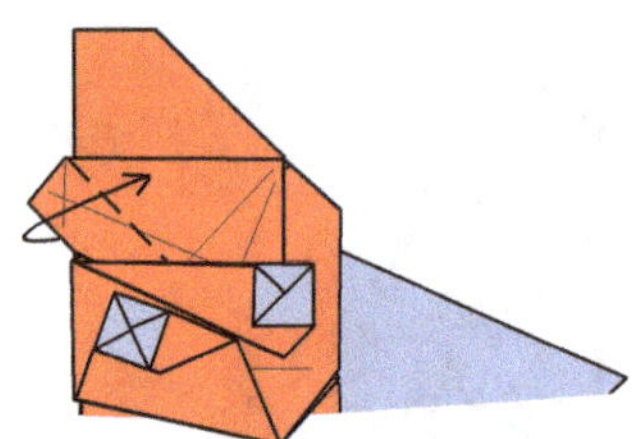

108. Swivel the top flap through.

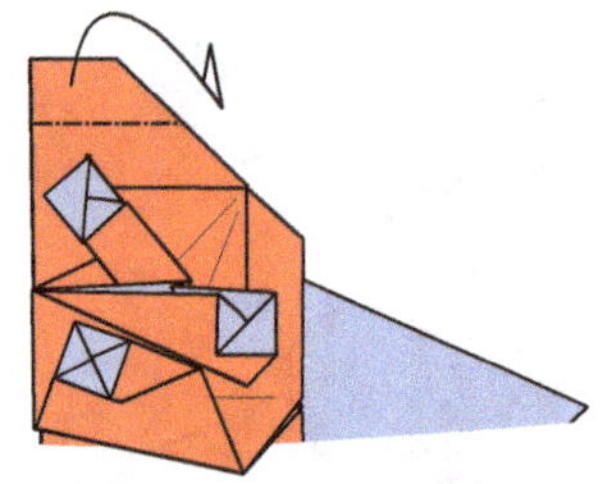

109. Mountain fold the top edge down.

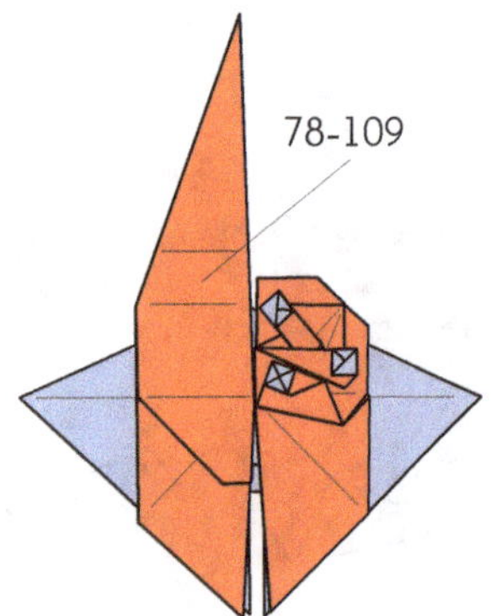

110. Repeat steps 78-109 in mirror image.

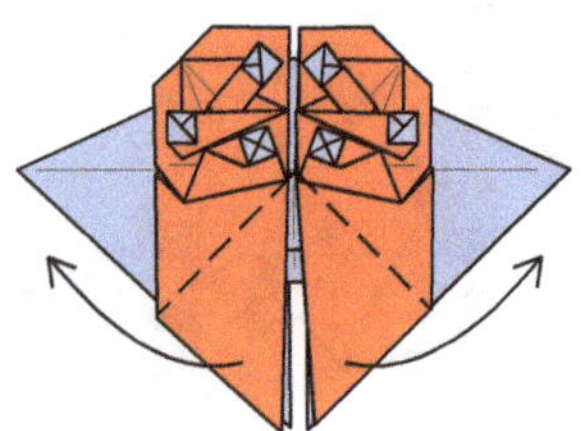

111. Valley fold the side flaps outwards.

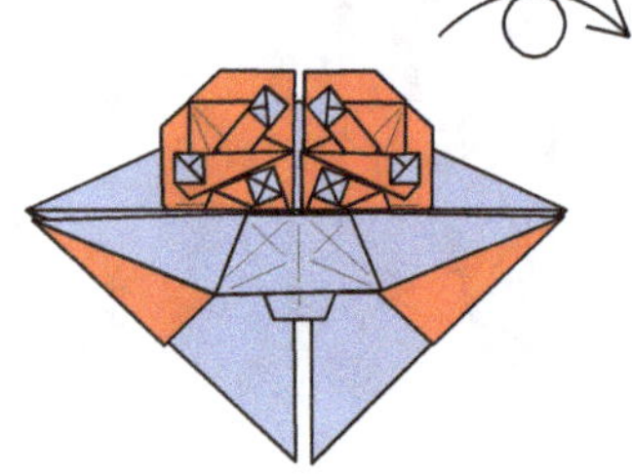

112. Turn over.

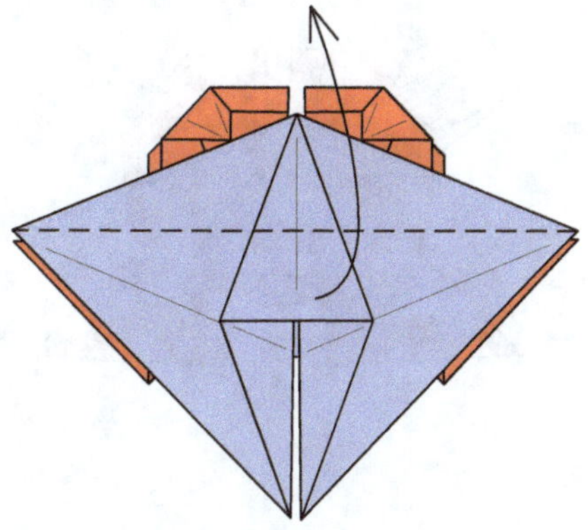

113. Valley fold up.

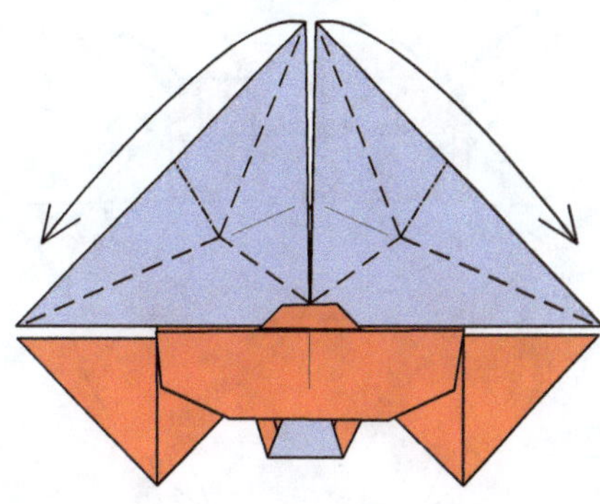

114. Rabbit ear the flaps outwards.

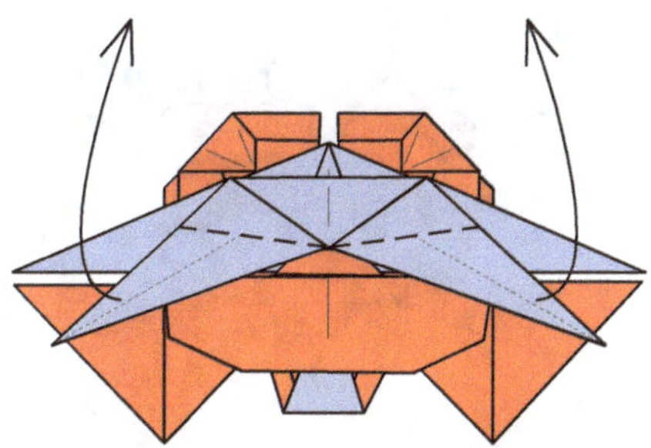

115. Valley the flaps up, allowing
one layer to swivel over.

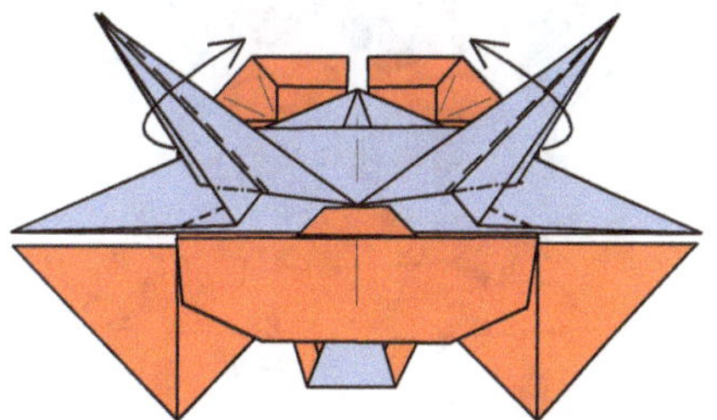

116. Valley fold the flaps in half,
allowing squashes to form.

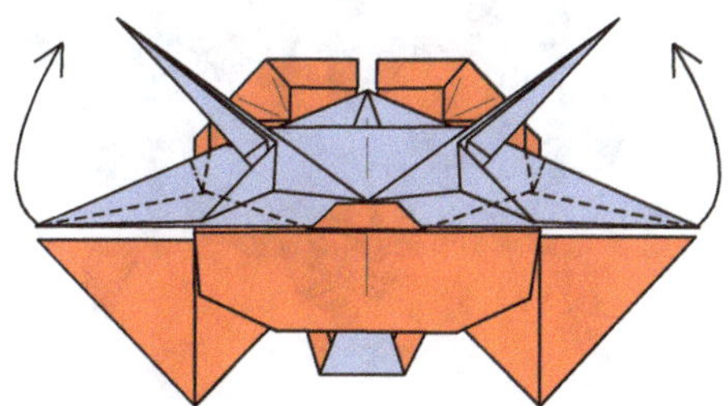

117. Rabbit ear the side flaps
upwards.

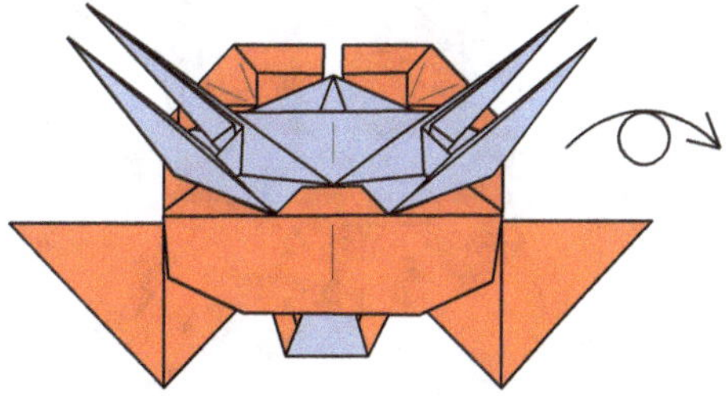

118. Turn over.

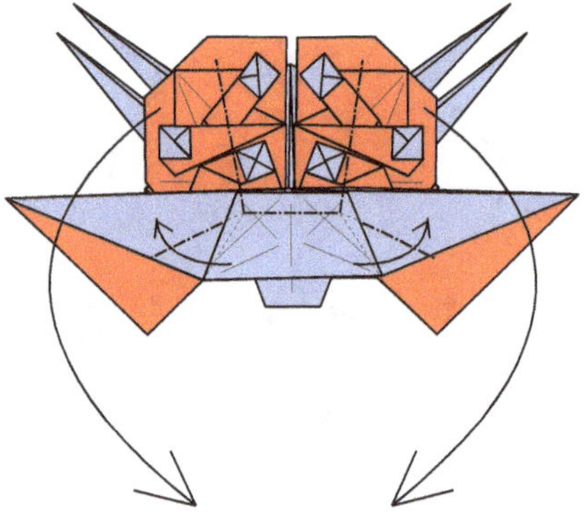

119. Crimp the top layer of the front legs, allowing the sides of the model to curve downwards.

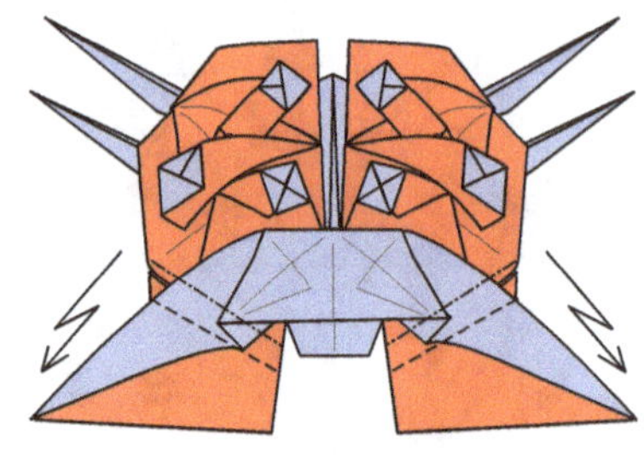

120. Pleat the front legs to lock.

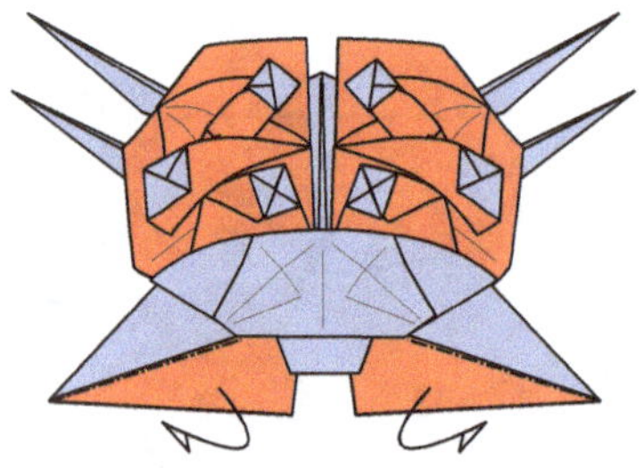

121. Swivel the lower layer of the legs underneath.

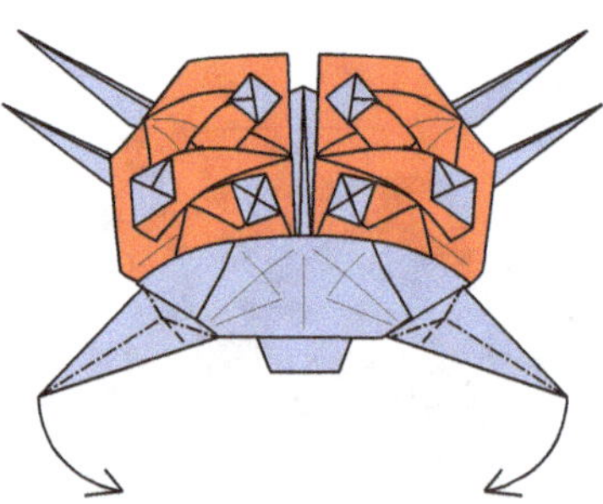

122. Rabbit ear the front legs forward.

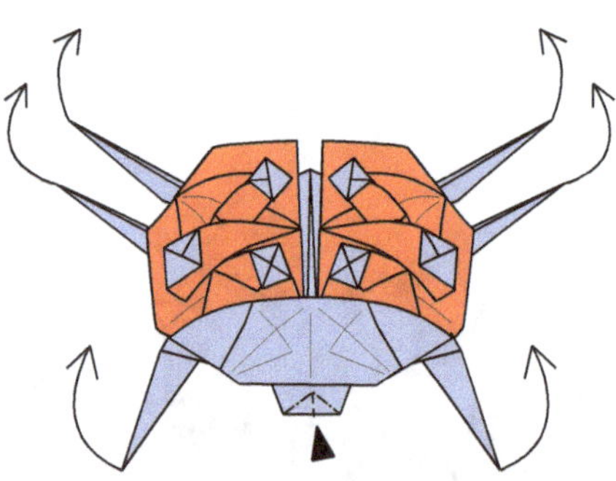

123. Reverse fold the front point. Round the body and shape the legs to taste.

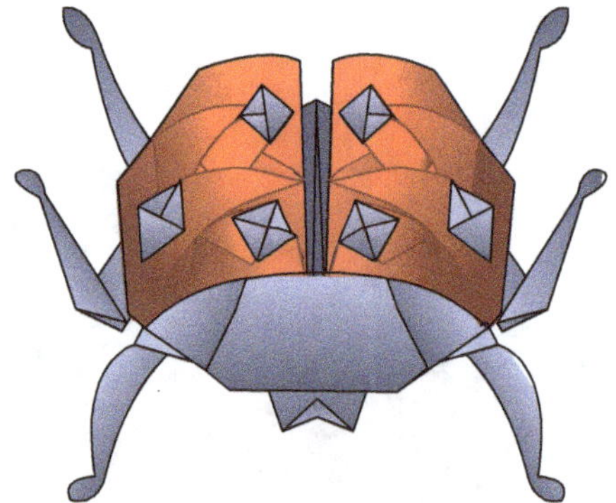

124. Completed *Ladybug*.

Materials and Methods

In theory, the only things required for origami is a piece of paper and a pair of hands. In practice, however, you will want to have the right materials for the project at hand. For initial practice attempts, you will want to use papers that are easy to fold, but not necessarily of presentable quality. The two most popular practice papers are commercial origami paper (sometimes sold as kami) and American foil. Both papers are available colored on one side, and white on the other. American foil is preferable as it holds its shape more easily. These papers feature a thin layer of decorative foil that helps your model hold its shape. Most of the origami supply houses sell a 10" version as their largest size, but some thinner wrapping paper can be used if you are looking for something larger. Japanese foil is thinner, and generally easier to fold than the American variety, albeit more expensive. Kami is better for those who have trouble with reverse folds and sinks. Both types of papers will yield adequate results, but almost invariably, more decorative choices will make your models look better.

For display-worthy efforts, you will want to use papers and methods that heighten the result, possibly at the expense of ease of folding. Such methods include foil-backing and wet folding, which includes the related technique of back coating. Both approaches allow the paper-folding artist to use material combinations to create interesting effects.

Foil Backing

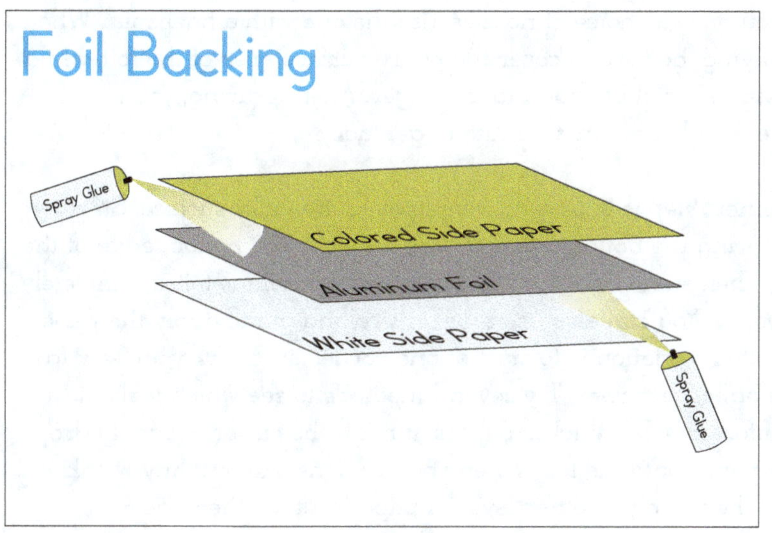

Foil backing is a great way to utilize nonporous materials, and papers with patterns that could get ruined with water (such as newsprint). Foil backing is the process of adding a layer of aluminum foil (yes, the same material you can find at virtually any grocery store) to paper, to give the resulting material unique folding characteristics. A common backing choice is tissue paper, which further enhances the folding properties of the foil (this combination is also known as "tissue foil"). Regardless of the backing material, the metal-like quality allows folds to instantly stay where they are placed. Spray adhesive is used to bond the layers together. This is also known as artist's adhesive or photo mounting spray, and it contains the same glue found on adhesive tape. You can find this at most art supply stores, but you will find it much cheaper at a hardware or office supply store. While you can usually use 3M's Spray Mount, some projects (typically involving very thick papers) will require something like 3M's Super77 Spray Adhesive. All work should be done in a well-ventilated area, as the glue is toxic. You will also want to protect your floor with newspaper. Place a sheet of foil on the floor. Leave the shinier side up first and use as the surface for the main color. In most cases, the foil will be the limiting factor as far as size is concerned, so use as large a sheet as necessary. Spray the glue onto the surface of the foil according to the manufacturer's directions.

If you have a choice of nozzles, use the one with a finer mist. When spraying, be sure to cover the entire surface area of the foil, while paying special attention to the edges. After spraying, you should give the glue about a minute to get tacky.

The next step is to apply your paper to the tacky surface. Start by adhering the bottom edge of your paper to the bottom edge of the foil. Then start working your way upwards until the foil is completely covered. You can also use a baker's rolling pin to apply the paper. Another variation is to start at one corner and work your way to the opposite corner. Try several methods to see which feels most comfortable. For thicker papers, it might be easier to simply drop the paper onto the foil. When you are done, rub out any wrinkles, and then apply another layer of paper on the other side.

To get the largest possible square, cut along the edge of the foil, which should be visible through the layers of paper, provided your papers are translucent enough. If you wish you can also tear through the foil, which is surprisingly accurate (and fun), provided you are using thin enough paper. First, score the paper, unfold, and turn over to leave the resulting crease in mountain fold formation. The paper can easily be torn in this position. Of course, you won't get the largest possible square this way, but it is easier to be accurate.

A rotary cutting board is recommended when tearing is not possible, or you cannot see the silhouette of the foil through your backing paper. While a traditional guillotine cutter might suffice, spending an extra $100 or so on a rotary cutter is worth the investment for the serious paperfolding artist. These can be purchased at better art supply stores or photography supply stores. A pair of scissors can be used when a paper cutter is not as convenient.

If you wish to make a square that is wider than your piece of foil, there is a way to accomplish this. First, you must adhere two (or more) strips of foil together. If you spray along the edge of one piece and attach the other piece along that edge, the results are remarkably seamless. Most likely, the paper you will want to use on the surface will be smaller than the foil piece you have prepared. There is a way around this hurdle as well. First, you should fold your foil in half. The resulting surface area should now be small enough for your paper. Before you use any adhesive, place a sheet of

newspaper between the fold to avoid getting any glue on the inner
layers. You can now adhere your papers on each side of the foil.
When you are done with the gluing part, use a scissor to cut along
the folded edge. After you unfold your piece, rub out the crease,
and the seam will almost disappear. You can repeat the same process
for the other side.

When folding larger models, you might find certain portions to be
flimsy. While wire is traditionally used to add rigidity, I have found
stuffing layers of foil to be even better. You can fold a piece of foil
over upon itself a few times to make it many layers thick. This can
be stuffed between the layers of the parts of the model that need
more rigidity.

If you are using tissue as the backing paper, where the properties
of the foil are at their most extreme, you are in for a radically
different folding experience. By themselves, foil and tissue make for
flimsy and weak folding materials, but together you have one of the
strongest and most resilient materials around. Also, when you make
a crease, it will hold very well. It will hold so well that it is difficult
to change its direction (i.e., valley to mountain). This makes procedures
that require precreasing, such as sinks, difficult to perform. You can
unfold the paper after precreasing, rub out the creases must be
changed, and replace them with new folds that are in the right
direction. Unlike commercial foil paper, you can rub out unwanted
creases without leaving a trace.

While it is true that foil backing will make folding your model more
difficult for most if its stages, its properties are fortuitous at the end
of a model's folding sequence. If your model has many layers, it can
easily be flattened. In extreme cases, a hammer can work wonders.
After your model is as flat as you desire, you can shape and pose
it any way you wish. Your model will hold that shape forever, until
you decide to reshape it, or someone or something inadvertently
reshapes it. The latter scenario is obviously undesirable. If you use
a slightly thicker paper (such as the Japanese papers), you will lose
some of the malleability but will have a much more solid looking
model, due to its increased thickness. It can still be bent out of shape,
but is acceptable if being displayed in a controlled environment.

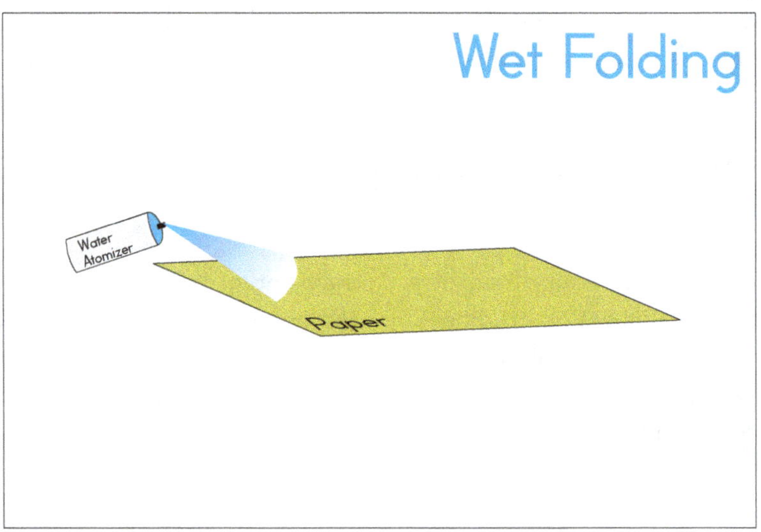

Foil backed paper looks great in person, but the camera lens often picks up the foil through the backing, even when the backing paper seems to be dense enough. This might be okay for some subjects, but to have a less reflective look, wet folding techniques are more effective. The process might be slower, but the results are more permanent.

Wet folding involves lightly dampening your paper during the folding process, so when it finally dries it will retain its shape. When paper is wet, the sizing (glue-like substance) that holds the paper fibers together is loosened. Once the paper is dry again, the sizing will hold the paper in its new position. Taking advantage of this property of paper enables the folder to hold shapes that seem to defy gravity. Not all papers contain a lot of sizing, so you might have to add a methylcellulose paste to your paper before folding. To do this, you first add the methylcellulose powder (which is sold at many art supply stores) to water and mix the compound until it is syrupy. You can use about a teaspoon for each cup of warm water. This paste can now be brushed onto your paper with a standard painter's brush. After the paper is dry, it will be even easier to wet fold. To speed up the drying process, you can use a table fan.

When wet folding it is important to realize your paper will
expand, often unevenly. This makes accurate folding much more
difficult. Also, reference fold crease lines become difficult to see
while paper is wet. For these reasons, you may prefer to delay
wetting the paper until key folds are in place. When you are
ready to wet the paper, it is important not to allow the paper
to get soggy. By using an atomizer's mist sparingly, a leathery
texture can be obtained from the paper. These spray bottles
can be found at many perfume sections; try to find one with as
fine a mist as possible.

Holding your model in position while drying can be a creative
challenge. Tools that work include twist ties (the plastic-coated
ones that are often used for electrical wire packing), portable
clamps, and painter's masking tape. As an example, you can
wind a twist tie around the legs of your insect model, bend them
into the desired position, and secure them to a flat surface with
masking tape. After further moistening your model with your
atomizer, it will retain its stance after it is dry and the bindings
have been removed.

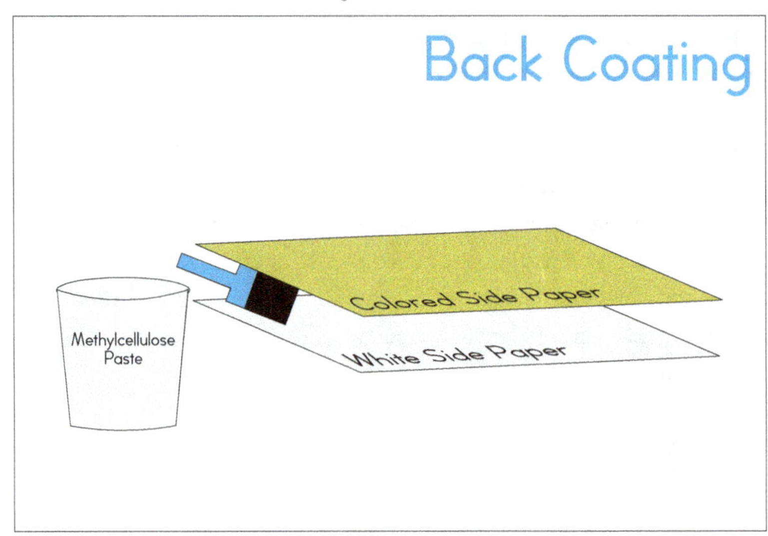

A related technique to wet folding is back coating. Since most specialty papers are monochromatic, the two-toned effect in many origami models is lost. You can use methylcellulose paste to adhere two complementing colors of paper together. Brush the paste on one paper, being sure to work on a smooth surface, as the paper will pick up any texture from your working surface. Apply the second sheet on top, brushing it into place. You can cut your square once it is dry, using a table fan to expedite the process. Again, a rotary cutter is recommended. The materials you chose to mate together should both be porous and fibrous enough to stay together, otherwise you might have to resort to foil backing.

Papers that work well include the Unryu variety (both regular and soft) from both Japan and Thailand. These papers might be labeled as containing mulberry or kozo fiber, but other fibers will work as well. You can also try Yatsuo papers from Japan, which are made from kozo and sulfite pulp, and have a much smoother look than the Unryu papers. These and other fine art papers can be found at better art stores and via mail order. You can expect to pay about three to four dollars for a 25" x 37" sheet.

Other important paper considerations include weight, which is how a material's thickness is described. To give you a gauge of what this means, standard copy paper is often at 20 Gr/M2 weight. Of course, you will double your thickness if you are bonding two sheets together. Try to keep the total thickness under 80 Gr/M2. When dealing with lighter colors, you might have to work with thicker papers just to get the right opacity (but you can mate them with lighter weight darker papers if you are trying to avoid additional thickness). As a test, you can hold the paper against a black surface to see how well it eclipses its backing. Sometimes, having the contrasting color show through is a good thing, as your color choices will seem to blend a bit. One thing you would like to avoid is having your paper bleed (having the dye run) when wet. The most temperamental colors tend to be reds and black, but it is a good idea to test out a sheet first if possible.

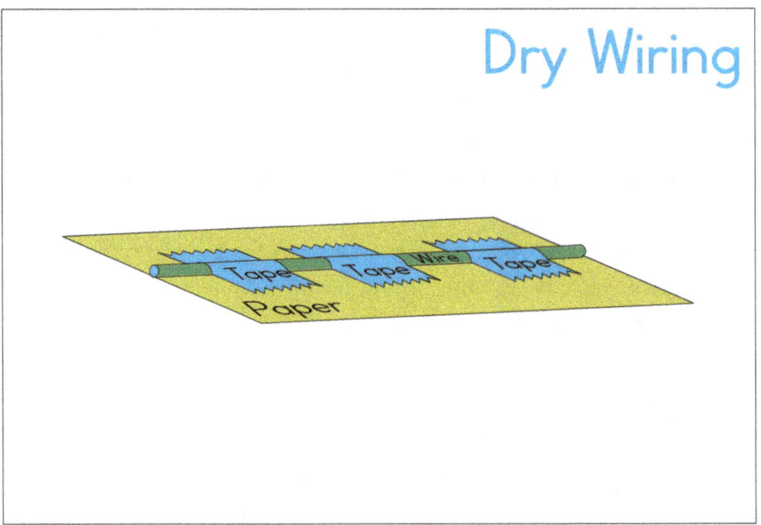

Both wet folding and foil backing will give your models a sculpted look. Sometimes is preferable to have a crisper look, where the paper looks less molded and more folded. Simply folding your paper without any of these special techniques will sometimes work, but for most models (especially those that are very complex), will have sections that will gradually spring apart. The solution is to strategically add wire to these troublesome sections.

For most models, florists wire will suffice. 26 gauge is a good thickness for most scenarios, and 22 gauge can be used where more strength is needed (lower numbers correlate with thicker gauges). The wire typically has a PVC coating (often green) that can be secured simply with a few pieces of scotch tape. For some heavier duty situations, PVC glue is useful. It can be cut with a pair scissors, but heavier gauges might be best trimmed with a wire cutter.

The wire has a palpable thickness, and it can sometimes be a challenge to avoid having it bulge through the surface layers of your model. It is best to lay the wire along a fold line that is on the underside of your model. In rare cases, you can cover the wire with multiple layers of aluminum foil to cover up the bulge.

It will be necessary to unfold and refold your model, adding wire as you feel it is helpful. Of course, this adds to the challenge of folding, but when done well, the results are worth it. As with foil backing, the final model can get bent out of shape, so special care is needed when storing. With enough experimentation, you should be able to conceive the perfect material for any model.

Ratio
Information

Housefly 0.15 0.13 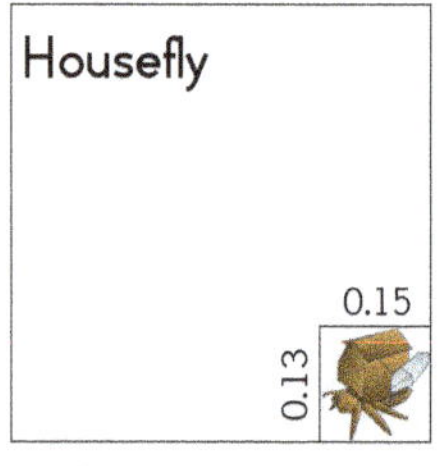	**Ladybug** 0.26 0.30 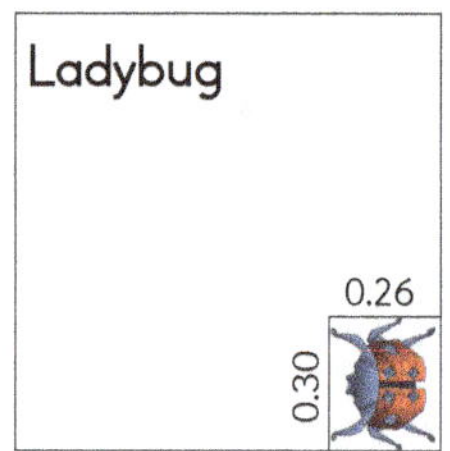	**Fly** 0.29 0.33 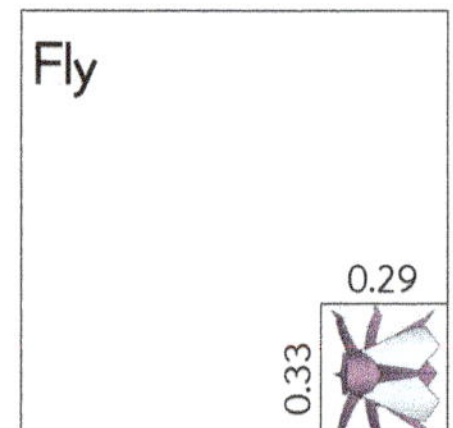
Beetle 0.30 0.35 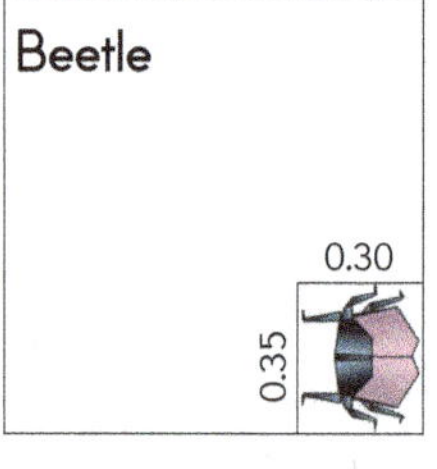	**Mosquito** 0.33 0.24 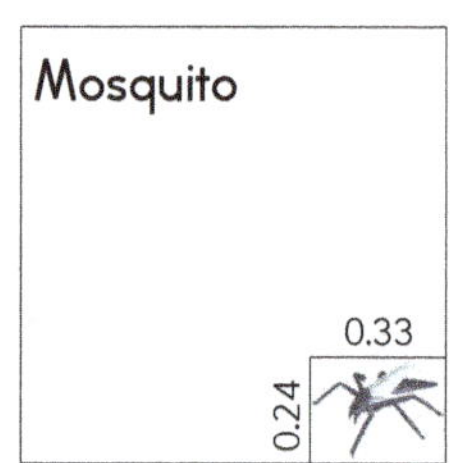	**Cockroach** 0.33 0.34 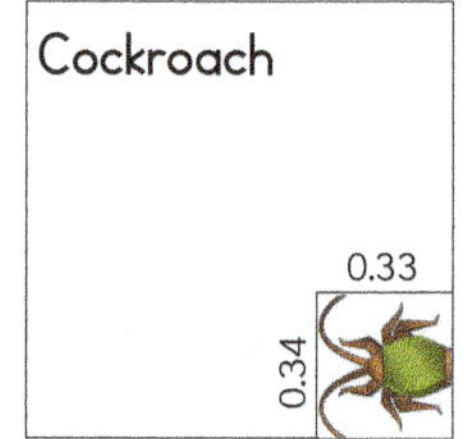
Bee 0.36 0.21 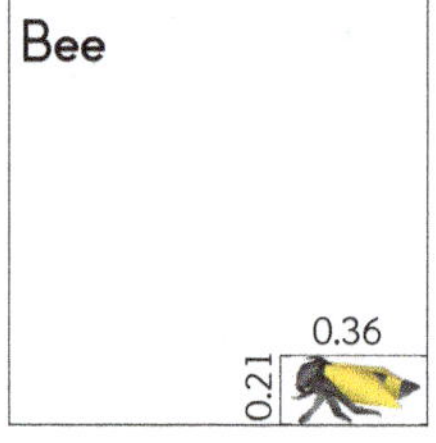	**Black Pine Sawyer** 0.38 0.60 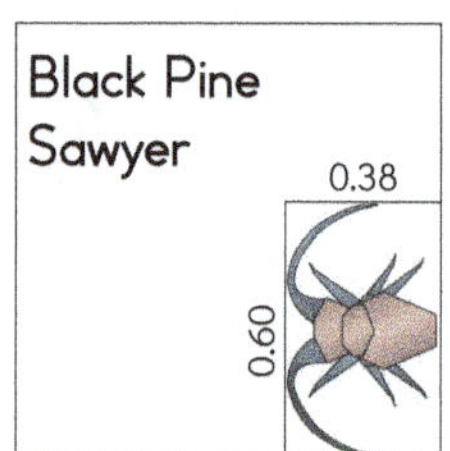	**Dragonfly** 0.39 0.48 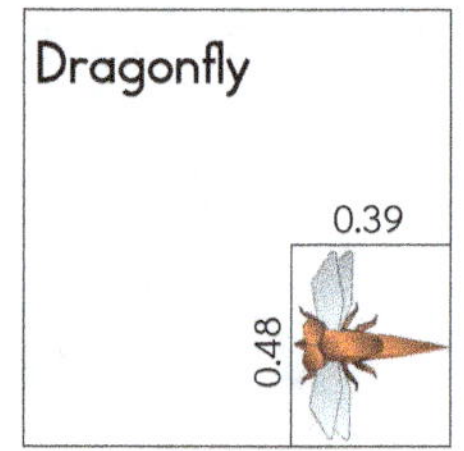
	Butterfly 0.49 0.27 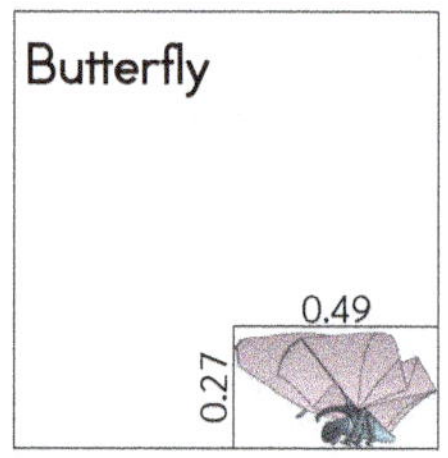	**Cankerworm** 0.58 0.16 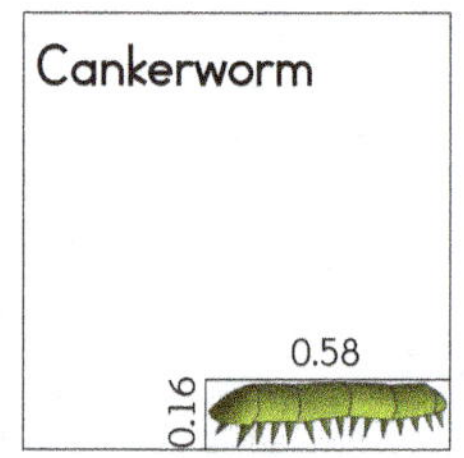